THE MODEL OF POESY

The Model of Poesy is one of the most exciting literary discoveries of recent years. A manuscript treatise on poetics written by William Scott in 1599, at the end of the most revolutionary decade in English literary history, it includes rich discussions of the works of Sidney, Spenser, Shakespeare, and their contemporaries. Scott's work presents a powerful and coherent theoretical account of all aspect of poetics, from the nature of representation to the rules of versification, with a commitment to relating theory to contemporary practice. For Scott, any theory of literature must make sense not of the classics but of what English writers are doing now: Scott is at the same time the most scholarly and the most relevant of English Renaissance critics. In this groundbreaking edition, Gavin Alexander presents a text of *The Model of Poesy* framed by a detailed introduction and an extensive commentary, which together demonstrate the range and value of Scott's thought.

GAVIN ALEXANDER is a University Senior Lecturer in the Faculty of English at the University of Cambridge, and a Fellow of Christ's College. His publications include *Writing After Sidney: The Literary Response to Sir Philip Sidney, 1586–1640* (2006), *Sidney's 'The Defence of Poesy' and Selected Renaissance Literary Criticism* (2004), a co-edited volume *Renaissance Figures of Speech* (2007), and numerous articles and book chapters on literary and musicological topics. He teaches at undergraduate and postgraduate level across a wide range of topics, from ancient to modern literature, with a particular emphasis on Renaissance literature, the history and theory of literary criticism, and textual studies. His online early modern palaeography course 'English Handwriting' is widely used around the world. In 2008 he was awarded a Pilkington Teaching Prize for excellence in teaching at the University of Cambridge.

Marcus Gheeraerts the Younger, *Queen Elizabeth I* ('*The Ditchley portrait*'), oil on canvas, *c*.1592 (detail). © National Portrait Gallery, London.

WILLIAM SCOTT

THE MODEL OF POESY

Edited with an introduction and commentary by

GAVIN ALEXANDER

CAMBRIDGE
UNIVERSITY PRESS

CAMBRIDGE
UNIVERSITY PRESS

University Printing House, Cambridge CB2 8BS, United Kingdom

Cambridge University Press is part of the University of Cambridge.

It furthers the University's mission by disseminating knowledge in the pursuit of education, learning and research at the highest international levels of excellence.

www.cambridge.org
Information on this title: www.cambridge.org/9780521196116

© Cambridge University Press 2013

First published 2013
3rd printing 2014

Printed in the United Kingdom by Print on Demand, World Wide

A catalogue record for this publication is available from the British Library

ISBN 978-0-521-19611-6 Hardback

In Memory of F. W. Walbank (1909–2008)

CONTENTS

ILLUSTRATIONS

PREFACE

The Model of Poesy (*c*.1599) by William Scott is one of the more significant literary manuscripts to come to light in recent years. Its existence and authorship were known to E. K. Chambers in the 1930s but the manuscript was not heard of again until Stanley Wells announced its rediscovery in 2003. It is now British Library Additional Manuscript 81083 and is edited here for the first time. I have included a substantial Introduction and Commentary, since the *Model* is a scholarly work with a rich context, and because I have been able to discover a great deal about its author that was not previously known. The Introduction and the Commentary work in tandem, the latter supplying the details and the former offering more continuous narrative and broader brushstrokes. I recommend any reader to begin with the text itself, however: the *Model* must earn attention because of its (I believe) very considerable interest and importance as a work of Elizabethan literary criticism.

'For things once finished well, soon enough finished are', says Du Bartas in William Scott's English translation, a wisdom perhaps lost in this era of research measurement. I am indebted to the AHRC for a research leave award and to the Isaac Newton Trust for two short-term research assistance grants; these have enabled me to complete this edition both sooner and better than would otherwise have been possible. It is a pleasure to acknowledge the assistance of the skilled and knowledgeable curators and staff of the British Library, the Cambridge University Library, the Folger Shakespeare Library, the Canterbury Cathedral Archives, and the departmental and college libraries of Cambridge, especially the English Faculty Library. I am grateful for the support, interest, and stimulation of my wonderful colleagues and students at Cambridge, and especially to Hester Lees-Jeffries, Sarah Howe, and above all Michael Hetherington, who acted as my occasional research assistant and from whose forthcoming work on Scott and logic I have very much benefited. I owe a great debt to Sarah Stanton at Cambridge University Press for fostering this project, and to her team for their superb work. Many colleagues and friends have helped by asking or answering questions and making suggestions, or by reading portions of my work. I should particularly like to thank Sylvia Adamson, Peter Auger, Joseph Black, Abigail Brundin, Colin Burrow, Alec Cobbe, David Colclough, Andrew Hadfield (who earns especial thanks for drawing my attention to a miscellany at the Folger that proved rather useful), Paul Hammer, Robert Harding, Nick Hardy, Roger Kuin, Micha Lazarus, Rhodri Lewis, Celia Pilkington (Archivist at the Inner Temple), Nigel Ramsay, Lisa Sampson, Sue Simpson, Tiffany Stern, Dorothy Thompson, Andrew Thrush, Philippa Walton, Stanley Wells, Alison Wiggins, and Andrew Zurcher. I also gained much from responses to talks about Scott that I gave at the Universities of Cambridge, Oxford, Sheffield, and Sussex; at the University of Massachusetts (Amherst); at the Folger Shakespeare Library; and at the Renaissance Society of America annual meeting.

I began working on this project shortly after the death, at the age of ninety-eight, of my grandfather Frank Walbank. From him I got the love of puzzling out what words and texts mean that has made this project so absorbing and enjoyable. He taught me the small Latin and less Greek without which many of Scott's sources would have been closed books. And he showed me what scholarship, and the scholar, should be. This edition is dedicated to his memory with love and gratitude.

REFERENCES AND ABBREVIATIONS

The following list of abbreviations includes the works most frequently referred to in the Introduction and Commentary, but is not a complete bibliography. See 'A note on sources and references' below for further details of referencing conventions and the texts of certain authors. Dates of composition and/or original publication are given in square brackets for vernacular works of rhetoric and poetics, where these are cited in modern editions.

ABBREVIATIONS

Adagia	Desiderius Erasmus, *Adages*, ed. and trans. Margaret Mann Phillips *et al.*, 7 vols. (Toronto, 1982–)
Ad Herennium	Anon., *Rhetorica ad Herennium*, in Harry Caplan (ed. and trans.), *Ad C. Herennium de ratione dicendi* (Cambridge, Mass., 1954)
ALC	D. A. Russell and M. Winterbottom (eds.), *Ancient literary criticism: the principal texts in new translations* (Oxford, 1972)
Ars poetica	Horace, *Ars poetica*, in H. Rushton Fairclough (ed. and trans.), *Satires, epistles and ars poetica* (Cambridge, Mass., 1929)
Art	George Puttenham, *The art of English poesy* [1589], ed. Frank Whigham and Wayne A. Rebhorn (Ithaca, NY, 2007)
Babrius	Aesopic fables, in Ben Edwin Perry (ed. and trans.), *Babrius and Phaedrus* (Cambridge, Mass., 1965)
BCP	Brian Cummings (ed.), *The book of common prayer: the texts of 1549, 1559, and 1662* (Oxford, 2011)
Binns	J. W. Binns (ed. and trans.), *Latin treatises on poetry from Renaissance England* (Signal Mountain, Tenn., 1999)
Blundeville	Thomas Blundeville, *The art of logike* (1599)
Burton	Robert Burton, *The anatomy of melancholy*, ed. Thomas C. Faulkner *et al.*, 6 vols. (Oxford, 1989–2000)
Butler1	Charles Butler, *Rameae rhetoricae libri duo* (Oxford, 1597)
Butler2	Charles Butler, *Rhetoricae libri duo* (Oxford, 1598)
CCA	Canterbury Cathedral Archives
Chambers	E. K. Chambers, *Sir Henry Lee: an Elizabethan portrait* (Oxford, 1936)
Cox	Baldassare Castiglione, *The book of the courtier* [trans. Thomas Hoby], ed. Virginia Cox (London, 1994)
CWBJ	David Bevington, Martin Butler, and Ian Donaldson (eds.), *The Cambridge edition of the works of Ben Jonson*, 7 vols. (Cambridge, 2012)
Dethick	Henry Dethick, *Oratio in laudem poëseos* [*c*.1575]: text in Binns
Diomedes	Diomedes, *Artis grammaticae libri tres*: text in Keil, 1; translations mine
Directions	John Hoskyns, *Directions for speech and style* [written *c.* 1599], in Louise Brown Osborn, *The life, letters, and writings of John Hoskyns, 1566–1638* (New Haven, 1937)
Donatus	Aelius Donatus, *De comedia*: Latin text in Wessner; English translation in Preminger

DP — Sir Philip Sidney, *The defence of poesy* [written *c*.1580; first published 1595]: text in *SRLC*

Du Bartas — Urban Tigner Holmes, Jr, *et al.* (eds.), *The works of Guillaume de Salluste Sieur du Bartas*, 3 vols. (Chapel Hill, 1935–40)

Durling — Robert M. Durling (ed. and trans.), *Petrarch's lyric poems* (Cambridge, Mass., 1976)

ECE — G. Gregory Smith (ed.), *Elizabethan critical essays*, 2 vols. (Oxford, 1904)

ERLC — Brian Vickers (ed.), *English renaissance literary criticism* (Oxford, 1999)

Evanthius — Evanthius, *De fabula*: Latin text in Wessner; English translation in Preminger

FQ — Edmund Spenser, *The faerie queene*, ed. A. C. Hamilton, 2nd edn, revised (Harlow, 2007)

Fracastoro — Girolamo Fracastoro, *Naugerius, sive de poetica dialogus*, trans. Ruth Kelso (Urbana, Ill., 1924)

Fraunce — Abraham Fraunce, *The Arcadian rhetorike* (1588)

Gascoigne — George Gascoigne, *Certain notes of instruction* [1575]: text in *SRLC*

Gentili — Alberico Gentili, *Commentatio ad Legem III Codicis de professoribus et medicis* [1593]: text in Binns

Gilbert — Allan H. Gilbert (ed. and trans.), *Literary criticism: Plato to Dryden* (Detroit, 1962)

Goyet — Francis Goyet (ed.), *Traités de poétique et de rhétorique de la Renaissance* (Paris, 1990)

Gravell — Thomas L. Gravell watermark collection at the University of Delaware Library (www.gravell.org)

Hannay *et al.* — Margaret P. Hannay, Noel J. Kinnamon, and Michael G. Brennan (eds.), *Domestic politics and family absence: the correspondence (1588–1621) of Robert Sidney, first Earl of Leicester, and Barbara Gamage Sidney, Countess of Leicester* (Aldershot, 2005)

Harington — Sir John Harington, 'A preface, or rather a briefe apologie of poetrie, and of the author and translator' [1591]: text in *ECE*

Hart, *Methode* — John Hart, *A methode or comfortable beginning for all unlearned, whereby they may bee taught to read English, in a very short time* (1570)

Hart, *Orthographie* — John Hart, *An orthographie, conteyning the due order and reason, howe to write or paint thimage of mannes voice, most like to the life or nature* (1569)

Haydocke — Gian Paolo Lomazzo, *A tracte containing the artes of curious painting carvinge and buildinge*, trans. Richard Haydocke (Oxford, 1598)

Heawood — Edward Heawood, *Watermarks, mainly of the 17th and 18th centuries* (Hilversum, 1950)

HMC De L'Isle — *Report on the manuscripts of Lord De L'Isle and Dudley preserved at Penshurst Place*, Royal Commission on Historical Manuscripts, 6 vols. (London, 1925–66)

HMC Hatfield — *Calendar of the manuscripts of the Marquis of Salisbury, preserved at Hatfield House*, Royal Commission on Historical Manuscripts, 24 vols. (London, 1883–1976)

Holland — Pliny, *The historie of the world. Commonly called, The naturall historie*, trans. Philemon Holland, 2 vols. (1601)

HoP — *The history of Parliament: the House of Commons, 1558–1603*, ed. P. W. Hasler, 3 vols. (London, 1981)

HoP2   The history of Parliament: the House of Commons, 1604–1629, ed. Andrew
                  Thrush and John P. Ferris, 6 vols. (Cambridge, 2010)
Keil   Heinrich Keil (ed.), *Grammatici Latini*, 8 vols. (Leipzig, 1855–80)
KHLC   Kent History and Library Centre, Maidstone
Kuin   Roger Kuin (ed.), *The correspondence of Sir Philip Sidney*, 2 vols. (Oxford,
                  2012)
Leech   John Leech, *Certaine grammar questions for the exercise of young schollers
                  in the learning of the accidence* ([c.1590])
Liddell and Scott Henry George Liddell and Robert Scott, *A Greek–English lexicon*, rev.
                  Henry Stuart Jones and Roderick McKenzie (Oxford, 1940)
Lomazzo   Gian Paolo Lomazzo, *Trattato dell'arte della pittura, scoltura et architet-
                  tura*, in Roberto Paolo Ciardi (ed.), *Scritti sulle arti*, 2 vols. (Florence,
                  1974), II
MED   *Middle English Dictionary* (2001), online version, September 2012
                  (quod.lib.umich.edu/m/med)
Meres   Francis Meres, *Palladis tamia, wits treasury* [1598]: text in *ECE*
Mulcaster   Richard Mulcaster, *The first part of the elementarie which entreateth chefelie
                  of the right writing of our English tung* (1582)
NA   National Archives
NA   Sir Philip Sidney, *The countesse of Pembrokes Arcadia* (1593)
Natalis Comes   John Mulryan and Steven Brown (trans.), *Natale Conti's Mythologiae*,
                  2 vols. (Tempe, Ariz., 2006)
North   Plutarch, *The lives of the noble Grecians and Romanes*, trans. Thomas
                  North (1579)
OA   Sir Philip Sidney, *The Countess of Pembroke's Arcadia (the old Arcadia)*,
                  ed. Jean Robertson (Oxford, 1973)
ODEP   F. P. Wilson (ed.), *The Oxford dictionary of English proverbs*, 3rd edn
                  (Oxford, 1970)
ODNB   *Oxford dictionary of national biography*, online version of September 2012
                  (www.oxforddnb.com)
OED   *Oxford English dictionary*, online version of June 2012 (www.oed.com)
On animals   Albertus Magnus, *On animals*, trans. Kenneth F. Kitchell and Irven
                  Michael Resnick, 2 vols. (Baltimore, 1999)
Oratio   John Rainolds, *Oratio in laudem artis poeticae* [c.1572], ed. William
                  Ringler (Princeton, 1940)
Padelford   Frederick Morgan Padelford (trans.), *Select translations from Scaliger's
                  'Poetics'* (New York, 1905)
PCC   National Archives, Prerogative Court of Canterbury
Peletier   Jacques Peletier, *Art poétique* [1555]: text in Goyet
Phaedrus   Aesopic fables, in Ben Edwin Perry (ed. and trans.), *Babrius and Phaedrus*
                  (Cambridge, Mass., 1965)
Physiologus   Michael J. Curley (trans.), *Physiologus* (Austin, Tex., 1979)
Pigman   George Gascoigne, *A hundreth sundrie flowres*, ed. G. W. Pigman III
                  (Oxford, 2000)
Pliny   Pliny the Elder, *Natural history*, ed. and trans. H. Rackham *et al.*, 10 vols.
                  (Cambridge, Mass., 1938–62)
Poetics   Aristotle, *Poetics*: translation in *ALC*
Porphyry   Porphyry, *Introduction*, trans. Jonathan Barnes (Oxford, 2003)
Preminger   Alex Preminger, O. B. Hardison, Jr, and Kevin Kerrane (eds.), *Classical
                  and medieval literary criticism: translations and interpretations* (New York,
                  1974)

Prose | Katherine Duncan-Jones and Jan van Dorsten (eds.), *Miscellaneous prose of Sir Philip Sidney* (Oxford, 1973)
Quintilian | Quintilian, *Institutio oratoria*, ed. and trans. H. E. Butler, 4 vols. (Cambridge, Mass., 1920–2)
Reardon | B. P. Reardon (ed.), *Collected ancient Greek novels* (Berkeley and Los Angeles, 1989)
Rhetoric | Aristotle, *Rhetoric*
Ringler | W. A. Ringler, Jr (ed.), *The poems of Sir Philip Sidney* (Oxford, 1962)
Ronsard | Pierre de Ronsard, *Abrégé de l'art poétique français* [1565]: text in Goyet
Russell | D. A. Russell, *Criticism in antiquity* (London, 1995)
Scaliger | Julius Caesar Scaliger, *Poetices libri septem* (Lyon, 1561); for details of editions used see 'A note on sources and references' below
Scott | James Renat Scott, *Memorials of the family of Scott, of Scot's-Hall, in the county of Kent* (London, 1876)
Sébillet | Thomas Sébillet, *Art poétique français* [1548]: text in Goyet
Shepherd | Sir Philip Sidney, *An apology for poesy*, ed. Geoffrey Shepherd; 3rd edn, revised R. W. Maslen (Manchester, 2002)
Shorter poems | Edmund Spenser, *The shorter poems*, ed. Richard A. McCabe (London, 1999)
Sieben Bücher | Julius Caesar Scaliger, *Poetices libri septem. Sieben Bücher über die Dichtkunst*, ed. Luc Deitz and Gregor Vogt-Spira, 6 vols. (Stuttgart-Bad Cannstatt, 1994–2011)
Skretkowicz | Sir Philip Sidney, *The Countess of Pembroke's Arcadia (the new Arcadia)*, ed. Victor Skretkowicz (Oxford, 1987)
Smith | Sir Thomas Smith, *De recta et emendata linguae Anglicae scriptione, dialogus* (Paris, 1568)
Snyder | Susan Snyder (ed.), *The divine weeks and works of Guillaume De Saluste Sieur Du Bartas, translated by Josuah Sylvester*, 2 vols. (Oxford, 1979)
Spingarn | J. E. Spingarn (ed.), *Critical essays of the seventeenth century*, 3 vols. (Oxford, 1908)
SRLC | Gavin Alexander (ed.), *Sidney's 'The defence of poesy' and selected Renaissance literary criticism* (London, 2004)
STC | A. W. Pollard *et al.*, *A short-title catalogue of books printed in England, Scotland, and Ireland, and of English books printed abroad, 1475–1640*, 2nd edn, 3 vols. (London, 1976–91)
Summa theologiae | St Thomas Aquinas, *Summa theologiæ*, Blackfriars' edn, 61 vols. (Cambridge, 1964–81)
Talaeus | Audomarus Talaeus [Omer Talon], *Rhetorica* (Paris, 1572)
Tilley | M. P. Tilley, *A dictionary of the proverbs in England in the sixteenth and seventeenth centuries* (Ann Arbor, 1950)
Vida | Ralph G. Williams (ed. and trans.), *The 'De arte poetica' of Marco Girolamo Vida* (New York, 1976)
View | Edmund Spenser, *A view of the state of Ireland*, ed. Andrew Hadfield and Willy Maley (Oxford, 1997)
Viperano | Giovanni Antonio Viperano, *De poetica libri tres* (Antwerp, 1579); English translation in Philip Rollinson (trans.), *On poetry* (Greenwood, SC, 1987)
Webbe | William Webbe, *A discourse of English poetrie* [1586]: text in *ECE*
Weinberg | Bernard Weinberg, *A history of literary criticism in the Italian Renaissance*, 2 vols. (Chicago, 1961)

Wells	Stanley Wells, 'A new early reader of Shakespeare', in Richard Meek, Jane Rickard, and Richard Wilson (eds.), *Shakespeare's book: essays in reading, writing and reception* (Manchester, 2008), 233–40; revised version of 'By the placing of his words', *The Times literary supplement*, 5243 (26 September 2003), 14–15
Wessner	Paul Wessner (ed.), *Commentum Terenti*, 3 vols. (Leipzig, 1902–8)
Wills	Richard Wills, *De re poetica* [1573], ed. and trans. A. D. S. Fowler (Oxford, 1958)

A NOTE ON SOURCES AND REFERENCES

In direct quotations from early printed sources, usage of i/j and u/v has been regularised, 'ß' has been replaced by 'ss' and ampersand by 'and' or 'et', and contractions and abbreviations have been silently expanded. In direct quotations from manuscript sources, supplied letters are italicised, but otherwise a similar approach is taken. The exceptions in both cases are certain examples in the Textual Introduction, which are treated more diplomatically. Lost or illegible manuscript text is given between curly brackets. Place of printing for pre-1700 books is London unless otherwise indicated. Page or leaf numbers are used in references to early printed books, where present and reliable; otherwise references are to printed signatures. References to poems are to (i) poem number or book and (ii) line number(s) in the form '2.278–9'. Similarly, references to acts and scenes of plays or to books, chapters, and sections of prose works are standardised to a sequence of arabic numerals separated by full-stops (e.g. 'Quintilian, 12.10.6'). References to classical texts are to their conventional numbering and only (additionally) to page numbers where a reference to a modern edition is also given.

Certain categories of source need further explanation:

1. Works of reference
Extensive use has been made of Charlton T. Lewis and Charles Short, *A Latin dictionary* (Oxford, 1879); Liddell and Scott; *ODNB*, for all British biographical details, unless otherwise indicated; and Simon Hornblower and Antony Spawforth (eds.), *The Oxford classical dictionary*, revised 3rd edn (Oxford, 2003), for all ancient biographical details.

2. Bibles
There is no certain evidence of what English Bible Scott used, but the Geneva Bible is the likeliest; all quotations come from that source, in a modern facsimile of the Cambridge edition of 1591: *The Cambridge Geneva Bible of 1591: a facsimile reprint* (Cambridge, 1992). Greek and Latin texts consulted are: *Septuaginta*, ed. Alfred Rahlfs, 3rd edn, 2 vols. (Stuttgart, 1949); *The Greek new testament*, ed. R. V. G. Tasker (Oxford, 1964); and *Biblia sacra iuxta vulgatam versionem*, ed. Robert Weber, 2 vols. (Stuttgart, 1969).

3. Classical texts
Greek and Latin texts in the volumes of the Loeb Classical Library series have been used unless otherwise stated in the Commentary or here. The Loeb translations are also used, unless otherwise stated, though sometimes these have been silently adapted for clarity. Other texts and/or translations are used instead or in addition as follows:

(i) Plato
English translations: John M. Cooper (ed.), *Plato: complete works* (Indianapolis, 1997).

(ii) Aristotle

Greek text of *Poetics*: Rudolf Kassell (ed.), *Aristotelis de arte poetica liber* (Oxford, 1965).

English translation of *Poetics*: M. E. Hubbard in *ALC*; with occasional use of Stephen Halliwell's translation in the Loeb volume *Aristotle, Poetics. Longinus, On the sublime. Demetrius, On style* (Cambridge, Mass., 1995).

English translation of *Rhetoric*: *The art of rhetoric*, ed. and trans. J. H. Freese (Cambridge, Mass., 1926).

All other English translations: Jonathan Barnes (ed.), *The complete works of Aristotle: the revised Oxford translation*, 2 vols. (Princeton, 1984).

(iii) Horace

Loeb texts and translations are used, but textual information is supplemented by D. R. Shackleton Bailey (ed.), *Opera* (Stuttgart, 1985).

(iv) Plutarch

I have made use of the contemporary translations of the *Lives* ('North') and the *Moralia* ('Holland'). The important essay *De audiendis poetis* is quoted in the translation in *ALC*. Otherwise, the relevant Loeb volumes are used.

(v) Plotinus

I have used Stephen MacKenna (trans.), *The enneads*, abridged John Dillon (London, 1991).

4. Continental texts

Translations from early modern texts are mine unless otherwise indicated.

(i) Scaliger

I have used Julius Caesar Scaliger, *Poetices libri septem*, facsimile of 1561 edn (Stuttgart-Bad Cannstatt, 1987), checking against the edited text with German translation in *Sieben Bücher*; the text of the 1561 edition is printed in two columns, with marginal letters dividing the page into quarters, enabling reference by page number, segment of page, and column: '168d2' thus refers to the bottom quarter of the second column of page 168. *Sieben Bücher* includes the page numbers from the 1561 edition, so either edition can be used to follow up references given here. It should be noted, however, that chapter references to Book 3 are to the numbering in the 1561 edition, which lacks a tenth chapter, and not to the corrected numbering in *Sieben Bücher*. Where a passage is translated in Padelford, that translation is used and a reference will be found. Otherwise, English translations are my own.

(ii) Viperano

See the list of abbreviations above, 'Viperano', for bibliographical details. Translations are Rollinson's unless otherwise indicated. Page references are to the English translation except where the Latin text is quoted, when the reference is to both texts, in the form '[Latin page]/[English translation page]'. These are often preceded by references to book/chapter.

(iii) Lomazzo

Italian text: Lomazzo; English translation: Haydocke for Books 1–5; otherwise mine. The frequent italics in quotations from Haydocke's translation are original.

(iv) Ariosto

English translations are taken from: Ludovico Ariosto, *Orlando furioso*, trans. Guido Waldman (Oxford, 1974).

(v) Tasso and Guarini

Scott's translations from Tasso have been checked against Ettore Mazzali (ed.), *Opere*, 2 vols. (Naples, 1970); for Guarini's *Il pastor fido* I have used the parallel text with Richard Fanshawe's English translation of 1647: J. H. Whitfield (ed.), *Il pastor fido* (Edinburgh, 1976).

5. English texts

(i) Chaucer

All references are to the texts and line numbering in Larry D. Benson (ed.), *The Riverside Chaucer* (Oxford, 1988).

(ii) Wyatt

All references are to the texts in Kenneth Muir and Patricia Thomson (eds.), *Collected poems of Sir Thomas Wyatt* (Liverpool, 1969).

(iii) Sidney

Quotations from the *Arcadia* are taken from *NA*; the corresponding pagination in Skretkowicz or *OA* is also given. I have used Ringler for all poems.

(iv) Spenser

All references are to the texts in *FQ* for *The faerie queene* and *Shorter poems* for the other poems.

(v) Shakespeare

All references are to the texts and line numbering in G. Blakemore Evans (ed.), *The Riverside Shakespeare*, 2nd edn (Boston, Mass., 1997).

INTRODUCTION

William Scott (c.1571–c.1617)

The author of *The model of poesy* was the product of two leading Kentish families: the Scotts and the Wyatts. His mother was Jane Wyatt, daughter of Sir Thomas Wyatt the rebel, granddaughter of Sir Thomas Wyatt the poet. His father was Charles Scott, the second son of Sir Reginald Scott of Scot's Hall. The Scott family had been based at Scot's Hall in Smeeth and the neighbouring parish of Brabourne since the early fourteenth century and its past generations had included prominent servants of the county and the country.[1] The Wyatts were not William Scott's only connection to the world of literature: Reginald Scott, the enlightened author of *The discoverie of witchcraft* (1584), was his father's cousin;[2] he may even have had a distant family connection to the clown Will Kemp.[3]

Scott's date of birth has been reported as c.1579,[4] which would make the *Model* the work of a younger man than it is. In fact, Scott was born in the early 1570s, possibly in 1571. We know that he had been born by 1574, because the visitation of Kent in 1574 recorded a William as the second son of Charles Scott and Jane Wyatt.[5] 1574 was also the year in which Charles Scott acquired the manor of Eggarton, above the village of Godmersham in the Stour valley, and related lands. When he bought Eggarton he was living at Challock,[6] but a search of the Challock parish register between 1560 and 1574 finds no Scotts,[7] so the family must have been living elsewhere before this when their first children, including William Scott and his older brother Thomas, were born. The parish records for the area of Kent dominated by the Scott family are patchy for these years. Godmersham, for example, is represented only by the Bishop's transcript, with a gap between 1571 and 1576/7. The baptism of a William Scott on 20 April 1571 is, however, recorded in the parish register (and the Bishop's transcript of the same) for Boughton Aluph parish,

---

[1] *ODNB*, 'Scott family (per. c.1400–c.1525)'.   [2] *ODNB*, 'Scott [Scot], Reginald (d. 1599)'.

[3] See *ODNB*, 'Kemp, William (d. in or after 1610?)' for the putative connection of Kemp to the Kempes of Ollantighe, near Ashford in Kent. Scott's paternal grandmother was Emmeline Kempe: *ODNB*, 'Scott, Sir Thomas (1534x6–1594)'.

[4] 'SCOTT, William (c.1579–aft.1611), of Godmersham, Kent', in *HoP*, III, 358–9, and thence by Stanley Wells (Wells, 234). It is not clear where the date of 1579 originates, but it is also associated with another William Scott, the distant kinsman from Chigwell, Essex who became the Blessed Maurus Scott: see Bede Camm, *Nine martyr monks: the lives of the English Benedictine martyrs beatified in 1929* (London, 1931), 186–7.

[5] W. Bruce Bannerman (ed.), *The visitations of Kent, taken in the years 1574 and 1592*, Harleian Society 75 (London, 1924), 30.

[6] *Scott*, lxviii: record 87, 22 May 1574.

[7] CCA-U3/27/P154B. I have searched the registers of a number of adjacent parishes without finding anything other than what is detailed here.

but this child is described as a son of Sir Thomas Scott (Charles Scott's older brother).[8] There is no other record of a son of Sir Thomas Scott named William,[9] and that this William should be baptised in Boughton Aluph is perplexing, since it is close to where Charles Scott was living at this time (it is the parish between Challock and Godmersham) and rather further from Scot's Hall, where Sir Thomas lived. The William Scott born at Boughton Aluph is more likely to be the son of the as yet itinerant Charles Scott, living in that area, than of Sir Thomas Scott, firmly ensconced in Scot's Hall several parishes away. But that would require a slip of the pen from the parson.

William Scott, then, may have been born in 1571 and was certainly born no later than 1574. He was brought up at Eggarton in Godmersham, a village that would be well known to Jane Austen 200 years later.[10] Scott's brother Thomas (*c.*1566–1635) 'probably went to Canterbury grammar school as a commoner and afterwards to university', and we can assume a similar path for William.[11] There are records of a Thomas Scott being admitted as a pensioner (that is, self-funding) at Corpus Christi College, Cambridge in 1582, and an unnamed Scott being admitted fellow-commoner at the same college in 1583.[12] Either or both of these may be William Scott's brother, an attractive possibility as it would see him following two years behind Christopher Marlowe from The King's School in Canterbury to Corpus Christi in Cambridge.[13] But the evidence is inconclusive, and the only William Scott recorded at Cambridge in the period is another man entirely: the future Maurus Scott, Catholic martyr, a sizar at Trinity in 1594, who transferred to Trinity Hall in 1596 and received the LLB law degree in 1600.[14] We know that many Scotts of the Scot's Hall branch studied at Oxford, especially at Hart Hall (now Hertford College); in the Oxford records, however, the only Williams in the period are from other counties.[15] Nevertheless, Oxford seems more likely than Cambridge, not only in view of the family connection but in the light of William Scott's interests in the intellectual culture of Oxford, which are explored below.

From university William Scott went to the Inns of Court in London, a typical path for a gentleman. He was admitted to the Inner Temple on 21 May 1595, and the admission was confirmed by the Inner Temple Parliament on 1 June 1595.[16] While he was a law student, he produced the scribal manuscript, now British Library Additional Manuscript 81083, that contains his treatise on poetics, *The model of poesy*, along with a partial translation of the poem of the Creation by the French protestant poet Du Bartas,

---

[8] Parish register: KHLC-P36/1/5. Bishop's transcript: CCA-DCa/BT/22.

[9] For pedigree see Robert Hovenden (ed.), *The visitation of Kent, taken in the years 1619–1621*, Harleian Society 42 (London, 1898), 128–9.

[10] As the home of the Knights, who adopted her brother Edward: see *ODNB*, 'Austen, Jane (1775–1817)'.

[11] Peter Clark, 'Thomas Scott and the growth of urban opposition to the early Stuart regime', *Historical journal*, 21 (1978), 1–26 (3). There are no records of commoners (as opposed to scholars) at The King's School, Canterbury before the eighteenth century.

[12] John Venn, *Alumni Cantabrigienses*, Part I, 4 vols. (Cambridge, 1922–6), IV, 33.

[13] See *ODNB*, 'Marlowe [Marley], Christopher (*bap.* 1564, *d.* 1593)'.

[14] Venn, *Alumni Cantabrigienses*, IV, 33; Camm, *Nine martyr monks*, 188–91.

[15] Joseph Foster, *Alumni Oxonienses . . . 1500–1714*, 4 vols. (Oxford, 1891), IV, 1324–5.

[16] The Inner Temple Admissions Database (www.innertemple.org.uk/archive/itad); F. A. Inderwick (ed.), *A calendar of the Inner Temple records*, I (London, 1896), 405.

La sepmaine. He dedicated the latter to his mother's brother, George Wyatt of Boxley. The *Model* he dedicated to Sir Henry Lee, the former Queen's champion and a kinsman from whose patronage Scott might hope to gain, if he was not benefiting already. It is important that the manuscript given to Lee contains both the *Model* and the Du Bartas, since they combine to demonstrate Scott's linguistic abilities (French, Latin, Italian, some Greek) as well as his intellectual power and Protestant commitment. Aside from the considerable importance and interest of the contents, then, we can see the manuscript as a demonstration to Lee of Scott's qualifications for employment, either on Lee's business or that of England. And the demonstration was successful: we can surmise that Scott's future career was guided by Lee's hand, and we find Scott close to Lee a decade later when the older man died. How much the two men had to do with each other in the meantime we can only conjecture. But Scott's next appearance in the historical record is a certain demonstration of Lee's patronage, for he served, once only, as Member of Parliament for New Woodstock in the Parliament of October–December 1601.[17] Lee was high steward of New Woodstock, and the borough's two seats were in effect in his gift. The two members had been Lee's kinsmen John Lee and Lawrence Tanfield in the Parliaments of 1588, 1593, and 1597 (Tanfield had filled one of the places in 1584 and 1586 too), and Lee's half-brother Richard would get a chance in 1604, but in 1601 it was Tanfield and Scott, the latter clearly a kind of temporary substitute for a Lee.[18]

Our next certain reference to Scott comes a few years later,[19] when we find him benefiting from a connection to another prominent Kentish family, the Smythes, and travelling to Russia. Thomas 'Customer' Smythe (1522–91) was a wealthy merchant and financier, with dealings in Muscovy and a specialisation in collecting import taxes and duties. He had married into a Kentish family and bought further lands in Kent, where his principal property was the manor and castle of Westenhanger (or Ostenhanger), a few miles south-east of Scot's Hall along the Folkestone road. His second son Sir Thomas (*c*.1558–1625) followed him into business, becoming a governor of the Muscovy and Levant companies, and first governor of the East India Company.[20] In June 1604 Sir Thomas Smythe was sent on a special embassy to the Tsar of Russia Boris Godunov, returning around June 1605; William Scott went with him. The Smythes and the Scotts were close: when William Scott's cousin Sir John Scott married for the second time it was to Katherine Smythe, sister of Sir

---

[17] *HoP*, III, 358–9; W. R. Williams, *The parliamentary history of the county of Oxford* (Brecknock, 1899), 197. Scott's brother Thomas would later be an MP for Canterbury; his manuscript discourse on parliamentary reform of *c*.1626 starts from a premise of disgust that the Commons includes so many burgesses who never live, much less hail from, the counties they represent (Clark, 'Thomas Scott', 16).

[18] *HoP*, I, 227–8 (New Woodstock); II, 447–50 (the Lees); III, 475–6 (Tanfield).

[19] We can discount the following: one William Bird wrote in around January 1604 to Cecil about a William Scott in Hertfordshire who had said a few scurrilous things about Cecil and recited a doggerel 'jest'; Cecil endorsed the letter 'An idle information' (HMC Hatfield, XVI 14). *HoP*, III, 359, mentions this as a possible reference to Scott, but the name is common enough for us to assume that it is a different William Scott.

[20] *ODNB*, 'Smythe [Smith], Thomas (1522–1591)' and 'Smythe [Smith], Sir Thomas (*c*.1558–1625)'. See also 'SMYTHE, Sir Thomas (*c*.1558–1625)', in *HoP2*, VI, 363–8.

Thomas Smythe; their brother Sir Richard Smythe, in turn, married Elizabeth Scott, Sir John Scott's sister.[21] The Smythes were not Scott's only connection to Muscovy, however. Sir Henry Lee's (illegitimate) brother Richard had travelled to Muscovy and was likely engaged in trade as a member of the Muscovy Company. He had been an earlier ambassador to Boris Godunov in 1600–1,[22] and would take Scott's place alongside Tanfield as the second Member of Parliament for New Woodstock in the 1604 Parliament when Scott in turn went to Russia. Although the patronage of Sir Henry Lee must have been ongoing – as we shall see – the Smythe connection seems to have been fruitful too. It explains why William Scott was living in Westenhanger – the Smythe manor – in 1611–12, after Sir Henry Lee's death.

The Russian embassy is the occasion of Scott's only surviving letter, and raises some intriguing questions about his literary activities over which we should pause. Sir Thomas Smythe's embassy was an eventful one, for a civil war came almost from nowhere within days of their arrival, and would drag on long after their departure. Scott wrote about the embassy in a letter to Robert Cecil, King James's secretary of state; that letter survives in the National Archives (SP 91/1) and is transcribed in Appendix 2 (249–53). Somewhat implausibly for a man in his early thirties who had already served as an MP, Scott claims that this embassy represents 'the maidenhoode of my travell, the first fruites of my reducing my study to matter of accion' (250). Scott tells Cecil that he has written an extensive discourse about the embassy: 'Because of the strange accidentes (strange even to prodigeousnes) falling out this yeere of Sir Thomas Smyths negociacions in Russia, and because of the manifold differing surmises and rumers thereon, me thinkes it worth labour to doe somewhat to assure and informe the world of soe important an affaire.' What he presents in the letter is a sort of executive summary, which he describes in the language of *The model of poesy*:

> The summe and argumente of the discourse is the Image of the ambassadors negotiacion, the discription of the Landes and Territories under and adjoyning to the Russe Empier, the mappe of their mannors and facions and last the story of theis Two last confercions in govermente, or rather in the governers, of all which (dedicated to yowr Lordshippe in private) I thought good to offer this summery following Comprizing the breefe of the mayne or Cardenall accident that fell out betwene theis turns (as understanding by Sir Thomas Smyth yowr Lordshipps desire that waye) till the larger Can be trancescribed.   (250)

The long reign of Ivan the Terrible, the first Tsar, had ended with his death in 1584. His son, Feodor I, succeeded him but, because of his physical or mental ill health, the *de facto* ruler was his wife's brother Boris Godunov. Feodor's younger brother Dmitry and his mother were sent away from the court and Dmitry died of a (possibly self-inflicted) knife wound in 1591. When Feodor died childless in 1598 Boris became Tsar. What happened in 1604–5 was extraordinary. A pretender to the throne had appeared a few years earlier, claiming to be Dmitry (an imposter having been substituted and having died in his stead in 1591, the story went). Having gathered support and a small army this Dmitry moved against Boris in June 1604, just after Smythe and Scott had arrived. The first of two engagements with Boris's army went Dmitry's way, the second decisively against him, but then Boris died in April 1605 and Dmitry's cause gained new energy. Boris's wife and only surviving son, the new Tsar Feodor II, were imprisoned and then murdered in June 1605, and Dmitry acceded to the throne, to reign for less than a year. There Scott's story ends, though the 'Time of Troubles' had many twists and turns yet (including two more 'false Dmitrys').

Schiller, Pushkin, and Mussorgsky were not the only ones to see the literary potential in these events. In 1605 appeared a fascinating volume offering an account of the embassy that deserves some consideration because of its similarity to the longer work that Scott promises Cecil. It also happens to be a major source for John Milton's *A brief history of Moscovia* (possibly written in 1648).[23] Its full title is 'Sir Thomas Smithes voiage and entertainment in Rushia. With the tragicall ends of two Emperors and one Empresse, within one Moneth during his being there: And the miraculous preservation of the now raigning Emperor, esteemed dead for 18. yeares.' This recognition of the literariness of events, here packaged as the sort of combination of tragic death and romance rebirth interesting Shakespeare at this time, is continued in the work itself. An anonymous editor who was not on the embassy has pieced together his account 'from the mouths of divers gentlemen that went in the Journey, and having som good notes bestowed upon me in writing, wrought them into this body', and he makes clear, too clear perhaps, that he has published the account without the permission of these gentlemen or of Sir Thomas Smythe.[24] The work is a patchwork, first a rather dull travelogue occasionally (and probably subsequently) seasoned with purpler prose and literary allusions, and then an account of the sensational events very much in the style of the regime-changing narratives of Book II of Sidney's *Arcadia*. Its range of contemporary literary allusion is impressive – Sidney,[25] Shakespeare, Jonson, Greville – and is exemplified in one of the few passages of this work to have received much notice.[26] It describes Feodor II's demise:

> his fathers Empire and Government, was but as the *Poeticall Furie in a Stage-action*, compleat yet with horrid and wofull Tragedies: a first, but no second to any *Hamlet*; and that now *Revenge*, just *Revenge* was comming with his Sworde drawne against him, his royall Mother, and dearest Sister, to fill up those Murdering Sceanes; the *Embryon* whereof was long since Modeld, yea digested (but unlawfully and too-too vive-ly) by his dead selfe-murdering Father: such and so many being their feares and terrours; the Divell advising, Despaire counselling, Hell it selfe instructing; yea, wide-hart-opening to receive a King now, rather than a Kingdome; as *L. Bartas* devinely sayth: *They who expect not Heaven, finde a Hell every where.*   (K1ʳ)

---

[23] See the list of sources in *A brief history of Moscovia* (1682), 109.
[24] *Sir Thomas Smithes voiage and entertainment in Rushia* (1605), A2ʳ.
[25] Examples of allusions: *The defence of poesy* (c2ᵛ); *Arcadia* (D4ʳ, E1ʳ⁻ᵛ).
[26] See, e.g., Margreta de Grazia, *Hamlet without Hamlet* (Cambridge, 2007), 45–8.

Shakespeare, Sidneian compounds, Du Bartas, the use of *model* as a verb, the (Aristotelian) dramatic plot as embryo: these are, as we shall see, all things found in Scott's *Model* as well as in this brief passage, and it is hard to imagine that they could come together very often. The impression that Scott is hovering close to this writing is only made firmer by another extraordinary passage, which follows almost immediately:

> Oh for some excellent pen-man to deplore their state: but he which would lively, naturally, or indeed poetically delyneate or enumerate these occurrents, shall either lead you thereunto by *a poeticall spirit*, as could well, if well he might the dead living, life-giving *Sydney* Prince of *Poesie*; or deifie you with the Lord *Salustius* devinity, or in an Earth-deploring, Sententious, high rapt Tragedie with the noble *Foulk-Grevill*, not onely give you the *Idea*, but the soule of the acting *Idea*; as well could, if so we would, the elaborate English *Horace* that gives number, waight, and measure to every word, to teach the reader by his industries, even our Lawreat worthy *Benjamen*, whose Muze approves him with (our mother) the *Ebrew* signification to bee, *The elder Sonne*, and happely to have been the Childe of *Sorrow*: It were worthy so excellent rare witt: for my selfe I am neither *Apollo* nor *Appelles*, no nor any heire to the *Muses*: yet happely a younger brother, though I have as little bequeathed me, as many elder Brothers, and right borne Heires gaine by them: but *Hic labor, Hoc opus est.*   (ĸ1ᵛ)

The examination of '*Benjamen*' traces the etymologies and biblical allusions that Jonson manipulates in the as yet unpublished Epigram 45, on the son who had died in 1603.[27] Scott was of course a 'younger brother' literally as well as figuratively (translator and critic, not original poet), but was he in a position to read Jonson in manuscript? If we knew Scott to be the writer of this passage we would be encouraged to imagine him, in 1605 as well as in the late 1590s when he wrote the *Model*, not looking at the contemporary literary scene from the outside but belonging to it. The pairing of Sidney and Du Bartas ('Lord *Salustius*') was not Scott's alone: Sylvester saw his Du Bartas translation as a continuation of Sidney's work (see below, xxxiv). Nor is the kind of knowledge of contemporary literature shown here something we should only expect from Scott, remarkable though it is. An appreciation of Jonson's Horatianism would be more more generally shared a decade or two later, but it is not so very prescient in 1605; knowledge that Greville wrote tragedies was more uncommon before the pirated publication of *Mustapha* in 1609; and any reader of Sidney's *Defence* might talk of Platonic ideas and quote Virgil, equating the reading and writing of fiction with Aeneas' journey back from the underworld (*DP*, 9, 22). We cannot, therefore, quite claim to see Scott's signature on this passage. Indeed, the style here and elsewhere is too enthusiastically Sidneian to convince one that it might be Scott's: the sort of precise and yet exaggerated imitation of Sidney's style managed by the Arcadian continuators like Gervase Markham and William Alexander is something Scott quite deliberately

---

[27] *CWBJ*, v, 134.

avoids in the *Model*.[28] But it is difficult to believe that Scott has nothing to do with this volume. If it is not by him, might it have been written *for* him? If he is not the editor, might he not at the very least be one of the witnesses collated by the editor?

We know little of Scott's activities in the years following the voyage to Russia, though evidently he worked more closely with Lee in the old man's last years, witnessing his will on 6 October 1609,[29] and composing (and signing) the beautiful biographical epitaph for Lee's funerary monument at Quarrendon after Sir Henry's death in February 1611, 'being a Sharer in his blood as well as in many his honourable Favours and an honourer of his vertues'.[30] Scott did not join the procession at Lee's funeral in April 1611, but 'Mr Scott's man' is first in the section of servants of Lee's family and retainers, walking alongside the servant of the chief mourner, Lee's son Henry, near the front of the procession.[31] That implies that Scott had by now some central importance in Lee's life and household. Scott received no specific legacy in Lee's will, but his own will tells us that he had already been granted a thirty-year lease on a farm (he does not say where) by Lee. Scott may, then, have been based for some of the period 1605–11 in Oxfordshire, with or close to Lee, but in an indenture of 6 November 1609 he is 'of Godmersham', evidently choosing to live close to his brother, and perhaps on family lands.[32]

In the visitation of Kent of 1619–21, Scott is recorded in his family tree as 's.p.' or *sine prole*, without issue, and therefore also dead.[33] But he did attempt to start a family in what turned out to be his last years. Scott married Barbara Tomlyn probably in 1610 or early 1611. Her father was a brewer and jurat (a Kentish alderman) in the town of Faversham, half a dozen miles north of Godmersham. The dowry included seven acres of land in Faversham, and seems to have involved some further complicated financial arrangements. An indenture of 24 February 1611 'Betweene William Tomlyn of the towne and Porte of Faversham in the County of Kent Beerebruer of thone parte and Thomas Scott of Egarton in the said County esquier and william Scott of Westinghanger in the fore said County gent of thother partie' sees the Scotts giving Tomlyn what is in effect a one-year loan of £100 at 10 per cent interest, secured against his brewhouse and orchards in Faversham, 'diuerse other good causes and consideracions him movinge'.[34] The terms of the indenture give Tomlyn the option of coming in person, or sending his assigns, to Eggarton, a year and a day later to redeem his property for £110, but an endorsement records that William Scott was there on 25 February 1612 and no one came. There was never any intention of taking over Tomlyn's business; it must just have been a gentle way of improving his father-in-law's liquidity, and Tomlyn continued to live and work at the brewhouse.

Scott, as that indenture indicates, had evidently moved with his new wife to live in Westenhanger, among the Smythes. A stillborn son was buried at Stanford (the parish

---

[28] On imitations of the *Arcadia* see my *Writing after Sidney: the literary response to Sir Philip Sidney, 1586–1640* (Oxford, 2006), esp. 262–82.
[29] PCC, NA-PROB 11/117, 326ᵛ–328ʳ.   [30] Chambers, 305.   [31] Chambers, 298.
[32] *Scott*, lxxiii, record 114, a land conveyance between Thomas and William Scott, and Ralph Ward (a family retainer who witnesses the Tomlyn indenture discussed below).
[33] Hovenden (ed.), *The visitation of Kent . . . 1619–1621*, 128.   [34] NA-E44/263.

into which Westenhanger had been merged in the sixteenth century) on 12 April 1611,[35] and a son William was baptised at Stanford on 2 August 1612. On that same day a son, John, of Scott's cousin Edward was buried there.[36] Edward Scott was a younger brother of Sir John Scott, and he would inherit Scot's Hall in 1616 when Sir John Scott died without issue.[37] At this date he was living in Postling, the adjacent parish to Stanford, and is mentioned as such in Scott's will (see Appendix 3, 255). He evidently offered William Scott some financial support, as the will makes clear, and his presence may have been another reason for Scott's living in this area in 1611–12. It was another temporary residence, however: we can sense that the Scotts' accommodation was not permanent in the Stanford parish register entry recording their son's baptism in 1612 ('William Scot, son*ne* to Mr William Scot of Eggertone'),[38] but it was in fact not back to Eggarton or Godmersham but to Brabourne that the family moved next, for the same son was, sadly, buried at Brabourne on 3 February 1614.[39] Evidently, Scott was also on good terms with his older cousin Sir John Scott, who had recently inherited Scot's Hall from his childless older brother Thomas,[40] and he may at that point have offered Scott somewhere to live nearby. Sir John is recorded shifting his lands and leases round from early 1611,[41] and an indenture of 6 October 1611, intended 'for the advancement and preferment of the heirs male of his brothers' and of his cousins, makes clear the order of succession to all the Scott lands, with Thomas and William Scott and their younger brother Antony bringing up the rear.[42]

Scott's date of death had been uncertainly placed at 'after 1611',[43] when the last thing known about him was his involvement in the commemoration of Sir Henry Lee. But in fact the date can be pushed back several years. Scott was alive on 13 June 1613 when his mother Jane made her will and left him plate, hangings, furnishings, and andirons.[44] Scott made his own will on 2 June 1615; here he is William Scott of Brabourne.[45] He leaves things to his wife 'and to the yssue of her, and my bodye (yf any be)', and, again, 'to the yssue of her and me (yf god send any)' and 'the yssue that may be yf yt please god of our bodyes'. At this point, the Scotts were childless and, after the death of young William, evidently a little desperate, but they had a daughter later in that year: Kathryn was baptised on 10 November 1615 in Brabourne.[46] Names were often taken from godparents, and a likely candidate is Sir John Scott's wife Katherine, the sister of Sir Thomas Smythe. Scott was still alive in 1616: Sir John Scott, in his will of 18 September 1616, gives 'unto my lovinge Cosen William Scott of Brabourne,

[35] Stanford/Westenhanger parish register: CCA-U3/253/1/1, 17ʳ.

[36] CCA-U3/253/1/1, 17ʳ; Bishop's transcript: CCA-DCb/BT1/222, 15.

[37] See 'SCOTT, Edward (*c.*1578–1645/6)', in *HoP2*, VI, 242–3.

[38] CCA-U3/253/1/1, 29ʳ; CCA-DCb/BT1/222, 15.

[39] Brabourne parish register: KHLC-P41/1/1.

[40] See *HoP*, III, 356, for Thomas Scott's death on 24 September 1610. On Sir John Scott see 'SCOTT, Sir John (*c.*1564–1616)', in *HoP2*, VI, 243–6.

[41] *Scott*, lxxiv, records 115, 116, 117, 119.   [42] *Scott*, lxxiv, record 116.   [43] *HoP*, III, 358.

[44] Consistory Court of Canterbury will register: CCA-DCb/PRC/32/44/348a.

[45] Archdeaconry Court of Canterbury will register: CCA-DCb/PRC/17/60/399. See Appendix 3.

[46] Brabourne parish, Bishop's transcript, CCA-DCb/BT1/31. From Thomas Scott's will we can infer that she must have predeceased her father.

my best geldinge'.[47] Sir John Scott died almost immediately, so we can hope that Scott got the horse.[48] Scott's mother Jane was buried at Godmersham on 3 March 1617,[49] and the will was proved on 17 April, but Scott may not have been around to collect that legacy. Scott's own will was proved on 12 August 1617, and Scott had evidently died before June 1617. Thomas Scott's will of 31 October 1633 includes a crucial detail. At some point in the Easter law term of James I's fifteenth regnal year (that is, between 7 May and 2 June 1617), 'because all my said Fathers sonnes except my selfe weare then dec*eas*d without issue' the various lands he had inherited from his father in fee-tail (that is, to pass to his brothers or their heirs if he died without issue) were transferred to fee-simple, making them his to bequeath without complicated entails.[50]

There is no record of Scott's burial and he may well have died abroad, since he made his will 'beinge then readye to take my Joyrney into the partes beyond the Seas' (254). 'Beyond the Seas' simply meant 'abroad',[51] so this may have been a trip to the continent, but in view of Scott's connections it was more likely to be the new world. Sir Thomas Smythe, with whom Scott had travelled to Russia in 1604–5, and in whose family's manor Scott had lived in the period 1611–12, was the treasurer of the Virginia Company and was heavily involved in Bermuda (known then as the Somers Islands). He had become governor of the Somers Islands Company, which was formed in 1615, the year of Scott's voyage, to oversee the Bermuda venture separately.[52] The American project was struggling both as a result of internal conflicts and because of dwindling numbers of colonists, and it is certainly conceivable that Scott might have been deputed to do some work there on Smythe's behalf. The Wyatts too had interests in the new world: we might note that Scott's younger cousin Francis Wyatt (the son of George Wyatt, to whom Scott's Du Bartas was dedicated) would in 1618 marry Margaret Sandys, the niece of Sir Edwin Sandys, a key member of the Virginia company, and go on to become governor of Virginia in 1621;[53] those travelling there with him in 1621 included his brother Hawte Wyatt and William Scott's nephew Henry Fleete, the son of his sister Deborah.[54]

A daunting trip to the new world and the contemplation of long separation from his family may explain the amplification of Scott's own sincere religiosity into the fervent opening sentences of what is his last literary composition – that part of the will where writers might compose their own variations on the necessary theme of the soul's and the body's separate destinations. Scott wills the latter '(yf I dye in England) to be buryed among my Ancestors in Brabourne' (254), maintaining the loyalty to his family

---

[47] PCC, NA-PROB 11/131, 57[v].

[48] Not 'about 28 December 1616' (*ODNB*) since Robert Sidney mourns him in a letter of 25 September 1616 (see below, li); the Brabourne parish register records his burial at Brabourne as 17 September 1616, one day before [*sic*] the date of his will: KHLC-P41/1/1.

[49] Godmersham parish register: CCA-U3/117/1/1.

[50] Consistory Court of Canterbury will register: CCA-PRC/32/51, 217[v]–19[v] (219[r]); reproduced in G. D. Scull, *Dorothea Scott* (Oxford, 1883), 199–203 (201–2).

[51] *OED, sea*, n., 11.   [52] *ODNB*, 'Smythe [Smith], Sir Thomas (*c*.1558–1625)'.

[53] *ODNB*, 'Sir Francis Wyatt (1588–1624)'.

[54] *ODNB*, 'Fleete, Henry (*c*.1602–1660/1)', stressing the strong Kentish component of the Virginia Company.

and his county that is the basis of his career and one message of his literary work. What little we know of Scott's later life, then, ties him closely to Sir Henry Lee and to Sir Thomas Smythe and gives him global horizons, but it also keeps him based firmly in Kent, the home of the Sidneys, the Scotts, the Smythes, and the Wyatts. That is the trajectory of a career that begins with an essay on poetics and a translation of Du Bartas.

The *Model* in context

SCOTT IN THE 1590S

It is possible to date *The Model of Poesy* with some precision to the summer of 1599. (The evidence for this dating is presented below, xxxvi–xxxvii.) The *Model* therefore belongs to a particular, and a particularly exciting, moment in Elizabethan literary and political history. It is also possible to place its author William Scott in more precise relation to the events, texts, and personalities of the late 1590s, thanks to evidence internal to the manuscript of the *Model* as well as external to it, and in particular to a family miscellany on which Scott seems to have worked in these years.

The Folger Shakespeare Library in Washington, DC has in its manuscript collections a 'Miscellany on religion and state affairs', MS v.b.214. Still in its original binding, it includes, among pen exercises, doodles, and jottings on its front and rear endleaves, the names of William Scott and his elder brother Thomas, who helpfully writes on the front endleaf (and contents page) 'Thomas Scott of Eggerton Gent'. The miscellany evolved in three distinct stages, confirmed by changes in hand, blank pages, and a contemporary contents page that lists only those texts copied into the miscellany before the third stage of compilation. The first stage must have been the work of Scott's father Charles, since it shows a particular interest in church politics of the 1580s. We can surmise that the volume was inherited by Thomas Scott after Charles Scott's death in 1596, because most of the documents in the second stage of transcription date from between 1597 and the brink of the Essex rebellion of early 1601; this stage includes a copy of Spenser's *A view of the present state of Ireland* (dated 1597 in the manuscript), and is likely to have involved William and Thomas directly. The third stage has an even more intent focus on Essex and Ireland, raking over the events of 1599–1601, and may, also or instead, have been the work of other names written in the volume – including John Knatchbull (a kinsman and Thomas Scott's future father-in-law), and a Richard Greene who signed the front pastedown and dated it 1 July 1601. The manuscript itself is complex and will repay further study.[55] Because we lack an extended specimen of William Scott's hand (we have only signatures in his italic hand at the end of the *Model* and Du Bartas dedications and of the letter to Cecil; short corrections in both documents, which in any case mimic his scribes' hands; and a signature in his secretary hand in the Folger miscellany), it is not possible to identify his with certainty as one

---

[55] An earlier study is interested primarily in the Essex context and does not identify the Scotts: James McManaway, 'Elizabeth, Essex, and James', in *Elizabethan and Jacobean studies*, ed. Herbert Davis and Helen Gardner (London, 1959), 219–30.

of the hands responsible for the volume's contents. However, his contribution is very likely indeed. I shall return to this volume at several points in this section.

The miscellany throws light on Scott's religious background. The first thing to be copied into it (though since lost or removed) was the 'Bishops' Articles'; seven items that follow respond to the Articles or concern the immediate fallout from this key episode in the history of Elizabethan puritanism. The three Articles were formulated by John Whitgift, on becoming Archbishop of Canterbury in 1583, and clerics were required to subscribe to them.[56] The first Article asserted the supremacy of the Queen in ecclesiastical matters and the third stated that the Thirty-nine Articles of 1563 were agreeable to the word of God; endorsing these two Articles was unproblematic for most. But the second Article was the sticking point. In asserting the authority of the 1559 Prayer Book and the episcopal hierarchy, and insisting that only the Prayer Book could be used in services, it reignited tensions between the bishops and the hotter sort of protestants who came to be known as puritans. Many in Parliament and the Privy Council objected, seeing in the Articles an Inquisition-style trap, since those puritans unable to endorse the second article were *de facto* failing to endorse the other two. The Articles reduced the room for manoeuvre of nonconformist or puritan clerics, led to the suspension of some churchmen, and were accompanied by a subtle crackdown on subversive religious publications.[57] The Scott family were against them: William Scott's father Charles Scott has been described as 'a committed puritan' who 'patronized young radical clergy and joined other sympathetic gentry in defending the county's godly ministers against Whitgift in 1584';[58] and his uncle Sir Thomas Scott addressed the Privy Council and led a delegation of Kentish gentlemen in a meeting with Whitgift at Lambeth Palace.[59] That puritan heritage has a long legacy. Scott's brother Thomas's 'life was dominated by an intense commitment to godly religion',[60] witnessed in the diaries and unpublished writings surviving from his later life; his daughter Dorothea Gotherson was to be a Quaker pamphleteer and preacher in the 1650s and early 60s.[61] A puritan tone can be heard in some passages in the *Model*, such as the long digression on pagan deities in literature (41–3), but also the pragmatism in William Scott's case of a man who respects bishops and other mainstream churchmen when they are pious or learned. Thomas Scott may have been a committed puritan, but the religious politics inherited by William Scott were those of a gentry family with local loyalties and responsibilities. Scott's is a pure kind of protestantism, most evident in his love of Du Bartas, but he shows no signs of a puritan mislike of poets and players.

---

[56] Henry Gee and William John Hardy (eds.), *Documents illustrative of English church history* (London, 1896), 481–4.

[57] For an extended discussion of this episode see Patrick Collinson, *The Elizabethan puritan movement* (London, 1967), esp. 243–88.

[58] Clark, 'Thomas Scott', 3.

[59] Collinson, *Elizabethan puritan movement*, 257, 258–9.

[60] *ODNB*, 'Scott, Thomas (*c*.1566–1635)'. See also 'SCOTT, Thomas (*c*.1566/7–1635)' in *HoP2*, VI, 246–52.

[61] *ODNB*, 'Gotherson [*née* Scott; *other married name* Hogben], Dorothea (*bap.* 1611)'.

The Folger miscellany also helps to fill in the gaps in Scott's biographical record, lending support to the hypothesis that he studied at Oxford (see above, xx). The second section of the miscellany includes a Latin speech of the Queen to the Polish ambassador from 25 July 1597. Squeezed into the blank space left on the opening that contains it, in an italic hand that may be Scott's, is a copy of a Latin speech delivered by the Queen to the heads of Oxford colleges on a visit in September 1592.[62] As discussed above, we have no record of the university education of Thomas (who would have been around twenty-six in 1592) or William (who would have been between eighteen and twenty-one), but if one of the two was at Oxford in 1592 it would have been William. William would have appreciated the speech's scholarly Latinity, and seems the more likely to have added to this politically minded volume an oration whose interest is limited to its occasion and literary quality; the same could be said of the inclusion of Henry Savile's oration for the same royal visit (71[r]). There was no standard age for university attendance, but twenty-one was old to be studying for the BA, just as twenty-four was old to begin legal training. The evidence is of course thin, and depends to an extent on our leaning towards a date of birth in 1571 rather than one closer to 1574, but it suggests the possibility that Scott stayed at Oxford for more like the seven years required for the MA; that possibility in turn helps to make sense of the scholarly depth demonstrated in the *Model*. Also related to Oxford is an interest in the Calvinist-leaning theologian John Rainolds, who from the late 1580s had held a special lectureship at Oxford in controversial theology and in the 1590s was to become engaged in an ongoing exchange with first William Gager and then Alberico Gentili which was printed in 1599 as *Th'overthrow of stage-playes*, and which William Scott read (see Commentary, 48.30–2n.). Two short controversial pieces by Rainolds, including his response to Richard Bancroft's 1589 sermon on the divine origins of episcopacy (57[r]), mark the start of the miscellany's second section, and a little later come Rainolds's arguments against Whitgift's position that Christ's soul (and not his body only) descended into hell (68[v]). In that visit to Oxford in 1592 Elizabeth 'schooled Doctor Reynalds for his precisenes, willing him to follow her lawes and not to run before them'.[63]

By the time of his father's death in 1596, William Scott was already a law student at the Inner Temple. This is a location of particular significance to our understanding of the *Model*, since Scott tells us explicitly that he wrote the *Model* and the Du Bartas translation during one of the law vacations (see Appendix 1, 248); as will become clear, this was probably the long vacation between 28 June and 8 October 1599.[64] The Inner Temple gave him access to works in manuscript. Scott quotes from a manuscript tractate by Richard Hooker (see Commentary, 66.24–5n.) that was not to be printed

---

[62] Folger MS v.b.214, 67[v]–68[r]; see Elizabeth I, *Collected works*, ed. Leah S. Marcus, Janel Mueller, and Mary Beth Rose (Chicago, 2000), 332–4 and 327–8 (English), and Elizabeth I, *Autograph compositions and foreign language originals*, ed. Janel Mueller and Leah S. Marcus (Chicago, 2003), 168–9 and 163–5 (Latin).

[63] *ODNB*, 'Rainolds [Reynolds], John (1549–1607)'.

[64] During the law terms students would attend the courts; during the vacations they would study and receive tuition (Inderwick, *Calendar*, I, xxxvi).

until 1612. It was based on sermons given by Hooker in the mid 1580s while Master of the Temple (that is, priest at the church used by Inner and Middle Templars), a role he had been appointed to by Archbishop Whitgift.[65] At another point Scott quotes directly from the *Directions for speech and style* of the Middle Templar (and friend of Ben Jonson) John Hoskyns, a treatise written for a young Templar probably only a matter of weeks or months before Scott was writing (see Commentary, 68.1–4n.); there are signs throughout the *Model* that he read Hoskyns carefully, and the two works have a surprising amount in common. Hoskyns writes a rhetorical treatise using literary examples, Scott a rhetorically informed work on poetics, but for both writers Sidney's *Arcadia* is the key text. And as we shall see, both works can be dated by casual references to the Earl of Essex's Irish campaign, over the spring and summer of 1599. Scott's awareness of late 1590s satire, his interest in Shakespeare, his impressive study of much of the most current literary writing, were enabled by his presence at the Inner Temple. It does not seem to have exposed him to the poetry of John Donne, as it would many young lawyers, but it did give him access to the bookshops and perhaps the theatres of London. The Inner Temple sits close to the Thames to the west of the old city walls, less than half a mile from where in Scott's day the booksellers crowded round St Paul's to the east, and with the theatres of Bankside just across the river to the south-east.

Scott had been admitted to the Inner Temple in 1595 at the request of Lawrence Tanfield (*c*.1551–1625), who had been made reader there earlier in that year.[66] He probably knew Tanfield because both were kinsmen of Sir Henry Lee (1533–1611), Queen Elizabeth's former champion and the dedicatee of *The model of poesy*. Tanfield married Lee's niece and was, as we have seen, a long-serving MP, under Lee's patronage, for the Oxfordshire borough of New Woodstock. His only child Elizabeth (1585–1639) may well be the 'young, more than hopeful gentlewoman and by me much to be respected kinswoman' (23) to whom Scott had given a copy of Plautus' *Menaechmi* prefaced by his short poem versifying the standard, supposed Ciceronian, definition of comedy (see Commentary, 23.37–24.8n. and 78.34–5n.). She was to become Elizabeth Cary, Viscountess Falkland, the writer and translator, and she, like Scott, presented a literary manuscript to Sir Henry Lee in these years, a translation of Abraham Ortelius' *Le miroir du monde* (1579).[67]

Lee, like Scott, was a Wyatt on his mother's side: Lee's mother Margaret Wyatt was the sister of the poet Sir Thomas Wyatt, and Wyatt (Lee's uncle, Scott's great-grandfather) took a hand in Lee's education.[68] Though Lee was from a Buckinghamshire family, the Queen's grant to him of the lieutenancy of the royal manor of Woodstock, and his acquisition of Ditchley, based him firmly in Oxfordshire, but always with those Wyatt ties to Kent too. As William Scott was later to write in the lengthy epitaph-cum-biography that he composed to sit near Lee's tomb

---

[65] *ODNB*, 'Whitgift, John (1530/31?–1604)'.   [66] Inderwick, *Calendar*, I, 405.

[67] At some point before her marriage in 1602: see *ODNB*, 'Cary [née Tanfield], Elizabeth, Viscountess Falkland (1585–1639)'.

[68] *ODNB*, 'Lee, Sir Henry (1533–1611)'.

in the chapel at Quarrendon, Lee 'served five succeedinge princes and kept himself Reight & Steady in many dangerous Shockes & 3. utter Turnes of State'.[69] Lee was never the politician, always a soldier first and courtier second, and this helped him survive. He was a Wyatt, though, in his love of the arts. I shall discuss Lee's patronage of painters below when I consider Scott's interest in the visual arts. As for Lee the poet, only a few short lyrics can now be ascribed to him with anything approaching confidence.[70] One of these is found on a portrait of Lee with his dog.[71] Three more are found in printed songbooks,[72] and the first of those was sung by Robert Hales in the tiltyard in 1590, at the Accession Day tournament at which Lee passed the baton of Queen's Champion to George Clifford, Earl of Cumberland.[73] Other poems, inscribed in prayerbooks or on his tomb,[74] may be by him. What role he played in devising the entertainments presented to Elizabeth when she visited Woodstock in 1575 or Ditchley in 1592 (during the same progress that took her to Oxford) is also impossible to tell.[75] But what becomes clear is that poetry lived for Lee in the company of music and the visual arts, in the tiltyard, and in courtly show.[76]

Lee is credited with the creation of the annual Accession Day tilts, around 1570 or 1571.[77] As Scott puts it, Lee was

> adorned with those flowers of Knighthood, Courtesie Bounty Valour, which quicklye gave forth their Fruicte, as well in the Feilde . . . as also in Court wher he shone in all those fayre partes became his profession & Vowes, honouring his highlye gracious M^ris with Reysinge those later Olimpiads of her Coronation Justs and Tournaments (Therby Tryinge & Treininge the Courtier in those Exercises of Armes that keepe the Person bright & steeled to Hardinesse, That by Softe Ease Rusts & Weares) wherin still himselfe lead and Triumphed, caryinge away the Spoyles of Grace from his Soveraigne & Renowne from the Worlde for the fairest Man at Armes & most complete Courtier of his Times[.][78]

Lee was a friend of Sir Philip Sidney, another keen tilter and deviser of *imprese* and allegorical entertainments; Lee accompanied Sidney on his 1577 embassy to the Emperor Rudolph, and Sidney worked the older knight's tiltyard persona of Lelius into

[69] Chambers, 305.

[70] For a discussion see Steven W. May, *The Elizabethan courtier poets* (Columbia, Mo., 1991), 355–7.

[71] Chambers, 83.

[72] Edward Doughtie (ed.), *Lyrics from English airs, 1596–1622* (Cambridge, Mass., 1970), 80–1 and 466–8 (Dowland, 1597); 102–3 and 478–9 (Dowland, 1600); and 350–1 and 587 (Dowland, 1610).

[73] See William Segar, *Honor military, and civill* (1602), R3^v–4^r.   [74] Chambers, 42, 303.

[75] For discussion see Chambers, 84–91 and 145–50, and appendix E, 276–97, for an edition of the Ditchley material. See also below, lxiv.142.

[76] For a study of these connections see Anthony Rooley, 'Time stands still: devices and designs, allegory and alliteration, poetry and music and a new identification in an old portrait', *Early Music*, 34 (2006), 443–64.

[77] See Segar, *Honor military, and civill*, R3^r. For a full account of Lee and the tilts see Frances Yates, 'Elizabethan chivalry: the romance of the Accession Day tilts', in *Astraea: the imperial theme in the sixteenth century* (London, 1975), 88–111.

[78] Chambers, 304–5.

the *Arcadia*. It is of course possible that the *Model* was Scott's bid for Lee's patronage, and that Scott was little known to his older kinsman: Scott's dedicatory epistle speaks of 'dutiful regard and honouring affection' but not of debt or gratitude; Lee's courtesy has been shown 'in some measure towards myself, in much, much more towards some of my nearest and most dear respected friends' (3). But the Tanfield connection as early as 1595 suggests that Scott was already under Lee's wing. We can therefore look in the *Model* for material that suits it to Lee, but also for evidence of Lee's influence. The engagement with the visual arts and the mention of *imprese* are just that, but the dominance of Scott's map of both the theory and the practice of poetry by Lee's friend (and Scott's distant Kentish kinsman) Sidney is also significant in this very particular respect too, however truly it may also reflect Scott's own literary tastes and theoretical commitments.

We see the same nexus of family, place, and poetry in Scott's relations with his uncle George Wyatt. George Wyatt of Boxley (1553–1624) was, in David Loades's words, 'the obscure son of a famous father, and the obscure father of famous sons'.[79] His political and poetic writings, preserved in a collection of family papers now in the British Library, show a pride in his Wyatt heritage, and his verse includes sonnets, a 784-line stanzaic poem on the Messiah, and a Latin paraphrase of the Song of Songs.[80] Scott quotes one of his sonnets (55)[81] and dedicates his Du Bartas translation to him (see Appendix 1), with a significant allusion to the epistle in which Sidney had dedicated his *Arcadia* to his sister. Sidney had described his composition of the *Arcadia*: 'Your dear self can best witness the manner, being done in loose sheets of paper, most of it in your presence, the rest by sheets sent unto you as fast as they were done' (*OA*, 3). And Scott describes his work on the Du Bartas: 'Nowe in the revisinge this my translation, I easely acknowledge my selfe faultye of much hast; (as onely hauinge one vacation to spend about it, and my discourse of the Arte of Poesy, as your selfe can best wittnesse).' Even on its own, but even more so when we detect the echo, this suggests that Scott was working in some proximity to his uncle. And we can see from the religious themes of some of Wyatt's poems that the two men had much in common. Indeed, this was not Wyatt's only connection to the project of translating Du Bartas into English. Josuah Sylvester's translation of *La sepmaine*, printed in 1605, includes in one of those translator's interjections of which Scott only partially approves (see Commentary, 72.34–73.3n.) the attribution of an impresa made from an anagram of 'Elizabeta Regina' to 'my deere *Wiat*', terms that suggest the two men were more than acquaintances.[82] Sylvester at another point works in a tribute to '*HARDY LAELIUS*, that Great *GARTER-KNIGHT*, | Tilting in Triumph of *ELIZAS* Right'.[83] These connections make sense when we notice that Sylvester too was from

---

[79] *ODNB*, 'Wyatt, George (1553–1624)'.

[80] On the Wyatt papers (British Library, Add. MSS 62135–8) see Agnes Conway, 'The Wyatt MSS. in the possession of the Earl of Romney', *Bulletin of the Institute of Historical Research*, 1 (1923), 73–6, and *The papers of George Wyatt*, ed. D. M. Loades, Royal Historical Society, Camden 4th Series, 5 (1968).

[81] See further my 'William Scott and the dating of George Wyatt's sonnets', *Notes and queries*, 59.1 (2012), 58–60.

[82] Snyder, I, 190 (Day 3) and II, 783.   [83] Snyder, I, 223 (Day 4, also first printed in 1605).

Kent. Also included in *Bartas: his devine weekes and workes* (1605) was a shape poem 'Lectoribus' ('To the readers'), a pyramid crowned with the Sidney heraldic arrowhead and porcupine and representing Sylvester's task as a parallel attempt to, rather than a completion of, Sidney's own translation of Du Bartas.[84] Sidney, Du Bartas, and Kent clearly belonged together, and not only in Scott's eyes.

*

The original contents page of the Scott family miscellany is a numbered list, in a single hand, of those items copied into the manuscript in the first two stages of transcription; the same hand has adapted this list by giving additional marginal numbers to items relating to the Earl of Essex, creating a second sequence; the manuscript's third phase of compilation then followed, and it was almost entirely concerned with Essex. Scott mentions Essex twice in the *Model* (44 and 52–3) and his connections to Essex deserve some consideration.

Robert Devereux, second Earl of Essex (1565–1601) fostered a view of himself as the military, political, and cultural heir of Sir Philip Sidney, whose widow Frances he married.[85] He served in the Low Countries when only twenty, and participated in the skirmish at Zutphen in which Sidney was mortally wounded. Sidney (the 'Stella' of whose sonnets was Essex's older sister Penelope) left Essex his best sword in his will, and the Earl of Leicester's step-son (as Essex had become when Leicester married his mother Lettice in 1578) took over from his nephew Sidney as the focus of English militant, internationalist protestantism. He also in time took over Sidney's role as an enlightened and engaged patron of artists, scholars, poets, and other young men on the make. From his return to England in October 1586, the month of Sidney's death, he became the Queen's new favourite, and for the rest of his life was engaged in a difficult, and in many ways passionate, relationship with the Queen, as each sought to control the other. Titles, lands, properties, honours, and other rewards followed, repairing the family finances crippled by his father's colonial and military efforts in Ireland. Essex became a leading figure in the tiltyard, and led various campaigns and raids in Portugal, France, and Spain, becoming in time Elizabeth's Earl Marshal and principal military leader. Essex was popular with puritan writers, who saw in him a chance for support against Whitgift, though his support for puritans was restricted to individual cases; like Sidney he was able to separate his personal religious beliefs (which seem to have been puritan) from his politics (which were more tolerant). He became a privy councillor in 1593 and gradually built up his political operation, hoping to succeed Lord Burghley as Elizabeth's leading councillor, and, as early as 1594, seeking covertly to secure the succession to the throne of James VI of Scotland. He was popular among university men, who might hope for employment with him among his growing army of secretaries, intelligencers, and chaplains. His success in leading the assault on Cadiz

---

[84] Snyder, II, plate 2, facing 889.

[85] The following account of Essex is indebted to Paul E. J. Hammer's biography in *ODNB*, 'Devereux, Robert, second earl of Essex (1565–1601)'. See also Hammer's *The polarisation of Elizabethan politics: the political career of Robert Devereux, 2nd Earl of Essex, 1585–1597* (Cambridge, 1999).

in 1596 (rather than the failure of the Azores voyage of 1597) was exploited to create the image of the general whom Scott hymns in the *Model*.

But things were already starting to go wrong as Scott wrote. Essex had withdrawn from court in mid-1598 after an angry quarrel with Elizabeth over whom to appoint as Lord Deputy of Ireland. Tyrone's rebellion was gathering momentum, forcing Edmund Spenser, for one, to flee Ireland at the end of 1598. Ireland was a familiar battleground, and political nightmare, for the Sidneys and the Devereuxs. Essex's father Walter Devereux had spent two-and-a-half years campaigning in, and attempting to colonise, Ulster before his death in 1576, and Sidney's father Sir Henry Sidney had acted as the Queen's Lord Deputy in Ireland. Essex continued to believe that his best route to power was through military leadership rather than politicking, and so reconciliation with Elizabeth came with his appointment as Lord Lieutenant in Ireland at the very end of 1598. He finally left with his army at the end of March 1599, but what was intended to be a swift campaign moved slowly and ended in a truce with the Earl of Tyrone, which Elizabeth could not accept. Essex felt he was being undermined at home, and decided to return to England, against Elizabeth's orders. Travelling quickly, he sailed on 24 September and reached the court at Nonsuch on 28 September, rushing straight to the Queen's chamber. After two subsequent meetings that day he never saw her again. Under house arrest, and in a state of mental and physical collapse, Essex had fallen utterly. He was no longer a potential patron for puritans, or scholars, or would-be servants of the state like Scott. Treason charges were put aside in early 1600 and Essex was given back some freedom, but he was banned from the court, and Essex House on The Strand in London started to become the centre of a gathering of disaffected nobles, puritans, and others who felt marginalised or outmanoeuvred in the factional politics of these years. The infamous, absurd rebellion of 8 February 1601 followed; Essex was executed on 25 February.

The Folger miscellany shares with many such manuscripts of the late Elizabethan and early Jacobean years a fascination with the politics of England seen in relation to Essex. Such miscellanies preserved for study and further dissemination documents which could not be printed: letters, reports, legal speeches and opinions, memoranda, treatises too sensitive to print. But did William Scott have a closer association with Essex? As Master of the Ordnance, Essex made Sir John Davies (whom he had knighted at Cadiz) Surveyor in January 1599, and took him with him to Ireland. Davies came back again with Essex in his precipitate return in September 1599,[86] and the lieutenant of the Ordnance Sir George Carew tried at that point to sideline Davies and replace him with his own clients. We have a letter from one of these, George Harvey, to Robert Cecil describing the occasion in April 1600 when he was ejected from the Ordnance by Davies and his servants 'William Scott, and another ruffianly fellow'.[87] This William Scott was at Essex House with Davies on the day of the Essex rebellion of 8 February

[86] *ODNB*, 'Davies [Davis], Sir John (1560x63–1625)'.
[87] HMC Hatfield, x, 100. See Chambers, 123–7, for an account of this episode, ignoring the William Scott connection (which may mean Chambers assumed it was a different Scott). The connection was first made in *HoP*, III, 359. See also Wells, 235.

1601, evidently without much clue as to what was going on. Davies tried to send him to a nearby gunmaker to acquire more guns, but by this point Essex House was locked down (a fortified refuge with hostages), and Sir Gelly Meyrick refused to let Scott out on his errand. He was subsequently held at the King's Bench prison and examined by Lord Chief Justice Popham.[88] As servant to the (Catholic) Davies, this William Scott had probably been in Ireland over the summer of 1599 when the *Model* was written and the Du Bartas translation polished. It seems impossible that the two William Scotts are the same man. Others implicated in the rebellion and imprisoned in its aftermath include people with connections to William Scott – Captain Thomas Lee (Sir Henry Lee's cousin), and Scott's own cousin Sir John Scott. So Essex's fall may have been close to home for Scott, but it was not *that* close.

A serious interest in Irish politics led Scott to get hold of and read Edmund Spenser's *A view of the present state of Ireland*. Probably completed in 1596, and including in its analysis an apparent argument for Essex's appointment as lord lieutenant,[89] the *View* was entered in the Stationers' Register on 14 April 1598 but not printed until 1633.[90] That edition attributes the work to Spenser, but the manuscript copies are silent, except for two that attribute the work 'E.S.', and one that attributes it to Spenser in what may be a later hand.[91] Yet Scott clearly identifies 'Master Spenser' as its author in the *Model* (19), and in the Folger manuscript it is 'Spensers Ireland' on the contents page. Thomas Lee, Sir Henry Lee's cousin, may have been the Scotts' source – their miscellany also includes a copy of a letter from him to Richard Lee (probably Sir Henry Lee's half-brother) written in 1597. Thomas Lee was a soldier in Ireland for most of the 1580s and 1590s and was executed for his part in the Essex rebellion.[92] When the *View* was transcribed into the Folger manuscript is uncertain, but it was probably during or after 1600, the date of a letter from Essex to the Queen that precedes it and does not appear to be a later addition.

*

The evidence for dating the *Model* to the summer of 1599, just before Essex's endgame, is simple:

(i) Printed works

Scott refers to a number of works printed in 1597 and 1598, by authors including Shakespeare, Drayton, Chapman, and Sylvester, as well as to the satirists being printed in 1598 and 1599 (24–5); he also appears to glance at the resulting Bishops' Ban on

---

[88] *Calendar of state papers, domestic series . . . 1598–1601* (London, 1869), 549, for the report of Popham's examination; *Acts of the Privy Council of England*, XXXI (1600–1) (London, 1906), 160, for the imprisonment.

[89] Andrew Hadfield, *Edmund Spenser: A Life* (Oxford, 2012), 335.

[90] *A view of the state of Ireland . . . By Edmund Spenser*, printed with *Two histories of Ireland* (Dublin, 1633).

[91] For a survey and sceptical reading of the manuscript evidence for attribution as it then stood see Jean R. Brink, 'Constructing the *View of the present state of Ireland*', *Spenser studies*, 11 (1994), 203–28 (esp. 217); for a riposte see Andrew Hadfield, 'Certainties and uncertainties: by way of response to Jean Brink', *Spenser studies*, 12 (1998), 197–201. See also Hadfield, *Spenser*, 520n.1.

[92] See Chambers, 185–202, and *ODNB*, 'Lee, Thomas (1551/2–1601)'.

satire of 1 June 1599 (see Commentary, 79.32–4n.). The latest printed work that Scott refers to or quotes is *Th'overthrow of stage-playes, by the way of controversie betwixt D. Gager and D. Rainoldes* ([Middelburg], 1599): see Commentary, 48.30–2n.

(ii) Use of Hoskyns

Scott quotes John Hoskyns's *Directions for speech and style*, which must itself date from early to mid-1599, due to its own reference to Essex's expedition into Ireland (see Commentary, 52.41–53.4n.).

(iii) Essex

Scott's references to Essex may well include an allusion to the Irish campaign but are made in terms that would be impossible after Essex's return from Ireland at the end of September 1599 (see Commentary, 52.41–53.4n.).

(iv) Scott's own remarks

Scott tells George Wyatt that he had only had 'one vacation to spend about [the Du Bartas translation], and my discourse of the Arte of Poesy' (248). This does not preclude drafts of either or both being written at some earlier point. The law terms in 1599 were as follows: Hilary term, 23 January–12 February; Easter term, 25 April–21 May; Trinity term, 8 June–27 June; Michaelmas term, 9 October–28 November.[93]

(v) Material evidence

Watermark evidence is rarely conclusive, but in this case the exact match (see below, lxxiii) of an unusual paper stock with a letter from the Queen of 4 August 1599, sent from the court at Nonsuch (ten miles south-west of the city), is significant. This was during a period of fears of a Spanish invasion, and Sir Henry Lee was at court in late August 1599.

Composition (or at least revision and completion) before 1599 is therefore impossible (i and ii), and composition after 1599 is unlikely, since no later works are referred to. Composition after Essex's fall at the end of September 1599 is unlikely, and composition during his Irish campaign likely (iii): he was best described as 'that famous general of the army of the most famous prince' (52–3) between March and September 1599. Such reference also makes transcription unlikely after that date. If we are to look for a single law vacation in which Scott could have composed and/or worked up the *Model* and the Du Bartas (iv), we have 13 February–24 April, which may be long enough but is probably too early; 22 May–7 June, which is surely too brief; and 28 June–8 October, which is the latest, longest, and likeliest. That date is also supported by watermark evidence (v).

---

[93] See *A Handbook of Dates*, ed. C. R. Cheney; rev. Michael Jones (Cambridge, 2000), 117, 125, 133, 141.

SIXTEENTH-CENTURY POETICS AND RHETORIC

Though Scott's biography has in itself many claims on our attention, the *Model* has to stand not because of its supporting historical context but because of its strengths as a work of poetics and criticism. It was written at the end of a century, the end of a monarch's reign, the end of a period of revolution in the arts and in intellectual culture, and the end of one of the richest decades in English literary history. It may not be quite the last word on all of those things, but it is a work of genuine power and reach. In the sections that follow I will examine the *Model*'s relations to the writings and ideas that give it its particular shape and texture, starting with the general background of Renaissance rhetorical poetics and literary criticism.

Scott's aim in the *Model* is to provide an outline account of poetry: what it is, how it works, what it does, what makes a poet, what the different kinds of poetry are, what the means are to effective and correct writing in each of those kinds. This sort of complete *ars poetica* had been attempted by only one other Englishman before Scott: George Puttenham in *The arte of English poesie* (1589). It had been attempted by many more on the continent of Europe, both in ancient Greece and Rome and in modern Italy and France, but in seeking to write usefully about modern English literature Scott was in almost uncharted territory. He has a number of advantages over Puttenham. Like Puttenham he has a mastery of the classical theory of rhetoric and its early modern offshoots; access to early English attempts to theorise English versification, and the French treatises of the mid-century that lie behind them; immersion in Horace's verse epistle known as the *Ars poetica*; and the example and insight of some powerful modern writers, notably Julius Caesar Scaliger. But unlike Puttenham he has things to say about the English language that he has learned from a generation of writers on the language (primarily the spelling reformers or orthoepists). He has an interest in, and a detailed mastery of, the most important text in effect rediscovered in the sixteenth century, and a work unused by Puttenham: Aristotle's *Poetics*. He can take inspiration, as Puttenham could not, from Sidney's brilliant *Defence of poesy*, which shares Scott's attention to Aristotle, and no doubt inspired it. And most crucially, Scott was writing a decade after Puttenham's treatise was printed, and more than two decades after much of it had been written: the literary map had been redrawn in the meantime.

The ancient critical legacy continued to evolve in Scott's lifetime. The earlier humanists had made crucial discoveries: among the most important was that of a complete manuscript of Quintilian's *Institutio oratoria*, found in a monastic library by Poggio Bracciolini in 1416.[94] The printing press facilitated the dissemination of these and other lost or neglected texts – most notably Aristotle's *Poetics*, first printed in a Latin translation in 1498 but only gaining significant notice after Pazzi's Greek–Latin edition of 1536.[95] Scholars reexamined the relations between ancient texts too: the simplest and most powerful stories about the development of Renaissance criticism concern the

---

[94] George A. Kennedy, *Classical rhetoric and its Christian and secular tradition from ancient to modern times* (Chapel Hill, 1999), 229.
[95] See Weinberg, I, ch. 9, esp. 361–73.

attempt to reconcile or synthesise Horace and Aristotle.[96] Ancient thought about poetry and the arts of language is found in various kinds of writing: philosophy (Plato notably); poetics (Aristotle above all, Horace in some respects); rhetoric (Aristotle, Cicero, Quintilian, and others); grammar (Diomedes, most comprehensively); commentary (on Virgil, Horace, Terence, and others); and in a large and open field that we can label rhetorical criticism and that includes not only Horace but such writers on style as Dionysius of Halicarnassus, 'Longinus', and Demetrius, their subject neither clearly oratory nor literary writing but both, and their quotation and criticism of poets more insightful than almost everything found in those other kinds of writing. Some of these ancient writers had commanded attention throughout the middle ages; others were newly available; and some were as yet little known. There is no sign of Longinus in Scott, and the influence of Dionysius and Demetrius is second hand; in this he is not unusual.

Renaissance critics wrote modern versions of ancient works, or translated them, or wrote commentaries on them, and so that rough sketch of kinds of writing can be replicated to an extent for the sixteenth century. But they also attempted two different, new projects. One was the grand synthesis of all that was known and might be said about poetry on a scale not seen in ancient writing on imaginative literature, and only comparable to works in other disciplines, such as Quintilian's twelve-book treatment of rhetoric or Pliny's thirty-seven books on natural history. Scaliger's *Poetices libri septem* (1561) was the leading example, and by poetry in such cases was almost always meant classical poetry and/or Latin poetry (which might then include modern neo-Latin verse). The other project was to theorise and regulate modern, vernacular writing. In France this saw various *arts poétiques* being offered in the mid-century, and some serious new thinking about aims and means from the poets of the 'Pléiade'. In Italy it saw an extraordinary output of treatises defining or defending the new genres (tragicomedy, heroic poetry), accounting for the older ones (madrigal), and sometimes offering theory on the lines of Aristotle, Horace, and Scaliger (and therefore ostensibly most applicable to ancient writing) that did not exclude, and perhaps was intended to foster, modern vernacular writing. The strong classical tinge to much literary theory was not necessarily at odds with practice, since much modern literary writing was just as concerned to build on and relate itself to ancient writing, though more creatively. Spenser's *The faerie queene* may be *sui generis*, an extraordinary syncretic tumbling together of ancient, medieval, and modern plotlines and modes of writing; but that does not mean that Aristotle or Scaliger cannot help us get a purchase on it. Before the rigid French-influenced neoclassicism of the late seventeenth century came the vibrant, open-minded, eclectic, and creatively distorting classicism of the late sixteenth century.

Since many of Scott's classical and continental sources had to be read in editions imported from the continent, we can expect to learn little from knowing which texts were also available in editions printed at home (or in the Low Countries for an English readership). But a brief survey helps us see more clearly which were the established

---

[96] See Marvin T. Herrick, *The fusion of Horatian and Aristotelian literary criticism, 1531–1555* (Urbana, Ill., 1946) and Weinberg.

and which the coming writers and texts. None of the relevant texts of Plato had been printed in Britain. An edition of the *Nicomachean ethics* (1581) and a translation by John Dickenson of the *Politics* (1598) were among a scattering of Aristotle's texts printed locally; there would be no edition of the *Rhetoric* until 1619 (Greek–Latin) and of the *Poetics* until Goulston's Latin translation of 1623. Cicero was very popular at the British printing presses, with scores of editions of his separate works in the sixteenth century, including many of the *De officiis* of course. Melanchthon's edition of *De oratore* and the *Orator* (or 'De perfecto oratore', as this edition calls it) was printed in 1573, the *Tusculan disputations* in 1574, 1577, 1591, and 1599, and a Cambridge edition of *De oratore* in 1589. A nine-volume (and probably never completed) printing of Denis Lambin's complete Cicero of 1566 was begun in London in 1585. Its first volume included all the works on rhetoric (every one of which Scott shows signs of having studied), and included the anonymous *Rhetorica ad Herennium*, no longer attributed to Cicero, which was itself separately printed (as Cicero's) in 1574. Horace was printed less frequently but what was printed is still significant: scholarly editions of all the poems with annotations, life, and descriptions of his different metres appeared in 1574, 1578, 1585, and 1592. Donatus' essay on tragedy and comedy, commonly found in editions of Terence, was included in *Pub. Terentii Afri Comoediae sex* (1583). The grammarians Diomedes and Priscian were ubiquitous in continental editions, though they were printed less as the century wore on. There were no editions of Demetrius or Dionysius or Longinus, though all had become at least scantily available in continental editions. Longinus' *On the sublime* would do better in the seventeenth century: a Greek–Latin edition was printed in Oxford in 1636, 1638, and 1650, and the first English translation followed in 1652. That the English were no laggards in making Longinus available can encourage us to look for signs of his presence earlier (and we will find some). Of Scott's modern sources, only the *Rhetorica* (first printed in 1548) of Petrus Ramus' collaborator Audomarus Talaeus was available in a British edition. It was printed in Cambridge in 1592 (*STC* 23659.3), and rhetorics based closely on it were also available: Dudley Fenner's *The artes of logike and retorike* (Middelburg, 1584; 1588); Abraham Fraunce's *The Arcadian rhetorike* (1588); and Charles Butler's *Rameae rhetoricae libri duo* (Oxford, 1597) and *Rhetoricae libri duo* (Oxford, 1598). Scott probably used one of Butler's versions.

Scott may also have used other sixteenth-century rhetorics, such as Susenbrotus' *Epitome troporum ac schematum* (Zürich, 1542; and printed in London in 1562, 1570, 1574, and 1586), but he is less interested in the figures (Talaeus or Butler offer a useful enough crib when he just wishes to list a few) than in larger issues to do with style, as well as the preliminary rhetorical stages of *inventio* and *dispositio*, and many sixteenth-century rhetorics sideline such issues in concentrating on itemising the rhetorical figures. Some of those rhetorics were by Scott's day in English: Richard Sherry's *A treatise of schemes and tropes* (1550), Henry Peacham's *The garden of eloquence* (1577; 1593), the appendix to the 1592 edition of Angel Day's *The English secretorie*, and indeed the third book of Puttenham's *Arte*. The only full, properly Ciceronian rhetoric, was Thomas Wilson's *Arte of rhetorike* (1553 and much reprinted). But such English rhetorics were aimed at those whose Latin was flawed or rusty, and Scott's was fluent: he sticks for the most part to Cicero and Quintilian.

Scott had access to family libraries – his own, almost certainly George Wyatt's, probably Sir Henry Lee's. He had access to the London booksellers, and to the culture of manuscript exchange and recopying through which unpublished texts like Hoskyns's *Directions* circulated at the Inns of Court. A base in Kent, close to such major ports as Dover and Folkestone and a short hop across the English Channel from France and the Low Countries, also helped Scott to access books printed on the continent. It certainly seems to have fostered his sense of connection with continental culture, as it did for many Kentish men, for whom travel to or service on the continent was always more likely than for those from counties further afield.

One of the things that is most striking about Scott is his scholarliness. Not only did he prepare to write the *Model* by reading copiously, but he is far more assiduous than many of his contemporaries in citing his sources. Rather than rely on a well-stocked memory or commonplace book, he has books open on his desk as he writes, and he quotes them, translates from them, and sometimes argues with them. That does not mean that he will not on occasion borrow a detail, even lift a phrase, without acknowledgement, but it does mean that we encounter Scott's account of poetry, his vision of the art, emerging in dialogue with a number of different, always intelligent and intelligently chosen, sources: the work is a unique, well-judged, and potent synthesis of existing scholarship. Scott's respect for the integrity of his sources also means that the *Model* is not what apparently learned works of Renaissance scholarship can often be: unregulated assemblages of citation, testimony piled on testimony, with very little in the way of prose, much less thought, linking them together.

This scholarly critic also did something new in relation to existing works of criticism in English, few though they were: he read them, and he thought about them. Sidney has not read an early draft of Puttenham in manuscript, and Puttenham, in revising his *Arte*, has no access to a manuscript of the *Defence*; Gascoigne was in print and is ignored by both. Harington mocks Puttenham (admiring only the typeface his printer used)[97] and plagiarises Sidney. Only when writers were engaged in detailed thought about prosody did they find it helpful to cite each other, as Webbe does Gascoigne and the Spenser–Harvey correspondence,[98] or show signs of attempting to build on earlier work. This difference in practice can be put down to the perception that the theory of English versification really was uncharted territory. The assumptions that must have guided these early critics when they looked at issues that were not language-specific are not necessarily false: the real thinking had been done by ancient and modern writers on the continent; modern English work could be safely ignored. Sidney changed that, though, by writing an English work on poetry of power and originality; and Scott builds above all on Sidney.

That line of influence I will consider separately below, but more needs to be said here about Elizabethan literary criticism. It comes in works of various shapes and sizes. The shortest, and often the most shapeless, are the many brief prefaces, prologues, and dedicatory epistles to literary works. These are often the source of valuable insights and

---

[97] See Harington's note to his printer, reproduced in Philip Gaskell, *From writer to reader: studies in editorial method* (Oxford, 1978), 24n.11.

[98] Webbe, in *ECE*, I, 275, 245–6.

brilliant *aperçus*. In the dedication to George Whetstone's *Promos and Cassandra* (1578), for example, we get the first glimpse in English of the dramatic unities.[99] In Nashe's preface to the unauthorised edition of Sidney's *Astrophil and Stella* printed in 1591 we get some extraordinarily imaginative writing which responds to the dramatic qualities of Sidney's sonnet sequence: it is a 'tragicommody of love performed by starlight' on a 'paper stage'.[100] In Robert Southwell's dedicatory epistle to *Saint Peters complaynt* (1595), a poem Scott refers to (20), we find a short manifesto for religious verse[101] to which Scott could not have taken exception had he known that the anonymous author was by now a Jesuit martyr. Michael Drayton would become a specialist in the condensed critical prefatory essay and some of his writing in that mode does brilliantly what Scott and few others attempt, in writing relevantly about modern vernacular writing in the inherited terms of classical poetics. But the first notable example comes in the preface to *The barrons wars* (1603). Ben Jonson is another whose critical thinking – in *Discoveries*, in his prologues and prefaces, in his plays themselves – just postdates Scott, though there is one possible moment of overlap (see Commentary, 76.41–77.1n.).

Verse treatises or discursive epistles in English on the lines of Horace (if one ignores Drant's translation of 1567, *Horace his arte of poetrie, pistles, and satyrs Englished*) also belong to the period after Scott – one cannot count Churchyard's versification (and unintended travesty) of Sidney's *Defence*, *A praise of poetrie*, printed in *A musicall consort* (1595). The most common mode is the apology, often explicitly rhetorical, in some cases certainly polemical. Thomas Lodge responds to Gosson's puritan strictures against poets and players with a Defence (the title page is missing in both surviving copies) that is general in terms and ethical in focus. All poetry is divine in inspiration and if it seems morally questionable it must therefore be allegorical. It was an old message, and most of Lodge's work was lifted without acknowledgement from an old work.[102] In this mode too is John Harington's lively triple apology for poetry, for Ariosto, and for himself as translator prefixed to his *Orlando furioso* of 1591. Sidney's *Defence* (also printed as *An apologie for poetrie*) was written in the manner and form of a legal speech.

The less rhetorically active works include Gascoigne's ground-breaking *Certayne notes of instruction*, printed in 1575 and therefore the first published work of criticism in English. Apart from some general pointers about poetic *inventio*, Gascoigne's focus is on versification. He borrows from the Latin grammarians' discussions of how to pronounce Latin (with three degrees of accent) in an attempt to theorise the newly regular accentual-syllabic line that his own verse exemplified with paradigmatic rigour. That genealogy explains why what is a useful start is therefore not yet a true account of what is going on in the English verse line. To that Scott will come much closer. In describing verse form, however, Gascoigne lifts with questionable relevance from the French *arts poétiques*. Also more simply bent on communicating information and analysis is William Webbe's excellent *A discourse of English poetrie* (1586). The less

---

[99] *ECE*, I, 59.   [100] *ECE*, II, 223.   [101] *ERLC*, 395–7.
[102] By Badius Ascensius in 1502: see William Ringler, 'The source of Lodge's reply to Gosson', *RES*, 58 (1939), 164–71. Text of Lodge (abridged) in *ECE*, I, 61–86.

useful half of this is a general account of poetry that juggles the usual commonplaces from the ancient writers. But when Webbe turns to discuss versification he makes some progress on Gascoigne, in describing how long lines (eight, seven, and six feet) may be understood as pairs of short lines (of four or three feet), an intuition that has been more fully worked out in modern times, and leads one to regret that Webbe seems to have escaped Scott's attention.

The three books of Puttenham's *Arte* are on (i) poets and poesy; (ii) proportion, i.e. verse form; and (iii) ornament, i.e. *elocutio*. The first offers a general account of poetry, its history, and kinds, which Scott leans on occasionally for confirmation but uses little as a source, since much of it is derived from the more authoritative Scaliger; in its closing history of English poetry, however, it offers balanced assessments of earlier writers that Scott happily cites: the two critics share a generous wish to give earlier poets like Chaucer and Wyatt their due, rather than to penalise them for not being Elizabethans, as Webbe does. Puttenham's second book includes some powerfully original work on verse form, which Scott summarises briefly, and some confused thought about metre; here Scott borrows details whilst undertaking his own original (and much better) analysis of how the English verse line actually works. Puttenham's third book is the most celebrated, and is original in offering a textbook account of the rhetorical figures aimed explicitly at poets. This is something Scott does not wish to do, and in that he is more of an Aristotle, respecting the integrity of the art under discussion, than a totalising Scaliger; nevertheless there are engagements with and borrowings from Puttenham's third book throughout the *Model*.

Puttenham's kind of hybrid poetical rhetoric is what we also get in Fraunce's *Arcadian rhetorike* and Hoskyns's *Directions for speech and style*. The former is really just a translation from Talaeus, and Scott reads that in the Latin (probably in one of Butler's adaptations), but Fraunce adds examples from Sidney to illustrate every point, and this method he shares with Hoskyns and, to an extent, with Scott. Hoskyns's stated aim is to teach a young man how to write stylish prose through the study of an annotated copy of Sidney's *Arcadia*, but what emerges is more than that, including some powerful thought which sheds light on Sidney's fictive imagination, on his powers of characterisation, on the aesthetic effect of his rhetorical figuration. Scott probably got access to Hoskyns late in the day: there are points of contact, one certain borrowing, and other moments where an influence may be felt, but nothing on the scale of the extensive copyings out of Ben Jonson (in the *Discoveries*) and the hand-me-down plagiarisms of the seventeenth-century rhetoricians Thomas Blount (1654) and John Smith (1665), which saw Hoskyns's own unpublished critical voice heard in print.

What had wrongfooted Puttenham as a prosodist was a notion (from the French) that English verse might only be syllabic, and a sympathy, shared with Webbe as well as Sidney and many others, for the idea that English verse might better (or also) be written according to the quantitative rules of scansion that applied to Greek and Latin poetry. In this system, syllables would not be accented or unaccented, but long or short. Where stress or accent remains somewhat (and magically) ineffable, quantity is simply about the duration of a syllable, with a long syllable lasting twice as long as a short one. Spenser and Harvey had deliberated the virtues and details of this system in an entertaining correspondence printed in 1579–80, and it would be the subject of a decisive battle between two exceptional poets, Thomas Campion and Samuel Daniel, in 1602–3. Scott has no time for it, an unusual position for a classicist. Since we do not measure quantity in the English verse line, we can either think of all feet as spondees, he argues, or ignore the quantitative system altogether. He even demonstrates how some of Sidney's lines in quantitative metre work as well if construed as accentual-syllabic (he does not say that they perhaps work so well originally because of this double life, but that point can be inferred).[103]

There were also Englishmen whose engagement with thought about poetry was conducted in Latin. This includes the rather predictable and derivative university exercise in praise of poetry from *c.*1575 attributed once to a youthful John Rainolds (on whom see above, xxx) and more recently to Henry Dethick,[104] as well as a thoughtful short treatise *De re poetica* appended to a volume of Latin verse by Richard Wills printed in 1573.[105] It also includes a work from 1593 until recently overlooked, because apparently one of legal theory, by the Oxford lawyer Alberico Gentili.[106] But the more interesting development was in a different kind of classicism. Scott writes a year after the first fragmentary translations from Homer of George Chapman, one or both of which Scott has certainly looked into (see Commentary, 53.1–2n.). The dedication of *Achilles shield* (1598) to Essex is a long essay in praise and defence of Homer, which includes criticism of 'soule-blind Scalliger' for his marked preference for Virgil over Homer and a redressing of the balance: '*Homers* Poems were writ from a free furie, an absolute and full soule, *Virgils* out of a courtly, laborious, and altogether imitatorie spirit.'[107] Scott may not have felt qualified to adjudicate this dispute. He had clearly studied Greek, but probably not to a level where he was comfortable reading without a facing Latin translation (the form in which he appears to have read the *Poetics*), and it may be that he had no access to Homer in this form. The *Model* includes only a single quotation from a Greek poet, Pindar, one of whose odes Scott must have worked through. The majority of the Greek prose works he cites are read in translation, whereas it is clear from his practice throughout the *Model* that he preferred to read poetry in the original and would not have trusted his judgement of the poetic merits of a translated text. Scott would therefore have relied on Scaliger's painstaking and scholarly demonstration of Virgil's superiority to Homer (however deluded or distorting we might now think this to be), and Scaliger was – as we shall see – one of his most important authorities. This sign in Chapman, if it is even that, of a preference for a Longinian, inspired, artfully artless sublime over a measured, Horatian, evidently achieved correctness does not therefore inspire Scott to throw out his Sidneian rationalist rulebook. But then it would not others too, for the next century was to be more Horace's than Longinus'.

---

[103] On this aspect of Sidney's practice in writing in quantitative metres see, e.g., Derek Attridge, *Well-weighed syllables: Elizabethan verse in classical metres* (Cambridge, 1974), 177–83.
[104] See *Oratio* and Dethick.   [105] See Wills.
[106] *Commentatio ad Legem III Codicis de professoribus et medicis*: see Gentili.
[107] *ECE*, II, 301, 298.

CLASSICAL AND CONTINENTAL SOURCES

Plato and Aristotle had been held in balance by Sidney, but Scott is a thorough Aristotelian. Sidney had read a number of Plato's dialogues, which makes his theory of the poetic '*idea* or fore-conceit' not only a response to Plato's later classical readers, like Cicero and Seneca, and to Renaissance Neoplatonism, but a fresh reading of Plato too. Scott is less attentive: he parodies Socratic dialectic (7.27–8.1), and on two occasions when he does cite Plato (16.17–19, 32.41), he is relying on a secondary source. Nevertheless, there are many signs that not only Plato's thought but his language has left its imprint in Scott's work, and Scott must have read either *Ion* or *Phaedrus* (or both) and the *Republic* to form his view that the *furor poeticus* is not the entirety of Plato's account of how and why poets write (7.16–17, 7.28–9, 10.6).

Aristotle's name, on the other hand, is invoked fifty-one times, more even than Sidney's (thirty-five). Scott has a thorough grounding in Aristotle's works on logic (the Organon), and makes good use of the *Nicomachean ethics* (on the nature of an art), and the *Rhetoric* (for how metaphors work), although his reliance on the paradigms of Roman rhetoric will have limited what he could get from the latter. There are signs of use of the *Physics*, the *Metaphysics*, *De anima*, and some of the treatises on natural history, though in these cases the learning may be second hand. Much of Scott's Aristotle comes from his university years, and is less conscious and scholarly and more a matter of basic assumptions and habits of thought and method. But it prepared him to give the most thorough and intelligent reading of the *Poetics* of any sixteenth-century Englishman. Scott does not just follow in Sidney's footsteps as a reader of the *Poetics*; he looks more closely at those ideas and passages that Sidney had drawn on, but also develops his own reading of the work. On many points his is the first English account we have. Among those questions broached by Aristotle in the *Poetics* that Scott covers, always intelligently and judiciously, are: what poetry is (imitation, not versification); man's instinct for imitation and the nature of our pleasure in contemplating imitations; the nature, relations, and origins of epic, tragedy, and comedy; the tragic effect; the dramatic unities; the analogy of poetry and painting; the primacy of plot; poetry's imitation of universals; poetry's philosophical superiority to history; the tripartite division of poetry by mode of delivery; organic form and unity; unity of action versus episodes; *desis* and *lusis*, *peripeteia* and *anagnorisis*; *hamartia*; the role of wonder; and verisimilitude. There are some occasions when in citing Aristotle Scott is not looking at the *Poetics* but at one of his modern sources – Viperano or Scaliger – but these are few. The majority of more than fifty citations of the *Poetics* show that the book – in probability a Greek–Latin parallel text such as Casaubon's two-volume *Operum Aristotelis... nova editio* (Lyon, 1590) – is in front of Scott as he works. Scott has a fundamental sympathy with Aristotle that Sidney lacks, and this is most evident in Scott's understanding of the form of a plot as something quasi-organic; that attention to structure – as is the case in Aristotle too – extends to questions of analytical and expository method. To Sidney's poetics of exemplary character Scott attaches (and reconciles) an Aristotelian poetics of form, and we see this in Scott's translation of *hamartia* as 'some one remarkable error and passion' (77.9). Though probably deriving simply from a Latin translation, it still gets closer to Aristotle's meaning (a plot-necessitated going wrong that is not necessarily the fault of the hero or the consequence of any moral shortcomings) than many subsequent accounts of *hamartia* in the English tradition.

The rhetorical basis of later classical and Renaissance accounts of poetry means that even as Scott moves English poetics back (or rather forwards) towards Aristotelian formalism he sees an extensive role in his work for rhetorical theory, which remained a coherent and beautifully formulated account of argument, expression, persuasion, and all the arts of language that both poets and their characters must employ. The two central authorities were Cicero, in his seven separate works on rhetoric (plus the pseudo-Ciceronian *Rhetorica ad Herennium*) and Quintilian, in his great synthesis of the Roman rhetorical tradition, the *Institutio oratoria* (to which some added Tacitus' *Dialogus*, which Justus Lipsius, and Scott, believed might be Quintilian's lost work on the causes of the corruption of eloquence). Cicero is cited by name twenty-seven times in the *Model* and Quintilian thirty-five, but there are dozens more points where Scott learns from or depends on these two authorities. I have already observed that Scott does not see a need for his treatise to itemise the rhetorical figures as Puttenham and Scaliger had, although he does include some selective discussion of the figures. He is interested in larger ideas, including the nature of the poet (the parallel accounts of the orator's knowledge, virtue, and *ēthos* or performed moral character were readily borrowed); the relative importance of art and nature to poetic (or rhetorical) skill; the relations of beauty and utility; the ordering and arrangement of any linguistic performance (speech, play, poem); procedures of definition and division of a subject; use of new, old, and borrowed words; ways of moving or otherwise affecting the audience/reader, including the generation of wonder; the different kinds of style and their differing effects on audience/reader; the rhetorical ways of representing (or simulating) emotion; vivid description; and decorum. Those in the second half of that list belonged to the third stage of rhetoric, *elocutio*, but most received less attention in the modern rhetoric books than in the ancient ones because so much space tended to be given to itemising and illustrating the rhetorical figures. Scott's focus is one sign that he is little influenced by Ramism. He shares the Ciceronian view that rhetoric comprehends philosophy (since the orator must be wise) and logic (since the orator must be able to think analytically) and is therefore happy to go to Cicero or Quintilian for cribs on questions (like definition and predication) that he has studied previously in philosophical or logical sources. Scott translates or paraphrases extensive passages from both authors, and occasionally takes issue with them. It is likely that Scott had read all of Cicero's rhetorical works: certainly each of them is the origin of at least one point or usage in the *Model*. But he concentrates on three. He uses two extended passages from *De optimo genere oratorum* ('On the best kind of orator'), and refers at numerous points to passages of the longest of Cicero's rhetorical works, the three-book dialogue *De oratore*. His favourite source, though, is Cicero's last rhetorical work, the shorter *Orator*, of which he makes extensive use, perhaps preferring its single authorial voice and tighter organisation to the more diffuse dialogue *De oratore*, but also seeing a theoretical kinship between the *Orator*'s project of delineating a perfect orator and his of modelling the perfect poet. There is little sign that he used the *Ad Herennium*, perhaps accepting that it was not Cicero's, but he makes good use of other works by Cicero, including the *Tusculan disputations* and *De officiis*.

It can almost go without saying that Scott is familiar with Horace's *Ars poetica* and is therefore able to cite it frequently in the *Model*, quoting and offering his own verse translations of seventeen lines in all. But it can hardly be said that Horace is a key source of ideas, since everything in Horace had been separately developed by earlier or later writers whom Scott has read thoroughly. Sidney, too, shows little interest in a project that attracted other contemporaries more wedded to Horace, that of reconciling Horace and Aristotle.[108] Nevertheless, Scott shares his contemporaries' love of Horace's verse treatise, and uses it not only to clinch many arguments but to give the *Model* its last words, telling ones at that: *lucidus ordo*, clear order. What Horace offered was more important than doctrines on wisdom as the origin of good writing, or decorum, or where to begin a story, or how to move an audience: the *Ars* is a rhetorical poetics and proof for Horace's followers of the inseparability of poetics from the art of rhetoric.

There are many other classical authorities on Scott's bookshelves, but the last one to merit separate mention here is the prolific late first-century to early second-century Greek writer Plutarch. Scott makes frequent use of anecdotes from Plutarch's *Lives* (Theseus, Phocion, Themistocles), and from various parts of the *Moralia*, especially the *Apophthegmata Laconica* ('Sayings of Spartans'), which he raids several times. In some cases, it is quite possible that an intermediary source has been used, but Scott's wording shows that he is looking at a copy of North's celebrated translation, *The lives of the noble Grecians and Romanes* (1579), when he cites Themistocles' conceit about speech resembling a rolled-up tapestry (66.5–9), and again (a page later, with the book still in front of him) when he borrows from the Life of Phocion a comparison of words to coins (sometimes the smaller is the more valuable) and then an anecdote about Demosthenes (67.13–16, 67.18–25).

The most valuable corner of Plutarch for a student of poetics, though, is one that neither Scott nor Sidney is fully at ease in: the superb essay, known as *De audiendis poetis*, on how the young should be taught to interpret poetry. Sidney and Scott believe that morality in poetry should be black and white: character should be exemplary, the good clearly good, the bad clearly bad. Aristotle had said that 'the poet's job is saying not what did happen but the sort of thing that would happen, that is, what can happen in a strictly probable or necessary sequence' (*Poetics*, 1451a). Sidney, however, is tempted throughout the *Defence* to turn subjunctive possibility into moral imperative, 'the divine consideration of what may be and should be' (*DP*, 11). He is able to contemplate exemplary evil on the stage, but when it comes to heroic poetry, he prefers only to imagine the representation of how we *should* behave (like Aeneas or Cyrus) and not how we should not. In a similar slippage, the thought that it is 'better'

---

[108] A contemporary example is Antonio Riccoboni's *De poetica Aristoteles cum Horatio collatus* (Padua, 1599): see Weinberg, I, 54, 240–2. Ben Jonson's translation of the *Ars poetica* survived the fire that damaged his library in 1623, but he tells us that a commentary on it, 'lighted by the Stagirite' [Aristotle], was lost: see 'An Execration upon Vulcan', ll. 89–91 (*CWBJ*, VII, 171), and, for a summary of the evidence, the editorial introduction to Jonson's translation of Horace (*CWBJ*, VII, 3). The commentary was first announced in the preface to *Sejanus* (1605): *CWBJ*, II, 213.

for our 'use and learning' to represent things as they could be rather than as they are or were (*DP*, 19) turns into the account of poetry as 'making things . . . better than nature bringeth forth' (*DP*, 8). Scott gives a more coherent account here, whilst beautifully preserving and justifying Sidney's terminology: 'some [poems] are made as things be (for the substance), others better or as they should or may be, without regard or eye to any extant ground; for evermore I hold the worsing of bad things is a kind of bettering of them, because thereby things receive perfection (as I may say) of deformity' (11–12). Make Thersites really abominable, and then we will know not to emulate him; make Pyrocles really virtuous, and then we will know to model our behaviour on his. The problem with this position is that very few works of literature really come up to its standards (and a good thing too), including of course Sidney's own: not only is Astrophil a melodramatic, randy fool, but Pyrocles and Musidorus are victims of passions that they fail, at crucial points in the *Arcadia*, to keep under control, thus endangering their own lives and the lives of those they love, and requiring a kindly author to rescue them. Plutarch knows this, and offers a much more pragmatic theory of how we might learn moral lessons from poetry: 'it contains much that is pleasant and profitable to the young mind, but just as much that is confusing and misleading, if study is not properly directed'; 'Poetry . . . is an imitation of the manners and lives of men, who are not perfect, pure, and irreproachable, but involved in passions, false opinions, and ignorance . . . we must accustom ourselves to commenting with confidence, and saying "wrong" and "inappropriate" as often as we say "right" and "appropriate"'.[109] His account is the suppressed subtext of Renaissance poetics: what Renaissance defenders of poetry did not dare to admit, and how Renaissance poets expected to be read.

Among many modern writers referred to, Scott makes notable use of Castiglione (several points including *sprezzatura*, 47); Vives (an extensive passage on 'vicious and noughty affections', 70–1); and the strictures against romance of the popular Huguenot general François de la Noue (70). But three works are referred to time and again: the *Poetices libri septem* (1561) of Julius Caesar Scaliger; the *De poetica libri tres* (1579) of Giovanni Antonio Viperano; and the *Trattato dell'arte della pittura, scoltura et architettura* (1584) of Gian Paolo Lomazzo. Scaliger's work was widely read, but the other two were little known in England, which also means that Scott for once felt able to borrow ideas without always attributing them, and occasionally to use them as stylistic models.

The *Poetices libri septem* (Lyon, 1561) of Julius Caesar Scaliger (1484–1558) was written towards the end of Scaliger's life and printed posthumously (with further editions that Scott might have used appearing in 1586 and 1594). Its seven books are named (i) *historicus* (historical), (ii) *hyle* (*hulē*, matter), (iii) *idea* (form), (iv) *parasceve* ('preparation', a book on style and ornament), (v) *criticus* (critical: judgements of authors), (vi) *hypercriticus* (further criticism), and (vii) *epinomis* (appendix). They cover, in 364 tightly printed, double-columned, folio pages, pretty much the entirety of what was known and thought about ancient and neoclassical poetry: the historical origins, nature, and evolution of the genres; versification; rhetorical *inventio*, *dispositio*, and

[109] *Moralia*, 15c, 26a–b.

elocutio; stylistic affect; a comparative concordance of Greek and Roman poets; and a history of Latin poetry, ancient and modern. Scaliger's treatise engages with Aristotle but also goes in opposite directions.[110] His is self-evidently a fusion of rhetoric and poetics, where Aristotle kept the arts separate, and although *mimēsis* is central to Scaliger's definition, it is not so much nature or universals that the poet must imitate as Virgil. The rhetorical dimension means that Sidney and Scott find in Scaliger a Horatian poetics of delighting and teaching rather than an Aristotelian poetics of catharsis. But Scaliger is also Aristotelian in other ways that would have appealed to Scott, notably in dividing his treatment according to Aristotle's four causes, the efficient and final causes in book 1, the material cause in book 2, and the formal cause in book 3.[111]

Scaliger's earliest significant influence was in fact in England, where Richard Wills plundered Scaliger's early pages for his *De re poetica* of 1573.[112] Sidney mentions Scaliger four times in the *Defence* (*DP*, 32, 40, 42, 53), citing Scaliger's treatments of Plato's banishment of the poets in the *Republic* and of the question of whether verse is essential to poetry, and using his authority to bolster commonplace points. A number of other details may derive from Scaliger without acknowledgement: Sidney has clearly at least dipped into *Poetices libri septem*. But Sidney's greatest debt, like Wills's, is to the opening pages of Scaliger's treatise. Scaliger's first chapter offers all of the ingredients of Sidney's well-known definition of poetry ('Poesy, therefore, is an art of imitation, for so Aristotle termeth it in the word *mimēsis*, that is to say, a representing, counterfeiting, or figuring forth – to speak metaphorically, a speaking picture – with this end: to teach and delight', *DP*, 10). And from the end of that chapter Sidney takes the inspiration for the famous 'golden world' passage of the *Defence* and its poetic 'second nature' (*DP*, 9): all other arts are reliant on nature, mere 'actors and players, as it were, of what nature will have set forth', Sidney says; 'Only the poet, disdaining to be tied to any such subjection, lifted up with the vigour of his own invention, doth grow in effect into another nature, in making things either better than nature bringeth forth or, quite anew, forms such as never were in nature' (*DP*, 8–9). Compare Scaliger:

> the poet depicts quite another sort of nature ... he transforms himself into a second deity. Of those things which the Maker of all framed, the other sciences are, as it were, overseers [*actores*]; but since poetry fashions images of those things which are not, as well as images more beautiful than life of those things which are, it seems unlike other literary forms, such as history, which confine themselves to actual events, and rather to be another god, and to create.[113]

Scott cites Scaliger on thirty-three occasions, never vaguely, always with the book open in front of him, and he follows or learns from him at scores of other points. The most

---

[110] See, e.g., Bernard Weinberg, 'Scaliger versus Aristotle on poetics', *Modern philology*, 39 (1942), 337–60; Weinberg, II, 743–50; and Luc Deitz, '"Aristoteles imperator noster ..."? J. C. Scaliger and Aristotle on poetic theory', *International journal of the classical tradition*, 2 (1995), 54–67.

[111] See Deitz, '"Aristoteles imperator noster ..."?', 61–2.

[112] See Wills, 25–9. On Scaliger's English reception, see *Sieben Bücher*, I, xxxvi–xlii.

[113] Scaliger, 3d1; Padelford, 8.

significant borrowing is of the four poetic virtues of proportion (or decorum), variety, sweetness, and *energeia* (33), which Scott uses to organise much of the second half of the *Model*. The most striking use lies behind Scott's extraordinary thoughts about the relations between poetic style and the sounds of vowels and consonants (51–2). Unlike Wills and Sidney, Scott ranges widely and thoroughly through Scaliger, making significant use of each of books 1, 3, 4, 5, and 6. That his engagement with Scaliger is not uncritical, however, but rather in the service of his own ordered account of poetry, is due not only to his own intelligence and theoretical ambition, but also to the strong influence of Sidney and the work of another later reader of Scaliger: Viperano's *De poetica*.

Giovanni Antonio Viperano (1535–1610) was a former Jesuit and client of Philip II's Secretary of State, Cardinal Granvelle, to whom his *De poetica libri tres* (Antwerp, 1579) was dedicated. Viperano achieved some early fame with a book on the writing of history (*De scribenda historia*, 1569) and wrote numerous other works, always in Latin, over the subsequent three decades, on biography, providence, and virtue, among many others, as well as a volume of his own poems. Shortly after the *De poetica* came a rhetoric and a commentary on Cicero's *De optimo genere oratorum* (1581). Scott's close study of Viperano (he is the first writer in England to make use of the *De poetica*) proves to be of great significance to the *Model*'s success, since this is one of the most intelligent, organised, and closely worked-out treatises of the period, synthesising Horace, Aristotle, and Scaliger on a manageable scale.[114] Considerable use is also made of Viperano in *L'Art poétique françois* (Paris, 1597) of Pierre de Laudun D'Aigaliers, most of it unacknowledged.[115] That Viperano was likewise little known in England seems to have encouraged Scott too to use Viperano as a sort of crib. He names him only three times, but uses him dozens more, and at some crucial points as a shortcut to a moment in Plato or Aristotle that is not open in front of him as he writes. Viperano also gives Scott the outline for the closing sentence of the *Model*.

That tribute to a key source is mirrored at the opening of the *Model* when Scott takes inspiration from Lomazzo's *Trattato* (see Commentary, 5.2–36n.). This work of art theory seems an unlikely source, but it speaks to Scott's determination to interrogate and expand upon the analogy between poetry and painting incidental to Aristotle's *Poetics* and Horace's *Ars* and fundamental to Sidney. Gian Paolo Lomazzo (1538–92) was an Italian painter who turned to writing after he went blind. His massive *Trattato dell'arte della pittura, scoltura et architettura* (Milan, 1584) is one of the key works of later Mannerist art theory,[116] offering a rigorous and detailed seven books on (i) proportion, (ii) actions and gestures, (iii) colour, (iv) light, (v) perspective, (vi) practice, and (vii) story (that is, kinds of subject matter). The first book includes an intelligent and detailed definition and division of painting; the second is primarily about all the human emotions that can be represented by gesture and expression. There was much here for Scott to learn from, both in the details and in the method. The 'great philosopher and painter Paul Lomaz' (31) helps Scott think about *verba*

---

[114] For an account see Weinberg, II, 759–65.   [115] See *Sieben Bücher*, I, liii.

[116] See Anthony Blunt, *Artistic theory in Italy, 1450–1600* (Oxford, 1962), ch. 9, esp. 152–3.

and *res*, with material on surface and substance (31–2); he gives him analogies for *energeia* in his account of perspective and three-dimensionality (65), and for decorum in his discussion of 'proportion' (35), which Scott adopts as his term. Scott also takes from Lomazzo his detailed anecdote about Leonardo's 'Last supper' (36). As with Scaliger, Scott draws from material throughout a lengthy work: in the main from book 1, but also from books 2 and 7, and possibly 4. It is to be doubted that Scott read the entire work, but he certainly read deeply in it, and very evidently used the Italian text despite the availability of an English translation of the first five books by Scott's contemporary Richard Haydocke (or Haydock): *A tracte containing the arts of curious paintinge carvinge and buildinge* (Oxford, 1598). That there was something of a visual turn in the late 1590s is due in no small part to the poetics of images of Sidney (the *Defence* was first printed in 1595) as well as to the poems of Shakespeare, Spenser, and others. It is not impossible that Queen Elizabeth's own partial translation of Horace's *Ars poetica* (ll. 1–178), which survives in her hand and dated 1598,[117] is a part of this story. Elizabeth is one of the interested discussants whose questions are reported in Nicholas Hilliard's *A treatise concerning the arte of limning*, a supplement to Lomazzo requested of Hilliard by Haydocke and perhaps dating from 1598 or 1599; Sidney is another.[118]

SIDNEY

The Sidneys were a part of William Scott's world, and the two families were distantly related. Scott's cousin Sir John Scott commanded a company of footsoldiers in the Low Countries,[119] alongside Sir Robert Sidney (who had a company of horse), with Sir Philip Sidney one of the force's leaders (as Governor of Flushing); Sidney refers to 'cosin scots company' in a letter.[120] When waiting for the weather to clear so that he could make the crossing from Dover in late December and early January 1593–4, Robert Sidney had stayed at Scot's Hall ('at Sr. Th. Scots').[121] Robert Sidney seems to have become a close friend of John Scott, saving him from trial when he was imprisoned for his part in the Essex rebellion, and also helping Scott pursue money still owed him for his service in the Low Countries.[122] John Scott married the sister of William Scott's patron Sir Thomas Smythe, and in 1626 Robert Sidney married Smythe's widow. When John Scott died in 1616 Robert Sidney wrote: 'I am infinite sorry for Sir John Scott: for he was a wise and worthy friend unto me, and such a one as I shall hardly find the like again. But I trust the friendship between me and that house will still remain, which of my side shall be carefully maintained.'[123]

---

[117] In Elizabeth I, *Translations, 1592–98*, ed. Janel Mueller and Joshua Scodel (Chicago, 2009).
[118] Nicholas Hilliard, *The arte of limning*, ed. R. K. R. Thornton and T. G. S. Cain (Manchester, 1981), 84–6, 17–18, 82.
[119] HMC De L'Isle, III, xxxii, xxxiv.
[120] Sidney to the Earl of Leicester, 22 November 1585: Kuin, II, 1128. By 'cosin' Sidney simply means 'kinsman'.
[121] HMC De L'Isle, II, 146; Hannay *et al.*, 39 and 41.
[122] *ODNB*, 'Scott, Sir Thomas (1534x6–1594)'.
[123] Robert to Barbara Sidney, 25 September 1616, in Hannay *et al.*, 200; HMC De L'Isle, V, 409.

We might therefore explain Scott's devotion to Philip Sidney's writings as a matter of Kentish loyalty, or a way of making his work more appealing to Sidney's friend Sir Henry Lee, or the tribute of one kinsman to another; and of course it is all of these things. It was also inevitable in a treatise of this sort that Sidney would be centre stage: the 1590s were Sidney's decade, more than Shakespeare's or Spenser's or Marlowe's, and there was no better example of the relation of literary theory to literary practice than the man seen as the leading exponent of both. But Scott's love of the *Arcadia* and his mastery of the *Defence* go further than this: he is one of Sidney's best-attuned and most sympathetic readers.

Scott refers only indirectly and in passing to *Astrophil and Stella*, Sidney's hugely influential sonnet sequence, and only quotes from it in his discussion of metrics. This attitude is shared by others: Sidney's friend Greville ignores *Astrophil and Stella* in his life of Sidney (*A dedication to Sir Philip Sidney*) as does Sir William Alexander in his *Anacrisis*.[124] The reason is that these authors are concerned to reconcile Sidney's literary theory in the *Defence of poesy* with his practice as a writer, and *Astrophil and Stella* appears to be an obstacle. It is *The Countess of Pembroke's Arcadia* that can best be related to what Sidney says in the *Defence*, because his is a theory of literature as a force for moral good.

The *Arcadia* was the first of Sidney's works to be printed after his death in 1586. Sidney had written it in around 1580, dividing it into five books of prose narrative interspersed with poems. It was after writing the *Arcadia* that he seems to have composed both the *Defence* and *Astrophil and Stella*, before he returned to the *Arcadia* and started vastly to expand it. He got no further than most of the way through a completely new third book, and it was in the revised and incomplete form in which he had left it that the work was first printed in 1590. This version, known as the 'new' *Arcadia*, was reprinted in 1593 with the addition of an ending supplied from books 3–5 of the original version. Finally, in 1598, came an edition of the *Arcadia* that was in effect Sidney's collected works: the composite 1593 *Arcadia*, the *Defence* (which had been separately printed in 1595), *Astrophil and Stella* (in print since 1591), and some short early works. Scott uses the composite *Arcadia* (Hoskyns prefers the 1590 version)[125] in either the 1593 or 1598 printing (probably the former). He calls the *Defence* Sidney's '*Apology*' (77.2) and may be reading it in the version published by Henry Olney in 1595 as *An apologie for poetrie* rather than that published by William Ponsonby later in the same year (and reprinted in the 1598 *Arcadia*) as *The defence of poesie*.[126]

---

[124] *A dedication to Sir Philip Sidney* (*c*.1610–14), in John Gouws (ed.), *The prose works of Fulke Greville, Lord Brooke* (Oxford, 1986), esp. 8–12; Sir William Alexander, 'Anacrisis: or, a censure of some poets ancient and modern' (*c*.1634), in Spingarn, II, 181–9 (187), and *SRLC*, 298–300 (300).

[125] *Directions*, 115.

[126] Unfortunately, the recent identification as Scott's of a copy of the 1598 edition of Sidney's *Arcadia* (in effect his complete works) now in the Cambridge University Library (Syn.4.59.12) must be rejected on palaeographical grounds. The signature 'Will: Scott' on the title page is in an italic hand clearly different from that of Scott's signatures, and in appearance belongs to the later seventeenth or eighteenth century, as does the (re-)binding, which accounts for the lack of original endleaves on which earlier marks of ownership might have been found; the handful of marginalia and underlinings, mostly found in the *Defence*, belong to a second hand, also different to Scott's and in appearance of the earlier seventeenth

For Scott the *Arcadia* is what Virgil is for Scaliger, an entire universe of exemplary writing: the two are 'absolute patterns of decorum' (57.37). Sidney shows us how to plot, organise, and order the narration of a fiction, how to represent character, thought, emotion, and speech, how to surprise, terrify, delight, move, and teach. The *Arcadia* is a source of ideas too, with its discussions of the nature of love and virtue. It is a handbook of versification, prose style, language use, and rhetorical ornament, a guide to how to write pastoral poetry. 'The *Arcadia* hath excellently limned the faces of all virtues and affections' (19.39–40), Scott says. Repeatedly in the *Model*, therefore, the *Arcadia* provides the example to illustrate the point. We can also see moments where Scott says something more loosely but nevertheless still distinctively Sidneian. Sidney is a writer who loves form and structure, and likes to use different orders of form as metaphors for each other. One of the *Arcadia*'s habitual tricks is to compare the form of some sequence of events, thought, moral position, even gesture, to the structure of a sentence. In the *Model* Scott offers a striking analogy between plot and sentence structure that seems like his imaginative response to this feature of Sidney's writing: 'Such are those pretty turnings of your sentences from the apparent bent of your phrase that are, as it were, models of the *peripeteiae*' (40.8–9). Scott's key-word, *model*, we see here, implies a possibility of analogy between different levels of poetic structure – plot, episode, sentence, word. Scott also likes to draw attention to those moments in his paradigm texts where the language of poetics is explicitly used. In explaining what *peripeteia* is and later how tragedy works he refers in detail to two separate scenes in the *Arcadia* in which the effect of events on bystanders within the fiction is described in the language of Aristotelian poetics (39 and 78); when he shows the importance of decorum at the level of plot he points to a moment in Heliodorus when the heroine Charikleia seems all too aware of the kind of story she is in and the need to play by its rules (36). This attention to theoretical language within literary texts is Scott's way of insisting on the purchase theory can give us on practice, and it is a direct response to Sidney's example.

The model of poesy is in many ways a commentary on *The defence of poesy*, adopting its basic theory, filling in its gaps, interrogating and weighing its sources, glossing and elaborating its difficulties. But it is also a very different sort of work, a much more ambitious and comprehensive exercise inspired by the *Defence* but not bounded or constrained by it. That inspiration, though, remains substantial. Sidney's is a poetics of character, of image, and of ideal forms. Poetry, by which he means fiction in verse or prose, is an art of *mimēsis* or representation, which presents in the actions and characters it portrays 'notable images of virtues, vices, or what else' (*DP*, 12), a vivid 'speaking picture' (*DP*, 10) that will delight, teach, and move the reader to emulate the idealised good that has been depicted and shun the bad. Because it can give examples and not only precepts, it teaches morality better than philosophy can; because it can create its own examples instead of relying on the flawed and compromised examples of history, it is a more effective teacher than history. What the reader should get from the poet is

---

century. For the attribution see Hannah Leah Crummé, 'William Scott's copy of Sidney', *Notes and queries*, 56 (2009), 553–4.

something like a Platonic ideal form, except that where for Plato the ideas were beyond the reach of mere imitative artists, for Sidney the artist accesses directly or creates the '*idea* or fore-conceit' (*DP*, 9), and that is his most important imaginative labour, because the authorial idea is the model not only for fictive plot and character but for the future life and ethos of the transformed reader. Sidney's poetics is a fusion of many classical sources, led in key areas by Scaliger (especially towards the idea that the poet does not imitate nature so much as create a 'second nature', *DP*, 9). From Plato come the ideas, with the Neoplatonic twist that makes them the strength and not the flaw of good art. From Aristotle comes a positive theory of *mimēsis*, a formalist approach to the construction of a story, a respect for the differences of genres, an emphasis on the shaping of plot material into something universal, instructive, and moving that generates wonder but is also believable. Horace reinforces some of those points and adds an insistence on decorum (of genre, of character, of language) and a mantra of teaching and delighting, both of which are drawn from the theory of rhetoric. And from that rhetorical background comes Sidney's additional emphasis on the third of the traditional triad of rhetorical aims and means: *logos*, *ēthos*, *pathos* (argument, speaker's character, emotion); *docere*, *delectare*, *movere*; teach, delight, move. 'For [poets] indeed do merely make to imitate, and imitate both to delight and teach, and delight to move men to take that goodness in hand, which without delight they would fly as from a stranger, and teach to make them know that goodness whereunto they are moved' (*DP*, 11).

All of this is in Scott too, as his opening definition makes clear:

> All antiquity, following their great leader Aristotle, have defined poetry to be an art of imitation, or an instrument of reason, that consists in laying down the rules and way how in style to feign or represent things, with delight to teach and to move us to good; as if one should say with the lyric Simonides (after whom Sir Philip Sidney saith) the poem is a speaking or wordish picture. . . .   (6)

Of Scott's many additions to Sidney one is especially striking because it, too, seems to come from an intelligent reading of Sidney's own literary works. Sidney is fascinated with the Platonic theory of love, whereby to love was to begin to glimpse the ideal form that lies behind the particularities of human beauty and virtue. There is within the *Defence* an occasional acknowledgement that a Sidneian reader may need to be something like a Platonic lover, but in both *Astrophil and Stella* and the *Arcadia* there are episodes that make clear – turning this equation round – that a lover is very much like a Sidneian reader. Scott draws material from these metaphorical exchanges in Sidney in his detailed account of poetic creation as a writerly and readerly falling in love with an idea (15–16). We can start to see that the *model* in Scott's title is, among many things, a sign of Sidney's particular bringing together of Neoplatonism and Aristotelianism: it is structure, idea, universal, form, example, speaking picture, 'an imaginative ground-plot of a profitable invention' (*DP*, 35).[127]

---

[127] See further below, lxix–lxx.

DU BARTAS

Scott's other literary hero may seem a less obvious choice, but the French poet Guillaume de Salluste, Sieur du Bartas (1544–90) was one of the most celebrated writers in England in the 1590s. Sidney (*DP*, 10–11) divides poets into three groups: (i) religious poets, (ii) historical and philosophical poets, and (iii) 'right poets', who create works of fiction. With the exception of his partial translation of the Psalms, Sidney belongs to that third group, whilst Du Bartas works within the first two. Not only could Du Bartas perfectly complement what Scott could get from Sidney, therefore, but he was also a poet whom Sidney admired and translated. Du Bartas was a Protestant, and that fact is fundamental to his popularity in Britain. It also meant he had an awareness of the British, their monarchs and men of culture, that led to a two-way traffic of praise and translation.[128] He had extensive dealings with James VI of Scotland, each translating works by the other and James attempting to persuade Du Bartas to stay permanently at the Scottish court; he praised both the Queen and the 'sweet-singing swan' Sidney ('milor Cydné . . . cigne doux-chantant').[129]

Scott knows all of Du Bartas's principal works. *La muse Chrestiene* (1574) included *L'Uranie*, his poem describing a life-changing encounter with the muse of sacred poetry, and a short biblical epic, *Judith*, to both of which Scott refers. But Du Bartas's fame derived from his epic account of the Creation, *La sepmaine* (1578), and its projected continuation into the rest of human history, the unfinished *La seconde sepmaine* (first two days 1584, with further parts appearing posthumously). The poems base their accounts on the Bible but expand to include extensive scientific, theological, and moral elaboration and discussion, as well of course as poetic ornament, including an abundance of epic similes; within Du Bartas's lifetime they were being reprinted in scholarly editions with commentary by Simon Goulart. Sidney is believed to have translated a good part of *La sepmaine*, if not the whole of it; that work, although entered in the Stationers' Register by William Ponsonby in 1588, was never printed and is lost.[130] James VI's translation of *L'Uranie* was included in *The essayes of a prentise, in the divine art of poesie* (Edinburgh, 1584) and was complemented by *The historie of Judith* (Edinburgh, 1584), translated by Thomas Hudson at James's instigation. Among other English printings were a Latin translation of *L'Uranie* (1589) by Robert Ashley; a Latin version of *La sepmaine* by Gabriel de Lerm, *Hebdomas* (1591; first printed in Paris in 1583); *Babilon* (1595) and *The colonies* (1598) by William Lisle (from the second week); and an anonymous rhyme royal translation of *The first day* (1595). Also contemporary with Scott is Robert Barret's manuscript translation of *Judith* and most of the second week, *c.*1600.[131] But the lasting work of translation was done by Josuah Sylvester, to

---

[128] For Du Bartas's reception and influence in English literature see Du Bartas, III, 537–43, and Snyder, I, 72–95, esp. 73–4 for the many who praised, quoted, or alluded to Du Bartas in the 1590s and 1600s. For a fuller account see Anne Lake Prescott, *French poets and the English Renaissance* (New Haven, 1978), 167–234, and Peter Auger, 'The *Semaines*' dissemination in England and Scotland until 1641', *Renaissance studies*, 26 (2011), 625–40.

[129] Du Bartas, I, 19–22; II, 141.   [130] For a summary of the evidence see Ringler, 339.

[131] Folger Shakespeare Library, MS v.b.224, discussed by Prescott (*French poets*, 188–91), but neglected in *ODNB*, 'Barret, Robert (*fl.* 1586?–1607)'.

whom Scott refers. Sylvester's work began with *A canticle* (1590), an almost instant translation of the poem Du Bartas had written celebrating Henri of Navarre's victory over the Catholic forces at Ivry, and continued with *The triumph of faith. The sacrifice of Isaac. The ship-wracke of Jonas* (1592), and *The second weeke* (1598), a partial translation of *La seconde sepmaine*. Scott would not get to read Sylvester's translation of *La sepmaine* for some years: it was first printed in *Bartas his devine weekes and workes* (1605), with a completed translation appearing under the same title in 1608.

But then Scott preferred to read Du Bartas in French and to translate him himself.[132] We cannot know how much of his translation of *La sepmaine*, which follows the *Model* in Add. MS 81083, has been lost; in all probability only the remainder of the second day. Water damage has removed increasingly large portions of the text in the last twelve pages, starting with the odd syllable and ending with a third of the last page's text. What we have is still significant: forty-eight pages, a strict thirty lines per page, translating all 766 lines of the first day and the first 656 of the 1,160 of the second day into fluent and dynamic hexameter couplets, matching Du Bartas's form exactly save only for the addition of English accent. Scott adds three four-line digressions in his own voice as translator, but otherwise the translation is almost entirely line for line, couplet for couplet, with only the occasional exception, the disciplined method of Sidney's sister Mary, Countess of Pembroke in her translations. And Scott stays close to Du Bartas, diverging for only the occasional quiet Englishing, as when the rivers Rhône and Ticino become Thames and Medway, or when a dry thought about the various musical possibilities that can be produced from different combinations of the notes of the pentatonic scale is transformed into a delightful image of change bell-ringing.[133]

Scott uses the example of Du Bartas to illustrate his points scores of times in the *Model*. *Judith* is useful as a text to put alongside Xenophon's *Cyropaedia*, Sidney's preferred example, to illustrate how a character in a story can be an exemplary 'image' or 'model': 'Bartas his *Judith* is a worthy pattern of a religiously trained and virtuously living woman' (19). And *La sepmaine* is the best instance of philosophical poetry: 'our incomparable Bartas . . . hath opened as much natural science in one week, containing the story of the creation, as all the rabble of schoolmen and philosophers have done since Plato and Aristotle' (20). Scott does not tell us in the *Model* that he has translated Du Bartas, though he includes four passages from his translation, one to illustrate mid-word caesura and the other three no different from all Scott's many other quotations of verse in Latin, Italian, and French: Du Bartas first because of what he says, and then the translation to make sure we can understand it.

Scott's inclusion of his Du Bartas translation alongside the *Model* in the manuscript given to Sir Henry Lee requires us to ask whether and in what ways the two works might be seen as complementary. It is of course vital for Scott the theorist to demonstrate his qualifications as a poet, something the many short versified translations from Horace, Petrarch, and others in the *Model* had only to an extent enabled Scott to do; the Du Bartas also enables him to substantiate his stated preference for hexameter in epic verse,

---

[132] On the editions Scott used, see below, lxxxii.

[133] Add. MS 81083, 69[r], translating 2.183 (line references to text in Du Bartas, 1); 70[r], translating 2.251–4.

as well as to illustrate his points about accentual-syllabic metrics, caesura, and feminine and triple rhyme. Scott's deep religiosity, and the *Model*'s commitment to poetry that exemplifies virtue or treats religious themes, makes the translation of something from Du Bartas an ideal test case. But why not the *Judith*?

La sepmaine is a poem about making. The analogy between the poet (Greek *poiētēs*, 'maker') and God is present in Sidney: 'Neither let it be deemed too saucy a comparison to balance the highest point of man's wit with the efficacy of nature, but rather give right honour to the heavenly Maker of that maker, who, having made man to His own likeness, set him beyond and over all the works of that second nature' (*DP*, 9). And it is Puttenham's way of beginning his *Art*:

> A poet is as much to say as a maker. And our English name well conforms with the Greek word, for of *poiein*, to make, they call a maker *poeta*. Such as (by way of resemblance and reverently) we may say of God, who without any travail to his divine imagination made all the world of nought, nor also by any pattern or mold as the Platonics with their Ideas do fantastically suppose. Even so the very poet makes and contrives out of his own brain both the verse and matter of his poem, and not by any foreign copy or example, as doth the translator, who therefore may well be said a versifier, but not a poet.   (*Art*, 93)

Compare Du Bartas, well translated by Scott, beside the marginal gloss, 'The world made without pattern':

> This admirable workman did not tie his thought
> To some imaginary plot of work forethought
> Found out with much ado, nor farther did he choose
> Any more ancient world, which he had need to use
> To model out this one (as does the master wright
> Of some great building, who before his hand be pight
> Unto his charge makes choice of some great frame and fair,
> Whose costly matter, cunning work are equal rare;
> And, if one only building he shall miss to find
> Whole, uniform, and fair, he patterns in his mind
> Of one the front, another's pillars he compares,
> And in the third he marks the winding, stately stairs;
> Thus over all he goes, choosing each seemliest thing,
> And after twenty patterns makes his one building),
> But, having naught saving a naught whereby to frame
> This whole, the chief of this fair work, th'eternal name
> Without far ranging, without sweating toil or pain,
> Creates the air, heav'n, earth, and this low-flowing plain . . . [134]

---

[134] Add. MS 81083, 56ʳ, translating 1.179–96. I have modernised the spelling and punctuation in these quotations.

The old anecdote about Zeuxis painting a Helen by studying many different beautiful women is here translated into the terms of building. The language of Scott's poetics runs through the passage (imaginary plot, model, frame, pattern, whole, uniform), but in thinking of creation as architecture it recalls Scott's guiding metaphor of his *Model of poesy* as a building, and reminds us that the theorist too is a maker, as Cicero had shown when he used the Zeuxis anecdote as an analogy for his own eclecticism in formulating a work of rhetorical theory.[135] Poets and theorists both are in Scott idealising, quasi-Platonic makers, forming a perfect idea or model of a thing ('the idea or image modelled in their minds', 11.20–1) and then delivering it to the reader in such a way that it will reform him or her on its pattern. Du Bartas offers a vision of God before the Creation as a Platonic demiurge contemplating the ideal forms of his glory, justice, might, and providence, 'Et si tu veux encor, de ceste grande boule, | Peut estre, il contemploit l'archetype et le moule'. Scott goes one better with his synonyms: 'Or farther, so may be, contemplating, he view'd | The great idea, type, and mould of this round rude'.[136]

As a poem about making, *La sepmaine*'s first two days must consider the relations between form and matter. Those relations are also a theme of Scott's treatise. This comes in part from Scaliger: his second book (of the seven of *Poetices libri septem*) is named *hyle* (*hulē*, 'matter') and treats versification, and his third book, on the organising patterns of a poem, its plotting and figures of thought, is called *idea*. But it also comes from Scott's intensely logical method of proceeding (on which see below, lxvi–lxvii): poetry as an object of definition must be something with both form and matter. The second day of *La sepmaine* includes an extended set of variations on the theme of form and matter with, again, many points of verbal and imaginative contact with Scott's treatise.

Another of the *Model*'s key terms is *order*. The first two days of *La sepmaine* (covering Genesis 1:1–8) are about order and chaos, about first principles and their correct disposition, definition and division, about separating light from darkness (and there is contact there with Scott's poetics of visual images, or with his title page motto), and the heavens from the waters. When Du Bartas turns to the job of elaborating the opening verses of Genesis, Scott reminds us that Ovid is a poetic intertext: chaos for Du Bartas includes 'Une pile confuse' but for Scott that is 'an indigested heape', after Ovid's 'rudis indigestaque moles'.[137] This is a welcome feature of Scott's translation: a generous and sensitive literariness. Scott follows the metrical and verbal model of Du Bartas attentively, but he also helps to relate Du Bartas to the rest of the literary world. When he hears an echo in Du Bartas of Seneca's famous chorus from *Thyestes*, he remembers his great-grandfather Wyatt's translation of those lines ('Stond who so list upon the Slipper toppe | Of courtes estates'): 'Eschelle qui voudra les estages des cieux . . .'; 'Climb who so list the scaffold of the upmost sky'.[138] It is the same habit of comparing and collating that makes the *Model* such a productive conference of authorities.

[135] Cicero, *De inventione*, 2.1.1–2.2.5.   [136] Du Bartas, 1.63–4; Add. MS 81083, 54[r].

[137] Du Bartas, 1.224; Add. MS 81083, 56[v]; Ovid, *Metamorphoses*, 1.7.

[138] Wyatt, 240; Du Bartas, 1.105; Add. MS 81083, 54[v].

But it is the scrupulous attentiveness that makes for some of Scott's best moments as a poet. Compare Du Bartas:

> L'immuable decret de la bouche divine,
> Qui causera sa fin, causa son origine.
> Non en temps, avant temps, ains mesme avec le temps,
> J'entens un temps confus . . .   (1.19–22)

And Scott, managing to sound for a moment less like Milton and more like Eliot:

> But that firm-fast decree from out the mouth divine,
> That once will work world's fall, did once give world his prime.
> Not after or before time, but at once with time,
> I mean time undistinct . . .   (53^r)

Whether Scott also tried to compose anything as a 'right poet' rather than only a 'versifier' we do not at present know. But his Du Bartas is ample evidence of his ability not only as a linguist but as a poet.

LATE ELIZABETHAN LITERATURE

Scott's view of the literary map is an up-to-date one. The classical and continental works of literature that he discusses are the ones influencing the major works of English literature printed in the 1590s, and in some cases belong to fashions (like pastoral tragicomedy) yet to make their impact in England. It is no surprise that Virgil (thirty mentions by name) should be the most prominent literary writer alongside Sidney. Virgil is the hero of Scaliger's *Poetices libri septem*, one of Scott's key sources, but of course the idea of Virgil's preeminence was neither a new nor a faulty one. Among other classical authors, the prominence of Ovid and Horace is also to be expected. The use of Pindar, however, is noteworthy, showing a more developed interest in ancient lyric than was common. Scott's attention to Roman comedy, and especially Terence, fits his academic background, but is also interesting in view of the classical leanings of some 1590s comedy for the public stage, notably Shakespeare's *The comedy of errors*. Heliodorus' *Aithiopika* figures prominently because it is a key reference text for Sidney, both as example in the *Defence* and as model in the *Arcadia*. Scott's references to modern continental writers show a similar pattern: an investigation of the sources of late Elizabethan literature. Scott reads (and translates) Petrarch, who alongside his student Sidney was the efficient cause (and indeed the formal and to an extent material causes too) of the late-Elizabethan sonnet boom. Scott reads Ariosto and Tasso, and is therefore able to appreciate the relations to them of Spenser's *The faerie queene*. His interest in Guarini's *Il pastor fido* and Tasso's *Aminta* is more unusual: the latter had been translated by Abraham Fraunce in 1591 (in *The Countesse of Pembrokes Yvychurch*), and the Italian text of both works had been printed in England in the same year. *Il pastor fido* would appear in a translation by an anonymous kinsman of Sir Edward Dymoke, a sometime patron of Samuel Daniel, in an edition published by Daniel's bookseller (and friend) Simon Waterson in 1602. Daniel and Dymoke had travelled to Italy in 1590 and had met Guarini, and they were clearly instrumental in bringing his play, and its mode, to an English audience. Daniel contributed a commendatory sonnet to the 1602 edition, and would himself write two pastoral tragicomedies for court performance, *The Queenes Arcadia* (1606) and *Hymens triumph* (1615). As the title of the first of Daniel's plays suggests, English pastoral tragicomedy recognised and exploited its affinities with Sidneian pastoral romance; indeed Fraunce's translation from Tasso in 1591 had been part of another avowedly Sidneian project: the writing of English verse in classical metres, Scott's rejection of which is his most significant disagreement with Sidney. Scott's interest in this mode, therefore, is unsurprising in a devotee of the *Arcadia*. The love of Italianate pastoral tragicomedy at court continued in the 1620s and 30s: Scott has noticed something that is just about to happen.

Scott looks back as well as forward. As Sir Thomas Wyatt's great-grandson he has a vested interest in remembering Wyatt's contribution to the development of Tudor lyric, and Surrey is paired with him, as he is in Puttenham. Scott's approval of Buchanan's Latin plays, of the early Elizabethan tragedy *Gorboduc*, and of the *Mirror for magistrates*, repeats Sidney's and is standard wisdom. Chaucer had been easier to ignore, despite Sidney's insistence on his significance: 'Chaucer, undoubtedly, did excellently in his *Troilus and Criseyde*, of whom truly I know not whether to marvel more, either that he in that misty time could see so clearly, or that we in this clear age go so stumblingly after him. Yet had he great wants, fit to be forgiven in so reverent an antiquity' (*DP*, 44). Chaucer's works – frequently printed before 1550 – had not been reprinted since 1561 but Scott may have had access to a new edition by Thomas Speght first printed in 1598, and this may have led him to refer not only to *Troilus* but to *The legend of good women* and *The Canterbury tales*.

Scott's literary tastes and attentions are clearly guided by Sidney's criticism and literary works. But his immersion in the literature of the 1590s requires him to apply the lessons he has learned – from Sidney above all, but also from Scaliger and Aristotle – to the newest English writing. As he says of his poetics: 'we bind ourselves, in substance, not to vary from antiquity, but make it more appliable to our later and modern kinds' (18). Scott has read Warner, Drayton, Southwell, Chapman; he knows the sonneteers as well as the satirists whose books had been burned in 1599. He pays serious attention to Samuel Daniel's historical epic modelled on Lucan, *The civil wars*, the first instalment of which had been printed in 1595, and to Daniel's *The complaint of Rosamond* (printed with his sonnet sequence *Delia* in 1592). Spenser (nine mentions by name) is rightly prominent: not only some thoughts about the language of *The shepheardes calender* based on those of Sidney, but the use of *A view of the present state of Ireland* (discussed above, xxxvi), and proper attention to the often overlooked *Muiopotmos* (in Scott's discussion of mock epic); not only general appreciation of the 'moral invention, shadowed so naturally and properly under the persons in his *Faerie Queene*' (19), but comment on its imitative relations to Virgil and Tasso, assessment of the organisation of its opening, and a criticism on a point of historical inaccuracy. Scott makes it clear that his criticisms of celebrated writers are necessitated by his refusal to read less good work: 'And here because for illustration I am forced to bring instances of errors, I must entreat not to be branded with the dignity of a *critic* for culling out the imperfections of our best writers, because I have not had – and I repent me not that I have not had – leisure to read the trivial vulgar poets' (33).

A sign of Scott's assurance and value as a critic is his use of Shakespeare. Though Shakespeare was not yet being seen as a writer of the significance of Sidney or Spenser, his stock was rising fast, as can be sensed from his prominence in Francis Meres's comparative lists of ancient and modern writers in the various genres in *Palladis tamia* (1598). Scott selects two works by Shakespeare and makes points about both language and genre. The first is *Lucrece*, first printed in 1594 but available to Scott in the newly printed second edition of 1598, from which he quotes twice: a criticism of 'endless date of never-ending woes' (l. 935) as 'a very idle, stuffed verse' (53) to exemplify a point from Scaliger about lines padded out by unnecessary adjectives to fit their metre; and quotation of 'sorrow ebbs, being blown with wind of words' (l. 1330) out of context and for its virtues as a commonplace (28). Scott's use of *Richard II* (a 'very well-penned tragedy', 45) is more interesting. He discusses its representation of how sorrow can issue in play (45, a generic point about comic relief as much as a point about human passions), adapting the line 'Or shall we play the wantons with our woes . . . ?' (3.3.164). He admires an extended passage spoken by John of Gaunt (1.3.227–32, beginning, 'Shorten my days thou canst with sullen sorrow') in a discussion of rhetorical amplification, which sometimes 'is by heaping our words and, as it were, piling one phrase upon another of the same sense to double and redouble our blows that, by varying and reiterating, may work into the mind of the reader' (66). He rightly criticises for their grammatical ambiguity the lines 'That when the searching eye of heaven is hid | Behind the globe, that lights the lower world' (3.2.37–8): 'one would take it by the placing his words that he should mean that the globe of the earth enlighteneth the lower hemisphere' (54). And in his discussion of how pastoral extends beyond poems about shepherds, he praises the decorum of Shakespeare's representation of the gardener (3.2) 'in that well-conceited tragedy of *Richard the Second*' (22).

These few references to Shakespeare's writings may seem slight in comparison to the many to the *Arcadia*, but they are still important: the use of Sidney to illustrate rhetorical treatises and critical essays was expected; that of Shakespeare was unprecedented. But why these two works? It may be that Sidney's use of Lucretia as a paradigm in the *Defence* drew Scott to Shakespeare's great poem. But it has many features that match it to a Sidneian taste and aesthetic, and we might single out three things in particular that Scott must have admired about *Lucrece*: its dense rhetorical texture; its tight neoclassical plotting and unity of action, the 'Argument' filling in the before and after; and its intense pictorialism, culminating in the celebrated Troy painting ekphrasis. Scott's selection of *Richard II* may also be due to a perception that it was in closer conformity to classical paradigms than many contemporary tragedies. We should note that the category 'history play' has no meaning for Scott (or for Shakespeare): *Richard II* is a tragedy. If we imagine Scott seeking a tragedy by Shakespeare to use for examples (and therefore in print by 1599), we see that his choice would have been small: *Titus Andronicus* (1594), perhaps *3 Henry VI* (printed in 1595 as *The true tragedy of Richard Duke of York*), *Richard III* (1597 and 1598), *Romeo and Juliet* (1597 and 1599), and *Richard II* (1597, with two further quartos in 1598). Only the last of these has the singularity of focus and relatively constrained plotting to sit comfortably alongside Scott's Aristotelian analysis. He needed the fall of a single great man, through *hamartia* or, as Scott puts it, 'for some one remarkable error and passion' (77), and that he found in *Richard II*.

That Scott's neoclassicism rules his response to Shakespeare is evident in a passing mention of *Lucrece* in what is a valuable attempt to theorise the Elizabethan short epic or *epyllion* (an old name that has only recently been applied to these works). From Aristotle comes a vocabulary of 'acts' (76.33–5, 77.12) as continuous sequences of action: though an epic may have several, a tragedy can have only a single such sequence if it is to have unity of action. Scott recognises that the short epic has a similar singularity, so that it can be understood as analogous to tragedy in comprising material equivalent only to a part of an epic poem. This Aristotelian and dramatic analysis yields the following:

> Again, they are to be comprehended under the *heroic* that of late are so graciously entertained of our graceless age, and which in solemn verse (not fit for music) handle narratively the misfortunes of some unhappily raised or famous person, thorough error, vice, or malice overthrown. Such are the *Mirror of Magistrates*, *Rosamond*, *Lucrece' Rape*, *Peter's Denial* (first in Italian, now imitated in English); I think, indeed, these answer to the *rhapsody* above mentioned and are as it were one act of the heroical. Chaucer's *Troilus and Criseyde* is in this rank, and his *Legends*. (20)

We can set aside the scholarship that recognises the Italian source of Southwell's *Saint Peters complaint* (1595); Scott is the only one of his contemporaries to do so. And we can suspend consideration of the connection between complaint and epyllion, with their different narrative methods but similar combinations of tragic action and subsequent lament; as of the connection back to Chaucer. All of that provokes new thoughts and opens up lines of enquiry. But perhaps the most useful feature here is that analogy of short narrative poem to tragedy, with Aristotle's great analysis of epic and tragedy lying behind it. It is an unprecedented theoretical treatment of Elizabethan shorter narrative poems and it helps us to see, for example, how and why we should attend to the tragic and dramatic dimensions of *Lucrece*, how its rhetorical excesses and obsessive gazing can be connected to the Shakespearean theatre.

Scott's preference for certain authors and works and his access to manuscript writings by Spenser, Hoskyns, and Hooker (see above, xxxvi and xxx–xxxi) may simply be the result of the casual textual encounters and wanderings among the bookshops of St Paul's that were the common experience of bookish young law students in late-Elizabethan London. Or they may be a sign of some genuine inwardness with the literary scene of the late 1590s, of the kind that we saw in 1605 in *Sir Thomas Smithes voiage and entertainment in Rushia*, with its possible connections to Scott. 1599 was the year Spenser died, the Globe was built, and the Bishops banned printed satire; it was the year after Sidney's complete works had appeared, and Francis Meres had offered his sketch of the new English canon in *Palladis tamia, wits treasury* (1598); the year before the appearance of two other publications sponsored by John Bodenham, *Englands Helicon* (1600) and *Belvedere* (1600), along with Robert Allott's *Englands Parnassus* (1600), which together confirmed Meres's view that the English now had a body of work that was comprehensively excellent – and able in the latter two cases to provide a comprehensive dictionary of commonplaces – across the range of poetic kinds. Scott is confident that the modern English poets can illustrate his poetic theory, and confident that it is right to develop that theory further to account for their writings. That confidence is of its moment. We should therefore ask if Scott intended the *Model* as a contribution to that moment. The *Model* has a separate title page, in clear imitation of print conventions, but this is no certain sign that he wished to have the work printed. Both the *Model* and Scott's Du Bartas are equipped with dedicatory epistles, a feature less usual in manuscripts than in printed books (where the epistle both anticipates a cash reward for plumping up its dedicatee and gratifies the reader by letting them witness an epistolary act that is private in its mode and origins). Of course, Add. MS 81083 is a presentation manuscript for Sir Henry Lee (see below, lxxvi), and so the epistle to Lee has a clear primary function, but Scott also includes the epistle dedicating his Du Bartas translation to his uncle George Wyatt, which – even if only in this unique manuscript copy – therefore ceases to be the private letter received and becomes the epistle overheard. Scott may have been thinking of further readers for these acts of dedication and for the works themselves, and we may – now that we have the *Model* and the Du Bartas again – feel genuine regret that they were not printed in their day. Whether Scott intended or hoped for either to be printed we cannot know, but it is not unlikely.

THE VISUAL ARTS

The portrait is full-length, and vast: eight feet high and five feet wide. The Queen stands almost square, hips, arms, shoulders, and head angled to her right, so that she both embraces and seems the source of the sunlight that illuminates her face, and so that her back is for now turned on the stormy darkness of the picture's right-hand side. She is as dressed and adorned as it is possible to be, the junctures of the trellis-work pattern of her white gown marked by pearls, rubies, or diamonds set in gold; the three stones, the diamonds painted as black as her eyes, decorate her hair and neck too, as well as the edges of her wired veil and hanging sleeves, whose outlines seem rather like the wings of an avenging angel. There are chains of pearls round her neck both inside and outside her lace ruff; above her left breast a pair of roses, not heraldic Tudor red-and-white but living pink; hanging from her left ear an armillary sphere, to signify her power and connect her to her servant, Sir Henry Lee, whose sleeves had been decorated with the same device in an earlier portrait of him by Antonis Mor in this same colour scheme:[139] Elizabeth's colours of black and white (and his, black and silver), plus the red of devotion and of life. In her right hand a fan, in her left a pair of gloves, her left little finger, the only one beringed, pointing to her feet and her feet standing on a map of England which is also the island itself, the horizon arcing away behind her dress. More precisely, she stands on Oxfordshire, and Lee's manors of Ditchley and Woodstock therefore. In the darkness of the right foreground are London and Kent, boats coming from and going to their ports, trading fabrics and

---

[139] National Portrait Gallery, NPG 2095 (from 1568).

books perhaps, or bringing war. Latin mottoes scattered around the portrait tell us of the Queen's magnanimity and power, a power that could be vengeful but is withheld; a sonnet (by Lee, perhaps) represents her as sun, storm, isle, and ocean. Everything comes from her and all thanks must return to her.[140]

This famous portrait was at Ditchley, with the manuscript of Scott's *Model* (see below, lxxv–lxxvi), until given to the nation by Viscount Dillon in 1932, and probably relates to the Queen's visit to Ditchley in 1592. It was painted by Marcus Gheeraerts II, 'The most important painter working in England between *c.*1590 and *c.*1620',[141] whose principal patron in the 1590s was Sir Henry Lee. Both the 1575 entertainment for the Queen at Woodstock and that in 1592 at Ditchley featured a hall hung with allegorical and emblematic pictures,[142] and in the latter case the Queen's ability to unpick the hidden meanings is what wakes the aged knight who guards them (Lee) from his enchantment. Lee, like Sidney,[143] was unusual for a non-noble in commissioning a large number of portraits of himself; in both cases this speaks more of connoisseurship than of vanity. Lee's include not only the Mor portrait from 1568, which is one of the finest representations of an Englishman of the sixteenth century, but several by Gheeraerts, including a portrait in his garter robes from 1602 and one with his faithful dog from a few years earlier.[144] Gheeraerts was also employed to paint Lee's cousin Captain Thomas Lee, and that portrait, with symbolically Anglo-Irish dress, impresa, and landscape background exemplifies several things that feature in Gheeraerts's work for Lee: technical innovation, for the landscape setting was introduced by Gheeraerts in English portraiture, and he was instrumental in popularising work on this larger scale;[145] ability to execute a patron's allegorical programme (for Lee is clearly the designer of these portraits' allegories); and the connection to the self-representations of the tiltyard, with meaningful costume and impresa, word and image. The 1590s is a period of impresa portraits,[146] and continued an interest in elaborate armour fostered by Lee, as Master of the Armoury and deviser of the Accession Day tilts.[147] Lee's patronage evidently commended Gheeraerts to Essex – a fine portrait survives – and other courtiers, including the Sidneys and, in the Jacobean period, Queen Anne.[148]

In the preface to his translation of Lomazzo, Haydocke tells us that English collectors ('some of our Nobilitie, and divers private Gentlemen') had worked hard to gather

---

[140] National Portrait Gallery, NPG 2561: see frontispiece. For a fuller description of Elizabeth's clothing in this portrait see Janet Arnold, *Queen Elizabeth's wardrobe unlock'd* (Leeds, 1988), 42–7.

[141] Roy Strong, *The Elizabethan image* (London, 1969), 70.

[142] *The Queenes Majesties entertainement at Woodstock* (1585), B4ᵛ; Chambers, 281–2; this latter entertainment might have been at Woodstock too, though Chambers argues convincingly for Ditchley. Further discussion and text of the Ditchley entertainment in Jean Wilson, *Entertainments for Elizabeth* (Woodbridge, 1980), 119–42.

[143] Roy Strong, 'Sidney's appearance reconsidered', in M. J. B. Allen *et al.* (eds.), *Sir Philip Sidney's achievements* (New York, 1990), 3–31 (16).

[144] See Karen Hearn, *Marcus Gheeraerts II: Elizabethan artist* (London, 2002), 17–18.

[145] Hearn, *Gheeraerts*, 18–21 and 9.

[146] See Alan R. Young, *Tudor and Jacobean tournaments* (London, 1987), 140–3.

[147] See Roy Strong, 'Fair England's knights: the Accession Day tournaments', in *The cult of Elizabeth: Elizabethan portraiture and pageantry* (London, 1977), esp. 129–33.

[148] See Hearn, *Gheeraerts*, esp. 21–2, 29, 34–5, and 51.

works by the old masters, 'as may appeare, by their Galleries carefully furnished, with the excellent monuments of sundry famous ancient Masters, both Italian and German'.[149] Scott had access through Lee and perhaps Wyatt to pictures that exemplified the theories and rules in Lomazzo. Sidney – Lee could have told him – had been a connoisseur of painters, employing John de Critz (Gheeraerts's future brother-in-law) and, in Italy, vacillating over whether to commission Titian or Veronese to paint his portrait, opting for the latter.[150] In tracing Sidney's footsteps through the metaphors and actualities of painting's relations to poetry, Scott must have done more than read Pliny and Lomazzo. We can see Gheeraerts's innovations, or some contact with continental paintings, in Scott's wonderful comparison of digressive episodes to the background details of paintings:

> And though they be but circumstances, yet necessarily they accompany the well doing and reporting of any thing or action: such are descriptions of countries, towns, buildings, fortifications, ships, jousts, pomps, funerals, and certain digressions into discourses of any science or art, as in painting you may observe most stories adorned with woods, rivers, birds, beasts, or the like; you shall commonly have no person drawn without some page, some child, some arms, favour, impress, or the like.   (37)

Gheeraerts's early portraits have a rather stiff programmatic style, but from the mid-1590s on he develops an extraordinary capacity to capture life and character. An experience of this evolution may lie behind Scott's appreciation of more expressive portraiture. Scott cites both Pliny and Aristotle on the painterly representation of 'those features and graces of sensible life and passion, those sweet forms of countenance and presence' (17–18), and has learnt how to articulate these qualities from Lomazzo's detailed treatment, in the second book of the *Trattato*, of the painter's skill of 'expressing the inward affections by the outward motions' (10).

Scott's love of painting is best seen in the extraordinary outburst of accumulated scholarly interest that comes from the mere mention of Sidney's 'speaking picture', on only the second page of the *Model*. Poetry is an art of imitation, in style, that teaches and moves to good:

> as if one should say with the lyric Simonides (after whom Sir Philip Sidney saith) the poem is a speaking or wordish picture, as on the other side he calleth the picture a mute or speechless poem, both painter and poet lively representing, to our common sense and fancy, images of the works of nature or reason, and reason guided by virtue, or misguided by passion, the one by the eye only in colours, the other by the ear in words: the one counterfeits the sundry motions and inward affections in the outward forms of behaviour and countenance (the mind's glasses), the other pictures the same person's mind and manners in the delivering of his life and actions, and therefore Petrarch saith of the poets 'pingon

---

[149] Haydocke, ¶5ᵛ.
[150] See, most recently, Elizabeth Goldring, 'A portrait of Sir Philip Sidney by Veronese at Leicester House, London', *The Burlington magazine*, 154 (2012), 548–54.

cantando', they paint whilst they sing. And thus indeed Horace links them in a very near affinity when he saith 'ut pictura poesis', poesy and painting are almost one and the same thing; only so much more worthy is the poet than the painter, by how much words (the proper servants of reason) are more immediate and faithful unfolders both of the scope of him that imitates and of the thing portrayed in the imitation than those dead and tongueless shapes set out in colours only, where the painter cannot presume to be understood in that he hath artificially expressed, much less in all he would have thereupon inferred; and then far better it agrees with the poet which is (in some degree truly) said of the painter, that he discovers neither more nor less but just as much in the imitation as the reasonable soul enjoins. Whatsoever we say of their likeness and agreement, it is most true that the fittest illustration of either is by other, which thing Aristotle by his practice approves. (6)

'Dead and tongueless shapes': this is a striking elaboration of Simonides' proverbial speaking picture/mute poesy. Scott's vividness as a critic, and his ability to pursue the analogy between poetic and painterly representation and expression, comes not only from his reading but, surely, from the training of his eye among Sir Henry Lee's pictures.

Form and method

POETICS, LOGIC, RHETORIC, AND THE MEANING OF 'MODEL'

Scott's treatise is exceptionally well organised. Because that organisation is not marked out in numbered books and chapters or any system of headings and subheadings, I have given a detailed outline below. This may give the impression that the *Model* is all structure. It is not, but it is vital nevertheless not only to understand Scott's many interesting ideas within their place in his larger scheme, but also to ask why the *Model* has the form and the method it does, which is what I address here.

Sidney's *Defence*, it is well known, is constructed according to the accepted plan of the classical oration: exordium, narration, proposition, division, confirmation, confutation, (digression), and peroration. It is an argument by the lead counsel for a team of poet-theorists, against rival teams of lawyers representing philosophy and history, before a judge who is the reader, and all readers. This rhetorical method was, at Sidney's request, subjected to an exhaustive and somewhat destructive logical analysis by a young, former Cambridge academic called William Temple.[151] Temple had become the best-known English champion of the revisionist logic of the French protestant Petrus Ramus, and came to Sidney's attention after dedicating to him an edition of Ramus with commentary, *P. Rami Dialecticae libri duo* (Cambridge, 1584). Sidney took Temple on as his secretary, a role he filled until Sidney's death in 1586, and set him to the analysis of the *Defence*; Temple was later secretary to the Earl of Essex, from

---

[151] See John Webster (ed.), *William Temple's 'Analysis' of Sir Philip Sidney's 'Apology for poetry'* (Binghamton, NY, 1984).

1594 until Essex's own death. This was not the only connection of Sidney to Ramism, that attempt to redefine and demarcate rhetoric and dialectic by giving the latter some of the territory that had belonged to the former. Abraham Fraunce was another, more literary, Ramist who came under Sidney's wing.

Method was a key Ramist word;[152] that Scott never uses it – preferring words like *order, frame,* and, indeed, *model* – points towards a sympathy with other, more traditional, schools of logic. Ramism had cleared away some of the paraphernalia of Aristotelian logic, and also redefined what are the overlapping relations of logic and rhetoric in Aristotle. Scott does use a Ramistic rhetoric book at one point, but only as a convenient source for the rhetorical figures, and in no way that shows a commitment to Ramism's theoretical bases (*inventio* and *dispositio* belonging to logic and not rhetoric). Nevertheless, Scott was clearly interested in logic, and in what logic might bring to poetics, independently of Sidney's own, somewhat vicarious, curiosity about these questions.

Scott's opening move in the *Model* is therefore to define poetry and then to break apart or divide this definition according to the predicables of genus, species, difference, and property. Quintilian gives an example: 'if you wish to define a horse ... the *genus* is animal, the *species* mortal, the *difference* irrational (since man is also mortal) and the *property* neighing'.[153] In the case of poetry, the genus is that it is an art, the species that it imitates in style, and the differences and properties are what distinguish the different genres from each other. Because, in Aristotelian logic, an art must have an end, Scott makes his initial definition, and the first of three sections of the *Model*, a matter of genus, difference, and end: an art of imitation in style, with the end of, through delight, teaching and moving to good. That is a definition recognisable from Sidney's *Defence*, but its logical underpinnings are made clear. The vocabulary of logical analysis is to be found everywhere in the *Model*: phrases like 'differences and several properties' (68.30), 'special properties' (76.18), 'differences and properties' (78.7) have very specific meanings. Of thirty-two occurrences of the word *difference*, around half are in the restricted logical sense.

For Scott poetics is a 'faculty', a distinct area of study, a separate branch of knowledge; he uses the word in this way sixteen times. 'It is neither possible nor needful', he tells us, 'to set down so absolute a frame of rules in the institution of our poet as shall be able to direct him to every particular circumstance required and belonging to the setting forth and dressing of every poem, because then we should grow infinite and run through all arts, even more than Quintilian in his *Oratory* or than Scaliger in our faculty' (29–30). Scaliger, as Scott acknowledges (58.32–4), did deal with much that falls within the province of rhetoric, but Scott is certain that he must not do this. Scaliger's first book of seven is historical, his second is on versification. In this he is

---

[152] For the suggestion that 'Whenever the word "method" appears in the writings of the late sixteenth century in England, it amounts almost to a confession of the author's awareness of Ramus' see W. S. Howell, *Logic and rhetoric in England, 1500–1700* (Princeton, 1956), 263. Howell offers a useful introduction to Ramus' reforms, 146–72, and to English Ramism, 173–281. On *method*, see especially 152–3 and 160–5.

[153] Quintilian, 7.3.3.

copied by Puttenham. But Puttenham had then lost sight of the project of writing an ordered poetics when his third book became simply a treatise on rhetorical *elocutio*, with no attempt to adapt rhetoric to the requirements of the different poetic kinds. Scaliger, on the other hand, had absorbed rhetoric into poetics in his third and fourth books, listing the figures among many other aspects of narrative form and poetic style, and emerging at the other end to apply this wisdom to the criticism of Greek and Latin poetry.

Rhetoric is everywhere in the *Model* and nowhere. It is there of course in the Sidneian triple aim of teaching, delighting, and moving. But Scott is careful never to dwell long on *inventio*, *dispositio*, or *elocutio*, and not to treat any of these separately. Rather, he divides rhetorical material up within his larger framework. So, to take the example of the *elocutio* that had waylaid Puttenham, we find that the figures crop up several times, in the service of a Scaligerian poetic virtue like 'sweetness' or *energeia*. Towards the beginning of Scott's discussion of style he turns from a point about natural or conventional meaning to a brief sentence about rhetorical tropes (53). Under 'variety', Scott defines *figure* and gives examples (without naming figures) of schemes and tropes: 'Thus need we only to give the general description and point out the fountain of all figurative speech, sending the reader to the rhetoricians for the variety both of the words and phrase' (58). Under 'sweetness', and as an appendix to his discussion of versification, he turns briefly to the effects of sound achieved by 'the grammarians' figures' and by the rhetorical schemes or as Puttenham called them 'auricular figures pertaining to clauses of speech' (64; cf. *Art*, 246). Under '*energeia*' he treats amplification (66–7), always resisting the boundaries of the various rhetorical categories and figures in play, and delivers a rapid summary of a section of the Ramistic rhetorics dealing with figures of thought (67–8). Scott follows, variously, Quintilian, Puttenham, and Talaeus, at least. All divide up the figures differently, so Scott's eclecticism is no sure way to ensure that everything is covered. But he does know what he is doing: redistributing those figures usefully analysed by rhetoricians, and defamiliarising them by taking them out of their place in the rhetorical system and depriving them where possible of their well-known names. It is all rather devious.

In structure, the *Model* is less like Scaliger's rhetorical poetics (with its hundreds of chapters and its larger categories transcending the poetic genres) and far more like Viperano's plan (replicated in other *artes poeticae* and not unlike the typical French *art poétique*): historical and general material first, moving towards specific treatments of the genres. Where Scott differs – and this is where he does bear comparison to Scaliger and the rhetorical tradition – is in dividing his treatment between first matter and then manner. The *Model* is – in one of its guiding metaphors – a house of poetry:

> And thus in our 'Model of Poesy' we must proceed (if we will proceed orderly) first to lay the foundation, to define it in general; which explained we may show, by division, how all several kinds of poetry as the divers rooms and offices are built thereon, how the general is dispensed into the particulars, how the particulars are sundered by their special differences and properties, that as walls keep them from confounding one in another; and lastly what dressing and furniture best

suits every subdivided part and member, that thereby direction may be given
how to work in which of the kinds our nature shall inform us we are most apt
for.   (5)

And we must 'proceed orderly', as theorists of poetics and as poets. The analysis of
narrative order, the correct disposition of parts within the whole, the quasi-organic
form of the properly made poem – these are what Aristotle gave to poetics, what Horace
found in the Aristotelian poetics he inherited, and what he passed on, now preserved
in the salt of rhetoric. The Elizabethans often missed the point of poetics because of
their love of rhetoric. Scott gives us what Puttenham lost sight of, what Sidney knew
but never wrote, and what Harington lacked the patience to develop: an Elizabethan
poetics. It is fitting, then, that he gives Horace the last word and the last word is *ordo*,
order.

Why did Scott call his work *The model of poesy*? The word *model* was relatively
new in English, though its French, Italian, and Latin forms were well enough known
to linguists like Scott. Its senses included plan, likeness, and object of imitation (for
further details and examples see Commentary, 1.1n.). Scott is fond of the outline or
summary – that is what his letter to Cecil offers in respect of a longer account of
the embassy to Russia; it is what we see in the diagram of the poetic kinds (69); and
it is what is promised in the *Model*'s subtitle, 'the art of poesy drawn into a short
or summary discourse'. The *Model* is therefore an outline plan of a larger structure
or territory, a guide to a long history and a complex theory. It is also a set of rules
and guidelines for the poet to follow: a plan of theory and a plan for practice. But
the relation of *model* to *poesy* runs both ways in Scott's title: we can model poesy
and poesy can make models. The title therefore forces us to recognise the affinity of
Scott's method as theorist to the poetic procedures he describes and theorises: parallel
activities of model-making (*poesis*). The word *model* encompasses the Platonic *idea*
imitated by the Sidneian poet; the shape that idea takes in the work itself, which
provides a model for readerly imitation; and the Aristotelian *universal*, a generalisation
arrived at by observing reality and abstracting from it a model of moral behaviour
or a model sequence of events, models which must be true to life or, in Scott's
Aristotelian terms, 'necessary or probable or possible' (34). *Model* is also a word that
takes us into visual representation and architectural measurement (where it is cognate
with *module*, the unit of measure that ensures the proportionate relation of parts to
whole). It therefore embraces the 'speaking picture' that poetry is for Sidney and Scott;
the formal, measured structure of the poem as versified form; and the well-ordered,
judicious *mimesis* that matches represented language, moral nature, and action to each
other according to the principles of *decorum* or, as Scott tellingly calls it (telling because
it is Puttenham's word for verse form itself), *proportion*. We have seen something of
this range of meanings in dynamic motion in Scott's translation of Du Bartas's account
of the Creation (above, lvii). Scott's *Model* shows us that poetic creation depends
upon the vital, mutually supporting and constitutive, relations between the poetic and
narrative forms of Aristotelian poetics and the ideal forms of Platonic philosophy. It
requires our attention to the ways poetry delineates the forms of thoughts, feelings,

characters, virtues, vices, moral states, and actions, and gives them form, ordering them in such a way as to maximise both aesthetic and didactic effect. These are the models that poetry makes.

AN OUTLINE OF THE *MODEL*

After a methodological introduction (5), the *Model* is divided into three sections, which Scott describes as first laying the foundations of the building, then building the walls that separate the various rooms from each other, then furnishing those rooms.

1 Definition examined by genus, difference, and end (6–17)

In the first section Scott offers a definition of the art of poetry: it is an art of imitation, in style, that uses delight to teach and move us to good (6). He also offers his key analogy, to which he will return repeatedly: the poem is a speaking picture (6). This definition is examined by genus, difference, and end (6). The *genus* (or matter) of poetry is that it is an *art* (6–7); this requires discussion of the *furor poeticus* (7–8) and the balance of art and nature in poetic skill (8–11). The *difference* (or form) of poetry is that it is an art of *imitation in style* (11); this requires discussion of the difference between copying something in the world and copying something only in the mind (11–12), and of whether it is verse or fiction (or both) that is required to make a poem (12); some further detail of this discussion is lost in the missing gathering (13). The *end* of poetry is that through delight it teaches and moves us to good. Most of this material, which happens to be the bulk of what Sidney discusses in the *Defence*, is lost. It might have included such questions as: what the *good* might be that poetry teaches; the ways of teaching of the philosopher and historian compared to that of the poet; fiction as lying or truth; the importance of *moving* in addition to Horace's paired teaching and delighting (in Sidney's terms: moving with desire to be taught and with desire to do what is taught). The text resumes during a discussion, after Aristotle, of the delight in imitation and in harmony from which poetry arose, and which made poetry mankind's first source of teaching (13–14). There follows a consideration of the qualities of mind and temperament required in the poet (14–15), and of how poetic creation occurs, understood as a sort of falling in love (15–17).

2 Origins and nature of the different kinds: heroic, pastoral, tragedy, comedy, satire, and lyric (17–29)

The second section begins by considering whether we should talk in terms of different kinds of poets or different kinds of poems, preferring the latter (17–18). Though following an inherited set of generic categories, Scott undertakes to demonstrate their relevance to modern writing ('In which division we bind ourselves, in substance, not to vary from antiquity, but make it more appliable to our later and modern kinds', 18). Scott's genres are defined by mode (narrative, dramatic, mixed), subject matter, and end, their history is discussed, and points are, wherever possible, illustrated with both ancient and modern examples. He discusses, in order: (i) heroic or epic, including its history, biblical analogues, and its subgenres epyllion and mock epic (18–21); (ii) pastoral, with again a historical account and a widening of the genre (21–2); (iii) tragedy, and (iv) comedy, the two dramatic kinds being treated alongside each other, ending with a consideration of related subgenres tragicomedy, satyr play, and mime (22–4); (v) satire, briefly, but with mention of its contemporary popularity (24–5); and (vi) lyric, at much greater length, broadening the category out to include all short poetry (notably elegy) and dividing the historical account of lyric by the different emotions represented (25–9).

3 (a) Matter, (b) style, and (c) rules for each genre (29–83)

The third section accounts for almost two-thirds of the *Model*. Rhetoric can be left to the rhetoricians (29–30), but Scott nevertheless aims to include discussion of everything that tends towards the threefold end of poetry – teach, delight, and move – and all governed by decorum (30–1). A distinction is made between (i) the subject matter or ground or argument; (ii) the device itself; and (iii) the clothing of the device. (This distinction, Scott does not say, corresponds to the rhetorical stages of invention, arrangement, and elocution.) But the material that follows is divided in two – first (a) matter (which sometimes includes its arrangement) and then (b) style, with the section (c) on rules by genre a sort of appendix, including much material on narrative structure. Once again, Scott tries to balance ancient and modern examples.

(a) Beauty (which is defined, 32) is required to create delight, and Scott borrows from Scaliger four virtues of poetic composition that tend towards beauty and 'are required as well in the device and invention as in the clothing of the device or style'. These are (i) proportion, (ii) variety, (iii) sweetness, and (iv) *energeia* (33), and they are considered in turn. Proportion requires accordance to reality (verisimilitude), in Aristotelian terms of probability and necessity; and self-consistency, including of character (33–6). Variety is of episodes and also of narrative ordering (36–8). Sweetness is a catch-all for effective plotting, but is also distinguished as a gentler twin of *energeia* (38); peripeteia, recognition, comic relief, similitudes (fables on the larger scale, metaphors on the smaller) are all routes to sweetness (39–41); here, Scott includes a lengthy digression against the use of pagan material to express Christian ideas or as subject matter in its own right (41–3). *Energeia* is about making an impression, and includes strong emotions and vivid descriptions or *enargeia* (43–5).

(b) After a discursive opening on finishing touches, the importance of style, and the value of restraint and apparent artlessness (45–7), Scott discusses words – how and to what extent to select, coin, borrow, and remake them (47–50) – and then style as something that comes into being when words are joined into sentences (50–1). The traditional three styles are introduced (51), and are examined first of all in terms of the sounds of words (51–2). Scott then provides further material on stylistic decorum at the level of word (52–3) before turning to the level of phrase and sentence, and introducing six stylistic graces, selected from many more in Scaliger: (i) perspicuity, (ii) purity, (iii) fullness, (iv) plentifulness, (v) softness, and (vi) sweetness (54–6). After a fuller consideration of the three styles (56–7), Scott returns to Scaliger's four poetic virtues, now to be considered at the level of style. Proportion requires the representation of emotion and speech in accordance with verisimilitude and decorum, and also includes sound that echoes sense (57–8). Variety is of phrase and therefore shades into rhetorical figuration (58–9). Sweetness, to distinguish it from the smaller-scale stylistic grace of sweetness just discussed, allows Scott to consider rhythm and sound; the former can include prose rhythm but is primarily the occasion for a lengthy treatise on versification (59–64); the latter can be considered both as rhetorical scheme (64) and as rhyme (62–3). *Energeia*, finally, is about vivid, expressive, forceful style; again, Scott's discussion touches on relevant rhetorical taxonomies (64–8).

(c) Scott opens this final subsection by reiterating and representing in chart form (69) the Aristotelian division of genres by subject matter, mode, and media (68–9). He then considers each of the genres in turn, with some inevitable overlap with the second section of the *Model*: (i) heroic, including lengthy discussion of proper subject matter (69–72), of the sections and arrangement of an epic poem according to the analyses of rhetoric (72–4) and poetics (74–5), and of the versification suited to epic (75); (ii) tragedy, and (iii) comedy, again considered first together and then separately, in terms of subject matter, structure, and versification (76–9); and then (iv) pastoral (79–80), (v) satire (80–1), and (vi) lyric (81), all more briefly. Scott then considers kinds of poetry that include a 'material' component – emblems and *imprese* (81–2). Finally, Scott returns to the question of the moral nature of the good poet (82), before a brief peroration (83).

Textual introduction

DESCRIPTION OF THE MANUSCRIPT
London, British Library, Additional MS 81083: William Scott, 'The Modell of Poesye' followed by a partial translation of Du Bartas's *La sepmaine*

Contents
1^r title page: '{THE MODEL}l | OF POESYE | Or | The Arte of Poesye drawen into a short or Summary Discourse'; 1^v blank; 2^{r-v} dedicatory epistle 'To the Right Honourable S{*ir*} Henry L{ee} | knight of the most Noble Order of the | Garter'; 3^r–49^v 'The Modell of | Poesye'; 50 blank; 51^{r-v} dedicatory epistle 'To the worthye Gentleman my very good | Vncle George Wiatt Esquier.'; 52 blank; 53^r–65^v 'The First DAYE of the first WEEKE of WILLIAM | SALUST LORDE DU BARTAS | O Thou th*at* guid'st the course of the flame-bearinge spheares;' ... 'If he haue past the limitts of his natyue cell.'; 66^r–76^v 'The Seconde DAYE | Let best accomplisht witts in flattringe rymes declare' ... '(Impatient of such durance) goes, turnes, runnes all o're | His vnacquainted' [catchword]

leaves: ii + 76 + ii, foliated in pencil at the British Library in 2008 (see note on verso of first rear endleaf)

formula (the lost gathering is designated λ): 1^2 2^4 [λ^4] 3–13^4 14^2 15–20^4

Paper
Modern endpapers. The *Model* was written using three paper stocks:

(A) Sheet size 310–14 mm × 414 mm approx.; watermark of lion oriented horizontally, countermark of small cinquefoil in corner of sheet; chain lines approx. 30 mm apart.

(B)   Sheet size 313 mm × 414 mm approx.; a finer paper; watermark of lion oriented vertically, in centre of half-sheet, and 'GB' in corner, countermark of crossbow; chain lines approx. 28 mm apart. An exact match for this paper, probably of Italian origin, is found in a letter from Queen Elizabeth to the Earl of Nottingham, dated 4 August 1599, at the Folger Shakespeare Library (X.d.130): Gravell CRSBW.006.1, INIT.116.1, LION.002.1.

(C)   Sheet size 312–14 mm × 414 mm approx.; watermark of small Greek cross (?), no countermark; chain lines approx. 27 mm apart.

The Du Bartas translation was written using two, possibly three, further paper stocks, both markedly thicker, with no coincidence of paper stock between the two separate works. Progressively worsening damage makes determining the watermarks increasingly difficult:

(D)   Sheet size 317 mm × 414 mm approx.; watermark of cockatrice with crozier and house, similar to Heawood 842 (found in a document from 1611) and 844–5 (from 1644 and 1646); no countermark; chain lines approx. 27–8 mm apart.

(E)   Sheet size 315 mm × 414 mm approx.; feint watermark, possibly post or pot type; chain lines approx. 26–8 mm apart.

(F?) Sheet size and chain lines as (D); feint watermark, feint countermark.

Layout

Page size 310–17 mm × 207 mm approx. The text is written between vertical margins approx. 150–170 mm apart. These are ruled in pencil in the first part of the manuscript, most often on one side of the leaf only, though in places on both. The top and bottom margins (never generous) are left to take care of themselves. The ruling ceases shortly before the end of the *Model* (after fol. 46) and is absent throughout the Du Bartas, the scribe relying instead on prominent chain lines; this pattern may suggest that the Du Bartas was transcribed after the *Model* and not before. In much of the Du Bartas, feint double scoring is used to mark in the outer margin the area for marginal notes. The *Model* fits between 33 and 38 lines of text per page, with, in addition, catchwords on recto and verso (almost always in the same hand and ink as the text on that page), except for the first page of the dedication and the first page of the text proper, which lack catchwords. The Du Bartas, with more generous lower margins, fits a uniform 30 lines per page, with catchwords on the verso only, and marginal notes.

Condition

There is frequent damage to the upper leaf corner. The opening leaves are badly damaged, causing some text loss along the top edge. The closing leaves are badly damaged by damp or water; this is first seen in the third gathering of the manuscript and becomes progressively worse, indicating that it began at the end of the surviving manuscript and probably accounted for the loss of what would have followed. The leaves have been expertly conserved at the British Library, with Japanese paper repairs consolidating missing or fragile areas; typical repairs in the first seven gatherings are to the upper corner of the leaf and top edge; repairs from the thirteenth gathering onwards are to damp/water damage in the upper middle portion of the leaf. A worm hole is visible from the start of the manuscript in the top margin close to the gutter. Its change of position between the second and third gatherings provides physical evidence that at least one intervening gathering has been lost. This worm hole has been repaired in the first two gatherings, but not thereafter, dwindling in size until its last appearance at fol. 31. (See Figure 1, towards the left of the top margin, and Figure 2, towards the right; the former has been repaired, the latter not.) The supposition that only one gathering has been lost is based on what Scott tells us of the plan of the *Model* and a judgement about the likely extent of the portion of his discussion that has been lost (see the outline of the *Model* above, lxx).

The following table summarises the disposition of contents and paper stocks in relation to the structure of the separate gatherings.

fol.	contents	gathering	paper stock
1–2	title page, dedication	1^2	A
3–6	*Model*	2^4	B, A (outer sheet, inner sheet)
–	[missing gathering]	$[\lambda^4]$	–
7–10		3^4	A
11–14		4^4	A
15–18		5^4	A
19–22		6^4	B, A
23–6		7^4	A, B
27–30		8^4	A
31–4		9^4	C
35–8		10^4	A, B
39–42		11^4	C
43–6		12^4	C
47–50		13^4	C
51–2	dedication	14^2	D
53–6	Du Bartas 1	15^4	D
57–60		16^4	D
61–4		17^4	D
65–8	Du Bartas 2 [begins 66^r]	18^4	D
69–72		19^4	F?
73–6		20^4	E

Hand

The manuscript is written throughout in a single, careful italic characteristic of the period 1590–1610, with clubbed ascenders and descenders. The text is carefully justified, with occasional line fillers, and is corrected in numerous places. Two correcting hands can be distinguished, one neat, the other more cursive; the latter is almost certainly Scott's, and the former may be. The corrections include missed lines of text, and in a few places appear to represent authorial revision, though in most cases they merely correct mistaken transcription and details of capitalisation or punctuation. The more cursive hand also supplies words, usually in Greek, in spaces left by the scribe, including the Greek motto on the title page. The neater corrections are designed to imitate the appearance of the scribal hand, and since the distinction between the two correcting hands is not always easy to make, it may be simpler to assume that both belong to Scott. The scribal hand develops through the *Model*, becoming more cursive. The scribe uses small capitals for proper nouns, and some other key terms and short quotations, in the second gathering (i.e. the first gathering of the text proper); this practice ends abruptly at the end of the second gathering, before the lacuna, suggesting that a less sudden transition might have been visible in the lost gathering, and suggesting too that the transcription of the text proper preceded that of the dedicatory epistle, which does not use small capitals in this way. A similar pattern is observable in the more careful writing of the Du Bartas, with use of small capitals dwindling (though not disappearing altogether) as, again, the writing becomes more cursive; the dedication to Wyatt lacks small capitals and again the degree of cursiveness suggests that its writing followed on from the completion of the transcription of the Du Bartas. What is presumably another hand has used the foot of 51^r (the first page of the Du Bartas's dedication) for pen exercises. For further discussion of the scribal and correcting hands see 'Scott and his scribe' below.

Binding

Bound in dark navy calf at the British Library in 2010 (date stamped on rear pastedown), 327 × 216 mm, with raised bands and gilt tooling on the spine. Modern endpapers have been introduced. The binding is loose, enabling text close to the gutter to be read. Guard stubs have been introduced between the endleaves and the conserved manuscript, and between each gathering of the manuscript, with two stubs visible between the first and second gatherings and between the penultimate and last gatherings. The top edge is flush, with differences in height of leaf being apparent only on the bottom edge. Examination of the manuscript prior to conservation and rebinding revealed fragments of threads and stitching holes that were aligned throughout the manuscript, showing that the two works were bound together at some previous point in their history, though when this might have been and when they became disbound cannot be determined. The pattern of quiring (with single-sheet gatherings for dedicatory epistles) tells us that the manuscript was bound after and not before transcription; this also means that we cannot be sure that the *Model* was transcribed before the Du Bartas.

Provenance

The manuscript is mentioned in E. K. Chambers's 1936 study *Sir Henry Lee*. Chambers had gathered materials relating to Sir Henry Lee for *The Elizabethan Stage* (1923) but in preparing his Lee biography he was given access to the work on Lee of Harold Lee-Dillon, seventeenth Viscount Dillon (1844–1932). Viscount Dillon's forebear the eleventh Viscount had married the heiress of the Lees of Ditchley in 1744, and the house and its collection had remained in the family since then. Chambers mentions Scott's manuscript in his account of the celebrated Ditchley manuscript (British Library

Add. MS 41499) of tilt devices and entertainments related to Lee, given along with a manuscript of excerpts from Sidney's *Arcadia* (Add. MS 41498) to the British Museum by Dillon. The *Model* and the Du Bartas are listed among five literary manuscripts that, Chambers reports, Dillon in his notebooks 'describes... as also preserved at Ditchley'.[154] Ditchley was sold in 1933 after Viscount Dillon's death, and it was with other Lee-related papers that had been at Ditchley and remained in the family that the manuscript was re-discovered. The assumption seems reasonable, therefore, that this was Sir Henry Lee's presentation copy, and that the date of the manuscript is close to that inferred for the *Model*'s composition, i.e. 1599. It can be further assumed that the Du Bartas translation was always included along with the *Model* and that, therefore, a further presentation copy of the Du Bartas at least would have been prepared for that work's dedicatee, George Wyatt. See 'Scott and his scribe' below for evidence that the *Model* was copied from an autograph manuscript.

Despite the second-hand terms of Chamber's report, it is possible that he inspected the manuscript at some point. It was discovered in an officially printed envelope from the Board of Education, addressed 'On His Majesty's Service. 16 | H. M. Inspector of Schools, | (   ) | Board of Education, | Whitehall, | LONDON, S.W.' The Board of Education was established in 1899, but the envelope must date from after 1901 (the beginning of the reign of Edward VII after that of Victoria). In the pre-printed parenthesis has been typed 'E G A Holmes Esq'. Edmond Gore Alexander Holmes (1850–1936) was an Inspector of Schools from 1875, and Chief Inspector of Elementary Schools from 1905 until his retirement in 1910; the envelope therefore dates from between 1901 and 1910, and in all probability between 1901 and 1905. Between 1897 and 1903 Holmes was serving in Oxford, and might have met Dillon (who had succeeded his father as Viscount Dillon in 1892) then. Holmes was an opponent of the narrow utilitarianism of elementary teaching, who 'believed that it was through the teaching of English, especially literature and poetry, that the emotions could be cultivated and the child's imagination stimulated';[155] he was also a poet, philosopher, and critic. He might have enjoyed reading Scott. However, it is more likely that the envelope was being recycled by a later employee of the Board of Education, for E. K. Chambers was a civil servant in the Education Department and then the Board of Education from 1892 until his retirement in 1926. There he worked with Sir Maurice Holmes (1885–1964), Edmond Holmes's son, who became a principal assistant secretary after Chambers's retirement and eventually permanent secretary in 1937. If the *Model* did in fact leave Ditchley temporarily after Viscount Dillon had come across it, it might have passed through the hands of any or all of these men, and (being unbound) it might therefore have been stored in an old Board of Education envelope, before returning to Ditchley.

Within the Board of Education envelope was a second envelope, with the handwritten title 'Treatise on Posey | William Scott | [horizontal line] | M.S Epist. | [horizontal line]'. The hand differs from another hand, which has written in pencil on Scott's title

---

[154] Chambers, 268–9.   [155] *ODNB*, 'Holmes, Edmond Gore Alexander (1850–1936)'.

page, between the Latin and Greek epigraphs, 'Written by Will Scott who wrote | S^r H Lee's epitaph —— | Shakespeares Rape of Lucrece referred to— | therefore after 16', the half- and mis-remembered date left incomplete.

The manuscript was bought by the British Library through Maggs in March 2005.

SCOTT AND HIS SCRIBE

The manuscript of the *Model* tells us a great deal about the processes of composition, transcription, and correction. Scott's scribe writes elegantly, but is relatively inexperienced, and also not as well educated as the author. A likely profile is of a young person within Scott's own family or in the household of his uncle George Wyatt or his patron Sir Henry Lee, though it is also possible that transcription took place in London within the Inner Temple. It cannot be assumed that the scribe was a man: it might have been a young clerk, but is as likely to have been one of Scott's sisters (a calligraphic italic hand like the scribe's was often taught to young women of the gentry and nobility in the late-Elizabethan/early-Jacobean period).[156]

The scribe starts out with the best of intentions (see Figure 1), but soon relaxes into the task (Figure 2 is taken from the middle of the work). In the first gathering of the text proper (3^r–6^v), certain key words and quotations, and all proper nouns, are written in small capitals (see Figure 1, lines 2, 5, 10, 13, and 14); this system has been abandoned by the time we rejoin the text after the lacuna between 6^v and 7^r. By the end of the *Model* there are fewer lines per page than at the start, fewer words per line, and only three-quarters of the number of words per page. The scribal hand towards the start of the *Model* reveals constant slight adjustments to keep the line of writing level, and a greater tendency to break words at line-ends. By the end the lines undulate more fluently, and the scribe sees the line break coming from further out and adjusts the writing so as to maintain a (less) carefully justified right margin, compressing or stretching the script to avoid breaking a word at the line-end. Copy-book calligraphy has become handwriting.

The manuscript is frequently affected by eyeskip, whereby the scribe jumps from one occurrence of a word in the text from which s/he is copying back or forward to another nearby and repeats or omits text. Examples are between the two occurrences of 'ioye' at 14^{v}28–30 (26.21–2) and of 'personatinge' at 45^{r}9–13 (76.17–19).[157] Where text is repeated, as in these two instances, the scribe notices the error immediately and deletes the repeated text, but in cases where text is omitted the correction is usually made in another hand that may be Scott's, or that of a third party. Less serious errors are often corrected by the scribe as s/he writes: for instance, '~~vnspeak~~ vnseperable' at 16^{v}32 (30.3) or dittographic 'without ~~without~~' at 32^{r}10 (54.26). Very rarely the correction must be made by the editor: dittography over line endings as with 'to |

---

[156] Scott's sister Elizabeth, for example, who was baptised on 10 November 1583 (and so would have been fifteen in the summer of 1599) and buried on 17 March 1619 (Godmersham parish register, Bishop's transcript, CCA-DCb/BT1/97).

[157] All references are to the leaf (recto or verso) and line number(s) in Add. MS 81083 (line numbers correspond to the online original-spelling edition) and then to the page and line number(s) in this edition.

honour amonge the liberall sciences, to sit wth the meanest handle may dus; and all this they sayd truly not vnreasonably, as they mince the compasse of this tearme ARTE, restreyninge it to be onely conversant aboute thinges materiall and workeable, as are the servile handy craftes of clothinge, Buildinge and the rest; but we shall easely and fully agree, if by ARTE with vs (as we w ARISTOTLE, and the streame'y followe him in callinge it soe) in a looser sence, they vnderstande a frame and bodye of rules compacted and digested by reason out of observation and experience, behoofull to some particuler good ende in our ciuill life. When thus we haue expounded and (I hope) reconcyled our selues to these first objectors, immediatly vpstart they who perhaps ill construinge their intricate master PLATO, will saye, and will needes haue him saye, Poesie is onely a diuine furye, or inspired force, farre passinge the narrowe limitts of mans witt, and therefore not possibly to be comprehended vnder the streyts of ARTE, it is a worke raysed wholy by mans conceyte; in the meane tyme they see not howe they consume Nature quite, by drowninge ARTE in a furie; and with as good reason, and to as good purpose they may saye (for Poets haue sayd as much or rather as litle before them) that Poesie is a thinge, I knowe not what, powred downe from heauen into their quill, I knowe not howe, wth they haue noe abilitie to order or restrayne, I knowe not whye; and then others shall learne by their sayinges, I knowe not when. But I will deale Platolike with these vnlike Platonicke (for I thinke Plato nothinge accessary to this soe vnworthy a conceyte) and put certayne questions and interrogatoryes to them, that shall make them selues witnesse against them selues, at least teache them to vnderstand them selues and vs, an keepe them from impeachinge any whitt our Arte; I aske then is this Instinct, Furye, Influence, or what els you list to call it, is this, I saye, diuine seede infused and conceyued in the mynde of man, in dispight of Nature & Reason, as you would saye by rape; surely they will confesse noe; is it there shaped & fedde, without the strength and vigoure of our reasonable Nature? nothinge lesse; Is this birth prodigiously borne, the lymmes and ioyntes sett and disposed without the industrious midwiferie of reason? that were reasonlesse. Lastly hath this Issue his apparrell fashioned and fitted by any other wise & rule, then wth Reason and Arte tells becomes and agrees with his stature and qualitie? It were to Arte lesse to answere yes; Nowe then haue we as much as we affirme or desire, when we obteyne that the matter or substance must be admitted, mixed with, and molded bye our Nature and Reason; borne & disposed by the assistance of Arte and Judgement, as bye the midwife; adorned with those habiliments, which witt, discretion and rules of Reason shall shewe to be to Idols' at 24^{v}22–3 (43.3) or 'pieces of | of' at 43^{v}28–9 (74.23), for instance, or the occasional scribal misreading not corrected, as with 'immitable' for 'inimitable' at 5^{r}35 (10.2) or 'martifialnes' for 'inartificialnes' at 17^{r}24 (30.32), or simple oversight that gives 'as it like' instead of 'as it is like' at 23^{r}11 (40.18). The scribe fails to recognise an abbreviated form of 'Aristotle' at 17^{v}15 (31.18), copying it without the mark of contraction as 'Aristle'; this was not picked up, but the scribe him- or herself seems to have corrected the initial misreading of 'Arioso' as 'Aristotle' at 19^{v}29 (35.7). Significant instances of editorial intervention are mentioned in the Commentary. But usually even minor errors have been picked up and corrected in another hand, which shows that the manuscript was checked with some care: examples are the insertion of 'measure' in 'any other measure and rule' at 4^{r}30 (7.40; see Figure 1), and that of 'well-' in 'well-disposed conceipts' at 16^{v}15 (29.28), the correction of 'stronge passions' to 'stormye passions' at 25^{r}17 (43.30), and that of 'same' to 'suɱe' (i.e. 'summe') at 39^{r}7 (66.20). More significant corrections include supplying an entire missed line from 'and' to 'contrarye' at 20^{r}35 (36.3–4) and a line lost through eyeskip from one 'ende' to the next at 17^{r}9 (30.16–17); the crucial correction of eyeskip omission of 'necessary or probable or possible' at 19^{v}3 (34.19); and another lost line through eyeskip between one 'and' and another at 34^{r}5 (57.32–3). Scott's telling Puttenhamism 'Ambage' is misread as 'Ambassage' at 28^{v}2 (49.3). All these errors have been corrected by another hand.

There is a sound argument that a neat hand making some substantial insertions of accidentally omitted material (typically whole lines) is the same hand in which was written the putative manuscript from which this one was copied. It is likely that that hand is Scott's, but since it differs from the more cursive corrections that are almost certainly his, it may be that of a second scribe. This hand mimics the scribe's in an effort to preserve the appearance of the manuscript, but it differs markedly in using a notably left-rotated ampersand which is visible in a number of corrections, and which is easily misread as 'of'. An ampersand of that sort has clearly caused the scribe trouble in the first place. The ampersand can be seen in the added line mentioned above, 17^{r}9 (30.16–17), where 'cold & storme' really does appear to read 'cold of storme', and also in the added line at 20^{r}35 (36.3–4). In one passage on 35^r the error was made and corrected in this way three times (lines 20–1, 29, and 31–2): the scribe has seen an ampersand, transcribed it as 'of', and the error has been corrected by an ampersand resembling 'of' in 'pronunciation & | deliuerye' (59.29), 'certeyne & fast' (59.37), and 'precise & cer-|teyne' (59.39). To this non-scribal hand, which may be Scott's, may therefore be attributed not only many of the corrections in the manuscript but, crucially, the copy from which the scribe was working. It is certainly possible, therefore, that the scribal copy was made direct from Scott's autograph manuscript, a possibility that bears on the questions of dating examined above (xxxvi–xxxvii). The problematic ampersand may mean that the reading 'the beholders testify their compassion of joy' at 39.29 should be emended to '. . . compassion and joy', but since the reading as it stands is not certainly wrong, I have left it.

Scott's scribe could not read or write Greek, and so spaces are left for Greek words and phrases to be filled in later in the more cursive hand that I will from this point and followinge of agreement is of merveilous movinge delectablenes, The Rules of these drawinge similitudes and ymages of thinges are out of Aristotle, that when you woulde advaunce the Estimation of any thinge, you drawe them from the more worthye thinges, when you woulde disgrace from the more vnworthye; Still there must be a fittnes and agreement in the poynt they are brought to cleere and confirme; Neither must you drawe them from thinges highe and obscure above that you woulde illustrate thereby, or thinges equally doubted of as that you would proue; as he that woulde shewe howe the thorny afflictions of this life accompany vs, woulde needes illustrate it by tellinge of the Man in the Moone with a bushe of thornes vpon his backe; this was not worth the graue authority of the Pulpit; els you may take wayued Storyes or traditions for the ground of your simile, as that of the Phœnix contempt of the worlde, and the swans sweetly ioyous embracinge her death; againe (accordinge to Quintilian & Scaliger) you must not wade into filthy, obscene, and corrupt matters for similitudes, lest you be muddied more then instruct, Lastly you must not frame thinges to that which by relligion and diuine authority you are prohibited to resemble to any thinge; and this vnavoydably lights on them that will needes goe to schoole with the heathens to learne of them howe to Deifie theire creatures and certaine Qualities. Not much vnlike this faulte is the Investinge God with the titles of Ethincke Idols, Nowe we make Loue, Lust, fortune, water, Earth, what not? Gods, offringe them Insence of our prayers and thankes, Anone we call God Jupiter, Apollo, Neptune &c. heathnish Idols; But perhaps this scrupulous plainesse will haue fastned on it by some selfe-likinge Judge, the name of folly; It may be as a vertuous gentlewoman in a suite was once pleasantly tolde by a Courtyer, whoe honorably respected her and her cawse, that in the managinge her matters she shewed her selfe (honest soule) to be one of Gods fooles, she did belike soe stand on innocent directions; sic itur ad astra; In the way of such heauenlye folly and hurtlesse simplicity, is she nowe arived at the hauen of her Eternall rest.

on assume to be Scott's; these include the Greek motto on the title page (1^r9). Scott missed one only, at 9^v9 (ἀγαθὸς ἠθογράφος, 17.37), but his detailed discussion of the passage of Aristotle from which the quotation is taken makes supplying the missing words straightforward. Occasionally spaces are left for other reasons, perhaps because the words *looked* like they were Greek. Scott fills such a gap in supplying 'so feined' at 41^v11 (71.4), the second syllable of 'Melicke' at 14^v3 (25.37), and 'Brookes' at 21^r28 (37.23). One of the busier pages, 23^v, is reproduced here (Figure 2). The keen eye will make out a scribal insertion of 'the' in 'of the agreement' in l. 1; an authorial insertion of 'her' in l. 15; parentheses inserted by Scott in ll. 16–17; authorial correction of 'obsence' to 'obscene' in l. 17; an authorial correction in 'be mudle' in l. 18; correction (probably scribal) over an erasure in 'feine' in l. 19 and an authorially inserted 'be' in the same line; authorial insertion of 'ifie' to complete 'Deifie' in l. 22; correction, again probably scribal, of 'thus' to 'this' in l. 27 and authorial insertion of the terminal 'se' in 'plainesse' in the same line; authorial correction in 'some' in l. 28; authorial parentheses in l. 29; authorial correction of 'shewes' to 'shewed' in l. 31; and, finally, authorial correction of 'di-|rections' to 'di-|rectnes' in ll. 32–3. This sort of detail is found throughout the manuscript, and demonstrates both that the scribe had a limited grasp of the sense of Scott's prose, and that Scott checked his text carefully (and perhaps had it checked by the person responsible for the neater, non-scribal corrections). Many of the marks of punctuation in the manuscript are probably authorial, but since they are a reaction to the scribe's imperfect rendition of the sense, it cannot be claimed that the accidentals of the manuscript represent Scott's precise intentions. Some of the catchwords, too, were added in by Scott or another correcting hand.

The checking of the manuscript seems at one point to have been done without access to its original. A cross in the margin indicates that something is wrong (a line of missing text through eyeskip, it can be inferred) at 29^v21 (50.39) but the missing text has not been supplied. I have marked this instance with an ellipsis. Checking was also done without access to, or consultation of, the books open before Scott as he wrote: so a correctly transcribed passage from Sidney at 31^v21–5 (54.6–9) has been altered by Scott to remove what, when he reread the passage, seemed like an erroneous duplication; I have privileged his original rather than his second intention in this case.

In just a few places the manuscript records authorial second thoughts. At 43^r13 (73.18) 'vniuersall forme' is changed to 'vniuersall nature', perhaps for the sake of *copia*, 'forme' having been used at lines 9 and 10 above (73.14 and 73.15), but also as a leaning away from a Platonic vocabulary to a more certainly Aristotelian one. At 46^r23 (78.5) Scott adds 'in the fifth' above the line to clarify his discussion of five-act dramatic form. And at 31^r16 (53.9), Scott elaborates his criticism of 'a very Idle verse | in that very well penned Poeme of Lucrece her rape' by inserting 'stuffed' after 'Idle'. The 'dumbe borne' man in Sophocles at 19^v27 (35.5) was originally only 'dumbe'.

The scribe seems to have had access in some cases to copies of the texts Scott was quoting. The foreign languages, with the exception of Latin, evidently caused difficulties: Scott must correct 'caso' to 'cosa' in the quotation from Tasso at 4^v23 (8.29), for example. The relative accuracy of the quotations from Du Bartas might appear simply to represent careful scribal copying from Scott's original manuscript.

But there is evidence that the scribe was given a printed copy from which to transcribe, presumably to avoid the difficulties evident elsewhere in reading foreign languages in the hand of the authorial manuscript. Two passages from Du Bartas, at 32^{v}26–33^{r}1 (55.37–56.7) and 42^{r}28–31 (72.3–6), are especially revealing, indicating a likely source, and the use of a copy of a different edition to check the text. There are, according to the list in one modern edition of Du Bartas's works,[158] twenty-five editions of *La sepmaine* printed before 1599, and no modern critical edition has included adequate collation and reporting of variants from all of them. So any conclusions here are provisional. The spelling and punctuation of the manuscript are very close indeed to the 1588 edition[159] at 32^{v}26–33^{r}1 (55.37–56.7), with identical spelling and only slight differences in punctuation: the manuscript and the 1588 text have 'trefue' where the 1582 edition[160] has 'tréue'; 'animaux' where 1582 has 'animaus'; and, crucially, the variant 'peut' in the first line of the quotation, a variant new to the 1588 edition, where 1582 has 'pour'. The sense of Scott's translation indicates that it is made from this version of the text too. The scribe also seems to have used the 1588 edition to copy 42^{r}28–31 (72.3–6), and produced a perfect copy, with spelling and punctuation identical. But a second hand (probably Scott's) has introduced a comma to mark the caesura in the final line of the quotation, and that hand, or a third hand, has added 'l'ay' (i.e. 'J'ai') neatly above the line between 'tout' and 'destiné' in the first line of the quotation. That addition is needed more to make the metre than the sense, and so its lack in 1588 is not fatal. Scott's attention to metre is to be expected, so he might have noticed the problem even without a correct version of the line in front of him. But he (or the possible third hand) would still have needed to supply 'l'ay' from somewhere, and it is found in the 1582 edition. At this point, then, the manuscript text very clearly demonstrates faithful copying of two different editions of Du Bartas – one that lacks 'l'ay' and one that has it.

EDITORIAL PROCEDURE

Because the scribal spelling and, especially, punctuation of the manuscript present considerable obstacles to the understanding of Scott's words, the *Model* is presented here in a modern-spelling text. An original-spelling edition is available online: [www.cambridge.org/gb/files/1713/7458/6256/Original_Spelling_Edition.pdf].
The original-spelling edition attempts both to produce a readable text and to represent and record the appearance of the manuscript. It therefore preserves pagination and lineation, adds line numbers, and includes an apparatus recording scribal and authorial errors, alterations, insertions, and so forth. In the margin of the present edition's text will be found the leaf numbers of the manuscript, recto or verso, in square brackets alongside the line in which occurs the text that begins a new page in the manuscript. This enables ready comparison of the modern-spelling and original-spelling texts,

---

[158] Du Bartas, I, 70–4.
[159] *La sepmaine . . . en ceste . . . édition ont esté adjoustez l'argument général . . . et explications des principales difficultez du texte, par S[imon] G[oulart de] S[enlis]* (Geneva, 1588). Copy examined: British Library, 11475.a.45.
[160] *La sepmaine* (Paris, 1582). Copies examined: British Library, 240.c.46 and 1568/8115.(1.).

and the use of the present edition's Commentary alongside the original-spelling edition. The more significant manuscript errors, corrections, and insertions are discussed in the Commentary [www.cambridge.org/gb/files/1713/7458/6256/ Original_Spelling_Edition.pdf].

Orthography is modernised in this edition; Scott's language is not. It is no easy matter to adapt early modern English – with its variable spellings and rhetorical punctuation – to the conventions of modern English – with its fixed spellings and syntactic punctuation. Paragraphing is for the most part editorial, though Scott's scribe occasionally begins a new paragraph or marks a break in some other way. Punctuation is editorial, but inevitably is influenced by that of the manuscript: I have often preserved its parentheses, for example. The manuscript punctuation frequently clouds Scott's sense, which is why I have thought it worth the effort to modernise. In a few cases no punctuation can make perfect sense of the words, however; these are remarked upon in the Commentary, and readers who are in doubts over such points may find the original-spelling edition instructive. In modernising the spelling of words I have used the *Oxford English Dictionary* and have found it an almost infallible guide. If it gives two apparently similar forms separate entries, then these are distinguished: so each instance of *throughly* and of *thoroughly* in the manuscript is preserved without change; likewise *sometime/sometimes* and *further/farther*. In a few cases, the scribe gives a word in two spellings both of which are still current and acceptable, but which are treated by *OED* as variant spellings of a single word rather than as separate words (e.g. *ambassador/embassador*, *behove(ful)/behoove(ful)*, *connexion/connection*). In such cases I have selected one spelling – in most cases the more usually accepted – and been consistent. Interesting cases are discussed in the Commentary. Where an archaic form has a separate entry in *OED* no attempt is made to modernise it, though always of course, in these as in other cases, the *OED* standard spelling of that form is used consistently: examples are *appliable, Christenmas, impatiency, interessed, noughty, satisfice, sith, stonishing, straightway, unconvenient*. At four points (4^{r}23, 28^{r}1, 28^{v}24, and 29^{v}6 = 7.32, 48.11, 49.24, and 50.26) Scott's scribe uses the form *an* for *and*; since *OED* (*an*, conj. and n.) only recognises this as a representation of regional or nonstandard English, in the form *an'*, I have replaced these with *and*. In a very few cases I have gone against *OED* for reasons explained in the Commentary. Typically this is where a form is reported merely as a historical spelling, but appears to represent such a different understanding of a word's etymology, sound, or meaning that to use the accepted modern form would seem wrong: examples are *accompted* (not *accounted*), *caesure* (not *caesura*), *perfited* (not *perfected*), *flower delice* (not *flower-de-luce*, much less *fleur-de-lis*). Scott uses many words that are not in *OED*, because they are *ad hoc* compounds or unusual superlatives (e.g. *skilfulliest*), for example. In such cases a modern spelling can be settled by clear analogy with other forms. Where Scott's usage predates the first recorded usage in *OED* (and there are scores of such cases), I have recorded this in the Commentary.

Modernisation is also, perforce, extended to quotations in other languages, with any difficulties (e.g. neo-Latin forms of Greek words) explained in the Commentary. Usage of u/v has been regularised in Latin quotations. I have made a reluctant exception to my rule of modernisation in the case of titles of Spenser's works, which are conventionally treated as a class apart. Though Scott would have thought there was nothing especially antique or exacting about the spelling of the title of *The Faerie Queene*, it seemed too odd to have him refer to *The Fairy Queen*. In verse quotations, terminal *–ed* is sounded if present, silent if the *e* is replaced with an apostrophe. Titles of books and works are capitalised conventionally within the text, but with minimal capitals elsewhere in the volume, where the many titles quoted in long form would otherwise create an eyesore. The titles of books as Scott gives them sometimes happen to correspond with their original title pages, but often they are Scott's name or a received name for a work. Instead of attempting to distinguish between these, all are treated as titles and italicised.

The Model of Poesy

or

The Art of Poesy Drawn into a Short or Summary Discourse

Si quisquam est qui placere se studeat bonis
Quam plurimis, et minime multos laedere,
In his hic nomen profitetur suum.

Ἐκ τοῦ Σκότου ὁ σπινθὴρ

TO THE RIGHT HONOURABLE SIR HENRY LEE, KNIGHT OF THE MOST NOBLE ORDER OF THE GARTER

It is a common saying (Right Honourable) that of two apparent evils the least is to be adventured upon. The vulgar commonness of this saying no whit diminisheth the dignity of the truth but adds weight of certainty, because things universally affirmed seem to bring nature's passport with them, whereby they challenge free admittance at the gates of every man's judgement. The two inconveniences that beset me are, the one, a denying myself the benefit of acknowledging a dutiful regard and honouring affection that nature (in some degree) and election impose on me towards Your Honour; the other, a falling into a gross error by reason of a disproportion I cannot so much flatter myself as not to see between this slender and worthless present and the duty it should represent, so as instead of expressing the honour I would, and am bound, I should blemish the truth and worth thereof, which I would not. In this difficulty affection, easily leading opinion (the overruler of all human resolutions), banisheth the consideration and consequently the fear of the unworthy fitness of this present, so as taking advantage of that noble disposition to courtesy whence the courtier is named, which in some measure towards myself, in much, much more towards some of my nearest and most dear respected friends Your Honour hath honourably acquitted yourself of, I choose rather to discover my wants and poverty than not to satisfy my desire to give a testimony of duty by nature and reason accompted due, making use of the ground young Julius Secundus received from his grave, wise kinsman, who, seeing him at school, perplexedly pensive after three days' study about the exordium of a declamation, blamed him as being over-careful with this saying: that it was not expected he should do better than he could. In like sort, I content myself [2ᵛ]₃₀ with presuming you, Sir, will be contented with the most of my least ability.

Thus resolved, I offer Your Honour this 'Model of Poesy' (indeed but modelling my dutiful affection), the first fruits of my study, which if they be (as I need not make doubt but they be) small and scanty, it may be some argument of excuse that they are the first; if hard-relished and unpleasant, that they were hastened to ripeness rather by some unseasonable force than of their own natural growth. Only I

3

may be bold to commend them as the Corinthians commended their gift of a small town to Alexander, whose all-conquering mind scorned to be bound to any in way of beholdingness for the world, and so refused their tame kindness, till, being let to understand that such a gift was not ordinary, neither before ever offered to any but Hercules, he willingly accepted their rare present. In like manner, even for the rareness of these presented fruits (being well near without any precedent), they may be worth acceptance. In which presumption I gladly and humbly commit them to that honour, which I pray long and much may be honoured in this life till late it be honoured eternally. And so craving pardon for what I do, as well as for what I leave undone, I rest

Your Honour's in all observance of duty most devoted,

William Scott.

THE MODEL OF POESY

Because all doctrine is but the orderly leading of the mind to the knowledge of something convenient and possible for us to know which before we knew not, and the way wherein we are to be led by this clew of discipline is the space between ignorance and science, we are therefore to make this passage by certain degrees and steps, of necessity first taking that which is nearest our understanding and which giveth light to that that ensueth, still proceeding from things known to things unknown, until we have gone through all the mazy paths that might trouble or stop the voyage of our mind in discovery of those riches she naturally covets. Now those things are nearest our understanding which are most universal (that is, which, being most simple, are the groundwork whereon the knowledge of others dependeth, which do impart of their nature to the rest), and without knowledge of them we cannot distinctly know anything that is derived from them. The definition, then, being this universal – for it consists of the first, most general principles and is the foundation (as they speak) whereon we raise the whole frame of knowledge, and the whole doctrine is no more but the rearing, fit coupling, and distinguishing all the parts from this groundwork, as you would say the extent of the definition – we therefore are taught, by those great fathers of science Plato and his scholar Aristotle, to begin with the definition of anything we intend to deliver the knowledge of. And thus in our 'Model of Poesy' we must proceed (if we will proceed orderly) first to lay the foundation, to define it in general; which explained we may show, by division, how all several kinds of poetry as the divers rooms and offices are built thereon, how the general is dispensed into the particulars, how the particulars are sundered by their special differences and properties, that as walls keep them from confounding one in another; and lastly what dressing and furniture best suits every subdivided part and member, that thereby direction may be given how to work in which of the kinds our nature shall inform us we are most apt for. And this is the period of discipline and farthest scope, to assist and direct nature to work, as being ordained to reduce man to his former state of moral and civil happiness, whence he is declined in that unhappy fall from his original understanding and righteousness.

All antiquity, following their great leader Aristotle, have defined poetry to be an art of imitation, or an instrument of reason, that consists in laying down the rules and way how in style to feign or represent things, with delight to teach and to move us to good; as if one [3ᵛ] should say with the lyric Simonides (after whom Sir Philip Sidney 5 saith) the poem is a speaking or wordish picture, as on the other side he calleth the picture a mute or speechless poem, both painter and poet lively representing, to our common sense and fancy, images of the works of nature or reason, and reason guided by virtue, or misguided by passion, the one by the eye only in colours, the other by the ear in 10 words: the one counterfeits the sundry motions and inward affections in the outward forms of behaviour and countenance (the mind's glasses), the other pictures the same person's mind and manners in the delivering of his life and actions, and therefore Petrarch saith of the poets 'pingon cantando', they paint whilst they sing. And 15 thus indeed Horace links them in a very near affinity when he saith 'ut pictura poesis', poesy and painting are almost one and the same thing; only so much more worthy is the poet than the painter, by how much words (the proper servants of reason) are more immediate and faithful unfolders both of the scope of him that imitates and of 20 the thing portrayed in the imitation than those dead and tongueless shapes set out in colours only, where the painter cannot presume to be understood in that he hath artificially expressed, much less in all he would have thereupon inferred; and then far better it agrees with the poet which is (in some degree truly) said of the painter, that he 25 discovers neither more nor less but just as much in the imitation as the reasonable soul enjoins. Whatsoever we say of their likeness and agreement, it is most true that the fittest illustration of either is by other, which thing Aristotle by his practice approves.

But because the definition and so the thing may be better under- 30 stood and allowed, we will (as the logicians will us) clear the purport and truth of these three parts thereof: first of the general or *genus* (as they call that part which answers to the matter in bodily things); then of the *difference* or separating part, which (as the form) gives name and proper being to the matter; lastly of the *end* which in every 35 instrument ought to be expressed, as being the hinge whereon the difference dependeth.

For the first, the *genus*, it is comprehended in this word, an *art*, or (to speak more plainly and vulgarly) an instrument of reason, consisting in the prescribing certain sufficient rules how to work to 40 some good end; which I know there are some will mislike, out of

the quintessence of their own nice conceits, and account it no less
than high treason (forsooth) to that great regent Philosophy, and
more than dishonour to heaven-born Poesy herself, to entitle her
an art, because (they say) we thereby give her authority out of her
jurisdiction and throw her down from her high seat of honour among   [4ʳ]₅
the liberal sciences to sit with the meanest handmaids. And all this
they say (truly) not unreasonably, as they mince the compass of this
term *art*, restraining it to be only conversant about things material
and workable, as are the servile handicrafts of clothing, building, and
the rest. But we shall easily and fully agree, if by art with us (as we   10
with Aristotle and the stream that follow him in calling it so) in a
looser sense they understand a frame and body of rules compacted
and digested by reason out of observation and experience, behoveful
to some particular good end in our civil life.

When thus we have expounded, and (I hope) reconciled ourselves   15
to these first objectors, immediately upstart they who (perhaps ill
construing their intricate master Plato) will say, and will needs have
him say, poesy is only a divine fury or inspired force, far passing
the narrow limits of man's wit and therefore not possibly to be
comprehended under the straits of *art*, which is a work raised wholly   20
by man's conceit. In the meantime they see not how they consume
nature quite by drowning art in a fury; and with as good reason,
and to as good purpose, they may say (for poets have said as much
or rather as little before them) that poesy is a thing, I know not
what, poured down from heaven into their quill, I know not how,   25
which they have no ability to order or restrain, I know not why, and
then others shall learn by their sayings, I know not when. But I will
deal Plato-like with these unlike Platonics (for I think Plato nothing
accessary to this so unworthy a conceit) and put certain questions and
interrogatories to them that shall make themselves witness against   30
themselves, at least teach them to understand themselves and us,
and keep them from impeaching any whit our art. I ask, then, is this
instinct, fury, influence, or what else you list to call it, is this, I say,
divine seed infused and conceived in the mind of man in despite of
nature and reason, as you would say by rape? Surely they will confess   35
no. Is it there shaped and fed without the strength and vigour of our
reasonable nature? Nothing less. Is this birth prodigiously born, the
limbs and joints set and disposed, without the industrious midwifery
of reason? That were reasonless. Lastly, hath this issue his apparel
fashioned and fitted by any other measure and rule than which reason   40
and art tells becomes and agrees with his stature and quality? It

were too artless to answer yes. Now, then, have we as much as we affirm or desire when we obtain that the matter or substance must be admitted, mixed with, and moulded by our nature and reason; born and disposed by the assistance of art and judgement as by the midwife; adorned with those habiliments which wit, discretion, and rules of reason shall show to be suitable and decent. I grant the poet is born so; and know they likewise the art never arrogates the making of a poet, but tells the poet how he shall make himself a poet?

For the better understanding and proof of this, consider that in every art there must be a disposition and apt ability of nature before the habit or settled quality that reduceth the works thereof into being; for art doth work upon a disposed nature and perfecteth it – so saith Viperanus of poesy especially. Neither can everyone that hath the knowledge how to work any artificial thing straightway work it; as in architecture, the skill and knowledge is in them that be only modellers – that is, they know how to build and can direct – yet without the manuary habit of hewing, squaring, etc., the frame cannot be built. Horace saith of himself he, whetstone-like, sets an edge on others whilst himself is dull; he knows by the skill how it should be done, but Nature hath not lent her assisting hand; he wanteth some of the mean abilities that come between the knowledge and the practice; and so he saith:

> munus et officium, nil scribens ipse, docebo.

> Whilst others I instruct to write,
> Myself prove myself artless quite.

And then I conceive of this as Amyntas did of another thing when he said:

> fui prima amante ch'intendessi
> che cosa fosse Amore.

A man may have the disposition before he have the active habit or habitual understanding of poetry. It is enough for our art to join hand in hand with that particularity of nature or *genius* (as it is called) which inciteth and enableth art and is actuated and perfited by art, so nothing at all doth it advantage them, that some are so untoward and indisposed by nature that no instructions, no endeavour, can transform them poets. Sith even this falls out alike in oratory, as Quintilian saith in direct and peremptory terms (whatsoever the proverb say, *orator fit, poeta nascitur* – the orator is made so, the poet

born so), though yet, I say, not in the same degree, if poetry be the
nobler and higher faculty and by consequence not so commonly easy   [5ʳ]
to be attained unto. But I say, with Horace, nothing can be done
invita Minerva, in spite of nature; and to expect this worthy quality
in every nature were to match Praxiteles in his folly, who would carve   5
and grave figures in slate or chalk, that can never be polished.

Again, here am I in danger to be asked: how is it that some who
have no art or skill be or seem good poets? Consider then, with
Quintilian, that in every faculty there is required (which likewise we
touched before) the nature or mind disposed, as the subject for art to   10
work upon: there must be an inbred fertileness of the ground before
tillage can promise any fruit, and the first is of more simple necessity
(saith he) than the latter, for all the seed and husbandry bestowed on
beachy mould is lost, whereas good soil, even unmanured, will bring
forth some fruit, wholesome and meetly well relished. And hereupon   15
I conclude that a good and disposed wit, by common prudence, bare
imitation, and practice, may write in this kind much commendably,
but, as maimed of one wing, he cannot work into his natural height.
And therefore are such merely natural makers seen to mar oft, to
have great wants, errors, and superfluities, which yet are not seen   20
of the vulgar but are discerned by the eye of the clear-seeing artist
only. And Sir Philip Sidney, doth not he affirm this to be alike in
other faculties, when he tells you he finds divers artless courtiers to
have a more sound style than some professors of learning? Nay, some
otherwise very accomplished wits and judgements shall never attain   25
grace and soundness in style – it is too plain. Yet they will not desert
oratory, I hope. Then shall they, of courtesy, give me leave to say that
though Nature strike a great stroke, yet she is not all in all, since the
time Adam's tasting the fruit of knowledge of good and evil made all
his posterity have eyes that can see more error than they can avoid,   30
and that now men must dig and delve for that fruit of wholesome
knowledge which before naturally, without the tillage of art, grew
plentifully in the orchard of Eden. Philosophers prove that creatures
must needs have augmentation by some nourishment from without
them, because else they should be born full grown and ripe at once,   35
and so the elephant, that is now threescore year old ere he comes
to the period of his growth and strength, should even as soon as he
were cast be able to bear a castle and fighting men in it. Methinks
the like may be said of poets: if they did not take help and increase of
ability of art, then no poem should need any industry, but it should   40
drop out of their pens as certain creatures do from the middle region

of the air, being moulded in heaven first. And then what will they
esteem of Virgil, that inimitable glory and prince of poets, seeing it   [5ᵛ]
is said that the goodly birth of his *Aeneis* saw not the light, as not
being complete, till he was eleven years old, but every moment grew
to perfection by the sustenance of art and industry?   5

What if I grant (which is all indeed that Plato can demand and no
more than Aristotle approves) that there is somewhat of instinct in the
poet? Do I thereby take away the being of an art in that kind? We know
that Bezaleel is said to have the spirit of God, or an extraordinary
instinct, in the curious skill of working in metals; yet, without doubt,   10
instructions and practice (the necessary parents of all art) brought this
disposition and inspired ability into actual perfection. Natalis Comes
saith every excellent man in any quality (as Amphion in music) was
called the child of Jupiter, because he had some more refinedness
of nature, or some instinct above ordinary men. And the painter, in   15
expressing the inward affections by the outward motions, wherein
consisteth the grace and glory of his art, requires in the practiser 'forza
ingenerata seco e accresciuta con lui sino dalle fasce', an inbred ability
born and nursed in him even from his swaddlings; and this he calls
a *fury* and saith it is reputed a divine gift, not a whit afraid to match   20
it with the poetical fury. Yet I trust no artist is so overweeningly
conceited that he will neglect those artificial directions which bring
this natural propenseness and supernatural inspiring into actual and
habitual perfection. These things considered, at length I securely
conclude with courtly Horace, the skilfulliest and most naturally   25
sweet lyric the Latins have, who saith:

> Natura fieret laudabile carmen an arte,
> quaesitum est: ego nec studium sine divite vena,
> nec rude quid prodest video ingenium: alterius sic
> altera poscit opem res et coniurat amice.   30

> Doubt is, if poets art or nature make;
> A reconcilement thus I undertake:
> No soil yields fruit without art's husbanding,
> No art makes barren minds rich harvest bring,
> But, art embracing nature, nature art,   35
> They sweetly work together, none apart.

Only I will say it were best for those some of our undertakers, who
Sir Philip Sidney saith can endure by no means to be cumbered with
many artificial rules, still to defend that the poet needs no art, no nor

the reader neither, lest by some cruel mischance he find them to be
(as that knight calls them somewhere) poet-apes, that is unreasonable   [6ʳ]
creatures, with a very ridiculous unhandsomeness mocking, rather
than imitating, the highest and gracefullest ability of nature and art.
This of the genus.   5
    By the *difference* now, as by a particular form or signet, let us stamp
the matter, and show what is meant by these words of *imitation* or
of *feigning and representing in style*. First, it is plain by them we
sequester poesy from all faculties that consist not in feigning or
imitation – as that of oratory, history, and the sciences – or feign not   10
style – as painting, carving, and the like. By *style* here I mean the
matter of words, whether in speech or writing, which answers to the
brass or marble in the carver's work. *Imitation* I say or *feigning* or
counterfeiting resemblances, because in poetry we follow always an
example or pattern, either of things as they be indeed or really, or   15
as they be in our conceits or the general notions (as the schoolmen
speak) of our mind. Now that which is in the conception of the
mind only, men are said to feign or imitate equally: *feign* because
it is nowhere in act or practice; *imitate* because in so expressing
any thing or action they follow the idea or image modelled in their   20
minds and reasonable apprehensions. And therefore Aristotle saith
the poet hath no regard to describe things as they be or be done, but
as they should (saith he) or may be or is likely enough, that they may
be perfect patterns for our knowledge and virtue to succeed unto.
Euripides (surnamed Hate-woman) always brought bad ones on the   25
stage, Sophocles always good. The reason of this difference being
asked of Sophocles, he made this answer (saith Aristotle): 'I bring
them as they should be, Euripides as they be.' And indeed there is
little difference: both are imitators and both feign. If the poet take a
true ground as his subject, he makes it another thing (like Theseus   30
his ship) by that freedom of spirit that (saith Julius Scaliger) adds
fictions to truth, or else with fictions follows truth, and so by adding,
changing, and polishing he appropriates everything to himself:

                    pictoribus atque poetis
          quidlibet audendi semper fuit aequa potestas.   35

          The poet and the painter in this do agree,
          That equally they have both their inventions free.

    Yet we may more nicely distinguish, and then (saith Aristotle) as
pictures, so poems, some are made as things be (for the substance),

others better or as they should or may be, without regard or eye to
any extant ground; for evermore I hold the worsing of bad things is a
kind of bettering of them, because thereby things receive perfection
(as I may say) of deformity. And this is seen in that Alexander could   [6ᵛ]
find in his heart rather to be Homer's Thersites (who is set out with   5
only this good proportion, to have a passing misshapen mind married
to a deformed body, like Richard the Third) than to be himself, even
Alexander the Great, of a poet-ape's setting forth – so much did that
rare spirit seem to be delighted with the decorum of even hateful
things. They that lay down things as they be, more precisely tying   10
themselves to true narration, may more properly be called *imitators*.
Such are those that write only true story in metre – as Lucan, Daniel's
Lancaster and York – or the sciences in bare verse – as Empedocles
did natural philosophy, who (according to Aristotle) hath nothing
like Homer (that is, like poetry) but verse. The other, that feign, by   15
following their own conceits, how things may or should be, which
make new or perfecter works than corrupted nature bringeth forth,
who, with the silkworm, spin their web out of their own bowels, may
by a more peculiar privilege challenge the title and honour of *poets* or
makers. Yet because the first have commonly somewhat of their own   20
device, some poetical ornaments, the order inverted, at least write in
verse (which is the poet's livery or habit), we comprehend them under
the names of *poets*, and their works are *poems*, for the matter is then
first the poet's when it is restrained and digested into his form. And
for art, it is as well showed in drawing the true picture of Lucretia, if   25
it be truly drawn, as in imitating the conceit of her virtue and passion:
the difference is, one gives you more true knowledge of the person of
Lucretia in such a distressful plight, the other sets you out a perfecter
image of the look (as it were) of constancy and desperate sorrow in
an imagined beauty. So as where the one evermore makes the person   30
more eminent and conspicuous, the other fully recompenses that by
delivering an absolute form whether of good or evil to be followed
or fled. The copying out of truth, then, is but the plain ground; the
descant and, consequently, sweetness of music is the poet's delightful
ornament and fiction. Only, of the latter we may say that for the chief   35
end (that is for doctrine and delight) it is of more direct use and
availableness than the straight imitating true, real examples, because
we find no perfection objected to our sense but that our discourse
doth still reach to a more absolute. Tully could never see at the bar so
perfect complete an orator (he saith) as he could expect and describe.   40

If you should desire to see a pattern of some particular virtue, or a constant direct way of

[LACUNA – 8 pages missing]

noisomest affects and passions before the eye as it were, whether it   [7ʳ]
arise of that imparting quality every best thing is said to be affected
withal or of experience, that the sensible beholding of them in the   5
reflex or images, when they are out of us and afar off, breeds a more
delightful satisfaction, whereas many times the consideration and
feeling is tedious and irksome within us in the first subject and really,
as I may speak. Which reason the philosopher inclineth unto when
he saith we joy in the works of imitation because we delight to have   10
some express and sensible demonstration or resemblance of what we
otherwise know, as in contemplation whereof our understanding is
afresh informed and our minds more sufficiently fed with a thorough-
digested knowledge.

   Now that delight of harmony (wherein all creatures seem to chal-   15
lenge some interest), more especially agreeable to man's nature, soon
found out that musical kind of number which, running in limited proportions, measured by feet, and having apt and consonant cadences
and rhymes, makes our metre or verse. And of these two parts is
poetry in her highest perfection compounded: the one the soul and   20
form of poetry, the other the matter or rather the proper habiliments
and clothing – as we said before, the livery or habit. Thus I may
(with Viperanus) conclude there was no person could ever claim the
title of being the author of poesy. For there was no time without
some degrees of it, nor no nation so barbarous as it hath not left some   25
relics and prints of the use of it, though rude were the beginnings and
inartificial, as of other faculties, till observation and practice bettering
and seconding nature brought it within the compass of rules to an art.
So as, for anything I see, they err not who say knowledge and civility
were admitted in among the ethnics by the popular door of delight,   30
where stood very anciently, if not first, poesy as the porter, because I
conceive the poets, being so ancient, must have some subject always,
and then, being the best and most ingenious wits, it is not unlikely

they would take some profitable argument as the ground of their
poems. And we find no human writers before Orpheus, Musaeus,
Homer, etc., neither any deliverers of the sciences (as some gather)
before some of the Greek poets. Here, now, we may say that poets
were always, that there was no time when they were not, in some   5
measure, and that nature is the first mother, practice and observation
the nurses, and art the last schoolmistress of the poet.   [7ᵛ]

And here I will entreat not to be so mistaken by some of the furious,
as though I made poesy a vulgar thing because (with Aristotle) I
show nature generally disposeth mankind to this faculty. For though   10
I affirm man, as man, to have the seeds of it, yet I say not they
can all bring forth the fruits in their ripest perfection, no more than
Quintilian, with the same consequence of reason, may be convinced to
say every man can be a perfect orator (which he will not say) because
he affirms those men to be as rare and degenerate as monsters in   15
nature that are altogether uncapable of that discipline, making it as
proper and natural to the divine part of man, the mind, to be disposed
to raise herself in any understanding quality as it is to a bird to mount
on her wings (though I confess there be some *struthiocameli*, made to
digest iron, that can scant lift themselves from the earth, much less   20
work cloud-high into the eagle's place). For more direct induction
of what I said, consider that of all the infinite number that come to
the universities, there are so few that they may be called none who
are utterly unable to make a verse and in some sort, poet-wise, to
show imitation. But to be absolute poets they must have (for nature's   25
part) most pure and refined wits, most industrious and considerate
dispositions, and (which is an unbelieved point) most indifferent,
temperate, and constant affections: my reason, because whilst they
naturally and lively express so several contrary forms of passion, they
need themselves to be clear of all perturbation, that their powers may   30
be unitedly intentive on their special object.

The poet is to be that polypus, which in sundry shapes must
transform himself to catch all humours and draw them to virtue. And
then, as the eye were not able to take the species or images of so many
colours unless the crystal humour were of a more fast compacted   35
substance and altogether uncoloured, so neither is the mind fastly
capable of those expressive conceits in their diversity if it be flittingly
fantastical, or if it be not free from any violent impression of any
one passion, that necessarily troubleth and distracteth the fantasy it
possesseth. This Scaliger discovers when he saith Lucan had indeed   40
a very great wit but the violent swinge of his intemperate nature, the

impatient and unlimited heat of his mind, could not stand with that
rare temper which is expected in the poet, which was admirable and
divine (saith he) in Virgil; the want of which staidness makes Lucan   [8ʳ]
exceed all measure, and sometime lose himself. Over and above all
this Aristotle leads me to expect in some a fury or supernatural motion   5
to enkindle and stir up these sparks of nature, to awake the powers,
and give an edge to art; as it is said:

> est deus in nobis; agitante calescimus illo:
>   impetus ille sacrae semina mentis habet.

> A spirit moves within, inflaming us to write,   10
> And this fit takes beginning of th' eternal light.

And this I take to be an extraordinary thing (in truth), as it was in
David; though I say not it be utterly ceased.
   Our nature is likewise sometimes incited in particular kinds by
some lower motion; and then the hot-spirited satirist will say: 15

> facit indignatio versum.

The passion of angry disdain at the corrupt manners of men working
in him do force him to pour forth his reproaches of vice in verse.
And this is the reason love is heathenishly called and invoked as the
god of poesy, for this affection of love, whether it arise of sensitive,   20
reasonable, or intellectual apprehension of good, is the common root
that gives force and quickening to the disposition in us. By *sensitive
good* I mean that which lies open to the sense and appears under
the show of pleasant or profitable, stirring natural affections; by
reasonable good that which presents itself in manner of virtue and   25
honesty to the reasonable part and moves the will to the begetting
of moral affections; by *intellectual good* that which offers itself to the
understanding part, bringing forth in us contemplative and more
spiritual affections. Upon this I say the poet proceeds after this
manner. First, in his reasonable consideration whilst he ruminates on   30
the true loveliness of virtue, he seems to frame to himself an image
of her, which his own work, as the heathens feign of Pygmalion,
he grows enamoured of; from thenceforth he becomes her herald
and trumpeter, to blazon her, to summon the world to serve under
her colours. Hereto comes it that Sir Philip Sidney saith David   35
showed himself, in his divine spirit of poesy, a passionate lover of
that unspeakable everlasting beauty, to be seen by the eyes of the
mind, cleared only by faith. Indeed, as a truly-reverend bishop told

me once, his Psalms are an excellent practice of one that is possessed
with the true love of God: that is, the unfolding and particular
exposing of the affections, endeavours, life, and faith of the servant [8ᵛ]
of God – a perfect image of a zealously religious mind in all estates.
Now as this love and liking cometh always of some likeness, so the   5
perfecter the degree of this liking is, the nearer still it is joined to
his object, restlessly labouring and striving forward till it be entirely
united and even oned with the thing it affecteth. Hence it appears
true (which Musidorus saith) that the love of heaven maketh a man
heavenly, as the immoderate love of worldly and sensual things,   10
worldly and sensual; whereupon we evidently conclude that the love
of virtue and piety is of so much more worth than these lower-seated
loves, by how much those heavenly eternal exceed these earthly
momentary beauties. And I would to God this might be the scope
and end of the ends of all both poetry and other faculties, to make   15
men in love with, and so possessed of, piety and virtue. Then might
our art justly be called a divine instrument. Then might Plato entitle
poets the engenderers of virtue, the guides of wisdom, the parents of
instruction, the agents and sons of God.

Yet to descend lower to a more earthly consideration of good: 20
when our bodily eye falls upon any worthy and fit object he sets our
fantasy on work, which promoteth it to our will and appetite and, by
a proportionableness thereto, a liking and delight is bred that stirs a
desire, and this we peculiarly name *love*, which, if no circumstance of
unlawfulness cross, may well and honourably be pursued to enjoying.   25
Now in the prosecuting this love the difficulties and impediments
serve as fans to inflame the affection, according to that *quod non licet
acrius urit*. This love thus inflamed, as it pricketh the mind forward
to imitate, so it sharpens, by intending, the wit and spirits and makes
our imitation to be more proper and pregnant, whilst we ransack the   30
most retired corners of our heart to discover the several forms and
moods of the affections, whether longings, hopes, fears, despairs,
joys, or discomforts. And if, with the sensual and natural pleasure,
virtue be objected for the reasonable part to work upon, there must
needs be very marvellous effects, where sense spurreth reason, reason   35
giving the reigns to sense. Such love I define with the stoics, as Tully
saith, to be 'conatus amicitiae faciendae ex pulcritudinis specie',   [9ʳ]
an endeavouring desire, arising of the apprehension of some lovely
quality, in the straightest degrees of virtuous enjoying to possess the
so qualified object. And then, with them, I will not be afraid to affirm   40
'sapientem amaturum', that a wise honest man may be in love. But

if the natural affections unnaturally sway the whole man, if there be no virtuous consideration, this merely sensual affection degenerates, and for that lawless common changeling,

> 'Non mi toccar, pastor,
> io son di Diana',   5

as with a rare decorum Tasso makes distressed Silvia speak to her beloved, loving and fearful Amyntas, every good mind should say:

> Let not the lewd, unhallow'd dart
> Of foul lust pierce the chaste-vow'd heart.

Thus let us come to the progress and growth of the particular kinds   10 as they are divided.

Tully saith orators are like painters, whereof (he saith) there are no other differences than the degrees of their skill make. To prove this, he saith all orators strive to be like Demosthenes, as all painters may be said to labour to be like Apelles, or Hilliard; and this may be truly   15 said. But he will have the poets to be otherwise, because (saith he) Menander, the comical poet, affects not to be like Homer, that writes in the heroic kind. This difference I acknowledge not, as taking the poets to be herein also like the other two. For the distinction of heroic and comical poets is in the argument and subject, that makes them   20 write and handle their matter diversely, not in the poet, a perfect poet and artist being of excellency in all kinds, though yet commonly men employ their gift, and are naturally aptest and most inclinable (as Aristotle confesseth), to some one of the particular kinds: some to more noble and lofty, as the heroical and tragic, some to more   25 vulgar and trivial, as the lyric and comic; and this may be and is alike observed in oratory and painting. That famous painter Zeuxis drew at once a boy and a vine. The grapes were so naturally and properly painted that when the work was set abroad the very birds flocked to eat of them, which when this excellent workman saw, in a great chafe [9ᵛ]30 he blamed himself, saying he had meant, as the artificial grapes had allured the birds, cozened by their counterfeited show, so the painted boy should have kept them away and feared them from approaching, thereby acknowledging he had not uttered so exquisite art in the one as in the other, and that his faculty was greater in drawing plants than   35 sensible living creatures. And so much perhaps Aristotle would mean when he saith Zeuxis was not ἀγαθὸς ἠθογράφος, as Polygnotus was: he could not so well express those features and graces of sensible life

and passion, those sweet forms of countenance and presence; though
Pliny say otherwise of Zeuxis.

Now to say Menander doth not imitate Homer is no more than
to say one argument is not like the other – as *Gerusalemme liberata*
is not like *Amyntas*; but Torquato Tasso made them both, and both   5
excellently well as ever any in either kind. And why may not Menander imitate Homer, since (Aristotle saith) Homer's *Margites* was the
same to the comedy that his *Iliads* and *Odysseas* were to the tragedy,
namely a rule and precedent (saith he)? Tully's error, I take it, was
because in poetry he attributes that to the art which should have been   10
true of the poet or of the subject of the art, that differs in kinds; and
in oratory and in painting he seems to affirm that of the orator and
painter which agrees to the art. And I wonder how he slips from that
himself saith presently: they that reckon divers kinds of orators truly
say something of the men, 'de re parum', of the art little or nothing.   15
I say then, as the painters are distinguished by the diversity of the
subject, so (by this it is clear) poets are some handling good things,
some taxing bad, some discoursing of divine things, some natural,
some of moral. But the differences of poets, or rather poems, will
best be showed by the manner of handling and the particular end,   20
evermore alterable according to the subject or argument. In which
division we bind ourselves, in substance, not to vary from antiquity,
but make it more appliable to our later and modern kinds.

And then I say of poems: some represent by narration only, wherein   [10ʳ]
the poet himself speaks mostly – as the heroical or epic, which may   25
be defined to be a poem or imitation simply narrative of great and
weighty things in weighty and high style, to raise the mind by admiration to some glorious good. The difference peculiar to him, and
that sequestereth him from all kinds else, is in that in a continued
narration or discourse of weighty matter, in a worthy and grave style,   30
he seeks by a delightful admiration to raise the mind to the affecting
some more than ordinary pitch of good. And this contains in it all
manner of heroical poems, and secludes all the rest of the kinds:
the tragedy because it is an interlocutory and personating relation;
the pastoral, mean matter in mean style; the comedy, low things   35
personated; and so of the rest you may gather the difference.

Now this narration was first in recording human acts or the praise
of worthies, called heroes, or men of eminent virtue and prowess,
such as was David, Samson, and many dukes of the children of Israel,
and such is said to be Hercules. And these were repeated at public   40
solemnities, feasts, and triumphs, called by a general name *scolia*

because with cups they were (as rounds) sung by cross turns, or
encomia, as though publicly in open streets and villages proclaimed.
The *rhapsody* was the same which afterward was appropriated to
Homer's works when they collected pieces of them and severally
rehearsed them upon sundry occasions. In English, our old Chaucer's   5
word is a *romance* or *ballad*, which (one saith) means some short
historical ditty, yet stately set down and of worthy acts. Such was
that song of David wherein he is reported to have slain his ten
thousand; of this kind are the hymns of Pindar in his singing the
honour of those triumphers at the Grecians' games. There is a full   10
wry imitation of this in Ireland (as Master Spenser shows) by their
bards to this day; in Hungary, that warlike nation, they use this still.
And I think the music is but accidental, for sometimes these were
only repeated and so by the subject distinguished, that we confound
them not with the lyric.   15
   Afterward the like acts of virtue and valour were undertaken in a
larger manner, whether the poet list to amplify some true story or   [10ᵛ]
feign some invention of his own, to deliver (as it were) the images of
the virtues themselves in the person and actions of these heroes, and
this either in solemn verse (therefore called *heroic* because it carries   20
a certain majesty suitable to those heroes) or else in a grave prose.
This kind of poem is called *epopoeia*, as you would say the compiling
of praise or celebrating praiseworthy things. Of the first in verse is
Homer in Greek, Virgil in Latin; modern, Ariosto, Tasso, and those
that be more historical and less fiction (like Lucan) – *The Disunion*   25
of Lancaster and York, *Albion's England*. Those in prose are such as
Xenophon's *Cyrus*, Heliodorus, ancient; later, Sir Thomas More's
Utopia and the *Arcadia* (except you will make the last a mixed kind
as having pastoral and much verse). To these you may add Master
Spenser's moral invention, shadowed so naturally and properly under   30
the persons in his *Faerie Queene*. In some example or precedent,
feigned or true, they all endeavour by an admiring emulation to
direct and move us to virtue in particular or general. Xenophon
(as Tully acknowledgeth) in his Cyrus hath given us 'effigiem iusti
imperii', the true scantling of an happy estate of government. Aeneas   35
is an image of a perfect man for wisdom, valour, and piety, as far as
Virgil could imagine; Orlando of bold hardiness. That chaste story of
Theagenes and Chariclea gives a goodly model of a virtuously placed
and managed love. The *Arcadia* hath excellently limned the faces
of all virtues and affections. Bartas his *Judith* is a worthy pattern   40
of a religiously trained and virtuously living woman. But above and

before all these is that sacred and lofty poem of Job (written, some presume, by the divine spirit of Moses), a clear mirror of inimitable yet human piety and patience. Neither do I make it hereby a feigned thing, but the manner of penning is by the best divines confessed to be poetical and joined in that division with the Psalms, and Sixtus Senensis saith some of the learned rabbins affirm it to be written in hexameter verse from the second chapter to the forty-two, though the rules be not known perfectly.

Now, farther, this heroical kind handles sometimes natural knowl- [11ʳ] edge and philosophy by way of discourse or narration, as of old Empe- docles, later Palingenius. Hitherto must be reduced Ovid's *Metamor- phoses*, in narration clouding much natural and moral knowledge. In this kind last in time but first in worthiness is our incomparable Bar- tas, who hath opened as much natural science in one week, containing the story of the creation, as all the rabble of schoolmen and philoso- phers have done since Plato and Aristotle. Indeed methinks what Jerome Zanchius, that sound deep divine and refiner of true natu- ral knowledge (drawing all to the touchstone of truth), in his most divinely philosophical writings hath discussed and concluded Bartas hath minced and sugared for the weakest and tenderest stomach, yet throughly to satisfice the strongest judgements. These, delivering the knowledge of nature in so infinite variety and the infiniteness of every particular as it is to our conceit, lead us to the infinite God of nature and have knowledge for their end, never ending till it come to action.

Again, they are to be comprehended under the *heroic* that of late are so graciously entertained of our graceless age, and which in solemn verse (not fit for music) handle narratively the misfortunes of some unhappily raised or famous person, thorough error, vice, or malice overthrown. Such are the *Mirror of Magistrates*, *Rosamond*, *Lucrece' Rape*, *Peter's Denial* (first in Italian, now imitated in English); I think, indeed, these answer to the *rhapsody* above mentioned and are as it were one act of the heroical. Chaucer's *Troilus and Criseyde* is in this rank, and his *Legends*.

Lastly, to these we join such narrations as handle small-seeming matters in high and stately manner, such as are Homer's *Frog-mouse- fight*, Virgil's *Gnat*, Spenser's *Muiopotmos*, and the like, whether it be that, as Balthazar requires at the courtier's hand proof of valiancy in matter of no great consequence sometimes, so the poet will volun- tarily show the vigour of his wit now and then in trifles; or whether though such creatures be but silly and contemptible yet war is a noble

and high subject and such sad events, even in these worthless animals, ask a solemn and grave representation; or lastly whether under   [11ᵛ]
these narrations is shadowed some moral of greater consequence.

Now follows that kind of poetry which is for the most part by interlocutory relation and action, where the poet speaks little or nothing in   5
his own person, and this such as have subject bad matter (as comedy
and tragedy) or that handles, immediately, meaner things in meaner
and more vulgar sort by meaner persons. I say *for the most part by way
of interlocution and action* for sometime the pastoral is by narration of
the poet only; I say *immediately* because the next and literal subject   10
is mean and common, though in a farther scope this kind figures out
often times great matters in the proportionableness to those common
conceits, and so sometime raise their style withal as you may see
in Virgil's *Eclogues*. When, therefore, without much preparation in
such entertainment of private low persons, by discourse and dialogue   15
reduced to shepherdish and rustical imitation either natural, moral,
or historical knowledge is delivered, or divine (as I take it is plain in
Master Spenser's *Shepheardes Calender* to be meant), it maketh the
pastoral (so by a general name known because that is the worthier
and most used sort) and this is a kind of low comedy conversant in   20
country rustical matters without much counterfeited action.

And this some say was the first kind of poesy that was practised,
because they will have the first kind of life irregular or without
government and civil society (at the least past the family), every man's
nature and choice his rule and law. Then, honour and swelling pride   25
being unknown or unaffected, every best man lived best content in
following that trade of living which with most ease and least offence
might yield best sustentation to his earthly pilgrimage, and so all
living to themselves took pleasure to maintain that that maintained
themselves, accompanying with their harmless flocks and herds, and   30
that mixedly men and woman (in all this they seem to have divine
testimony consonant with them). Thus in a kind of idle easefulness
they gave occasion (say they farther) to those natural desires to seize   [12ʳ]
on them that made them not idle but thought-busied in procuring
what they desired and setting forth themselves to their loves one   35
before another in a low-pitched ambition and emulation, if they
chanced to be rivals; and this could be no way so answerable and fit
in anything as in some fruit of the wit, taking force from the root
of love, whereby they might challenge and combat one another but
especially win the high reward of the ever-partial judge's good liking.   40
Thus they say grew the pastoral.

Of this sort was Theocritus the chief of the Greeks, Virgil of the
Latins, who doth imitate and (as he useth) exceed his pattern. Modern: in other tongues many, in English the *Shepheardes Calender*, that
imitateth the ancient so well that I know not if he come behind any
for apt invention; only for his affecting old words and phrases Favor-   5
inus, in Agellius, would say he seems to talk with Evander's mother
whereas (saith he) Curius, Fabricius, and Coruncanius, our ancestors,
and, more ancient than these, the Horatii talked with their people in
plain and customary speech; neither affected they the words of the
Aurunci, Sicani, or Pelasgi, the first inhabitants of Italy, as it were   10
Saxons and Normans of England. But Sir Philip Sidney amendeth
this and leaves all behind him in the pastoral kind. Now these have
a common name, *eclogues*, because of the selecting some best ones,
howsoever some will (with singular learning) cross the stream of all
the learned and draw it from such a word as signifies goatherd-songs,   15
but wrestingly. These are subdivided as those by shepherds properly, called *pastorals*; by neatherds or creaght-keepers, accordingly
bucolics; of husbandry or husbandmen, therefore *georgics*; goatherd
kinds have their name agreeable; or if ought besides, as Sannazar hath
added those of fishers out of Theocritus (saith Scaliger). Chaucer's   20
Canterbury Tales (for ought I see) are to be quartered with these and
may be named of travellers or pilgrims, for the vulgar persons, and
for their manner is much after this. The gardener, in like sort, is with
a passing good decorum brought on the stage in that well-conceited
tragedy of *Richard the Second*.   25
   Now those kind of interlocutory poems which with more prepara-   [12ᵛ]
tion and business handle errors, abuses, and vices, as well attending
chairs of estate as the penniless bench, are by a general and common
name of the Grecians called *dramatical* (from the stir, saith Aristotle,
and running in action), as you would say personating poems, where   30
being altogether in dissembled action the actors are called in Greek
dissemblers or *hypocrites*, not such as they seem. These are either
comedy or *tragedy*. Tragedy (Aristotle saith) was first brought to perfection, and that by Sophocles, though it may seem to come from,
and after, the comedy, which lay rude and neglected a great while,   35
and both of them from the heathenish rites of worship (agreeable
to Aristotle). First, in a certain kind of service, they used dancing
with obscene tricks and thereamong certain verses called *phallica*,
containing for the most part reproaches and taunts of private men.
After, they grew to alter this to an ordinary kind of interlude, ridicu-   40
lously invecting against, carping, and taxing whatsoever absurdity

they pleased to observe in any private particular person, and this
from village to village, and so (Aristotle tells) the *comedy* took his
name, because it was used in hamlets and little country towns for a
clownish pastime (like our ales and May sports). Lastly, they marched
forward and were promoted into great towns and cities on wagons,   5
acted by disguised persons, and were admitted and tolerated to blaze
and reproach folly and wickedness in their counterfeited actions,
because this backbiting kind of scurrility restrained (as they thought)
men in order and honesty; neither went they above the clown's faults.

Such like beginning is reported of the tragedy (if he came not   10
of the liberty of this comedy – that more insinuated into popular
ears – by lifting itself above popular vices), and that was, as they
used to sacrifice to Liber (the heathen idol of vintage) they would
magnify him with certain songs or ballads called *dithyrambi* (a name
fitting their dull conceit of Bacchus), wherein they would mention his   15
power, by his acts inflicting calamities on great men, etc., and when
they lacked ground of their own examples they would step over to   [13ʳ]
their neighbours. These in like sort grew into villages (thereof at the
first obtaining the common name of *comedy* with the other) and they
came to be acted on wagons, the persons painted; which thing Horace   20
affirms when he imputeth the infancy of it to Thespis:

> Ignotum tragicae genus invenisse Camenae
> dicitur et plaustris vexisse poemata Thespis,
> quae canerent agerentque peruncti faecibus ora.

> Thespis is held the first that tragedy found out,   25
> And taught this uncouth kind first to be borne about
> On wagons, whilst the players did their face besmear,
> That they might sing and act disguis'd parts everywhere.

Thus, lastly, by adding persons, ordering and limiting the invention, they ere long arrived at the height they are; *tragedy* so named   30
because the reward was a goat (saith Horace). It may be thus defined
to be a personating poem, solemnly and sadly handling great and
unhappy actions, by fear and compassion to purge outrageous and
cruel affections. The comedy differs in that it handleth smaller fortunes pleasantly and vulgarly, the end always contentful, by merry   35
scorn and reproach purging peevish subtle and vicious dispositions.
I think these verses expressly describe the comedy, once given by me
to a young, more than hopeful gentlewoman and by me much to be
respected kinswoman, set before Plautus' *Menaechmi*:

> A comedy, the common errors' glass,
> Wherein we see by scorn and witty sport
> Presented vice and folly as they pass
> In mean abuses of the vulgar sort,
> That the reproach and ugliness of sin   5
> May make us loathe the vices we live in;
> > So read (sweet lady) as the good you know,
> > By foil of ill, more clear, more lovely show.

The Greeks have Sophocles and Euripides for tragedy; we have
in Latin Seneca and Buchanan. For comedy the Greeks have   10
Aristophanes, the Latins Plautus – for much wit somewhat uncivil –
and Terence – pure and much chaster – following and bettering   [13ᵛ]
Menander the Greek comedian. Of late days we abound in this kind
and I would it were not true enough of these times which either
Tacitus or Quintilian (neither of them men of ordinary conceit or   15
observation) saith was true of his age: the proper and peculiar vices
of our state are the great account of stage players, fencers, and horse
races, wherewithal the mind being mostly possessed, alas what leisure
can we find for study of ingenious and honest arts (saith he)? Indeed
Sir Philip Sidney saith naughty play-makers and stage-keepers have   20
made this kind (not only unfruitful but) justly odious, and so, like an
unmannerly daughter showing a bad education, this kind causeth her
mother Poesy's honesty to be called into question. This fertileness
hath brought forth a bastard kind of *tragicomedy*. Of great affinity to
these interludes are the ancient satyr and mimic, that were first parts,   25
one of the tragedy, and the other of the comedy, and after – worthily
shut out – they grew to be unworthy kinds by themselves. The
satyr taking his name from feigned rustical and boorish divinities,
so called, in like sort they represented unseemly gestures, lewd and
bitter scurrilities; the *mimic* from his apish fooleries, by gestures,   30
motions, and gross imitations, like our clowns, antics, or jigs in
plays. But I reckon these scum unworthy the countenance of poesy.
  Next followeth that kind which hath the end common with the
former, to make a loathing of any gross corruption or deformity of
behaviour and manners, arising of the ancient satyr, and is originally   35
the Latins'. It is either in a bitter open reproof, and then it is the *iambic
satire* (*iambic* signifieth as much as traducing or calumniating), or else
in a more mild gibing and witty scorn it laugheth the absurdity out
of countenance, and then it is called (nowadays) the *satirical epigram*.
It may be thus described in general to be a poem narrative or a short   40
conceited representation of the evil-favouredness of any fault or

crime, in open, odious, or scornful manner under a particular name,
as it were, pointing out and with a goad galling those that commit   [14ʳ]
notorious errors and vices, to drive them into a detestation of what
is unseemly or villainous. I here oppose narrative to personating.
Of this kind of old Quintilian saith Lucilius was the first, of whom   5
Juvenal saith, showing the nature of the kind withal:

> ense velut stricto quotiens Lucilius ardens
> infremuit, rubet auditor cui frigida mens est
> criminibus, tacita sudant praecordia culpa.
> inde irae et lacrimae.   10

> All as Lucilius with his fiery blade doth threat,
> His reader blusheth straight for cold and guilty fears;
> His heartstrings, with his secret guilt, do sweating fret:
> Hence wrath proceeds, that breeds remorseful tears.

After him Juvenal, Persius, Martial, and Horace, some more mild   15
and toothless, some more curst and bitter; surely Baal and Baal's
priests were in such a sharp manner girded by the prophet. We have
of our times and in English very riotous wits in this kind.

Lastly we fall into those poesies wherein we imitate and discover
our affections and moral or natural conceits, more sudden and short   20
yet pithy and profitable, which may be all reduced under the *lyric* by
the countenance of Scaliger, that so enlargeth the word. I remember
well I have before numbered the hymn, romance, or historical ditty
under the heroical kind, and to the indifferent that looks into the
nature of the heroic and considers that they lose little grace if they   25
want music – whereas these are for the most part low matter, principally the number fitted to melody – it will not breed much offence
if in anything they may (as they may) be distinguished. *Lyric* are
so called because properly they be appliable to music and song and
might be married to some instrument, as the harp, which anciently   30
was thought the fitliest agreeable to ditties and was (some write) first
devised by Amphion, who by his harmonious rhymes and sweet eloquence (saith Natalis Comes) so softened and suppled the minds of
the rude and savage people that he drew them to build the walls of   [14ᵛ]
Thebes and live in obedience to their laws; hence it is fabled that he   35
had power by his music to move and assemble stones. This is likewise
called the *melic* or melodious kind, and this sweet part of poesy is of
use in holy as well as civil matters.

Now those of this kind that represent affections are such as utter
joy, sorrow, desire, anger, hate, and those that depend on these.   40

Those of joy may be termed in a more peculiar sort the *lyric*, as being
of a natural merry sweetness. Those of desire and sorrow are called
elegiac or plaintive, for the poet, having pleasure for his scope (as one
saith), will not so much as utter grief but in form of pleasure. Those
of anger and hate may generally be ranged under the name of *dirae*,   5
as you would say the furious kind. The old heathens (as in all things
they obscured truth with some cloudy fables) did set out the horror
of guilty wicked minds as to be the work of certain furies, which
they feigned to be sent from hell to haunt offenders (indeed foul
offenders feel the first fruits of hell in this life, either first or last); in   10
like sort these kind of bitter upbraidings, with terrible imprecations,
they called *dirae* because they would grate and exagitate like furies,
or because they invoked them. Now those that have given themselves
over to a reprobate impiety may be by imprecation cursed (in some
sort) by these (as the Italians call them) desperate poems, if we know   15
our spirit; as is the 137 Psalm, against the sons of Edom, malicious
deriders of the Jews' captivity in Babylon. And because all those
of anger, disdain, and hate have some kind of cursing, defiance, or
detestation in them, they may not unfitly be reduced unto this kind
of *dirae*.   20

The first – of joy – receive distinction according to the divers
matter of our joy, which ariseth either of divine or worldly good.
Of the first the first is when by the clear-seeing eye of faith we are
made partakers of the very joys of heaven, and, in some sort raised
above and out of ourselves, we seem to prevent those eternal felicities,   25
which inflames our heart to set the tongue and pen a-work in blazing
that unutterable glory. From hence comes a second joy, when in the   [15ʳ]
assurance of the forgiveness of our heart-torturing sins we sing the
sweet peace of a good conscience and triumph over death and hell;
and this kind is principally and properly beseeming all Christians.   30
This hath of old stirred up the holy men, as especially David, to
sing his unconceivable joy in many hymns; this stirred up Mary and
Zachary to express the overflowing joy of their souls in apprehending
by faith the presence of their redemption; this is the true matter of
perfect joy, that makes us joy in all things we enjoy.   35

And so the fruition of the commendable good things of this world
do stir up in us a lawful worldly gladness which is expressed in
divers forms as the degrees be of the worthiness whereupon our
gladness is grounded, and have names according to the particular
causes of our joy: as those of victory over our enemies and (which   40
is the consequent of victory) peace and (which is the companion of

peace) plenty were called *epinicia, epipompeutica*, etc., and may be called *triumphals, pageant songs*, or *hymns of solemnity*, as it were lauds and magnifyings of the fountain of all earthly good, for they were most in the praise of God; such was the proto-hymn of Moses and Miriam and the heathen paeans. Those that record the birth are called   5
genethliaca or natal songs. Marriages have their *epithalamia*, so named of the bride chamber. All feasts and entertainments, whether public – as you may see in Dido's entertaining of Aeneas – or between those whom especial friendship and alliance assemble, have their songs or carols, as I have seen in some colleges in bringing up the boar's head at   10
Christenmas, and in the Inns of the Court some such thing. Virgil sets down the matter of these in Iopas his songs, of very virtuous use. But this kind suffers now a strange metamorphosis in our last, loosest age into crowed ditties lewd and scurrilous, having no ingenious conceit and most of them most abominably lascivious, such as the heathens   15
would not endure; and shame is it that they be suffered to disgrace our art and undermine our honesty.

Those lyrics that are of the affections of love and desire, if we will (and this will is best), may be of divine things: such are David's psalms of his love of God's hests and laws and the grace of his countenance,   20
but especially the Song of Songs expresseth the inexpressible desires and (if I may so speak) transcendent love of Christ and his spouse the   [15ᵛ]
Church. Or otherwise this desire and love is lower set, but perhaps more violently carried, of some object agreeing to our sense and appetite which in honourable and honest manner may be undertaken   25
and prosecuted, where virtue hath the managing of those eye-pleasing colours and apt proportions of feature which, with the sober sweet graces of behaviour, countenance, and presence, make up the perfect harmony of that beauty reason's eye can only discern. Now because desire is of things not enjoyed, or not sufficiently, and the heat of   30
love is most spent in the pursuit of this desire, therefore most of this kind consists in complaining the absence and want of something which possessed we persuade ourselves would be of pleasure and use to us, and so is joined with those of sorrow, taking a common name with them of *elegiac* or plaintive. Of this nature are in the first, most   35
worthy sort divers of David's psalms, containing complaints of the absence of God's countenance after which he thirstingly panted as the hart after the fresh waters. In the latter sort are the complaints uttered in the rhymes and sonnets of Petrarch, some say the father or refiner of our vulgar kinds. Indeed he is most curious, and of them   40
I have read (not many), or for aught I can hear observed of the rest,

there is nothing in him but may stand with honesty and virtue. We have some English admirers of their sundry stars with great felicity of wit that follow him; but it were to be wished some conceits had never been born or never seen the light to have eclipsed the virtue and worth of them whom they have unworthily succeeded.   5

Besides, we have other plaintiffs as we have other calamities and losses, whether of goods, honour, friends, health, or whatsoever worldly fading joy we hold dear. The end of these is a satisfaction of ourselves by a delight which naturally everyone hath even in the representing and limning these affections to behold them in the   10 image and reflection, though the passions themselves be grievous and dreadful within us; not unlike that (as Aristotle saith) which is in our nature whilst we behold outward bodily shapes, for (saith he) with a kind of troubledness and sad solicitude (λυπηρῶς) we abide to see savage and hideous beasts themselves, but their pictures and images [16ʳ]₁₅ we with a delightful gladness behold, and the gladlier if we have seen those monstrous creatures themselves. Besides, it is an ease to the person affected to unload the burden of his affections and pour out his passion in complaint:

> For sorrow ebbs, being blown with wind of words.   20

But the best of all uses is that which Petrarch in his very first sonnet expresseth, gathered by his beholding, in cool blood, the image of his past errors:

> Ma ben veggio or sì come al popol tutto
> favola fui gran tempo, onde sovente   25
> di me medesmo meco mi vergogno;
>
> et del mio vaneggiar vergogna è 'l frutto,
> e 'l pentersi, e 'l conoscer chiaramente
> che quanto piace al mondo è breve sogno.
>
> Lo now full well I see how to the blockish rout   30
> Long time I was a byword; this doth often make
> Myself, remembering it, shame of myself to take;
>
> From shame of that my vanity this fruit springs out:
> Repentance of my fault, and knowledge proving plain
> That pleasure of the world even as a dream is vain.   35

Now cometh the last kind of lyric, which is called so because it is brief and vulgar, though it have no particular suitableness to music; and this is either more seriously grave, insinuating shortly

a commendation of good or a discovery of false good, or else more
merrily light and conceited. Of the first are those moral precepts
and natural problems fit for instruction, such as are the Proverbs of
Solomon, such is Cato, such are Horace his *Epistles* and some odes;
and him doth Sir Thomas Wyatt in his lyrics, especially in two or   5
three epistles to Sir John Pointz, so happily follow as I think none
since hath bettered him in that kind for a sound conceit couched in
beseeming phrase and well-running metre (though that was not then
so curiously affected). Indeed I know none (in my small observation)
about his time for prose or verse of comparable sweetness and full-   10
ness, saving my Lord of Surrey, who hath written in this kind. And
as the fathers of those lyrics lived linked in love so these children
of those parents after them are jointly succeeded to eternize them;   [16ᵛ]
of both which one saith (being of good judgement and learning) he
reputeth them for the two chief lanterns of light to all others that   15
have since employed their pen upon English poesy. Of those lyrics
Sir Philip Sidney saith there are many things in them tasting of a
noble birth and worthy a noble mind. Likewise the *Heroical Epistles*
of Ovid, some of them discovering virtuous affections of love and
constancy, are to be numbered in this kind, and him one of our age   20
and nation well imitateth and honestly. Now those that are merrily
witty, being short and sweet yet pithy and of use, may be ranked
under the *lyrical epigram*, which commonly stretcheth not to beyond
a sonnet and is as much less as you will, leaving always a perfect
sense. They are called *epigrams* as being fit to be set on any statue,   25
monument, table, window, banner, shield, etc. Still they are tending
or appliable to instruction as coming from wit, figuring out pleasant
and well-disposed conceits. To these are referred epitaphs; poesies
in rings, jewels and the like; likewise mots in emblems and impresses,
of which we will speak somewhat apart.   30

   Thus I hope I have led you into all the several rooms of poetry
and pointed you to the least twig and scion of this fair plant; which
if I have been long in, I think it will so appear to give light to the
part ensuing, as here we may be much briefer. Thus let us come
to describe the furniture of poesy, the rules and laws the poet must   35
observe in his imitation.

   It is neither possible nor needful to set down so absolute a frame of
rules in the institution of our poet as shall be able to direct him to every
particular circumstance required and belonging to the setting forth
and dressing of every poem, because then we should grow infinite and   40
run through all arts, even more than Quintilian in his *Oratory* or than

Scaliger in our faculty. Besides there are many things which must, in so infinite variety of device and ornament, be left to the prudence and discretion which is to be an unseparable companion of the poet's. But as they that read physic presuppose their auditors to be already natural philosophers, so we presume that every undertaker in our faculty be a general good scholar in all kinds of learning (for so he must be) and namely a rhetorician. Then shall we need to prescribe those rules only which are peculiarly by him to be observed inasmuch as he is a poet, and are to be added to the rules of other sciences to make him a poet. Only by the way, if occasion fall out accordingly, we will touch those strange and bordering rules which in any sort may give light to those that are direct in our way.

Now, then, we know that every work is directed and overruled by the end. That is, by knowing and observing the end we gather what are the most convenient means to produce it: as they that would build an house must first know to what end the house is, namely to keep from cold and storm, so as to this end they must have such stuff as will hold out wind and weather; next, for the apt disposing and stowage of household stuff and such things as are to be kept dry and warm it must be built in such a form as is capable of those implements and necessaries; then it must be distinguished into divers rooms and offices for the better ordering and performing of sundry kinds of businesses; lastly, to the end it may please the eye as well of the owner as of the guest and passenger, it must be beautiful and uniform. Thus, then, we must remember what we proposed to be the end of this instrument or faculty, which we showed to be threefold: to delight, to teach, to move, and all these in imitation, in delight as in a pleasant alley to lead along to knowledge and virtue. So as whatsoever is behoveful to this triple end is required in the poet inasmuch as he is a poet; whatsoever swerves from this end of delighting, and by delight of teaching and leading to goodness, that is not of the art but of the inartificialness of the undertaker, of the abuse or ignorance of the art.

Scaliger saith that Virgil (which is easily the prince of all heathen poets) seems to him to know only what is indecorum or unfitly unbeseeming, and to have withal this resolution, rather to leave out many things that might bring grace than admit anything unpleasant or disgraceful. And nothing less (though with less reason) seemeth Horace to say of Homer when he saith 'nil molitur inepte', he did nothing without reason and discretion. Indeed as the common saying is out of Aristotle *rectum est sui index et obliqui* (right discovers both

itself and shows what is awry) so, on the other side, he that knows how
to avoid all error knows how to walk in the direct way, and then he
that hath nothing evil, superfluous, lame, harsh, unseemly, unorderly
may be registered among the absolute poets. And this perfection is   [17ᵛ]
rather to be laboured after than looked for, howsoever he that aims   5
at the noon sun shall shoot higher than he that levels at a landmark,
and it is the duty of art to give rules of perfection. Notwithstanding,
as divines say out of James (*sic parvis componere magna solebam*) true
religion consists not only in living unspotted from the world (which
is so far good as it yields no stench of ill) but more principally in   10
showing those fruits of faith in doing those deeds of mercy (there
described) which are as a sweet perfume in the nostrils of God and
man, so we must say of the poet (which Quintilian doth of the orator)
it is but his first virtue 'vitio carere', to be clear from faults, and
the oration or poem doth not challenge so much commendation for   15
wanting blemishes as for being graced with those beauties that not
only offend not but much please and delight, and move. And so
Aristotle saith Homer knows all that beseemeth or beautifies.

   Now because every poem consists of those two parts, of the subject
and ground of the device and of the device itself, we must first see that   20
this ground and argument be of use and substantial, according to the
degrees the divers kinds require. And, whatsoever kind we write in,
there must be no deformity, no evident or purposed harm or offence
in the main matter and ground. For how can that tree bear good fruit
whose poisoned root spreads vicious nourishment into every branch?   25
How can that move to good that in the very substance in the marrow
and pith is viciously offensive? That pleasure that wholly ends in
the pleasing and tickling the sense is no better than sensual; and
what singular thing is it to move the natural affections and appetite
(already but too prone) to follow the pleasure of sense-objects? To the   30
delight of a reasonable creature there must be something agreeable to
the reasonable part, and therefore the poet promiseth to enrich the
understanding with knowledge, to conduct the will, that noble part
of the soul, to the pursuit of virtue and good; and then Quintilian
will say there is more pleasure in beholding a rich cornfield than a   35
meadow diapered with fair lilies and violets, and that he would rather
enjoy the vine-embraced elm and the fat olive than the fair-spread   [18ʳ]
but fruitless plane or the neatly-cut myrtle.

   It is a true saying of the great philosopher and painter Paul Lomaz
that in painting the conceit and story doth more please the wise   40
beholder than the colours which are the object of the eye and serve

but to lead unto the consideration of the thing represented by those superficial forms. And the same thing, with the same truth of reason, he affirms of the poem, which, saith he, receives more commendation 'per i concetti e per la sostanza', by the goodness of the conceit and substance, 'che per quella armoniosa legatura di parole ch'esteriormente si sente all'orecchio', than by that musical connection and composition of words that beat upon and affect only the outward sense. So as that sauce of sweetness and eloquence which the poet useth doth but sharpen the stomach and awaken the appetite to receive that wholesome food which evermore breeds our growth and progress in good. And so they that under these flowers of poetry hide snaky wantonness and villainy bring poison in a golden goblet and are to be entertained as soul-murderers, whilst these their poems are (when they are best accomplished) only of the same value and estimation that Sabina Poppaea was, who being (as Tacitus saith) graced with all things but with an honest mind, for want of this only inward virtue (the king of all graces) her name is razed out of the check-roll of worthy woman and she is now famous only for being an exquisite strumpet; so they, having the pith corrupt and the heart adulterate (which disgraceth all other graces whatsoever), are to be banished the society of the honest, and being now but burnished dross not able to endure the touchstone of virtue it were good they might pass the trial of the fire till they were purified.

We must then have the subject and scope good. When we are thus far proceeded we are to consider farther that the more peculiar and proper duty of the poet is out of this argument and ground to frame a well-proportioned body, and then to present this goodly body in her fair and holiday attire that she may (with a Judith-like temptation) allure men to affect her, which cannot be otherwise procured than by the mediation of delight, which always ariseth of[18ᵛ] some beauty or sensible object, suitable to our appetite or will; and then we say this outward dressing is no more but the harbinger to lodge the liking and love of the matter and conceit in men, as the beauty of the virtuous Parthenia was to constant Argalus. So as now we must seek what is required to the making a thing beautiful. We describe *beauty* to be a quality arising of an apt and graceful featuring and disposition of the parts and members between themselves to the composing of the whole; that is, beauty consists (as Aristotle saith) in the convenient quantity and bigness of the whole, in the correspondency and mutual proportion of the parts, and lastly (saith Plato) in the colours' agreeableness to our sight.

Great Julius Scaliger (as great Bartas calls him) restrains and seems
to apply these general conditions to the beauty of the poem, whilst
thoroughly looking into the nature of poetry. He observes that to
strike with the pleasure of our poem the doors of men's senses these
four virtues are especially requisite: first a *proportionableness* or uni-   5
formity; secondly *variety*; thirdly *sweetness*; lastly that *energeia*, force,
effectualness, or vigour, which is the character of passion and life of
persuasion and motion. Now all of these are required as well in the
device and invention as in the clothing of the device or style, and that
severally may be observed. I make here a difference (with Scaliger,   10
after Aristotle) between the *device* and *argument*, above mentioned,
the device being but the appendix (as he saith) of the argument and
subject, and serves for the opening, setting forth, or any way accomplishing it. For example, the argument is the valour and virtue of the
two princes; the device is that which Sir Philip Sidney hath conceived   15
of their particular adventures in arms and love with all the appurte-
nances to express the other by. First, then, because the orators say
those things whereby we labour to persuade are in nature first, we
will show how these four virtues, in order, may be in the invention,
and then the clothing and adorning of our persuasive conceits may   20
be attended. And here because for illustration I am forced to bring
instances of errors, I must entreat not to be branded with the dignity
of a *critic* for culling out the imperfections of our best writers, because   [19ʳ]
I have not had – and I repent me not that I have not had – leisure
to read the trivial vulgar poets. And I always think, with Scaliger,   25
Homer must not be the rule of poetry but must be ruled by the rule
itself which is the art, and if Homer sometimes sleep and Horace be
offended with that, surely he that understands the art shall see other
meaner poets, and shall grieve to see them, in so heavy sleep and
security of errors.   30
    The *proportionableness* of the matter and conceit is two ways (as
Scaliger seems likewise to note): in the agreeableness and conformity
of the device with the thing and in the correspondency of the parts
among themselves to the framing of the convenient whole. For the
first, our apprehension of any real thing in our mind is the *idea* or   35
image of the thing, which must needs be proportionably answering
the truth, and so you must always apprehend the thing as it is in
his proper being and nature's. Hence, then, it is a rule that if you
take a copy or true ground of some story or description, you must
not lay down any part otherwise than the precedent will bear, as in   40
story or narration you must not bring in a person of another age or

country to be a present actor, no more than you would describe an elephant without joints in his feet. Some herein will blame Virgil for reporting Dido to be in a wanton kind of love with Aeneas when she lived not at that time and was a virtuous temperate woman. Whether it be a fault or no in him, that tied not himself to declare things as they were done but took the liberty of his own feigning invention to show the assaults and constant virtue of Aeneas, let poets define; hereby my meaning may be known. But with more reason (perhaps) he is found fault withal for telling of harts in Africa, which place affords none. Scaliger blames Sannazar, that will bring the Magi out of Ethiopia when as the Scripture saith they came out of the east. Master Spenser may justly be indicted for infringing this statute when twice in one part of his works he saith 'the tomb Mausolus made', meaning that monument which his wife Artimisia, famous for the fervency of her love to her husband, after his death set Scopas and others (as Pliny reporteth) about, which being finished was held for one of the wonders of the world.

Otherwise, if you stand upon your own fiction you must invent things necessary or probable or possible. *Necessary*, as that a wise man should *futuris prospicere*, as you would say provide for after-times; the ordinary works of nature and conclusions of all sciences are necessary. Things are *probable* or *possible* which experience shows have before fallen out, the same causes being put; it is probable that a virtuous person should be unhappy, according to that of Aeneas when he thus speaketh to his little Ascanius:

> disce, puer, virtutem ex me verumque laborem,
> fortunam ex aliis.

> Of me, my son, learn virtue, how to do and bear
> In hard assays, but seek for happiness elsewhere.

This is that Aristotle means by *verisimile*, and this is that Horace commands:

> ficta voluptatis causa sint proxima veris,
> nec quodcumque volet poscat sibi fabula credi.

> Those things you feign for pleasure next true things must be;
> Presume not men's belief to every tale agree.

Yet remember it is true which Aristotle saith Agathon was wont to affirm: it is probable and likely something unprobable and unlikely may fall out. And so the poet hath liberty sometime for admiration to

pass ordinary and common reason, representing even wonders, but
then still the means must be extraordinary. It is very reprovable (saith
Aristotle) to feign anything void of reason; yea in tragedy (he saith)
they are to be hissed from the stage that counterfeit anything beyond
belief. Sophocles is blamed for feigning a dumb-born man to travel   5
from Tegaea into Mysia in three days and without a guide. Here
methinks Ariosto must needs be reprovable, that tells you of a man
that runs through half a dozen bodies of men with his ordinary lance
and carries them aloft in the air like so many gloves; and some things
more palpable he reports. These are so far from breeding admiration   10
as everyone will say with Horace 'incredulus odi', I abhor the hearing   [20ʳ]
so incredible a report. Hyperbolical speeches may be used, but they
descend not into particulars.

The other part of this *agreeableness* is in the correspondency of the
invention, so as it be still proportionable in itself. And this is that   15
Horace means when he compares such as forget this principal grace
to those idle painters that draw a fair woman's face on an horse's neck
with wings upon her back (like a bird), her lower parts filthily (saith
he) concluded in a fish. It is, saith the excellent painter, that symmetry
or conformity of parts proportioned *armonicamente* that pleaseth the   20
eye and mind of the beholder; so is it that suitable correspondency in
the parts of our poems that yields a sweet harmony to our ears and a
beauty to our eyes. The poem must be, according to Aristotle, as one
body of fitly-composed members that have a proportionable greatness
and dependency one with and upon another, and this Horace means   25
by his conclusion that your work must be 'unum' and 'simplex', it
must not be an hermaphrodite or mongrel; and this Scaliger means by
constancy when he saith imitation must follow the thing and constancy
the imitation.

You must make the device continually like itself, the persons one   30
and the same. The describing notes or *characters* (as after Theophrastus they may be called) of every particular must be constant and
answerable to the proposed form: Aeneas always devout, valiant, and
wise, his Achates faithful; Pamela in all her behaviour bearing state
and majesty in a virtuous resolution and so commanding an awed love   35
and a reverent respect; Philoclea in all her carriage modestly mild and
sweetly virtuous, so, as it were, wooing love and honourable regard;
Anaxius proud in all his gestures, swelling in his terms, and evermore
behaving himself as one that beholds everything under him; as for
Dametas, he is as constant as any, and nothing comes from him but   40
as needs must from a muddy-headed clown tossed with the too-full

wind of his own unsitting authority. These rules are broken by not observing circumstances of time and place and persons likewise: long speeches in great exigents; short conveyances and shuffling up of matters of great consequence, contrary to Chariclea's excellent conceit when Theagenes would have had her (according to the nature [20ᵛ]₅ of desire) suddenly acknowledge her self and state that more quickly they might enjoy their long-desired mutual joy – 'No, sweetest sir,' saith she, 'matters of great consequence must be brought about with much preparation and wrought out through many circumstances.' Our tragedies (nowadays) huddle up matter enough for whole *Iliad*s 10 in one hour.

Again, heed must be taken that you make not your second persons (as Horace calls them that are not principals) exceed in grace of expressing the first and chief. It is written of an excellent painter in Milan that undertook the drawing of Christ with all his Apostles 15 at the Supper how he so curiously and with such majesty set forth his Jameses that when he came to draw Christ himself he had spent the height of his skill so before that he was fain, after knowledge of his error, to leave his wonderful piece of work unfinished, and chose rather to have it unperfect than with disproportion to grace the dis- 20 ciples above their master. But especially you must not cross yourself by any contradiction. Was it not a fault to bring the messenger to give warning of Euarchus' approach within half a mile of the lodge and immediately (in Philanax his report) to make him two miles off, without intimating any reason why he differed from the former? Sir 25 Philip Sidney would not have so erred.

Lastly, the whole of any poem must be of competent quantity according to the several kinds, as Aristotle illustrateth by the like insensible objects which (saith he) if they be too great and vast the sight cannot at once comprehend their proportion, their entire beauty 30 is lost and slips out of the memory; on the other side, if the poem be over-little the mind overruns it and cannot rest thereon without wearisomeness.

The second virtue is *variety* and diverseness of matter or invention, that may with supply of news hold up the mind in delight, soon 35 quatted with satiety which makes even the best things seem tedious; and this is as well in the conveyance – in wrapping and inverting of the order of the same things (like the many traverses, wreaths, and crossings in the continued knot of a garden that feeds the eye with a [21ʳ] perpetual variety); and this is the poet's special privilege – as also in 40 the additaments of new accidents and devices. In the first, of *order*,

the poet must have especial regard that the breaking off and change
of narration for the time and matter befit, and hinder not the easy
passage and the distinct receipt of the whole discourse: the time must
not be confounded in proceeding too far forward with one particular
or (which necessarily follows thereon) in returning to fetch things   5
too high behind; your matter must not be led along all in one tenor,
but mirth interlaced with serious and sad matters, precepts with
narration. In this kind of orderly order Scaliger worthily commends
Heliodorus for a well-contrived invention as a pattern. For my part
I think it plain Sir Philip Sidney in the general gate of conveyance   10
did imitate him, and I think it as plain that he exceeds both him
and all other for a delightful easy intricateness and entangling his
particular narrations one with another, that makes them as it were
several acts, every one having a kind of completeness in itself, the final
issue so much more welcome by how much it is by the difficulties   15
and interruptions hid and held aloof from the longing mind. Again,
when you have the same things and actions to represent you must
set them forth in divers forms: divers knights, their persons unlike,
unlike qualities, habits unlike, unlike enterprises; so, many combats
none like other in show or issue; in like sort of all other things.   20
    Now, farther, this variety allows those supplies and additaments
which are called *episodia* as by-matters and complements, that (saith
Aristotle) consummates the poem and as so many brooks or rivulets
fall into the same channel, enlarging thereby the main stream of your
work. And though they be but circumstances, yet necessarily they   25
accompany the well doing and reporting of any thing or action: such
are descriptions of countries, towns, buildings, fortifications, ships,
jousts, pomps, funerals, and certain digressions into discourses of any
science or art, as in painting you may observe most stories adorned
with woods, rivers, birds, beasts, or the like; you shall commonly[21ᵛ]30
have no person drawn without some page, some child, some arms,
favour, impress, or the like. The rules in these *episodia* be first that
they come in naturally and easily, not wrested in, as he that Horace
speaks of, having a dexterity in drawing a cypress tree, would not
describe a shipwreck without that drawn in one or other part thereof;   35
did this any whit belong to the shipwreck, or whereabout grew it in
the sea, trow ye? Again, you must not dwell upon these digressions,
as when you have occasion to meddle with any schoolpoint or matter
of learning (except it be, as it may be, your purposed subject), you
must (as the dog at Nilus) touch and away; which rule Lucan is noted   40
to have broken whilst ambitiously he seeks to show his knowledge

in things impertinent, high, and abstruse. Especially you must avoid repetition of the same conceit; as in that commended tragedy of *Gorboduc* you may in one leaf observe, to the same purpose, the story of Phaeton twice to be alluded unto, as if the world afforded no other example to show the unhappy success of rash aspiring, or as if it could be proved no other way but by example. Lastly, you shall not need in a glorious vanity to heap up all can be devised to your purpose: it shall be enough to have a comely store of the more proper and substantial conceits. Quintilian shows this to be artless yet much pleasing the vulgar, that cannot see the difference between rude superfluity and competent plenty. Our vulgar poets are much accessary to this transgression.

The third virtue is *sweetness*, which I take to consist principally in those apt conceits and fairly-shaped images taken in the mind of the poet and shadowed in the style, for I am of Aristotle's opinion, who thinks those pictures that have no conceits or creature resembled by them but are only a flourish of exquisite colours disposed to please the sight are nothing so delightful as are those images which, though they be but barely lineated in white, yet give the representation of some known creature or story. The orators (among whom Quintilian [22^r]$_{20}$ most distinctly) make the principal part of their faculty to consist in moving the affections, and these affections they make to be of two sorts: either moderate and calm or else more violent and passionate. To the first they lead the judges by the gentle hand of pleasure; to the latter they seem to force them by the more forcible swinge of admiration. The poet in this end agreeing with the orator hath the same means with him to come to his end, so far (at least) as the orator joins with the poet, the poet at the last far outstripping him in this the glory of both their faculties. And then it seems those graces whereby they endeavour to produce these more appeased and temperate affections are no other than those that are contained under our virtue of *sweetness*, as the other that carry to those more forcible and warm affections seem to be comprised under that other virtue of *efficacy*; and, which Scaliger acknowledgeth with Quintilian, this of sweetness differs in degree only, in the remissness of the motion, from that of efficacy, which is more intended and powerful.

Now, then, the orators and poets place the sweetness of the conceit in the natural and proper device, ever possessing the mind of the hearer or reader with evidence and pleasure which makes him easily and cheerfully apprehend the thing delivered, whilst they utter expressively their intendments and free the mind from all

indisposition through sadness and displeasure which usually block
up the passages of attention and persuasion, the haven where both
orator and poet should strike sail. Thus the poet must strive to make
evident and clear his apt conceits, his main scope, and likewise season
all with a sensible pleasantness. And this latter, first to be handled in   5
this place, is chiefly in the smooth and cleanly alterations which by
reason of cozening the expectation (as Quintilian saith) are always
delightful, either with gladness if they be to the more glad and more
welcome part, or with astonishing admiration if they be turned to
more sad and unworthy events (which falls under the consideration   10
of the next last virtues). Such are those *peripeteiae*, as you would
say indirect compassings of matters, when the strange, unexpected   [22ᵛ]
issue of things falls out otherwise than the direct tenor or purport of
that went before and there is something properly and handsomely
brought about contrary to the bent of the matter or expectation of the   15
reader or beholder, as when friends by some unlooked-for accident
fall from one another or enemies are reconciled, which is ordinarily
by revealing of something which before was unknown or covered
and disguised, as, when the two friends Daiphantus and Palladius
combated one another, by the striking of Palladius his helmet   20
from his head Daiphantus knew him to be his entire Musidorus –
which accident, so to see friends meet, makes the readers, as they
are said thereupon to be, full of wonder and yet fuller of joy than
wonder.

This delightful alteration gives most times conclusion to comedies,   25
when matters are of troublesome and intricate grown to some glad
issue and calm end: as in Terence his first comedy, by the coming
of Crito Glycerium is discovered and all parties gladly appeased in
her enjoying Pamphilus; the beholders testify their compassion of joy
with a plaudite. Especially that comedy of the two brothers in Plautus   30
(now grown good English) hath all those delightful errors concluded
in Menaechmus and Sosicles their meeting and acknowledging one
another. Such are the intruding merry matters and persons in the
more serious acts of our poems, which doth (as Quintilian speaks)
'tristes solvere affectus', dissolve sad affections into delightful joys   35
and pleasure. Such are, in Virgil's fifth Book, the description of
the games after the doleful narration of the toils of Aeneas and the
tragical end of Dido. What a welcome pleasure breeds that change in
Heliodorus from the sad expectation of man-sacrifice to Theagenes
his wrestling with a beast, wherein are showed many delightful feats   40
of nimble activity! Such are the bringing-in Dametas and Mopsa to

play their fools' parts among noble personages in great and grave matters.

Besides, there is much sweetness in the witty conceits, apt sentences, proper allusions and applications to be dispersed in your poem like so many goodly plots of lilies and violets strewed all over   5
the new-springing meadows. Of these conceits most acceptable are those that are most nicely drawn and, as it were, beyond expectation.   [23ʳ]
Such are those pretty turnings of your sentences from the apparent bent of your phrase that are, as it were, models of the *peripeteiae* –
they are called *facetiae*, *sales*, and *lepores*, merry, graceful, and savoury   10
jests – which arise of the pleasantness and urbanity of our nature and of the occasion administered in the matter. In all things that discerning judgment of the poet must keep measure and decorum, that nothing exceed, that nothing be wrested in, but which naturally and voluntarily, as it were, offers itself to be entertained.   15

Of great, especial great, sweetness is that kind of invention which is grounded on likenesses, as when I conceive a thing not as it is in itself and own nature but as it is like another more familiar or sensible thing. And this pleaseth because it adds to our knowledge and doth store our understanding with the apprehension of divers things at once, as   20
saith Aristotle, bringing withal this example of a common metaphor or resemblancing speech, 'old age is stubble', whereby we learn that the one is stateless and withereth as that the other is without all vigour and beauty. Philosophy tells us that is only perfect knowledge of anything when we know the same thing every way it may be known,   25
as by the causes, proper affections, and effects, and by their neighbour nearness or reference to other things. Now the orator and poet well find this beholding of things in others more clear and ordinary, as it were in crystal glasses, are as several ways of informing us, and every way doth add clearness and proof to the other. Of this nature are   30
all *apologi*, parables, or fabulous resemblancing conceits, as those of Aesop. Of what force these are to convince, by insinuating into our untoward affections, may be seen by that one effect recorded in Holy Scripture, upon such an apt induction used by Nathan to David, which roused him from the deep sleep of his sin more throughly than   35
all the loud-crying of the prophets. Likewise of this suit are those fabulous narrations of Ovid, in some proportionableness agreeing to true moral and natural instructions. Of this kind are all allegories and the feigning of persons, as when wisdom is feigned in the Scripture
to be a woman; this investing of qualities with persons and following[23ᵛ]40
of the agreement is of marvellous moving delectableness.

The rules of these drawing similitudes and images of things are out of Aristotle, that when you would advance the estimation of anything you draw them from the more worthy things, when you would disgrace from the more unworthy; still there must be a fitness and agreement in the point they are brought to clear and confirm.   5
Neither must you draw them from things high and obscure above that you would illustrate thereby, or things equally doubted of as that you would prove: as he that would show how the thorny afflictions of this life accompany us would needs illustrate it by telling of the Man in the Moon with a bush of thorns upon his back; this was not worth   10
the grave authority of the pulpit. Else, you may take received stories or traditions for the ground of your simile, as that of the phoenix her contempt of the world, and the swan's sweetly joyous embracing her death. Again (according to Quintilian and Scaliger), you must not wade into filthy, obscene, and corrupt matters for similitudes, lest   15
you bemuddle more than instruct.

Lastly, you must not feign things to be that which by religion and divine authority you are prohibited to resemble to anything. And this unavoidably lights on them that will needs go to school with the heathens to learn of them how to deify creatures and certain qualities;   20
not much unlike this fault is the investing God with the titles of ethnic idols. Now we make love, lust, fortune, water, earth (what not?) gods, offering them incense of our prayers and thanks; anon we call God Jupiter, Apollo, Neptune, etc. – heathenish idols. But perhaps this scrupulous plainness will have fastened on it by some self-liking judge   25
the name of folly. It may be as a virtuous gentlewoman (in a suit) was once pleasantly told by a courtier who honourably respected her and her cause that in the managing her matters she showed herself (honest soul) to be one of God's fools, she did belike so stand on innocent directness; *sic itur ad astra* – in the way of such heavenly   30
folly and hurtless simplicity is she now arrived at the haven of her eternal rest. And for me, I think some of those things that fall under   [24ʳ]
my reproof are directly derogatory from His honour that sent us into the world only to do Him honour, of which He is so jealous that I am rather content to be a fool in fearing too much than so wise as   35
to presume any whit above my knowledge. These small-esteemed leaks if they be not stopped will make shipwreck of our true worship. Shall I say the heathen shall rise against us? Surely they turned all their excellent abilities in this kind to the honour of their supposed divinities, and what disproportion there is that we should not honour   40
our not supposed but known God, the true author of our being and

felicity, that still gives us (as Sir Philip Sidney saith) new-budding occasions to praise Him, I must confess I cannot see. And still I think the tongue and pen are instruments that ought to join in consent with the mind to make a melodious harmony in the ears of the Almighty, that exacteth at our hands as well the calves of our lips as the first 5 fruits of our heart, the reverence of the body as well as the bowing the knees of our soul. Neither will He know them in heaven before saints and angels that will not with reverend boldness confess His holy name before the sons of men.

The *Courtier* tells of one that in all his actions and gestures affected 10 to be like a great man of his time, and whereas the person imitated had a natural wryness of his neck this apish fellow would, with a very ridiculous grace, affect that withal. Do not our poets the same whilst they even tread in the wry steps of the naturally stumbling heathens, and so nurse those superstitious conceits which Sir Philip 15 Sidney thinketh was the reason why Plato would worthily banish them his commonwealth? But Christianity (saith that worthy knight) hath taken away all the hurtful belief and wrong opinion of the Deity among us, and why it should not in like sort take away all the wrong and hurtful confession of the mouth (which confession is the 20 unseparable companion of our belief) I (with divine Bartas) profess I see no reason. It was a reverend ancient father that said the Church saw, and sighed to see, herself grown an Arian; poetry may with like [24ᵛ] reason wonder and complain that she is become so wholly (almost) an heathen. We think nothing speeds well that is not undertaken 25 with the invocation of I know not what idols, neither doth anything sound well that is not graced with some of Ovid's gross fables of their esteemed gods, whereas Ovid cannot be defended not deeply to have faulted in that Scaliger justly taxeth Homer for when he saith he oftentimes speaks of their gods as of their swine, so unreverend are 30 Ovid's fictions of their divinities; and we throughly imitate them. I will grant as much as Tully when to another purpose he saith: in many things I worthily commend them these men say they imitate, 'etsi in eis aliquid desidero', although I must confess that, as heathens, they had wants; 'hos vero minime laudo qui nihil illorum nisi vitium', 35 etc., but those most of our poets I think worthy much reproof that imitate nothing but their imperfections and errors, are nothing so much, and so are great strangers from the good (saith he) they would entitle themselves unto.

Blame me not if I think these gay Babylonish garments anathema: 40 they are accursed in that Law which I think nobody will think transitory. And we know, or should know, that the Almighty Maker and preserver of all, in His jealousy, counts it equally dishonour to be called Baal (when it is once attributed to idols) as to have His uncommunicable name (much more worship) attributed to that worm-eaten tyrant Herod. Truly, I see not that Bartas wanteth any grace may be looked for in a poet though worthily he contemn these heathenish rags, garnishing his poem with most proper and sweet allusions, stories, and graces arising from honest truth and unsuperstitious conceits, as you may especially note in his *Judith*. And he craves pardon if he (haply) do not enough swerve from those misconceits of the gentiles, as being the first reformer and refiner of our corrupted faculties. If I could pluck this one weed out of the fair garden of poesy I would think my digression well bestowed. And I hope this will be enough, except we be as Heliodorus makes the Ethiopians to have been, of whom he saith that neither pity nor religion might break a long continued custom among them: so as, under pretence of supporting rotten antiquity, we care not how unmercifully we seduce and offend the ignorant and weak and spare not to offer sacrifice to idols.

The last virtue is that forcibleness or *energeia* which though it may seem to be in the expressive phrase, yet (with Scaliger) I take it principally to be in the invention and conceits that leave their print in the style, to convey the affection expressed into the bosom of the reader and beholder. It is not (saith Scaliger) but in *operosioribus poematibus*, in the more troubled and busy kinds of poetry (as which Quintilian names the tragedy), that are called also pathetical or passionate kinds; that is, it is most naturally and eminently in those and not but in the stirring and more busy parts of the other, since in the comedy likewise sometimes are to be found violent and stormy passions (according to Horace) and the very shepherd hath his strong motions of anger, loves, and sorrow, which all must be proportionably expressed both in the conceits and style. We showed in the last virtue (out of Scaliger and Quintilian) that this of efficacy is of great affinity with that of sweetness and differs in the degree from it, in that this worketh by the highest intention of delight by a stonishing admiration whilst the reader and beholder is as it were ravished and carried into the expressed passion, whether anger, hate, fear, compassion, zeal, or the like, and seems (as Quintilian saith of the judges moved by the orator) so to be interessed in the matter as if it were his own case, and then the persuasion is all one with the affection.

Now this efficacy and forcibleness consists chiefly (saith Quintilian) in the liveliness of expressing, I may say of imitation, when
you utter those moving affections in most apt and suitable conceits
so as the passion itself cannot entertain more feeling apprehensions
and more expressive images: as you describe fear by setting out the   5
person affected with pale face, ghastly staring looks, standing hair,
quaking and trembling limbs, starting and unconstant motion, faint   [25^v]
and breathless voice, speech distracted, broken, and not much pertinent; anger you paint in bloody colours, red and sternly furious in
his visage, rolling and piercing eyes, his body in violent and uncer-   10
tain motions, his voice loud, his speech interrupted and peremptory,
hastily tumbling out, one word devouring another. Courage, the child
of anger, at least attended by anger and wrath, raiseth a man so as
he thinketh nothing too high or too hard for him; impossible things
his conceit will compass and unavoidable things he will despise; in   15
the lowest estate, like the sun, he will show his glory greatest, and
then triumph most when he is most far from triumph, as though he
would force the vigour of resolution, as fire, out of the hardest rock of
despair, according to that of Statius: 'est ubi dat vires nimius timor',
in a noble mind the greatest cause of fear is the greatest whetstone of   20
resolute hardness. Was Aeneas ever more boldly resolute than when
he saw death, the dreadfullest enemy of nature, before him?

> 'moriamur, et in media arma ruamus.
> > ('Let's bravely die, rushing on our foes' arms . . .)
> una salus victis nullam sperare salutem.'   25
> > (One only ease remains to them that vanquish'd be,
> > No hope, no care of safety in themselves to see.')
> > > per tela, per hostis
> vadimus haud dubiam in mortem.
> > (Thus we our honour ransom whilst our breath we lose,   30
> > In passing through the spears and arm'd troops of our foes.)

In the most desperate point of danger there is one word of encouragement left to Leonidas wherewith he may breathe spirit and valour
into his few troops against the multitudes of the Persians: they shall
go by the passage of an honourable death to sup with those that are   35
immortally blessed. Of at the least equal gallantness of mind, but
upon firmer ground, proceeded that noble general's answer to some
that aggravated the danger of a hideous storm in a sea expedition:
'Doth not the sea yield up her dead as well as the earth?' (said he).
The Lacedaemonians ask not (saith their brave leader in Plutarch) [26^r]₄₀

how many, but where their enemies be. These conceits, as they are natural and proper to that virtue, so are they moving and forcible.

Hereto comes it that the poet must seek for apt comparisons and images that may glass the passion and make it more sensible, and therefore Quintilian, out of Tully, calls this vertue *evidency* or illus-   5
tration, when the thing is rather said to be showed and demonstrated, as it were, to the eye than spoken (saith he). For example, such a thing you may observe in Vasthi's passionate delivering the true form of her pitiful fortune, whilst she is made (by Peter Matthew) to consider herself in the most overthrown estate a dejected mind can imagine;   10
thus in English:

> Who sees the fair sweet blossoms of the newborn spring
> The garden with their beauties richly garnishing,
> The flower delice, the lily, primrose, violet,
> And rose of vermeil dye all in their borders set,   15
> How when the northern blasts, so sharp and cruel chill,
> Unwelcome winter sends from Hyperborean hill,
> These knots of borrow'd tires despoil'd appear straight ball,
> That now the discontented gardener therewithal
> Scant knows their changed hue, so eager cold doth nap   20
> And miserably waste their beauty and their sap:
> That man in them beholds Vasthi's disastrous state;
> Vasthi, whose matchless glory so excell'd of late,
> None will acknowledge now; her beauty's drooping cheer
> Hath lost the shining beams of all her former clear.   25

Sometime the person shall be so plunged into the passion of sorrow that he will even forget his sorrow and seem to entertain his hardest fortune with dalliance and sport, as in the very well-penned tragedy of *Richard the Second* is expressed in the King and Queen whilst

> They play the wantons with their woes.   30

David seems ravished and insulting in his divine joy when he makes the hills leap and skip, the floods clap their hands, and the like. All those *peripeteiae* and sudden changes that fall out unto the worse part are most forcible and moving, which may be understood by that we delivered in the other virtue of *sweetness*. Now come we to the style   35
and clothing our conceits.

Pliny reports that Parrhasius, the famous painter, who beguiled [26ᵛ]
Zeuxis as Zeuxis did the birds, was the first that invented and observed just symmetry and proportion in his pictures, and farther that he first represented the sweet forms of countenance and favour,   40

the beautiful elegancies of the hair, the delicate and lovely graces of the mouth, by which (saith Pliny) he carried the garland from all painters of his time by their own confession; for he affirmeth this to be the highest subtlety and most curious point in that art, well and gracefully to set forth those extremities of their work and by adding 5
so sweet a close to the ending picture to give the beholder occasion to conceive beyond that is expressed. So may I say, now we are come to the style of poesy we are come to those extreme and last beauties wherein consisteth the greatest grace and glory of the poet, the light and last shadows which are the life of our speaking picture, that add 10
complete grace and perfection to all the rest.

Quintilian saith it is agreed upon among all orators that the elegancy of style is far the hardest, as it is the chiefest, of the parts of oratory. For the invention and disposition (saith Tully), they are *prudentis hominis*, but for eloquence or graceful delivery, *id oratoris* – that 15
is properly the orator's. Quintilian will perhaps farther say invention is common oftentimes with the ignorant and disposition is of small learning and meditation, but this outward fit adorning, proper and powerful delivering our conceits is that that breeds admiration and reigns even in the worthiest learned judgements, and so, he concludes, the orator fights not only in strong but in polished arms. 20
All which fits as well, if not better, to the poet, that hath the same end with the orator: in style by delighting to teach and move. Both must have their speech beautified and polished to delight; distinct and proper to teach; apt and expressive to move. If then it be true 25
which Tully saith, that the orator and poet are of nearest affinity; if in the wordish consideration (as speaks Sir Philip Sidney) they agree; if (according to Quintilian) the orators and poets receive distinction [27ʳ]
of worthiness chiefly by this last ornament of style – we must (with the orators) take some more pains and, beginning at the beginning, 30
consider that to the coupling and framing of style goes the words as the matter and the connection or composition of these words in sentences and clauses as the form, in both which needs diligent choice in the poet.

But as one instructing parents in that duty of love to their children, 35
which is especially required, by way of wary prevention saith he had first need to teach parents how they should not love their children because they ordinarily offend in loving them too much, so I had need first to warn the poet how he should avoid that fond love and affection which too evidently shows they too often catch at shadows, 40
with Aesop's dog, and lose by neglecting the substance, when with the

orators they should consider that words are invented for the thing's
sake and that they are of no worth nor estimation farther than as they
serve to express our conceits. The undiscreetly loving father loves to
see his child brave and gorgeous, full of entertaining complement in
outward show and behaviour, but cares not for those substantial parts   5
of knowledge and virtue whereby he may benefit his country and raise
himself in fame and honour; so, many self-pleasing writers cover their
shallow-conceited births in glorious style and piece out their want of
matter with store of idle words and fustian terms, as they be called.
Tully said many followed Lucullus in magnificence of building but   10
few or none tread in the steps of his virtue. Many unproportionable
minds will assay to imitate Virgil's smoothly-running and richly-
beautified verse, but they care not to approach his apt and profitable
invention. Some that perhaps see it could afford to taste the sweet
milk, but they are loath with the cat (forsooth) to wet their foot, to   15
take the pains and thought to compass it. Others may dispense with
themselves because *quod supra nos nihil ad nos*, things above our reach
we leap not at. And these kind of men fight in painted paste-arms,
likely to win little honour whilst they do little good. For their poems,
a man may afford them all the commendations a Lacedaemonian gave[27ᵛ] 20
the nightingale when, having heard her sweet voice and seen her little
body, he cried out, 'A voice and nought else': so are their works bare
sounds without any proportion of substance in them.

   And, that this fault may be avoided, we will (even in the entry)
seek to prevent it by giving a general notice of the nature of this   25
affectation, whilst we describe it to be an endeavouring desire above
ability to appear extraordinary in the exquisite manner of delivery of
our conceits, in words and style unfitting the subject or circumstances
of person, time, and place; withal applying to our turn that golden
rule of the *Courtier*, who requires in the courtier in all his behaviour,   30
in all his exercises and actions, that nothing be done with labour and
contention but meekly and easily. So let the poet proceed naturally
of his own accord with a careless art or care-hiding art. Plutarch (out
of Philoxenus the poet's authority) in his instructions of attending
poetry saith: that meat is best pleasing to the delicious taste that when   35
it seems flesh is no flesh, and that fish that is no fish. So, a little to
wrest this observation of the cook's eloquence (as those dainties are
called), I may say that eloquence of the orator and poet is best that is
no eloquence, that art that conceals art.

   Now, then, we must look that our words, whereof as of timber   40
we build and compact the frame of our style, be such as may be

understood, or else they cannot reach any of the ends the poet aims
at: it is no more than if nothing were said where nothing is learned.
And here, since use is that, as Horace saith,

> quem penes arbitrium est et vis et norma loquendi,

at whose disposition is the level and line of man's speaking and well-   5
speaking wholly to be directed, we must use those words that be in
use, and by use we, with Tully and Quintilian, would be taken to
mean the use and custom of the best and best judicious who, as in
manners, must be followed, not of the rude and faulty. So as by this
we are forbidden to entertain those words which being warned out[28ʳ] 10
and unbilled as unserviceable soldiers must not by the poet be levied
anew and sent abroad with rusty arms, having no beauty nor vigour in
them; only reverent antiquity (as the ruins of old Rome) shows they
were once in account and estimation, but now custom hath made a
full conquest of them they rest buried in obscurity, and pity and foul   15
wrong were it to discover their mouldy carcases. Master Spenser is
worthily noted by Sir Philip Sidney to have erred this way, whilst he
exceeds good manners to draw those words to tread a measure in his
rhymes though the rattling of their bones proclaim their cripple age
and decay.   20
  Again, the poet must not, when our language hath words decent
and full of efficacy, enfranchise far-born strangers or, cashiering our
own tried companies, muster a new troop of untrained raw servitors
only for the fresh glistering shows of scarfs and plumes which dazzle
our eyes and betray our strength. Such are *procerity* of trees, *summity*   25
of evil, as though *length* and *height* would not serve their turn, *amass*
for *to heap together*, and the like. 'Be ye as azyms, for Christ our Pasch
is immolate,' say our seduced countrymen the Rhemists, whereby
(alas) how do they show the miserable blindness of their embondaged
judgements and prove, by putting away truth and singleness of heart,   30
they hazard the shipwreck of common sense and reason (as one saith
to another purpose)! Surely they meant not to translate, that is to
give the true English of the original to the benefit of the ignorant.
Yet I deny not but some ancient words may be admitted as well
as some new coined, at the least new stamped, so the last be done   35
(as Horace saith) sparingly and modestly and the first be not too
outworn. The certainest direction (out of Quintilian) is of old words
and accustomed to take the newest, of new and unusual the oldest:
the one bears a grave kind of majesty by his known soundness and
reverent antiquity; the other adds a delightful elegancy to our speech   40

by his unacquainted newness and apt variety. If we should make no
new words we should not be able to express our meaning in divers new   [28ᵛ]
inventions without much circumstance and ambage of speech, which
all languages labour to avoid, because the conceit, being so quick
itself, it is much pleased with the soon delivery and quick receiving   5
of the message sent by the tongue and pen (the ambassadors and
agents of the mind) and, contrary, is much perplexed and offended
with the tediousness and difficulty of long circumlocutions, unready
and ambiguous speech. Will we take of the Athenians, saith Tully, the
reforming of our diet and will we refuse their polished and reformed   10
speech? This were (saith he) to feed on acorns when we might have
corn. Therefore all tongues are allowed to reform and perfect their
dialect and fashion of speaking and the poet is he that may challenge
especial privilege, both in denizing strangers into the rooms of those
are old and weak and in repairing and strengthening our naturals by   15
addition or change, because this is readier and more acceptable than
creating can be, if it can be.

And as some tongues are apter than others, I think we shall find our
English to have every way as great an happiness as any, because we
can by easy change draw the words of any language to have the very   20
habit of English: sometime by addition, as *imitation* from the Latin;
sometime by taking away somewhat, as *galliard*, *cavalier* from the
Italian; sometime by exchange, as *extremity*; sometime by exchange
and contracting, as *patience*; sometime by altering accent, as all almost
of our many words we borrow of the French, that have their accent   25
never farther back than in the last syllable save one, whereas we
most times draw it more back if it be of more syllables: as *venison* –
the French hath an accent sharp on the middle syllable. From the
Dutch we borrow words, making them more gentle and smooth by
either changing the harsher letter into his milder confine, as those   30
which are called the *mediae* into the aspirate as in *father*, or by taking
away some of the consonants which they usually heap together, as
in *God*. Still, in our enfranchising or borrowing new words we must   [29ʳ]
be directed by these two: proportion and derivation. As, if one make
similitude of *similitudo*, another may make *aptitude* of *aptitudo*; if one   35
say *potent* another may make *clement*. But here needs discretion, for
always this cannot be presumed upon: it cannot well beseem to say
mightful because *spiteful* doth well, but *powerful* may supply there.

Again, we must use our words derived and borrowed to that sense
the original and primitive imparts to it: as, because an envious, sedi-   40
tious man is said to *incense*, one saith not unfitly he is an *incendiary*.

Yet we find some words by tract of time degenerate, as streams that differ from their fountain: so *priest* in English differs from his original acception, which was no more but an elder, doctor, or pastor of the Gospel, but we use it for a sacrificing and massing priest in opposition to the former. Else Marcus Caelius might have been allowed to term himself *frugal* when he was most excessively lavish and prodigal, for, as Quintilian notes, it comes of a word that signifies fruitful or plentiful, as you may say bountiful, but *frugality* is taken for the contrary virtue of moderate sparing.

Now for addition or change in our own words, we sometime do it by adding a particle or affix that intendeth and enforceth the signification, as *embolden*, *engrieve*, *dissever*, and such like. But our especial grace is in that coupling of words, as it were marrying of them, wherein we come little behind the Grecians – whose tongue therein followed the mother Hebrew and by that, chiefly, was made unimitable of the Latin, that hath no felicity this way – and have far the advantage of all modern tongues, except the French perhaps almost equal us. In these we express our meaning full as effectually in less compass, which as we say is ever affected. Besides, our speech sometimes beautified with these words runs more sweetly-easy; sometime, again, these add majesty and stateliness, according as they be chosen. This copulation may be sometime of mere adjectives, as *swift-sure*; also of mere substantives, as *star-gazers*; of substantive and verb, as *handfast*; or of substantive and participle, as *rose-coloured*, borrowed of Homer that calls it *rose-fingered morn*; likewise of the particle and participle, as *never-ending*; or of two particles and a participle, as *never-enough-praised*; and sometime of the particle and noun, as *between-kingdom*, which Sir Philip Sidney presumes upon after the Latin *interregnum*. This of the words in general; we now come to the connection or conjunction.

By the joining of words in order and congruity (which, as being measured by grammar and the natural properties of every language, we are discharged from far entering into) arise those sentences and clauses, which deliver a perfect sense to the hearer or reader; and by continuation of them in a constant tenor and agreeableness of phrase is our peculiarity of style to be judged. For from this composition doth flow a certain *quality*, so called, which is no more but the outward figure and form – as you would say the favour and physiognomy – of our writing or discourse, arising of the constant and [. . .] sentences, alterable according to the subject and circumstances (as it were, the fashion of the garment), suitable to every state, degree, and affection.

And this is very aptly besides called *character*, for speech carries a certain stamp, impression, or image as well of the thing as of the nature or affection of the deliverer, according to that of Tully, where he saith every motion of the mind hath proper to it some countenance, behaviour, sound, or voice to be expressed by, and so he discerns as   5 many differences in style as there are persons that write, because everyone hath some peculiarity of nature and some difference of apprehension out of which he inditeth, and discovereth the same as well, at the least, in words as in the countenance and gesture. It is not seen that a fantastical fickle wit did ever write a grave or composed   10 style; neither doth a sober man write other. I remember it was said   [30ʳ] (by one able to judge) of one of noble blood in this land, he might be easily known to be an hot and impatient spirit because his gate and pace was evermore hasty and furious, like Jehu in his march, as an hot-mettled horse is described by 'stare loco nescit'; so in his writing   15 there is observed a stirring warmth and headiness, answerable to his nature.

But all forms of style are reduced to one of these three: either *high* or noble, *low* or base, *mean* or indifferent. For these are, as it were, the complexions of our speech, which receive outward constitution   20 chiefly according to the temper of the subject and argument, which is in the place of the humours to colour and animate our style; and thus though (as Tully saith) many that write in one of these kinds differ everyone from the other, and every style hath some degree of the properties of the other, yet they are to be ranged and denominated   25 under and according to the predominant quality and form. Now, that we may the better discern these differences in others and frame them ourselves, we must not disdain to consider the very first principles and grounds of distinction. First, then, observe that in words there are degrees in the greatness, indifferency, and lowness as well of the   30 sound as of the emphasis or force of sense. Words composed of some letters yield a more full and swelling sound, as where is *o* (a vowel) or *ou* and *oa* (diphthongs); others more indifferent and plausible, as where *a*, *u*, *y* (vowels) are or (diphthongs) *ai, ei, eu, ie*; lastly, some give a very small, slender, and easy noise, as words composed of *e* and   35 *i* (vowels). Of the first, examples may be *cormorant, prowess, broad*; of the second, *fame, fire, pure, beauty, rain, wry*; of the last, *penitent, iniquity*. Likewise, consonants have their differences: some gentle and mild, as those that are called tenues – *p, t, c*, or *k* – and the liquids *l* and *m*; some harder, as those that go for the aspirates, as *f, ch, th*, yet not   40 so hard as the mediae *b, d, g*, and *u*-consonant; but of all the hardest

and harshest are the double consonants *x* and *z*; *n* hath a tingling
sound, *r* a rough and rattling, but the doubling of these consonants
with themselves or one with another makes the pronunciation more [30ᵛ]
striking and more settled, and so of greater gravity and vehemency;
the single ones make it voluble and easy. 5

For sense and signification, as Scaliger notes out of Virgil very
great difference, so in English may be observed much: as *displeased*
is not so much as *anger*, *anger* as *wrath*, *wrath* as *rage*; *praise* is not so
much as *fame*, *fame* as *honour*, *honour* as *glory*. Again, some words are
more worthy, of more dignity, than others, as Scaliger notes in this 10
word *incedo* when Juno saith 'incedo regina', she treads like a queen
or imperiously: *credit* is not of so great a worthiness as *reputation*,
reputation as *honour*. The grammarians will needs note *mulier* to be
a word unworthy the majesty of the heroical poet because Virgil
never useth it but *femina*; surely many words may be observed to 15
be unworthy many places. Was it not unworthy in translating Virgil
to say Troy was 'squeezed'? Surely it was a very rotten phrase. The
same translator said, as unworthily, Aeneas 'trudged' from Troy, and
'improbe amor' he renders 'scurvy love': the unseemliness of these
attributes every eye may see. 20

And here, by the way, I may take just occasion to speak of the
epithetons or attributes, in whom resteth much of the garnishing, life,
and vigour of the style. And being as pages to the substantives, we
account this the best general rule, to make them suitable to their
leaders: if they mourn, these followers go sad; if they fight, these are 25
bloody; when they be merry, these are cheerful; when they grave,
these sober. To add a light and loose epitheton to a grave substantive
were as seemly and seasonable as to set a pied feather on a minister's
hat, which I confess I have seen, and farther I confess how ridiculous
the wearer was. Further, your epithetons must not be always sauce – 30
that is, only for complement – but sometimes they must be substantial
meat, of necessary sense and weight: as he that says *faithful diligence
is the whole duty of a servant* under *faithful* comprehends a great
branch of the servant's duty. Especially those attributes to persons
must be of choice and fit: Aeneas is called *heroical* Aeneas, *devout* [31ʳ]₃₅
Aeneas; Achates *faithful*. Herein that Chaucer of the Greek poets,
Homer, is by Scaliger not undeservedly blamed because he keeps
not always decorum: Achilles might be swift of foot, but to call
him *swift-footed Achilles* is a diminishing term for he should rather
have been denominated from some worthy quality of his great mind. 40
What honour or rather dishonour should I do to that famous general

of the army of the most famous prince, of whom one says he is the
true image of the Achillean virtues, to call him *swift-footed Essex* –
though perhaps he can run as fast as Achilles could – except there be
some occasion to use that particular active quality? And here Homer
exceeds himself in indecorum, for when Achilles' great heart was   5
overmastered of grief so as in his impatiency he seemed to melt in
tears, Homer saith 'swift-footed Achilles wept'. Again, you must not
have idle attributes only to fill up your metre (saith Scaliger): 'The
endless date of never-ending woe' – a very idle, stuffed verse in that
very well-penned poem of Lucrece her rape. Lastly, you must have   10
variety of epithetons for the same thing and person, which likewise
Homer fails in, cloying his reader with half a dozen times calling
Achilles *swift-footed* in a very few leaves. Evermore that prudence
and discerning dexterity of the poet must measure decorum in all
things.   15
   Again, we must observe, though the propriety of words (according
to Aristotle) be to be moderated and overruled by the will and pleasure
of the first institutors and speakers, that as they shall set down and
receive this word or that to signify this or that thing every word
thereafter is said to have his proper signification, and so no words are 20
natural, yet we may (with Tully) consider this difference: that some
are more proper and natural, born as it were together with the things,
and may claim some interest from their birth in the things; other are
more improper, artificial, of another set and stock, and are only for
some neighbourhood, affinity, and proportion sometimes adopted   25
and substituted in the rooms of the former. Tully saith these latter   [31ᵛ]
words were first used for necessity, because of the penury; indeed the
God of nature shows himself in this (as in all else) infinitely above
man, that could make things in their diversity with greater facility
than man could invent names to distinguish them by. Afterward   30
these came to be used as ornament and are called *tropes*, translated or
borrowed words, and, signifying by a certain kind of comely abuse
and sweet indirectness, they colour and beautify our speech being
marshalled in convenient stations – and by them very much is our
style distinguished.   35
   And as all these words single breed difference in our speech and
style, so there is more than much art and judgement required in
the connection, and the difference of the style mostly ariseth out of
this texture and coherence of words and sentences. The poet hath
especial great liberty in placing and ranging his words in divers forms: 40
he shall not always deliver his conceit in the forthright Dunstable

tenor of speech, but may leave out, transpose, and interpose with special grace. He shall not always say *they were not gone far in the wood* but, with more grace, *they had not left many trees behind them*; he shall not need always to say *all of us must do this* but sometimes *this do we must all of us*. 5

> The incomparable excellencies of yourself (waited on by the greatness of your estate) and the importance of the thing (whereon my life consisteth) doth require both many ceremonies before the beginning and many circumstances in the uttering, both bold and fearful

– there is much art in the contriving this insinuating conceit. Gen- 10 erally that phrase best maintains his dignity that is of somewhat a long return, where there is a kind of dependency of the sentences and clauses, one inferred upon the other and linked one unto the other. I think Sir Philip Sidney hath first attained the perfection of this grave form and I know not if any in any language be more than matchable 15 to him.

Farther, for the better informing of the poet in this so much missed mystery of style, we may very distinctly note (after Scaliger) some [32ʳ] common graces of our speech and affections (as they be called) that may be found in every kind. The first most common is *perspicuity*, 20 when our words are, as it were, thorough clear and transparent to convey the meaning or conceit to our understanding (as the object to our sense is carried by a convenient *medium*, as the school term is), which is by well-sorted usual words (as we showed before) and by fit and natural knitting of them, so as, having no ambiguous or obscure 25 phrase, the reader proceeds without let or rub to understand what is delivered. The contrary to this may be seen in him that thus lays down ambiguously a good conceit:

> That when the searching eye of heaven is hid
> Behind the globe, that lights the lower world 30

– one would take it by the placing his words that he should mean that the globe of the earth enlighteneth the lower hemisphere.

The next is *purity*, when the speech is proper and naked without ornament, and this thorough the handsome plainness much pleaseth. Scaliger brings that of Virgil for an example: 35

> Tityre, tu patulae recubans sub tegmine fagi, etc.
>
> O Tityrus that lies in shade of beechen tree, etc.

Methinks Sir Philip Sidney makes Lamon begin his pattern of pastorals, that narration of the love of Strephon and Klaius, in the same
purity.

A third grace of style is *fullness* or completeness, when nothing is
wanting, neither doth anything abound, as in Virgil's description of   5
security is observed:

> ille meas errare boves, ut cernis, et ipsum
> ludere quae vellem calamo permisit agresti.

> He suffers thus our herds secure in fields to stray,
> And thus with oaten pipe gives us free leave to play.   10

Another is *plentifulness*, when the style is fluent, more than full,
because it hath something (as you would say) superfluous, as a plant
whose boughs and branches though they may endure some pruning,   [32ᵛ]
yet being suffered to be on they add much grace. Virgil in this fruitful
plenty describes sleep and Sir Philip Sidney security: 15

> Whilst thus they ran a low but levell'd race,
> Whilst thus they liv'd (this was indeed a life)
> With nature pleas'd, content with present case,
> Free of proud fears, brave begg'ry, smiling strife
> Of climb-fall court, the envy-hatching place;   20
> While those restless desires, in great men rife,
>   To visit so low folks did much disdain,
>   This while, though poor, they in themselves did reign.

Likewise *softness* or smoothness is a grace, when the words easily
enter the ears, as in that virtuous sonnet of mine uncle George Wyatt,   25
beginning thus:

> The slender taper with the trembling flame
> The sliding shade of life that lightly flies,
> Resembles right we all from whence we came
> Return at last, oft when we least surmise, etc.   30

But the last and perfectest, that seems to contain all the rest, is
sweetness, that not only makes easy passage but seems to woo the
hearing sense to attention, so as Scaliger speaks of his delighting
in Herodotus his style – an ale-knight may more easily depart with
the sweetest liquor than he leave reading it. If I be not deceived, in   35
Bartas his description of the night this grace is especially to be noted:

> La nuit peut tempérer du jour la sécheresse,
> Humecte notre ciel, et nos guérets engraisse;

La nuit est celle-là qui charme nos travaux,
Ensevelit nos soins, donne trêve à nos maux;
La nuit est celle-là, qui de ses ailes sombres
Sur le monde muet fait avec les ombres,
Dégoutter le silence, et couler dans les os   5
Des recrus animaux un sommeilleux repos.
   O douce nuit, etc.   [33ʳ]

The night doth moderate the drought and heat of day,
Doth moisten our parch'd air and fat our tilled clay;
The night our travail charms, makes tedious labours cease,   10
Doth bury all our cares, and gives our mind free peace;
The night doth, by her drowsy, softly-soaring wing,
Dull silence on the earth and secure quiet bring,
And calmly doth infuse a soft and sweet repose
Into the tired limbs of what so life enjoys.   15
   Sweet night, etc.

Can anything be more clear, pure, full, fluent, soft, and sweet?

Likewise, all style is of a sharp quickness or stirring that proceeds
from the inward warmness of the affection, which we shall better note
in the particular conditions, before which it rests that we should, out   20
of these grounds, describe the particular forms of writing or style.
We say then, with Scaliger, *high* style is that character of speech
which ariseth of chosen well-sounding words, enriched and as it were
embossed with the most glorious figures, that holds up in a well-raised
admiration and even involuntarily ravisheth the mind thorough his   25
maintaining a perpetual dignity in words and phrase and thorough
those two affections of speech, *gravity* and *vehemency*, which this
kind is said to appropriate unto itself. *Grave* speech I describe, with
Scaliger, to be that that is of words weighty, figurative, and above
ordinary, properly knit and composed. *Vehemency* is when the words   30
are of good sound and somewhat slow in the pronunciation, as it were
walking out in state, when the phrase is passionate and violent, as in
interrogations and hot repetitions. This may be called the courtier's
gorgeous and rich garment, as Scaliger calls it the generous form.

The *indifferent* or *mean* style or character is that which ariseth of   35
calm and easy words taken from the more civil use, digested and
joined plausibly and set out with the more familiar and temperate
kind of figures, wherein (as in the beauty of Helen) everything is of
a choice fineness, so as if it want anything in majesty it supplies that   [33ᵛ]
defect with a greater proportion of pleasure, and where it strikes not   40
admiration it delightfully woos by the pleasing elegancy, everywhere

challenging volubility and smoothness, when the words are of easy,
soft, and sweet passage. And this may be as the citizen's neat habit,
which Scaliger calls the frugal form.

The lowest and basest style is that of very vulgar common words,
the phrase plain and popular, in all the carriage like Lalus, where   5
everything is comely because it is kindly, where rudeness cannot
make any deformity because it is suitable to the well-meaning subject
or argument, which is as the heart. And if at any time it be a figure or
ornament to have no figure or ornament, it must needs be here, where
simplicity and low-creeping security are called in as most graceful   10
properties, that is, where are no colours and nothing that is affected.
This is the plain-fashioned suit of the shepherd and ploughman.

Now, then, since we see what style is, of how many kinds, and
whence their differences arise, we will briefly apply all that hath been
said of the style in general to our first four conditions, required, as in   15
the conceit, so in the clothing of the conceit. First, then, we require a
proportionableness in the style: that is, when the words fit the subject
(which we showed to bear the chiefest sway in the differences of
style) and circumstances, when the style is suitable to the particular
kind or poem – as the heroic and tragic is suited with the high style,   20
the comedy and lyric with the mean, the pastoral and satirical with
the low or base. Likewise, the persons from whom and to whom, the
time and place, as in the conceit so in the uttering and expressing the
conceits must be especially regarded. Truth is always the mistress
of imitation. It is an especial grace to give the proper terms of all   25
artists, as of physicians, soldiers, seamen, and those that are inferior
handicraftsmen. We must observe with Tully every motion of the
mind to have a proper and peculiar kind of utterance: as anger (saith [34ʳ]
he) inditeth eagerly, with contention, the phrase cutted and short;
sorrow, contrary, hath a lowly, yielding phrase with some amplifica-   30
tion, and sometimes interrupted (saith he); fear brings forth dejected,
faltering, and uncertain speech; pleasure affords a careless remissness and facility with smooth, cheerful, and fluent phrase; pride
vehement, swelling, and insolent in the delivery with peremptory
absoluteness; courage hath a presuming and lofty phrase, bold and   35
assured; and so of the rest. Examples of all these easily may be taken
out of Virgil and the *Arcadia*, two absolute patterns of decorum. We
may further observe every thing and action to have a particular form
of utterance suitable and proper to it, to deliver, as I may say, the
true idea, species, or image thereof. Scaliger notes in those words of   40
Virgil, 'pro cumbit humi bos', such a lively character to stick in the

number and sound that he seems to see the very fall and tumbling down of the beast. And methinks in those verses,

> una Eurusque Notusque ruunt creberque procellis
> Africus et vastos volvunt ad litora fluctus,

first I hear the bustling of the winds arising, till anon the storm   5
appears fearful upon us and delivers over the hideousness of a sea tempest to the conceit of the reader. But to prosecute the particulars of fitness and decorum were an endless piece of work. We only touch that which the poet must dwell upon, employing all his skill and diligence to grace and make acceptable his wholesome poem: 10

> Scribendi recte sapere est et principium et fons.

> Wise knowledge is the fountain-head and spring
> Whence flows each poem's rightly ordering.

The next grace and virtue is *variety* of phrase, where the poet must have store and great exchange of words, as well to cull out the fittest   15
as to vary and diversify every kind, for this, while it much pleaseth, much moveth. In this place comes into consideration all figurative and borrowed words and forms of speech, that serve by their divers varying and a kind of indirect insinuation to steal into our dull and   [34ᵛ]
untoward affections. We generally thus describe *figure* to be a seemly   20
variety of speech, somewhat unordinary and irregular, as you would say a tolerable erring in word and phrase from the common and direct use. I will not always say *God*, but sometime *the eternal being*; I will not still say *Tully*, but sometimes *the orator*; I will not say an angry man's eyes are *red*, but *inflamed*; I will not say *sword* always, but sometime   25
take his general *weapon* or a more general *iron*; I will not say that *neither the greatest might or the most perfect holiness*, but that *neither the might of Caesar nor holiness of Christ could ever warrant a man not to be ill spoken of*, etc. Thus need we only to give the general description and point out the fountain of all figurative speech, sending the reader   30
to the rhetoricians for the variety both of the words and phrase – at the least to Scaliger, that hath so absolutely written that nothing seems to be wanting which may inform the poet in all the secrets of this faculty, all enlightened by examples. Only I must put the poet in mind that it is a variation and figure to be sometimes without   35
figure: if your speech be all coloured and gaudy it becomes affected and so offensive. And then this simplicity or naked plainness is to be accounted the ground or field (as the heralds speak) where you may

diversify your charge with eminent colours and devices; so must your flourish of figures appear distinct, not heaped one upon another, as it were metal upon metal, like our over-riotous gallants that load their apparel with lace and guards without any measure or order.

The third grace of style or virtue is *sweetness*, when a delight is   5
taken in at the ear by the proportioned and harmonious gracefulness of words. Now (that we repeat not what was above in the general affections of style advertised) we, with Tully, say there are two things 'quae permulcent aures', that delightfully affect the ears: the one is *number*, the other *sound*. And though sound be (as Scaliger saith)   10
the soul of number, yet we may consider it alone, both in figure   [35ʳ]
and rhyme. For number, there is no speech but is qualified with that stirring and motion which is measured by that divided, distinguished, or (as they call it) discrete quantity, number. And this numbrous stir is moderated by time (as all motion is), and of this time and   15
motion the ear is judge (as the agent of the mind), saith Tully, whilst it discerns each syllable to have either a slow staidness in delivering and sound, that takes up a long and full time, or a more voluble speed and currentness, which is uttered in a shorter time and moveth the sense a less space and less sensibly.   20

Now of the linking and joining these timed syllables in the least proportion ariseth a *foot*, whose office is immediately to move and measure syllables. Of these feet, coupled and fitly disposed, springeth another number, which if it be loose and uncertain is common with the orator and to be found in prose, and then this kind is no more   25
but 'apte verbis comprehensa sententia', a convenient number of feet aptly disposed and restrained within the compass of a *sentence*, which is such a part of speech as hath a kind of continuedness and dependency of pronunciation and delivery, uniform in itself – so that as, often times, the sense seems unperfect, in like manner the ear   30
rests unsatisfied if this sentence want his due extent. And this is that that is called *concinnity* or tuneableness of speech which Tully looks for in the orator, and saith the orators took it of the poets, whilst they observed their orations 'cum severitate audiri', to be heard with displeasure, whereas the poets were always attended with delight and   35
willingness.

But if these number of feet be certain and fast knit, as well in order or disposition as in the whole proportion or compass, they make a *verse* or *metre*, which is a more precise and certain comprehension and number of feet strictly disposed to affect the ear, differing from the   40
former because the numbers are certain and certainly disposed. And

now we must shake hands with the Grecians and Latins, who had
their verse consisting only in the stinted number and set disposition
of such feet as were distinguished only by time, which by reason
of the length of their words, and the lengthening of them in the   [35ᵛ]
variations by cases, moods, tenses, and persons, they were very apt   5
for. But our modern languages all of them wanting those cumbersome
differences that (saith Sir Philip Sidney) were a piece of Babylon's
curse – for indeed the Hebrew hath them not – but just as we
have our varyings distinguished by particles for the most part –
particularly the English, consisting most of monosyllables (as are   10
all almost of our Saxon appellatives) – we are not capable of those
variety of feet, because every such word will have a full or long
time, and so our feet (I mean that coupling of syllables that answers
to their feet) are distinguished by the *accent* or moderation of the
sound, every foot consisting of two syllables, so as the number of our   15
syllables are still certain. And that grace of tuneableness which they
had by the variety of currentness of their time-serving feet is fully
recompensed by another grace our modern kinds have, namely that
answerableness of the ends of our verses in likeness of sound which
we call *rhyme*.   20

The Now, then, we will in our verse consider three things: the *foot*, the
rhyme, and the *caesure*; in all which together, and truly I think in each
of them severally, it is plain we come not behind any modern tongue.
It is most true Sir Philip Sidney saith: we have only consideration
of the number of syllables and accent in our verse. For our foot is   25
restrained only to two syllables whereas the ancients had more, and
of these two syllables the accent evermore sits more sharp on the one
than on the other, and so lifteth up the voice which withal seems to
time it and draw it to a full or long delivery – at the least is answerable
to the long time; the other hath the accent depressed, and so answers   30
to the short-timed syllable. And thus we may be said to have only
spondees in our verse, or rather iambics if they be even-footed verses
and trochees if they be odd, which I think may be observed to be
perpetually observed.

The *iambic* foot consists of a short and a long syllable, the *trochee*   35
of a long and a short, which times our accents still answer unto.
For example, our even-footed verse (being that which hath no odd
syllable, but just either fourteen syllables, which make seven feet,   [36ʳ]
or twelve, which make our hexameter or six-footed metre, and so
downward): you may observe every second syllable to be more raised,   40
distinct, and full sounding than the former, that passeth away more

easily and as it were not stood upon – as in this fourteen-syllabled
verse of Sir Philip Sidney will appear if it be scanned:

Whose senses in so ill consort their stepdame Nature lays.

And in this of twelve:

Now was our heavenly vault deprived of the light.   5

Again, take those that are of odd syllables, as seven, which make three
feet and an odd syllable – you shall note the first syllable to have the
raised accent, the last pressed down, as:

Sigh they did but now betwixt

Him great harms had taught much care.   10

To which if ye will add one foot more, the verse keeps the same order
of accent – as to the first imagine were added somewhat thus:

Sigh they did but now betwixt their sighs.

Take away a foot, and the accent stands as it did:

Him great harms had taught.   15

Neither can these syllables be removed from their natural tenor, as
in words that are of many syllables you may easily discern by mis-
ranking them and putting the accent from his due place, as, in this
odd-footed verse,

Interchangeably reflected,   20

turned thus,

Reflected interchangeably,

there is an evident unnaturalness and harshness. This is without
doubt very generally true, that these our feet are most precisely to
be kept and distinguished by accent, and I see not but that our verse   25
runs as stately and solemn as the Latins, if not as volubly pleasant,
distinguishing the volubility according to the smallness of the vowels
and the singleness of our consonants, which may be quickly seen by
our hexameter that answers just to the Latin heroic.

Sir Philip Sidney for variety hath kept the very foot and number   30
of many of the Latin kinds of metre in his pastorals and, amongst the
rest, of their hexameter, as in this:

Unto a caitiff wretch whom long affliction holdeth.

This goes marvellous both stately and naturally, by reason it is most   [36ᵛ]
of spondees and our tongue suits very well to them, so as no accent
is missounded. Contract the two last syllables in *affliction*, as we use,
into one – it is just our six-footed verse with a female rhyme, as thus
you may see if you make another to rhyme to it: 5

> Unto a caitiff wretch whom long affliction holdeth,
> To him that his despair in plaining lines unfoldeth.

The next is not so easily changed, because he runs more on dactyls
and displaceth the accent:

> Grant yet grant yet a look to the last monument of his anguish.   10

I must confess my ear is as much pleased with the English foot as
with the Latin in the first hexameter, but the last is unproper. For
those kinds of measures are not natural to any vulgar tongue, and yet
our English is as appliable to them as any I know, and so saith Sir
Philip Sidney.   15
  Now our verse to make the delight more perfect hath to this
proportion of number added another ear-pleasing grace unknown to
the Greeks and Latins: the like sounding of the last words or ends of
our verses which we call *rhyme*. Tully saith the ear especially attends
the extremity and close of our sentence and there resteth satisfied;   20
therefore this close must not be without some especial tuneableness
of number (saith he), which is most precisely kept in our metres,
that evermore return within convenient distance an answerableness
of number and sound both. And this rhyme is of three sorts: either
in returning the same sound in the last syllable, which makes the   25
masculine rhyme (as it is called after the French), the accent being
upon it sharp; or in the two last syllables, which the French call the
feminine rhyme, when the accent is on the last save one; or in the
three last syllables, which the Italians call *sdrucciola*, when the accent
is in the third syllable backward. For the first, example may be *show*, 30
know, *low*; for the second, *treasure*, *pleasure*, *measure*; for the third,
carefulness, *warefulness*, *sparefulness*, or in divers words, as *framed is*,
named is, *blamed is*. Now the English is fit for all these sorts of rhyme
equally; the French and Spanish not so for the *sdrucciola*; the Italian
admits not the male. And yet further, by the varying and transposing 35
the rhymes to some convenient distance, we grow to have another
proportion of number called a *stanza* or *staff* that is of divers verses   [37ʳ]
in a proportionable return of the rhyme and number crossed and

intermingled, that gives a great delight to the ear. This staff may differ also in the measures: some short, some long, some rhymes returned in the middle, some in the end – the variety of all which is to be apprehended by observation only.

The third thing which is in verse to be observed is the *caesure*   5
(which likewise the Latins had) or pause, lighting upon some of your middle syllables, that serves as a breathing place where you seem somewhat to rest, in those verses that are from four feet upward. This the French and we have, the Spanish and Italian not; the accent must be there sharp. In the verse of five feet the caesure is in the   10
fourth syllable, as:

> Can Reason then ‖ a tyrant counted be?

– the rest is upon *then*. In the six-foot verse the pause is upon the last syllable of the third foot, as:

> Now was our heavenly vault ‖ deprived of the light   15

– the caesure is at *vault*. In the verse of seven feet (the longest that our tongue admits) the rest is at the last syllable of the fourth foot, as:

> Whose senses in so ill consort ‖ their stepdame Nature lays

– the pause is at *-sort* in *consort*. Now our monosyllables are very apt   20
for this rest, which will do the better if it fall upon such a one because it may take up a fuller sound, and also if the sense rest withal, in the shortest rest of a comma, it will be the pleasanter. At the least it would be most upon the last syllable of a word, yet sometimes for variety (which is ever to be attended of the poet) it is graceful to place   25
it in the former of a many-syllabled word, as to my ear the last of these two verses sounds best:

> I fear to tire myself ‖ if at first I proceed
> With two great journeys' has- ‖ ty unadvised speed.

And though I say verse be the habit or livery of the poet, and that it   30
is a part of that sweetness which generally we exact at his hands, yet I say not that all poesy must needs be in this strict number. Sir Philip Sidney saith well verse is no cause but an ornament of poetry, and he saith better, by way of illustration, that it is as a long counsellor's gown to a counsellor, which none wears but a counsellor, and yet[37ᵛ]₃₅
he may plead in a scholar's gown. Indeed the difference is only in the fashion, the stuff being the same. The most comely and decent

attire wherein the poet clothes his apt imitation (which Aristotle calls
the soul of the poem) is this metre, but since it may attain unto this
general end by another means – by that looser number, which hath
his grace of sweetness also – I see not why those excellent imitations
and inventions that are in prose should be shut out from the number   5
of poems because they are in purple and not in scarlet, because
they want this complemental cut. The key that is made of iron is as
properly a key as if it were made of gold, because it performs the end
of opening and locking as well as the other. So this kind of writing
in prose (numbrous also) perhaps opens and shuts the affections –   10
the passages to persuasion – as well as if it were in golden metre, and
then it may be used in the imitation without prejudice. And some
kinds of poetry seems to claim this looser kind of number as their
proper clothing – as the comedy – and some kind of poets have taken
this liberty in other kinds – as Pindar's number cannot be found to   15
be strict metre in his lyrics.

Rules of verse may be: that no accent be altered in your measures;
that your caesure fall natural; that your rhyme be not of the same
words or consonants but like sounding only or agreeing in the vowels
(which are the life of sound); that you alter not orthography or con-   20
gruity for rhyme or number – which all yet may be broken for variety,
so it be done with discretion and modesty. Again, for sweetness of
sound, *euphoniae gratia* (as they speak), and for the currentness of
number, the poet is allowed to add, transpose, and interpose parts
of words, letters, and syllables in the beginning, middle, and end,   25
which are the grammarians' figures – as, for example, *ydone* for *done*,
goldilocks for *gold-locks*, *spoken* for *spoke*; or to take away something
from the beginning, middle, or end – *twixt* for *betwixt*, *ta'en* for *taken*,
morn for *morning*, etc.

To this virtue of sweetness is reduced a great part of that grace   30
of repetition of sounds and words which makes the figures rhetorical   [38ʳ]
that are called *auricular*, for affecting the ear, when we seem to toss
and play with the same sound and word, catching it again and again
in the middle or in the end of the same sentence, in the beginnings,
middles, and ends of divers sentences, sometimes in part, sometimes   35
in whole – which are so ordinary as we need no division but send the
poet to his own sense and the rhetoricians' observations.

Now come we to the last virtue and grace in style: the *forcibleness*
and *efficacy*, when the conceit is so uttered and expressed as the
readers are moved and passionately affected with the lively quickness   40

of style. The painter (saith learned Lomaz) gives not only the true
measure and proportion of the length and breadth of the bodies he
represents in a plane but (saith he) by observing the perspective light
he can represent to your eye the third dimension, thickness, whilst
by artificial lines, shadows, and lights he gives the form, steepness,   5
height, and hollowness, setting it off so as like a very body it seems
embossed and embowed (as they speak). Methinks our virtue of
efficacy in some sort answers to this, when we express the images of
our conceits so properly and lively in style that the words and phrase
bear the true character and stamp of the moving passions, and seem to   10
deliver over to the sense of the reader the affection expressed. Tully
saith of orators they may be compared to wrestlers, whereof some
desire no more but to maintain health and therefore fit themselves
only to exercise 'in xysto', saith he, to deal in mean matters. Others,
over and above this soundness of body, seek to have fresh and fair   15
complexions and show force and vigour in their joints and sinews, and
these affect the Olympian games and honours, contending publicly
in weighty cases, this being the period and perfection of that faculty.
In like manner I may say of poets that to reach the triumphal garland
they must have, beside the proportion, variety, and sweetness which   20
are the beauties that seem only delightfully to affect the mind, a
certain sinewy strength and brawniness of style that may constrain the
reader and lead him captive. Now as we said before in the conditions   [38ᵛ]
of the conceit, that forcibleness was principally and most eminently
in the busy and stirring kinds, yet, likewise, the calmest poems may   25
entertain some strong passions with their passionate apprehensions,
so must the most appeased kind of poetry be allowed this forcibleness
of delivery and utterance, though not in that height and eminency
that the more passionate poems seem to appropriate – as, if you look
into that excellentest pattern of the pastoral in Sir Philip Sidney in   30
the person of Lamon, you shall easily see that sweet, becoming tale
to be graced with all elegancies and namely with much forcibleness
of style.

  Now we said above that the principal force and vigour was in the
conceit, invention, and matter, without which (Tully saith) words   35
or speech can have no station, are as it were of no service. And here
we may say (with him), likewise, words have their necessary use,
without which the conceits want their light, are as it were unborn.
So as now we must see how best we may proportion our style and
phrase to the thing, to make it lively and sensible, to give it lustre,   40

which Quintilian (tracing Tully) saith is affected chiefly by amplified speech: when we so follow our conceit with words as, by the propriety, we seem to set out the thing or action before the eye. Sometime we amplify by entering into particulars, breaking the whole into his parts, anatomizing every limb; and then speech (as Themistocles said to the King of Persia) resembles the imagery in a piece of arras, for in both the conceits and images are seen when they are unfolded and laid open but seem lost when they are wrapped up and straitened, though they contain all they did otherwise. As he that saith a city was sacked embraceth all in his conceit another doth who, descending into particulars, reckons up with Quintilian the flame and fire in temples and houses, the rattling noise of falling roofs, the united confusion of divers clamours and cries, the howlings, lamentations, and wringing the hands of women and children, old men complaining how they were kept unto an unhappy day, young men how they were born in an unhappy hour, the uncertain flight of some, the last constant embracement of others, the insolencies, robberies, and sacrilege of the conquerors, etc. Yet (saith Quintilian) this latter manner of report doth more pierce the affections than the other, which, as an hasty messenger, delivered the sum in a word and left the particulars to our imagination to work out. Every man understands what is meant when I say, in gross, *he took compassion*, but when one shall thus speak,

> he pitieth, he taketh up in his arms, he lovingly embraceth, he kisseth, and
> with more than fatherly tenderness tempers his words,

he seems to me to picture the personal behaviour of the compassionate, and by so plain and particular beating on the manner he conveys this affection into my mind.

Sometime our amplification is by heaping our words and, as it were, piling one phrase upon another of the same sense to double and redouble our blows that, by varying and reiterating, may work into the mind of the reader:

> Shorten my days thou canst with sullen sorrow,
> And pluck nights from me, but not lend a morrow;
> Thou canst help time to furrow me with age,
> But stop no wrinkle in his pilgrimage;
> Thy word is current with him for my death,
> But dead, thy kingdom cannot buy my breath.

Especially this heaping of speech works into the affection when there is a gradation in the words or sense, climbing higher and higher as it were by scale:

> He lost besides his children and his wife,
> His realm, renown, liege, liberty, and life.   5

Bartas, speaking of Thunder, saith:

> Sans cesse il tourbillonne,
> Il bourdonne, il frémit, il mugle, il bruit, il tonne.

Thus ambitiously translated:

> And without rest he tumbleth, rolls round over, under,   10
> Doth panting fret, groan, chafe, rage, fume, storm, bellow, thunder.

There is a contrary way of forcibleness in style, when we comprise [39ᵛ] and compact our conceits in short and pithy terms, and then (as Plutarch says) speech is like gold and silver, that the purer they be the less they be in quantity: so, saith he, the excellency of speech   15 consisteth in signifying much by few words. This is that Chaucer with a good decorum describes in the scholar of Oxford, that speaks quick and short and of high sentence (saith he). Phocion (in comparison of whom Demosthenes himself little esteemed all other orators, if we will believe Plutarch), walking on the theatre in a deep study,   20 was asked by one of his friends what he so seriously mused on. 'Marry,' said he, 'I am thinking with myself how I may abridge anything of that I have to say unto the people.' And so Demosthenes, whensoever he saw Phocion stand up to speak, he would say: 'See the mincer of my words.' This must needs be moving when the   25 mind so quickly apprehends so much. 'Veni, vidi, vici', saith Caesar: I have approached, viewed, conquered. Sallust is excellent for this compactedness of phrase.

Again, all coloured speech, as it delights, so it moves, as bold metaphors, presumptuous hyperboles: *pitchy night* is very forcible,   30 more than *black*, *frozen heart* than *hardened*, *an ocean of tears* more than *a flood*. Likewise, the habit or form of figurative phrase which the rhetoricians call of the sense or sentence, and say it is 'ad movendum et pervincendum', to constrain and force violently, is very powerful. Such are passionate exclamations, whether arising of despair, admi-   35 ration, desire, disdain, derision, or sorrow, which commonly begin

with some note of passion, as *Oh* or *Alas*, and many times with
interrogations, which is a very moving form of speech, and, as one
saith, a warm proposition, when we seem to be angry and take it hotly
to have that we propose doubted of:

> Pro deum atque hominum fidem, quid est si haec contumelia non est?   5
>
> O heaven and earth, if this be not an indignity what is?

> tantaene animis caelestibus irae?
>
> And is there then   [40ʳ]
> Such rancour in the hearts of mighty men?

saith Master Spenser in imitation of that of Virgil. The *epiphonema*   10
is of marvellous moving grace:

> tantae molis erat Romanam condere gentem.
>
> So great endeavour needed Rome's high state to rear.

Likewise, those forms are moving which make us correct the tenor of
our phrase and recall our words; and when our unsupportable passion   15
seems to silence us quite, making us end abruptly; the hasty turning
of our speech to some other person, that seems to grow of some
sudden apprehension, forcibly distracting us; the deliberating with
ourselves; lastly the feigning of a person, when we act the case of that
party that is affected, sometimes giving life and tongue to senseless   20
and dead creatures – these are all moving as the rhetoricians show
you. Again, to conclude this condition, as sweetness is in the conceit
differing in degree from the grace of efficacy, so is it with these
conditions in style, particularly number and metre: as they are sweet,
so are they moving – as Quintilian saith of the heroical verse that the 25
mind is raised and lifted up by the lofty stateliness of it.

We are now at the last to descend into the consideration of the parts
of poetry, applying the rules and restraining them to the particular
kinds. And here we must remember what we made above to be the
grounds of their differences and several properties, which we showed   30
to be the particular end and subject that give the distinctions of the
manner of handling, following herein Aristotle, who makes the kinds
differ one from another in some or all of these three: either in that they
imitate divers things or subjects; or secondly in that they imitate the
same things diversly or after a divers manner (because to a differing   35
end); or lastly (which we comprised under this last if it belong to
the poet) in that they imitate by divers means, as by verse, number,

music, and bodily motions. And we may now for our memory and
better proceeding lay you down the principal heads of that division
before your eye:

poems handle matter	good	by narration	solemnly – heroical
			vulgarly – lyric
		by personating	pastoral
	bad	by narration	satirical
		by personating	solemnly – tragical
			vulgarly – comical

And of each of these six somewhat we may say apart briefly,
beginning with the heroical – most worthily the first – that hath   5
(according to Aristotle) all the best graces alone that others have
between them, and that most eminently; wherein for our direction
we are to consider his subject and particular next end. For his subject
or matter, it is always good and high, or as high. His particular next
end is to stir admiration (saith Aristotle), and then (according to Sir   10
Philip Sidney) this kind not only teacheth a truth but the highest
and most excellent truth, drawing the portraiture of the most worthy
virtues and moving the mind by admiration (the highest degree of
delight) to the pursuit of some worthiest good. And here it will
be sufficient for us to stand upon the perfectest and principalest   15
kind, which is that where the poet, taking the liberty of his own
invention, feigneth the imitation of actions and virtues, which under-
kind containeth whatsoever best graces are common to all other of
the heroical poems; and the differences are very small betwixt this
and the other – those differences, I mean, which may challenge any   20
different cautions and rules. Thus, then, when the heroical imitateth
actions they must be great or of great persons, as Horace shows in
Homer, making him the rule of this kind:

> Res gestae regumque ducumque et tristia bella
> quo scribi possunt numero, monstravit Homerus.   25

Homer is the precedent that shows how the acts of kings and captains,
how sad wars are to be imitated. And as Homer hath thus gone before,
Virgil hath exceedingly well succeeded:

> Arma virumque cano.

And Tasso is a second Virgil:

> Canto l'arme pietose e 'l capitano.

And Spenser another Tasso.

Here, then, is no mention of love, dalliance, and courtship. I except
not the moral virtue but that passion – one of virtue's unruly ser-   5
vants – which doth womanize a man and more too, saith Musidorus.
The end of the heroic is to lift up the mind by some worthy and
manly affection to some more than ordinary pitch of virtue, not to
soften it with weak and maidenlike impressions, much less to steep
and drown it in wantonness and sensuality. So as here those carpet   10
poets that make their argument love and courting dalliance to stir
sensual and low-pitched affections are clean dismissed from the rank
of the heroical – yea some may be utterly unbilled from the service
of poetry as weak or treacherous. Such is *Amadis de Gaule*, of whom
Monsieur de la Noue (famous for that in war and peace he so well   15
both knew and did) nothing fears to affirm that those books are as
dangerous for youth to attend as Machiavel for the aged; and Sir
Philip Sidney worthily useth a diminishing term of that effeminate
invention. Surely the more of this weak and nice stuff possesseth
your leaves the less heroical your poem is, the less worthy worthy   20
minds. It is true the heroical poet, that he may the more enlighten the
beauty and form of virtue and prudence, is to bring vice and folly as
the foils, leading the virtuous, wise man thorough many temptations,
assaults, and difficulties to set the more garlands of triumph upon his
head. But still he must have regard to his main scope: that he inform   25
and fashion the reader's will and affections aright, which is the end of
instruction; that he make vice odious always as well as virtue lovely.
And this is to be observed in all kinds of poetry.

Here, then, for our poet's direction (once for all) we will with
Vives distinguish vicious and noughty affections (the root of bad   30
actions and manners) into two kinds: one sort are 'utilitatis et volup-
tatis cuiusque expertia', void of all pleasure or profit; the other 'in
corpus cum delectatione sensuum aliqua manant', are instilled into
us by some sensible apprehension of pleasure. The first sort may be   [41ᵛ]
expressed at large to the life, to object before our eyes (as he saith)   35
the foulness of them: such are pride, rage, hate, envy, that yield no
commodity or sweetness but, as furies sent from hell, they are the
scourges of themselves. The other kind of affections presently offering delight and profit to our sense and appetite (though indeed they
have no true loveliness) yet presenting sensual pleasures, 'hoc est   40

dulcem perniciem', sweet destruction, and being 'simulacrum quod-
dam naturalis desiderii', lively portraitures of men's natural prone
desires, these should be more sparingly and partially expressed and
the persons so feigned persecuted in some sort and taxed sharply,
principally to discover unto what loathsome inconveniences such   5
passions drive men, leaving shame and sting of conscience to succeed
after; whereas if you should lively and fully imitate these pleasurable
affections, you might instead of making them odious even breathe
and instil them into the mind of the reader, and prove in the end like
bad conjurors that raise the spirits you cannot lay again – these stick   10
so close to nature that it is easier to keep them from our knowledge
than, being known, to keep us from affecting them.

Apelles drew but the half face of Antigonus because he would
conceal the deformity of the want of one eye, but our Italian painters
and Italianate disdain to be his scholars and they will deliver the full   15
of better hidden shames. 'Pictoribus atque poetis', etc.: the poet (forsooth) and painter have liberty to undertake any representation, any
spectacle. And so, amongst them, Virgil is esteemed too scrupulous
and chaste who in his great prudence very well observed this distinction, whilst in expressing the love of Dido as a temptation to distract   20
constant Aeneas he so warily and wisely covers it as a man cannot
easily by him conceive the degrees of the passion or possession till he
come to the horrible event – and so he lets us see the stinging sharp-   [42ʳ]
ness of this passion in the detested end and issue, noting the violence
thereof *a posteriori* (as I may say) by the effects. If Tasso bring Armida   25
to the camp, he so sets her out as men have little motion in the reading
but to the abhorring her disguised behaviour and enticements, every
stanza almost branding her falsehood and seeming sweetness with
disgrace and reproach. If Heliodorus undertake a love of Theagenes,
it is a sober constant virtue, breeding and stirring up in him knightly   30
and honourable resolutions, not a wanton languishing passion that
enfeebleth the mind and disableth the body from undergoing any
high or hardy attempt. How much worthier is this proceeding than
that of Ariosto, in divers places unworthy any chaste ears? I will
boldly speak as much as self-convinced Ovid fearfully delivered to   35
another purpose: 'teneros ne tange poetas!' And as Bartas saith:
waste not your precious time and gifts in wanton argument. Ovid
was banished an heathen state, and why should our Christian poets
entertain that which caused his just exile? So if he confess that he
perished by his own wit, let not our poet's wit be as Uriah's letters: a   40
cause of destruction to the bearer. Let everyone resolve as divine

Bartas doth, after a worthy reproof of heathenish-conceited and loose poets:

> Or tout tel que je suis, j'ai du tout destiné
> Ce peu d'art et d'esprit que le ciel m'a donné
> À l'honneur du grand dieu, pour nuit et jour écrire 5
> Des vers que sans rougir la vierge puisse lire.

> For me (all as I am) I constantly decree
> The small skill and small gifts that heaven affordeth me
> To turn to God's high honour, always to indite
> In such phrase as chaste virgins shall therein delight. 10

Truly a resolution becoming a modest, virtuous mind.

Now we showed the heroical kind to be narrative, wherein we are to consider these parts: first, the *argument* or *proposition*; secondly, the [42ᵛ] *invocation*; lastly, the *narration* itself. The proposition is necessary in all narrations, and Bodin requires it in the history. It must be in 15 the poet modest and short. You must not profess too much in it, according to Horace, that blamed a poet for too high and arrogant a promise; surely, if Lucan be faulty for too lofty a proposition, our Master Daniel, that treads in Lucan's steps, even in this particular is not unreprovable. It needs likewise to be short, as being only to 20 prepare the reader with a summary apprehension of what ensueth, to get good liking and attention at his hands. The invocation, being to sanctify our works, to stir up ourselves, and breed a reverent regard in the reader, must be directed to the true infuser of all worthy graces:

> né si comincia ben se non dal cielo, 25

saith young Silvio in *Pastor fido*, that I may render it with better authority:

> Every good and perfect gift comes from above from the father of lights

– and this devoutly and shortly. Heathenish invocations, I hope, are proved offensive, which offensiveness – if at any time – in the 30 beginning is to be avoided, where we labour to purchase good will and audience for all that follows; and then must it be short too, lest it keep the reader too long from his promised matter. In the first fault most of our poets modern are faulty, as I take it. In the latter the invocation of Josuah Sylvester in that very well-laboured and commendable 35 translation of the *Second Week* of Bartas is blameworthy, whilst he detains his reader with matter that would have better befitted a preface than a translator's invocation (which is at the best but an

intruded thing), so disproportionable to his author that he is well
near ten times as great, if you consider the invocation separated
from the proposition or argument. Now some join the proposition
and invocation together, as Homer and Bartas; other have beside
both these a *proem* or transition, as Virgil; some again have a proem [43ʳ]₅
that serves instead of their proposition and invocation, as Spenser
in his *Faerie Queene*; and some have neither proem, proposition, nor
invocation, but these are in prose as the *Arcadia*.

When thus we have prepared ourselves and the reader, we
immediately fall into the narration, wherein you may consider it in   10
whole and in the parts. For the whole, it must be (saith Aristotle)
as an entire creature, proportionable and beautiful. And then this
narration is called a *fable* or feigning imitation of the actions of men,
with conveniency and aptness framed to answer the general form
of some particular virtues to be followed; which form is called the   15
allegory (saith Viperanus), whilst in the pretending a bare report of
some singular and particular accidents we (as by mystery) enwrap
and convey properly the universal nature of some moral or civil
virtue: as we showed above in Aeneas, who is not described as one
extant only sometimes and so mannered, but as an image and model   20
of such virtues of piety, wisdom, and valour portrayed in his carriage
in all fortunes – in war and in peace. Thus, then, not all the life or
actions of any person are to be delivered, but so much only as may
behove to the describing these virtues, all so invented and disposed
as nothing can be added, taken out, or misplaced without some   25
inconvenience and evident unshapeliness. And the artists further
give precept that this invention have some true ground, as Homer,
Virgil, and Tasso have, yet we see excellent poems have not: only
they have reference to some place and time being, and they keep
the due circumstances of them. So as though Aristotle say that the   30
heroical poem differs from the tragedy, in that this is not limited to
time as that is, it is expounded that he means not so narrowly. Some
will tie the story to be straitened within two years' efficiency, because
if it be much longer it must either, as Aristotle saith, repeat many
things tediously and grow withal too huge and vast, or else (which   35
is equally graceless) every action cannot have the due circumstances
and natural inducements: as may be seen by those that hasten so
much and divers matter within so small space and compass. And the
ancient heroical poets exceed not this time, as Homer, Virgil, and   [43ᵛ]
Tasso. For this Sir Philip Sidney was (without doubt) too artificial to   40
have intended his story or narration farther than to the knitting up of

the two royal couples' fortunes in bringing them into a settled estate
of marriage and mutual exchange of joy in enjoying one another,
for their virtues and affections with the issue was the main scope
of his whole invention. Surely about that space is fittest for the just
heroical poem.   5

Now for the parts of this narration or fable Aristotle makes it to
consist of two. The first he calls δέσιν, the other λύσιν, the collection
and the resolution – as you would say the conception and delivery, for
Aristotle so warrants to compare it. And then the conception is the
first part, growing greater and filling the womb of your poesy (as he   10
speaks) with the *episodia* or supplements till things are brought into
some anxiety and exigence, as it were fallen in labour, and thenceforth
all the difficulties, as the throes and pangs, are wrought thorough
in the delivery and issue, which is the resolution. Your collection
or conception must not take beginning (as Horace saith) 'gemino   15
ab ovo', from the first seed, but it must begin at some memorable
occurrent directly pertinent to the narration: it must take original
in some principal part, as it were the heart. And then (as Pindar
sang) the front of your poem, as of a building, must be τηλαυγὲς,
resplendently beautiful. Virgil, after this rule, sets out the fore-part   20
of that goodly frame of his *Aeneidos*, beginning at the sea-fare of
Aeneas from Sicily towards Italy, falling upon the coasts where Dido
reigned, which is one of the most pertinent and worthy pieces of all
his frame. Sir Philip Sidney, in like manner, begins his narration
at the recovery of one of the principal persons after the horrible   25
shipwreck, and leads him immediately into Arcadia, that was the
fountainhead of all chief adventures, the rendezvous of all worthiest
occurrents. From such beginning the birth still grows, the members
are still added and increased, till the number be convenient and
complete, till the matters be sufficient and grown to some proneness   30
and ripeness for the second part, which is the resolution or delivery,   [44ʳ]
where all difficulties grow to some change and issue, when there is
a cleanly conveyed turning of all things to some notable end and
conclusion that fully dischargeth the promise of the poet and satisfies
the reader.   35

Now (saith Aristotle), as these be the formal parts of your poem, so
the same may be considered as it is divided according to the discrete
quantity into sections and books. And this division (as Quintilian
speaks of that of the orator) hath the same use the stones in the high-
way have, whereon is inscribed the space or number of miles from   40
place to place to give the traveller instruction and encouragement in

his journey whilst he sees what is past as well as what is to come. In like manner, those that attend the poet are more directly informed and led along in their long and intricate way by apt sections and divisions that always follow the matter, which naturally will incline to a full point or station where a rest may be made. It must not be abrupt, in the middle of a story or action, for that were as unhandsome and unconvenient as the course an ambassador of great place (as I have heard) used to take in his travel who, μικροπρεπείας ἕνεκα, for small-seemingness, because he and his purse might pass invisible, would be sure to take up his bait and lodging in some dorp or scattered village, balking greater towns more fit for receipt and entertainment. Virgil is a very good precedent, and Bartas that follows him in his *Judith*; the *Faerie Queene* and *Arcadia* are very conveniently parted and cut into members, having a kind of completeness every part in itself. The numbers of these books and chapters cannot be strictly prescribed.

Lastly, for the clothing of this heroical invention: for your style, it must be rich and high, and then your verse must be hexameter (called *heroical* as most proper to this kind) because by the length thereof and kind of measure or feet the dignity and majesty is maintained (according to Aristotle), and when you come to more busy and troubled matter this verse is more capable of forcibleness and vehemency. And this stateliness and gravity is as well seen in our vulgar kind of hexameter as in the ancient (as we showed above). You may recompense this solemn drawing at length your vulgar metres by that proportion of the stanza, which for the interrupting and proroguing the rhyme (that is now especially attended) will maintain his state and weightiness in a five-footed verse as well as in the longer. And the heroical is most worthily sustained by staff, which is a proportion so uniform in itself as every one of them seems to have a kind of sufficiency of conceit, and for the delivery it closeth with an apt cadence of rhyme, commonly the two last verses immediately answering in likeness of sound, which, after the former crossed variety, seems to give the ear satisfaction and disposeth it to a pause or rest – and for this the staff is set alone, as though he were complete in himself. Some think when the rhyme falls immediate the seven-footed verse is the fittest number for the heroical poem; indeed he runs very grave. I think the five-footed metre in such soon return of rhyme is somewhat light, yet used. But I leave it to every man's judgement upon observation: only take heed of the common error Tully speaks of (indeed an error too commonly stumbled upon in every way of life) – that we restrain not our liking and commendations to so much only as we ourselves can best attain unto.

Thus much for this heroical kind. Whatsoever other under-kind of heroical the poet undertakes, it differeth only because he hath a subject ready framed to his hand, and, as it were, a real pattern of his picture, in drawing whereof he must approach to this former perfection and so is allowed to better his example (as Aristotle saith); or else it is a part of this, that keeps his uniformity in proportion answerable to the whole. If it be matter of knowledge only or bare discourse of the sciences the poet undertakes, he must strive to utter his conceits with all the graces we showed above in the general conditions, ever inflaming the mind by admiration to affect knowledge, which is always the noblest work the noblest part makes progress in.

The next kinds of poetry are the tragedy and comedy, the first of affinity with the heroical as borrowing his subject thence, the latter very near of kin to the former in the manner of handling, which is by personating. We will first consider them jointly, and then distinctly by their special properties. For their subject they handle bad matter, and by way of action or personating, or feigning persons, to deliver more sensibly the images of those vices are to be avoided. Especially here is first that distinction of vicious affections (before in the heroic mentioned) to be regarded, lest while we paint our naked shames we tempt the will rather than reform it: for this kind of personal resemblancing is most moving (as all agree), and then most dangerous is the limning of those inbred pleasurable affections.

For their formal parts in general, they are the same with the heroic. Every either tragedy or comedy is grounded on actions or things done (or likely to be done). And then you are allowed a *prologue* for an entrance, or some part answerable to the proposition for preparation; and the fable itself is no more but an apt and uniform imitation of some singular action or expedition and the accidents belonging to that one action, answerable to the general nature of some particular ill affections and vices to be shunned. And the fables or subjects of these poems are but as certain parts, acts, or special passages of the heroic, which contains the arguments of many tragedies and comedies both, for as Aristotle saith of Homer's *Margites*, I may say of Dametas, Clinias, Braggadocchio, etc., that they are (singled by themselves) the rule and argument of the comedy, as well as Dido, Argalus, and Parthenia of the tragedy. Here, likewise, are those parts of conception and delivery, the same which the former hath, the reason of the whole and his part being one. All must be within one day's efficiency, and you must begin at some principal point of your one act (as Sir Philip Sidney shows in his *Apology*, to whom I refer the reader as to one that hath absolutely delivered the rules to be observed in these two especially abused kinds, for more than all I say), and this single birth grows in proportion till by one turn of the wheel of imagined providence, by one *peripeteia* or change of fortune, it is brought to the issue or *catastrophe*, requiring few and direct *episodia* or additaments in the beginning, bringing the person in, only for some one remarkable error and passion, into a pack of troubles and jeopardy, and then concluding with some notable overthrow and punishment or recovery and contentation.

If it be above one act (though it may be such an act as all a man's fortunes depend on), it cannot in so little a time be represented with those due circumstances that necessarily accompany every such alteration and turn of estate and work it out. It will not be so truth-like, which (according to Aristotle) in this kind must especially be observed, because everything is here drawn to a more palpable delivery and receipt. The main end cannot be wrought – namely, the through discovery of ill guises and affections and their foul fruits and rewards, to stir us up to dislike and shun the like. But our times (as in much else) yield to the grossness of the vulgar, sense-tickled applauses, posting over in the imitation more in one hour or two than many ages could bring about in the true real action. This error of many actions in much time breeds error in the circumstance of place likewise, which confounds the readers and beholders, as at large Sir [46ʳ] Philip Sidney discovers, where Asia is of the one side and Afric on the other, and so many under-kingdoms, that the person acting must ever begin with telling where he is, etc.

Farther, now, these kinds being by action or personating not by narration, the division of them according to the discrete quantity differs likewise from the other of the heroic, and they are cut into acts and scenes (for this the Latins' partition we only choose to follow, as putting sufficient difference between the heroic and our now handled kinds). An act is such a part as comprehends some convenient passage of the device where things are carried in one tenor without evident change, distinguished in the tragedy by the chorus falling between every act, commonly making some application and use of the precedent act; in the comedy this distinction hath been by mimical and clownish representations. Horace commands just five acts. Again, each act is subdivided into scenes, which are distinguished by some change of persons and speakers. Some will

have but ten scenes in one act. If you will precisely order these acts, the first must be a summary uttering of the whole expedition, the second begins the narration or story, as it were, the third brings matters into difficulty, the fourth presents some mischief tending to the catastrophe or conclusion in the fifth, whether sad and unhappy   5
or contentfully pleasant. Thus far jointly, now by the more restrained subjects and ends we will see the mutual differences and properties of these personating kinds.

The subject of the tragedy is matter highly offensive in high persons, his end by fear and compassion to drive men into hatred of those   10
foul affections and manners that bring forth such sad events. And then – as Sir Philip Sidney saith of the tragical estate of Amphialus at his mother's unworthy yet deserved death and his own unmerciful fact upon himself – things are full of danger, the persons full of worthiness, the manner full of horror, evermore the mind is carried up in   15
an astonishing admiration proportioned to our will, that ariseth from   [46ᵛ]
our beholding those hideous dreadful things which in the representation, according to Aristotle, affect us with some kind of pleasure. So as here we see there is no reason to stir wanton affections, since there is so little suitableness and agreement betwixt them and the   20
dreadfulness and commiseration evermore to be maintained in the tragedy, in which are to be represented all the stormy and furious passions with their proper actions, as challenges, defiances, disgraces, fights, battles, murders, massacres, etc. For the style, it must always be high, even insolent for the most part, to suit those violent appre-   25
hensions and motions. The verse, methinks, is best that consists of five feet, and the rhyme each verse immediately returned, though neither always be observed – sometimes breaking verse, sometime missing rhyme, sometime the rhyme crossed, and the French use much a longer metre. But I think, there being so much vehemency   30
and violence in the tragedy, it is more suitable to have the verse hasty and the rhyme quick, answering the passion.

Now for the comedy, his subject is the common, trivial errors, follies, and abuses man's life is liable unto, Tully for this commending it as the glass and mirror of our manners and conversation; the persons   35
are the meanest of our civiller societies; the end by ingenuous mirth and sportfulness to work in men a scorn and hatred of those wayward and gullish affections and demeanours that bring them into difficulties and disgraces. Here, first, Sir Philip Sidney (worthily following Aristotle) puts difference between unchaste scurrility and extreme   40
doltishness on the one side, moving loud laughter, and that seemly

pleasantness and urbanity on the other side that breeds a delightful mirth and teaching delightfulness. And farther (from him), he
plainly forbids stirring laughter in sinful things, which are rather
execrable than ridiculous, or in miserable, which are rather (saith
he) to be pitied than scorned: as gaping at a wretched beggar and   5
beggarly clown that cannot mend his fortune, jesting at strangers,   [47ʳ]
against law of hospitality, for not speaking English as well as we –
these are mere mimical toys, idle barren imitations, without pleasure, without use. Of all things most hateful are the irreligious jests
at religion, for as it is against the law of comedy and received custom   10
(howsoever now countermanded) to represent the errors and follies
of high states and personages, lest the sacred majesty of the places
and dignities become contemptible for those personal faults, so neither must the errors of these high and holy mysteries be profaned
and vilified by vulgar reproaches, because, the case going so near as   15
the conscience of a man, these slips and errors are to be pitied and
tenderly tendered, not scorned and reproached. Neither are Scripture phrases to be caught up and broken into jests in these scornful
imitations, much less that reverent holy name (at the bare mention
whereof every knee should bow, at the least every religious heart do   20
homage) wretchedly torn or tossed, whether in passion or mockery.
But your argument should be the unbecoming forms of behaviour
and fantastical humours men discover in their civil outward guises
and demeanours, such as are seen in a busy courting gallant, in
a heartless threatening Thraso, a self-wise-seeming schoolmaster, a   25
wry-transformed traveller, a smell-feast Gnatho, a niggardly Demea,
a sordid Chremes, a crafty Davus – as Sir Philip Sidney almost fully
reckons them. Now for your style it must be familiar and easy, called
the *mean* or indifferent, grounded on common sayings, proverbs, and
fine plausible allusions. The number must be loose, in prose or very   30
neglected metre. For the action or personating, it nothing belongs to
the poet, as Aristotle seems to say, and if the statesmen and divines
find anything prejudicial to religion or honesty of manners, let them
determine about the lawfulness or unlawfulness of the acting.

   The next species or kind is the pastoral, evermore conversant[47ᵛ]₃₅
about country rustical matters, at the least handling all matters as if
they were no other, imitating virtues and affections as they are seated
in those clownish persons or delivering of the knowledges of those
rustical faculties belonging to the country life, reducing all to the
shepherdish guise: sometimes by conference and personating, with-   40
out much stir or counterfeited action, and then is it the peasant's or

boorish comedy; sometimes by narration or without action, where the
poet himself discourseth in his own person, which may be drawn to
the pastoral lyric; sometime beyond the immediate next sense there
is some higher and hidden meaning signified by those common conceits, which is called the *allegory* or mystical sense, and this is that Sir
Philip Sidney means when he saith the pastoral under the pretty tales
of wolves and sheep includes oftentimes the whole considerations of
wrong-doing and patience, that shows out of Meliboeus' mouth the
miserable people's estate under hard lords or ravening soldiers. The
rules are easily applied if you observe decorum of subject and particular end, which is to delight and teach by the comely simplicity
and homely expressing those low-creeping conceits. The phrase and
style must be the lowest and basest, such as the ploughman, shepherd, gardener, and the like use, yet sometimes Virgil will raise his
quill to a higher note; but I think it should never be above that that
may well be found in some fertile common conceit. The verse and
number may be and best seems to be light and loose, uncuriously
framed or artificially natural.

The satire follows next, consisting in taxing and reproof of the
more gross and foul vices. First, here, I may say of the poet as Quintilian saith of the orator: he should be more disposed and prone to
defend and maintain good than to accuse and impeach the bad. Yet
(saith he) shall he not abhor the name of an accuser so much as for
no respect of public or private duty he can be drawn to call men
'ad reddendam vitae rationem', to give an account of their life and
conversation, but he must not in this summons and arraignment
so proceed as if he were 'poenae nocentium cupidus', desirous of
the shame and disgrace of the offenders, but 'emendandi vitia corrigendique mores', as one that seeks only to correct vice and reform
manners. Neither are all kind of vices to be ripped up, lest the poet
seem to teach whilst he discovers such contagious sores as whose rot-
tenness will spread itself to the annoyance and touch of those are yet
untouched – such of which Quintilian saith 'nimium est quod intelligitur'. And I would our histories were not faulty this way with the
satire. Sometimes the reproof is more sharp and bitter, in the iambic
satire, sometime more gibingly sportful, in the satirical epigram, one
openly and palpably taxing vice, the other covertly and more tenderly
coming over the offence: the one makes the guilty person sweat, the
other blush. The style of the first is crabbed, harsh, and unpleasant,
the phrase almost sordid sometimes; the other's style neglected and
untrimmed but more plausible. The metre of the first may be riding,

5

10

15

20

[48^r]
25

30

35

40

uneven and untoward; of the latter more easy and current and will
best be drawn into a sonnet, which is a proportion of fourteen verses
and suits very well to any such uniform conceit as this is, that is
contrived with a continual dependency of sense till it receive the life
and completeness in the last verses.   5

Now lastly come we to the lyric, to which we assigned a large
jurisdiction, that handles matter of divine, moral, and natural consideration, imitating as well calm as violent affections and passions;
so as it would be too long a career for both (I fear) the wearied reader
and (I am sure) my wearied spirits, and withal somewhat superflu-   10
ous, to prosecute the particulars. Only as the cosmographers gather
the roundness of the body of the waters because every least drop
separated naturally falls into a globe and enrounds itself, upon this
ground, *eadem est ratio partis et totius* – without change of reason I may   [48ᵛ]
turn the argument and infer that this parcel and every smallest parcel   15
of poesy must keep the conditions of the greater and more complete
kinds in a proportion, though not so eminent, because every part
must answer the general reason or nature. And then I say: in the
invention and style still you are to keep proportionableness, variety,
sweetness, and efficacy in every least lyrical epigram. For the rest,   20
I leave the poet to his own observation of the particular end and
subject.

Thus far have we entreated of imitation in style, which is entirely
the poet's. Now it remaineth that we should proceed to that imitation
which admitteth some material object to the discovering the conceit,   25
where some manuary faculty doth join bodily representations, that
may more expressively and gracefully utter the invention of the poet.
And this is by *emblem* and more properly by that noble device of
impresa (especially of use in the court and camp), where the artisan
brings his portraiture as the body, the poet the speech and word   30
as the soul, neither being of use without the other, the body or
picture as a lifeless carcase if it be not informed and actuated by the
word as the spirit, the word as an idle, fantastical air that hath no
sensible existence, that cannot move the sense, unless it be organised
and embodied by some image or superficial portraiture objected to   35
the eye; all taking foundation in the simile or comparison, where
there must be proportional answerableness and sympathy in some
quality or affection betwixt the things representing and the things
represented. But this too large a field for me to ear in, as asking
greater ability and observation than I dare arrogate, I forbear to enter   40
into, especially before one so nobly famous for his accomplished skill

in feats of arms and chivalry – to which profession chiefly this is a
worthy appurtenance – and in this age in which the sweet sunshine
of our blessed peace under the happy reign of a most sacred majesty [49ʳ]
hath gilded so many wits that have brought forth so great plenty of
devices of this kind as for variety, subtlety, and grace of invention 5
they deserve to be conveyed in fame's golden records to all posterity.

Now from these rules to be observed in the art I turn to the artist,
and then I say, if Quintilian will – out of Cato – have the orator
to be a good man as simply necessary to his art, we must needs
look for as much in our poet, ever conversant in matters tending 10
to virtuous action and inward honesty, who proposeth his sugared
meats to unjudicious wits for the most part, and is therefore called the
vulgar philosopher. Indeed, as in natural generation the form must be
first in that that begets or imparteth it to another, so in this begetting
of virtue there must be a virtuous form or habitual form of virtue ere 15
it can be dispensed forth, and it is much what reasons Quintilian, by
the groping light of his barely natural reason, could gather to prove
his orator must be a good man, which are equally at the least appliable
to our poet. They want the life of their writing if they be not taken
with the passionate love or hate of what they would have others love 20
or hate; the intention cannot be great where there is no delight or
affection; and their device and invention must needs fail where the
mind is remiss. Nay, it is impossible (saith Quintilian) but he should
stick and trip in delivery whose words are sent without the counsel
and consent of the mind. And as one saith of behaviour I may say 25
of speech and persuasion: it can never come kindly from the person
whose mind is not proportioned to that he doth outwardly affect.
A cold, speculative knowledge such may deliver, but they, wanting
this sensible impression and feeling stamp of virtue in themselves,
cannot leave that character or efficacy in their style which is the 30
life of persuasion, the very chiefest scope and end of both orator
and poet. Lively and perfect description comes from the thorough
consideration and apprehending the object. Now if any thoroughly in [49ᵛ]
his mind consider and digest the beauty of virtue, he is very too much
sensual that is not touched to the quick with the love of her. Besides, 35
what an indignity it is that themselves should confute in themselves
the power of their so-much-proclaimed powerful faculty in that (like
bad-living preachers, who should be God's orators) the lines of their
life and doctrine run parallel, never meeting together! Surely pity
and shame is it, that these swinish generation be permitted, by their 40
impious reproachful living, to pollute so goodly pearls.

The poet being thus disposed by nature, informed by art, qualified by virtue, let him, in imitating the best, practise with the most, and then surely – not reaching above his height, not striving beyond his force – as Horace saith,

nec facundia deseret hunc nec lucidus ordo.   5

COMMENTARY

Cross-references are in bold and refer to the page and line numbers of the text (e.g. '**4.1–6**') or to the relevant place in the Commentary if suffixed with **n**. (e.g. '**12.4–10n.**'). Verse translations within the text of the *Model* are Scott's.

1.1 The Model of Poesy *Model* was a new word in English, having appeared in French and Italian earlier in the sixteenth century, derived from the post-classical Latin *modellus*. The first printed book to include the word anywhere in its title appeared in 1600 (*STC* 11634), and the first to use it in a sense similar to Scott's was John Yates's *A modell of divinitie* (1622). Its principal meanings when Scott wrote were: (i) a plan or representation of structure (typically architectural, and therefore relating to Scott's recurrent image of his art of poetry as a building); (ii) a likeness, especially on a smaller scale; and (iii) an (exemplary) object of (moral or artistic) imitation. These meanings of course shade into each other, and the latter two are especially close in Sidney's and Scott's poetics of exemplary images. Relevant senses distinguished in the *OED* are illustrated by some early uses in texts of importance for Scott: for the second sense, Shakespeare, *Richard II*, 1.2.28 (*OED*, model, n. and adj., 2a); and for the third, Sidney in *The defence of poesy* on the failure of *Gorboduc* to serve as 'an exact model of all tragedies' (9a, first recorded usage; *DP*, 45), and in the *Arcadia* on the sleeping Pyrocles and Philoclea offering 'a perfect modell of affection' (10, first recorded usage; *NA*, 2L6^r; *OA*, 273), as well as Du Bartas on paradise as a model ('modelle') of the pagan poets' Elysium (9a, in Sylvester's translation; *La seconde sepmaine*, day 1, 'Eden', 53). In Sidney Scott would also have found Philoclea as 'the modell of heaven' (*NA*, E3^r; Skretkowicz, 84), and the analogy in the *Defence* that compares philosophy to an architect's verbal description and poetry to a picture of 'the house... in model' (*DP*, 16). Puttenham, another of Scott's favourite sources, describes his treatment of the figures of rhetoric as 'a new and strange model of this art' (*Art*, 3.10, 243). Scott uses the word within his treatise: the third sense overlapping with the second at **19.38** and **73.20**, the second sense at **40.9**. He also uses the related verb at **11.20** in a Neoplatonic sense, the artist's idea being *modelled* in his mind (on this area of his theory see **15.29–33n.**), and the noun *modeller* at **8.16**, where those who model cannot necessarily move from theory to practice. The sense (*OED*, model, n. and adj., 1б) of an architectural unit of measurement, less relevant in its precise application than in its more general implications, is found in Lomazzo (see **10.15–21n.**), 1.4: '*Proportion is a correspondencie and agreement of the measures of the partes betweene themselves, and with the whole, in every worke.* This correspondencie is by *Vitruvius* called *Commodulation*: because a *modell* [*modulo*] is a measure which beeing taken at the first, measureth both the partes and the whole' (40; Haydocke, c2^r). For this definition of *proportion* cf. **33.31–4n.** In offering a *model*, then, Scott provides an analytical plan of the structure of the discipline of poetry, with an emphasis on the proportionate relation of the parts to the whole, and a depiction of the whole art of poetry that can serve as an ideal template for future poets, if they can put its lessons into practice. See also Introduction, lxix–lxx.

1.5–7 Si quisquam... profitetur suum Terence, *Eunuchus* ('The Eunuch'), prologue, 1–3: 'If there are any who are eager to please as many good men as possible and to offend as few as possible, this man wishes to enrol in their number.' The last line should read 'in his *poeta* hic...' ('... this *poet* wishes to enrol in their number'); Scott probably omitted 'poeta' so that the epigraph could refer to him as author of the *Model*, though it is possible that his scribe omitted it by mistake. Modern editions of Terence (who lived in the second century BC) favour early Latin orthography ('quisquamst... plurumis... minume... suom'), whereas those in Scott's day in effect modernised it to accord with classical Latin: see for example *Pub. Terentii Afri comoediae sex* (Cambridge, 1589) and *Publii Terentii Afri comediae sex* (1597). I have followed Scott and his contemporaries in this practice.

1.8 Ἐκ τοῦ Σκότου ὁ σπινθὴρ 'Out of the darkness the spark [*Ek tou Skotou ho spinthēr*]'. This epigraph appears to be Scott's invention, as its delightful pun (Scott/*Skotou*, darkness), promising us illumination out of Scott, suggests (the capital Σ in the manuscript is unnecessary but is preserved here since it draws attention to the pun). The idea of light coming from darkness has obvious biblical echoes, with analogues in both the Greek New Testament and the Septuagint: e.g. II Corinthians 4:6 ('For God that commaunded the light to shine out of darkenes [*Ek skotous phōs*]...'); Job 37:15 ('Diddest thou knowe when God disposed them? and caused the light [*phōs*] of his cloud [*ek skotous*] to shine?'). The word *spinthēr* is found nowhere in the Greek New Testament but is found with some frequency in the Septuagint: e.g. Isaiah 1:31, Wisdom of Solomon 2:2. The genitive form *skotou* is rare, *skotous* being the norm both in the Bible and in the Church Fathers, again suggesting that the word is being manipulated to point the pun. Plato is an alternative source. In *Cratylus*, Socrates observes, in discussing an etymology, that 'People welcome the daylight that comes out of darkness [*ek tou skotous to phōs*]' (418c–d); and in the allegory of the cave in *Republic*, 7 (514a–520a), the ability to learn and to comprehend the forms is represented through images of light and darkness: see especially 518a, on the temporary blindness of those who come from the darkness into the light ('ek skotous eis phōs'). The epigraph refers squarely to some of Scott's themes: of poetry as what Sidney calls 'the first light-giver to ignorance' (*DP*, 4), and of poetic inspiration as a divine spark or illumination, seen in Scott's discussion of 'these sparks of nature' and his translation of the commonplace from Ovid at **15.8–11** ('A spirit moves within, inflaming us to write, | And this fit takes beginning of th' eternal light'). In suggesting that Scott's methodical *art* of poetry is the source of illumination it relates to a tradition of describing method in terms of (sometimes Promethean) light: see, e.g., Petrus Ramus, *Dialectique* (Paris, 1555), Q4^r.

3.1–3 TO THE RIGHT HONOURABLE... GARTER On Sir Henry Lee (1533–1611) see Introduction, xxxi–xxxiii. Lee was made Knight of the Garter on 23 May 1597

(Chambers, 172). This kind of dedicatory epistle – and its attendant rhetoric – is almost always found in printed books of the period, but less consistently in manuscript works; it might suggest that Scott was preparing the *Model* for printing.

3.4–5 common saying ... adventured upon   The proverbial choice of the lesser of two evils: *ODEP*, 233; Tilley, E 207. In this case the two evils are (i) that of not offering Lee something (**3.10–12**) and (ii) that of the offering being as insignificant as the *Model* (**3.12–17**); the latter is found to be the lesser (**3.23–5**).

3.8–9 the gates of ... judgement   Spatial metaphors were common in ancient and early modern psychology. There was some variation in the scholastic accounts of the mind, but a common formulation identified three interior senses or faculties, concerned respectively with the past (memory), the present (judgement, intelligence), and the future (foresight); for examples with which Scott would be familiar see Cicero, *De inventione*, 2.53.160 and Spenser, *FQ*, 2.9.47–58. Judgement, however, might equally be the product of the combined workings of the various different faculties, and, again, Scott may be thinking of something like Aristotle's 'common sense' (see **6.8n.**).

3.20–1 that noble disposition ... courtier is named   The words *courteous, courtesy, courtier* all derive from *court* (courtiers are those found in courts; courtesy is the label for the model of good behaviour expected in courts). Scott deliberately confuses this etymological relation in order to give the virtue of courtesy greater conceptual stability and priority (courtiers are so called because they embody the virtue of courtesy). Even as Spenser observes, with better logic, that 'Of Court it seemes, men Courtesie doe call, | For that it there most vseth to abound' (*FQ*, 6.1.1.1–2), he still manages to give courtesy priority, the court simply affording the opportunity to give this pre-existent virtue a label. Book 6 of Spenser's *The faerie queene*, printed in 1596, is devoted to the question of the relation of courtesy to courts, at a time when the moral authority of Elizabeth's court – an authority with which Sir Henry Lee had been at least emblematically associated as her champion – was under scrutiny. Scott makes use elsewhere of Baldassare Castiglione's foundational text on the mores, values, and intellectual aspirations of the Renaissance court, *Il cortegiano* (1528), translated by Sir Thomas Hoby as *The courtyer* (1561): see **20.35–21.3n.**, **42.10–13n.**, and **47.29–32**.

3.21–2 much, much more   A Sidneian repetition, possibly lifted directly from the dedicatory epistle to Sidney's *Arcadia*, addressed to Sidney's sister the Countess of Pembroke, whose 'name ... (if much much good will doe not deceive me) is worthie to be a sanctuarie for a greater offender' (*NA*, ¶3ᵛ; *OA*, 3).

3.25 accompted   The archaic form *accompt* retained a separate identity from *account* until the nineteenth century, in technical usages. Although the third edition of *OED* removes the separate entry for *accompt* and merges it with *account*, the form is sufficiently different to warrant preservation here.

3.26–30 the ground young Julius Secundus... than he could An *exordium* is the opening of an oration constructed according to the classical pattern. A *declamation* was a kind of formal oration used in rhetorical education. Scott gives here a close paraphrase of Quintilian, 10.3.12–14, which continues: 'There lies the truth of the whole matter. We must aim at speaking as well as we can, but must not try to speak better than our nature will permit' (10.3.15). Scott thus introduces what will be an important theme: the influence and limitations of a writer's natural abilities. Julius Secundus, Quintilian's 'very dear friend' (10.3.12), came from Gaul and is praised for his oratory in this passage and an earlier one (10.1.120–21); he also features as a character in Tacitus' *Dialogus* (see **24.14–19n.**). He was secretary to Otho (AD 32–69), who was the husband of Poppaea Sabina (see **32.15–19n.**) and briefly emperor in the year of the four emperors.

3.34 modelling On *model*, noun, see **1.1n.** Its verbal usage was even newer than its usage as noun: one other sense in *OED* predates Scott (*OED*, *model*, v., †1), but his usage here predates all other examples cited, including that for the relevant sense (†2, first instanced in 1604).

3.34 first fruits The first products of husbandry in a season, customarily offered to God (see, e.g., Leviticus 2:14, Numbers 18:12). Within the Church, the first fruits were a payment (commonly the first year's income) made by an office holder to his superior, as by a bishop to the Crown. The metaphor is commonly used by young Elizabethan writers offering their labours to a patron or readership: see, e.g., John Florio, *Florio his first fruites* (1578). Scott uses the phrase again at **26.10** and **42.5–6**, and in his letter to Robert Cecil, describing his trip to Russia with Sir Thomas Smythe as 'the first fruites of my reducing my study to matter of accion' (see Appendix 2, 250).

4.1–6 the Corinthians... rare present This anecdote about Alexander the Great (356–323 BC), which Scott somewhat garbles, is found in Plutarch's essay 'On monarchy, democracy, and oligarchy', 2: 'Now the word *politeia* (citizenship) is defined also as "having a share of the rights in a State," as we say the Megarians voted Alexander the *politeia* (citizenship); and when he made fun of their eagerness, they told him that up to that time they had conferred citizenship upon Heracles only and now upon himself. Then Alexander was astonished and accepted the gift, thinking that its rarity gave it value' (*Moralia*, 826c–d). Megara was a city-state near Corinth. Alexander may have visited it towards the start of his reign, when he went to Corinth to summon a meeting of the organisation of Greek allies (the 'League of Corinth') that he now led: see Robin Lane-Fox, *Alexander the Great* (London, 1973), 69. Alexander's family claimed descent from Heracles (Hercules), and he was Alexander's role model.

4.7–8 rareness... precedent Scott may simply be emphasising that these first fruits really are his first, but his point is probably the larger one that this treatment in English of the subject of poetics is almost unpredecented. The precedents for Scott's undertaking were indeed few – principally the vernacular treatises of Gascoigne,

Sidney, Webbe, and Puttenham (see Introduction, xli–xliv). Viperano makes a similar point about the lack of precedents in Latin in the preface to his *De poetica* (1).

4.11–12 craving pardon . . . leave undone   An echo of the general confession from morning prayer in the 1559 *Book of common prayer*: 'We have lefte undone those thinges whiche we ought to have done, and we have done those thinges which we ought not to have done, and there is no health in us: but thou, O Lorde, have mercy upon us miserable offendours' (*BCP*, 103). Cf. Romans 7:15.

4.14 William Scott   The signature in the manuscript is Scott's autograph: 'Will: Scott.'

5.2–36 Because all doctrine . . . understanding and righteousness   In his opening Scott maps out his treatise and makes explicit its logical organisation. He leans heavily on Aristotle and the Aristotelian tradition both for the general outlines of his logical method and for particular details of its exposition. In addition, Scott's method finds a striking parallel in the opening chapters of Lomazzo's *Trattato*, one of his key sources (see **10.15–21n.** and Introduction, l–li). After a preface on 'the excellencie, original, and progresse of painting' (11–21; Haydocke, A1ʳ–4ᵛ), Lomazzo provides a lengthy essay on method, 'The division of the worke' (21–4; A5ʳ–6ʳ), in which he juxtaposes the order of nature (from particulars to universals) and the order of teaching ('l'ordine de la dottrina', from universals to particulars). Because

> our understanding . . . cannot comprehend all the particulars, which are infinite . . . it must beginne with the order of Teaching . . . This Method then proceeding from the universals to the particulars, may easily be understood of us, because our understanding is of that nature that it properly understandeth universals, in so much as the power of our minde is spiritual, and therefore willingly embraceth universall things separated from their matter.   (22–3; A5ᵛ)

Lomazzo then explains that he will begin, not with the first principles of logic and philosophy (*ab ovo*, and Lomazzo himself makes reference to Horace on narrative here; on which see **74.15–16n.**) but (*in medias res*) with the definition of painting, and examination of it by the predicables of genus, species, and difference. Book 1 then opens with a definition and an account of this by genus (= matter) and difference (= form). Its genus is that it is an art, its difference that it represents three-dimensional objects on a plane, and by representing actions and gestures expresses the affections and passions of the mind (25–8; B1ʳ–2ᵛ). In his second chapter Lomazzo proceeds to the division of painting, and from this analysis follows each of the remaining six books. Scott did not learn his logic from Lomazzo, but he took from him a clear example of how to apply it. Lomazzo only fails to set Scott on his way by not viewing painting clearly in terms of its purpose, as Scott, following Scaliger and Sidney, must do for poetry. Scott's, and Lomazzo's, emphasis on the order of teaching or *ordo doctrinae* ('all doctrine is but the orderly leading of the mind', **5.2**; 'if we will proceed orderly', **5.24**) reflects current debates about the relation between enquiry and teaching in the arts and sciences, and notably the influence of the Italian Aristotelian philosopher and logician Jacopo Zabarella (1533–89). Cf. also Viperano's complaint that Horace 'nullum ordinem doctrinae tenuit' ('followed no order of teaching'; my translation) in the preface to his *De poetica* (3–4).

5.2–5 doctrine . . . ignorance and science   Scott's opening sentence is full of words whose meaning has shifted: *doctrine* means (the act of) teaching (*OED*, †1a, 2); *convenient* means appropriate, fitting (*OED*, *convenient*, adj. and n., †3a, †4); *discipline* is instruction (*OED*, *discipline*, n., †1a); and *science* is knowledge (*OED*, *science*, 2).

5.5–10 clew of discipline . . . mazy paths   The image of the labyrinth was a common one in Scott's day both for life and for objects of understanding or enquiry. See, for example, Du Bartas on those who forego the guidance of faith and scripture (*La sepmaine*, day 1, 87–8), as translated by Scott: 'Whil'st of a pure chast vergin they forsake the thredde | Blynde guides, themselves with others theye in Mazes leade' (Add. MS 81083, 54ᵛ); and Scott's letter to Cecil, which offers 'a Clew to leade yowr Lordshippe oute of the Darke Laberynth toward the light' (Appendix 2, 251).

5.6–16 make this passage by certain degrees . . . derived from them   Compare the opening of Aristotle's *Physics*, the model here for both Lomazzo (who cites it, 22; Haydocke, A5ʳ) and Scott: we must start 'from the things which are more clear and knowable to us' and 'advance from universals to particulars' (184a–b). Scott's theory of knowledge is Aristotelian in its distinguishing of universals and particulars. *De anima* treats how we form concepts from sense impressions and the *Prior analytics* and *Posterior analytics* discuss the connection of these abstracted concepts by logical inference to form knowledge. On the distinction between arguments from particulars to universals (induction) and from universals to particulars (deduction or argument by syllogism) see *Posterior analytics*, 1.1, noting that the universals are proved rather than established in a process of induction: 'All teaching and all intellectual learning come about from already existing knowledge' (71a); cf. *Nicomachean ethics*, 1139b, on induction. Scott's Aristotelian method would be overtaken in the course of the next century by Bacon's scientific induction, but it is not at the time at which he writes outmoded, and indeed the elegance of its statement makes this a rhetorically as well as intellectually powerful opening.

5.18 frame of knowledge   On a special sense of *frame* see **7.10–14n**.

5.21–3 we therefore are taught . . . deliver the knowledge of   Plato and Aristotle stand here for a tradition of logic and rhetoric. On beginning an argument with definition see Cicero, *De inventione*, 2.17.53 and 2.18.55. This advice was repeated by Thomas Wilson in *The rule of reason* (1551): 'When we go about to expound any matter, first we must beginne with the definition, to know the very nature of the thing, the whiche we cannot do, except we first learne the predicables' (B4ᵛ); 'There is nothyng in all this whole art of logique more necessarie for man to know, than to learne diligentlye the definition, and division of everye matter that by reason maye be comprehended. For he that firste well understandeth what he doth go about . . . shall lesse erre in the whole discourse folowing' (D7ᵛ). Quintilian, in his discussion of definition, gives the sample definition of rhetoric itself (5.10.54); Cicero does the same with civil law (*Topica*, 2.9). This will only have encouraged Scott to put such emphasis on his definition of poetry. Scott's basic education in logic would have been centred on Aristotle. On the necessity of beginning an art with a definition of its end cf. Jacopo Zabarella's commentary on Aristotle's *Posterior analytics*: *In duos Aristotelis libros posteriores analyticos commentarii* (Venice, 1582), A2ᵛ.

5.24–31 we must proceed . . . every subdivided part and member   Cicero treats definition by division or enumeration in *Topica*, 5.28–8.34, and cf. the second book of Thomas Blundeville's *The art of logike* (1599) for a treatment of definition and division contemporary with the *Model* (47–55). For definitions by genus and species see Cicero, *Orator*, 33.116–17; *De partitione oratoria*, 12.41; *Topica*, 2.9, 3.11, 5.26–9. In traditional Aristotelian logic the kinds of statement about things that one might make (predicates) were organised into five classes known as the predicables or, as Thomas Wilson calls them, the 'common words' (*Rule of reason*, B4ʳ); without them, as Blundeville says, 'no true Definition nor good Division can be well made' (47). Aristotle (*Topica*, 1.4–5, 101b–102b) recognised four: *genus, definition, property, accident*. Quintilian, in his account of definition, gives Scott's four, genus ('the general'), species ('the particulars'), difference ('special differences'), and property ('properties'): 'For example, if you wish to define a horse . . . the *genus* is animal, the *species* mortal, the *difference* irrational (since man is also mortal) and the *property* neighing' (Quintilian, 7.3.3; cf. 5.10.53–64). In the later scholastic tradition, following Porphyry's *Isagoge* ('Introduction', third century AD), a fifth predicable – Aristotle's *accident* – was added: in Porphyry's example – man is a rational animal capable of laughing – animal is genus, man species, rational a difference, laughing a property, and white, black, sitting would be accidents (2.21–2: see Porphyry, 4). The predicables are omitted in Ramist logic, though a Ramistic account of definition is still close to Scott, especially in eliding species and difference: 'A perfect Definition or setting foorth of a thing, is that, which is made of the whole kinde or generall, and the proper difference of that severall sort which is defined, where the first part is called the generall, the other the proper or special difference' (Dudley Fenner, *The artes of logike and rhetorike* (1584), B3ᵛ). But all five predicables are still given in traditional treatises contemporary with the *Model*, such as Blundeville (5–11), and Wilson's earlier *Rule of reason* (B4ᵛ–5ʳ). Scott's logic is traditional, and may have been revised by consultation of Quintilian rather than the logicians. In thinking of poetics as a building Scott may be following Cicero, *De oratore*, 1.35.161–3, where the image is used for a body of rhetorical theory, but the image is commonplace. The definition of a house was a common example in Aristotelian logic: see, e.g., *Parts of animals*, 639b and 646b, and Blundeville, 49–50.

5.32–3 which of the kinds . . . most apt for   Cf. Viperano, 1.18 (62), building on Horace, *Ars poetica*, 38–40, on evaluating our talents and suiting our efforts to them.

Scott later makes an apparently opposite point, that we should avoid 'the common error . . . that we restrain not our liking and commendations to so much only as we ourselves can best attain unto' (see **75.40–76.2n.**).

5.33 period . . . scope (i) *period*: endpoint, outcome, goal (*OED*, *period*, n., †11, †12); (ii) *scope*: target, goal (*OED*, *scope*, n.², †1a, 2a, 3a).

5.34–6 reduce man . . . righteousness *Reduce*: lead back, restore (*OED*, *reduce*, v., †6). Scott is probably offering 'moral and civil happiness' not as the totality of what was lost at the Fall, but as a part of it. The idea that learning could reverse at least some of the effects of the Fall was common to Renaissance humanists, and a necessary stage in any attempt to reconcile classical learning with Christianity. Compare John Milton, *On Education* (1644): 'The end then of learning is to repair the ruins of our first parents by regaining to know God aright, and out of that knowledge to love him, to imitate him, to be like him, as we may the neerest by possessing our souls of true vertue, which being united to the heavenly grace of faith makes up the highest perfection' (*Complete Prose Works*, II (New Haven, 1959), 366–7). Cf. Sidney: 'This purifying of wit, this enriching of memory, enabling of judgement, and enlarging of conceit, which commonly we call learning, under what name soever it come forth, or to what immediate end soever it be directed, the final end is to lead and draw us to as high a perfection as our degenerate souls, made worse by their clayey lodgings, can be capable of' (*DP*, 12). A possible source for Scott, if one is needed, is Vives (whom he paraphrases at **70.29–71.7**), who states frequently his position that through learning we 'are restored to humanity, and raised towards God Himself' (*Vives on education*, 6; preface to *De disciplinis libri XX* (Cologne, 1536), $_\pi$2A3^v).

6.1–4 All antiquity . . . move us to good Aristotle does not define poetry in the *Poetics* but proceeds immediately to divide it: its genus is *mimesis* or imitation; the differences that distinguish its various kinds are differences of object, medium, and mode. He does, however, give a famous definition of tragedy which offers a model for Scott's definition: 'a tragedy is a *mimēsis* of a high, complete action . . . in speech pleasurably enhanced . . . in dramatic, not narrative form, effecting through pity and fear the *catharsis* of such emotions' (1449b24–8). Horace also omits a definition, although something resembling Scott's definition of poetry, with its didactic emphasis, can better be inferred in his case than in Aristotle's. The same can be said of many sixteenth-century continental critics, including Scaliger: most of the components of Scott's definition are found spread through his opening chapter. Scott's principal example is Sidney, whose definition he builds upon (by adding, following Aristotle's example above, reference to style) and quotes: 'Poesy, therefore, is an art of imitation, for so Aristotle termeth it in the word *mimēsis*, that is to say, a representing, counterfeiting, or figuring forth – to speak metaphorically, a speaking picture – with this end: to teach and delight' (*DP*, 10). Book 3 of Diomedes' *Artis grammaticae libri tres* (late fourth century AD), devoted to poetry, opens with an influential definition, which, however, very evidently lacks the reference to imitation: 'Poetica est fictae veraeve narrationis congruenti rythmo ac pede conposita metrica structura ad utilitatem voluptatemque accommodata. distat autem poetica a poemate et poesi, quod poetica ars ipsa intellegitur, poema autem pars operis, ut tragoedia, poesis contextus et corpus totius operis effecti, ut Ilias Odyssia Aeneis' (Keil, I, 473: 'Poetic is the metrical arrangement of a narration, either fictitious or true, agreeing in rhythm and foot and suited to both use and pleasure. There is a difference between poetic, poem, and poetry, for by poetic we mean the art itself, but by poem we mean a part of a work, like a tragedy, and by poetry a continuous and more entire body of completed work, like the *Iliad, Odyssey*, or *Aeneid*'). For teaching and delighting see Horace (*Ars poetica*, 333–44) and Scaliger (1b2; Padelford, 2). Sidney had completed the analogy to the three aims of classical rhetoric (*docere, delectare, movere* – teach, delight, move: e.g. Quintilian, 3.5.2) by stressing poetry's ability to move. His definition itself, however, refers only to teaching and delighting. Tasso (*Discorsi*, 1594, in Gilbert, 467) was to argue that since a thing could not have two ends without one being subservient to the other, the end of poetry was to teach. Others dared to follow the less frequented classical path and argue that the end was delight: see **26.3–4n**. Scott manages to fit all three aims into his definition, and he also clarifies that we are to be taught and moved to *good*. Of those works of Renaissance poetics that give a definition Viperano is typical, and has the three components that Scott expands upon: 'poetry is rightly defined as the art which imitates the actions of men in rhythmical language in order to teach them to live' (3). Scott's definition is in part a definition of the art of poetry (i.e. poetics) rather than the practice ('an instrument of reason, that consists in laying down the rules and way how in style to feign or represent things'), leaning on the distinction between poetic, poetry, and poem in Diomedes above, and ubiquitous in sixteenth-century criticism (e.g. Viperano, 1.6, 17). For the Aristotelian definition of *art* (Greek *technē*) see **7.10–14n**. Aristotle's definition of *art* as 'a state concerned with making, involving a true course of reasoning' (*Nicomachean ethics*, 1140a) lies behind Scott's 'instrument of reason'. Lomazzo also emphasises that painting is 'an instrument [*instrumento*] of the *memory*, of the *understanding*, and of the *will*' (16; Haydocke, A2^v).

6.5–7 Simonides ... speechless poem   Sidney uses the phrase 'speaking picture' twice only (*DP*, 10, as quoted at **6.1–4n.**, and 16), but the first occasion is in his definition of poetry and the idea is clearly central to his poetics of exemplary images. Scott's attribution of the dictum 'poetry is speaking painting and painting silent poetry' to the poet Simonides (mid-sixth to mid-fifth centuries BC) follows Plutarch (*Moralia*, 346f; cf. *De audiendis poetis, Moralia*, 17f–18a). Scott would have been reminded of Simonides' saying by Viperano's discussion of it and its implications in his opening chapter (4); it also figures in Puttenham, 3.19 (*Art*, 293), as an example of antimetabole (after *Ad Herennium*, 4.28.39).

6.8 common sense and fancy   Two of the faculties in traditional psychology (cf. **3.8–9n.**). *Fancy* (a contraction of *fantasy*) is another word for the imagination (Greek *phantasia*), the part of the mind that processes mental images. The *common sense* (Aristotle's *koinē aisthēsis*, translated by Aquinas as *sensus communis*) receives the sense impressions from the five external senses and is sometimes equated with what Scott earlier calls 'judgement' (see **3.8–9n.**). See, for example, Robert Burton in *The anatomy of melancholy* (1621), 1.1.2.7: '*Inner Senses*, are three in number, so called because they be within the braine-panne, as *Common Sense, Phantasie, Memorie* . . . This common sense is the Judge or Moderator of the rest, by whom we discerne all differences of obiects; for by mine eye I doe not know that I see, or by mine eare that I heare, but by my common Sense, who judgeth of Sounds, and Colours' (Burton, I, 152). The later sense of *common sense* as natural understanding or plain wisdom was in evidence at this date but is not in play here.

6.8–10 images . . . misguided by passion   Scott quite elliptically introduces two key ideas. The first is whether the poet (or other artist) only imitates reality ('works of nature') or may represent things that do not exist ('works of . . . reason'). This distinction, between *ens reale* (the world of actually extant objects) and *ens rationis* (the realm of conceptual objects known only to thought), has a long history in logic and metaphysics reaching back to Aristotle. The second idea is the moral status of the poet or artist: virtuous rather than misled by passion, Scott hopes; see further **82.7–41**. The terminology of 'images' draws on Sidney as well as Viperano, e.g.: 'the poet . . . fashions images [*imagines*] out of what has never happened and makes the images of what has happened more beautiful' (Viperano, 1.2, 15/8).

6.11–14 the one counterfeits . . . life and actions   Cf. Viperano, 1.5: 'the good poet creates fictional actions in order to demonstrate mores, just as the good painter depicts the features of a face in order to express the disposition of the heart' (15). Scott is also thinking in the terms he has borrowed from Lomazzo: cf. **10.16** on the painter's ability to express 'the inward affections by the outward motions'.

6.14–15 Petrarch . . . sing   Petrarch, *Rime*, 308.7: 'I have often tried in vain to depict in song [*pinger cantando*] for the age to come her high beauties, that it may love and prize them, nor with my style can I incarnate her lovely face' (Durling). Scott changes the infinitive 'pinger[e]' to third-person plural 'pingono', with an elision to preserve the metrics of the quoted fragment.

6.16–18 Horace . . . same thing   The tag *ut pictura poesis* has often stood as a shorthand for the analogy between poetry and painting that is so central to the *Model*. Though Horace at the outset of the *Ars poetica* (1–13) develops the analogy in terms of fictive licence, this particular passage (361–5) is concerned with a very specific comparison: 'A poem is like a picture: one strikes your fancy more, the nearer you stand; another, the farther away. This courts the shade, that will wish to be seen in the light, and dreads not the critic insight of the judge. This pleased but once; that, though ten times called for, will always please.'

6.18–24 so much more worthy . . . thereupon inferred   In setting poetry against painting Scott mimics the *paragone* (comparison), a format popular in Italian Renaissance art theory, in which rival visual arts would be compared (painting versus sculpture), or the claims to supremacy of painting would be weighed against those of music or poetry. Always, as here, the question was which art form could better imitate nature. Lomazzo quotes at length from Leonardo's *paragone* of painting and sculpture (138–40; Haydocke, 2E6^v–2F1^r).

6.20 scope   Target, aim, purpose, theme (*OED, scope*, n.^{2}, †1, 2, 3).

6.28–9 the fittest illustration... practice approves   The analogy runs through the *Poetics*: for example when Aristotle observes of figure painters that 'though they make people lifelike they represent them as more beautiful than they are' (1454b9–11), and most famously in Aristotle's discussion of plot as more important than character, 'a relation similar to one we find in painting, where the most beautiful colours, if smeared at random, would give less pleasure than an uncoloured outline that was a picture of something' (1450a39–b3; see **38.15–20n.**). For Aristotle's related discussion of character depiction at 1448a see **11.38–12.4n**. Cicero also makes frequent use of the analogy between the language arts and the visual arts: see, e.g., *Orator*, 11.36, 19.65, 50.169. See also Quintilian, 12.10.1–9.

6.32–7 these three parts... dependeth   The procedure of definition by genus and difference here shades into the Aristotelian theory of causes. Scott follows the scholastic tradition in equating genus with matter (*hulē*) and difference with form (*eidos*): see Porphyry, *Isagoge*, 11.13–17 (Porphyry, 11, with commentary at 194–5). Compare Quintilian, 5.10.62, after Cicero, *Topica*, 3.13 and 7.30, where *forma* is Cicero's preferred word for species or *eidos*. Matter and form map on to two of Aristotle's four causes (*Metaphysics*, 1013a): the material cause (what something is made of) and the formal cause (what its form is). The treatment of end equates to Aristotle's final cause (the *telos* or goal of a thing); only the efficient cause (what makes it happen) is omitted from Scott's three-part procedure, and as Scaliger (6a1) and Lomazzo (18; Haydocke, A3^v) point out, that is the artist himself. The two kinds of definition are neighbours in, for example, Blundeville's *Art of logike*. He gives six kinds of definition, beginning with the essential and the causal. The essential consists of a statement of genus 'joyned with some speciall difference or property'; the causal definition uses one or more of Aristotle's four causes (48). For definitions concerned with *telos* or end see Quintilian, 2.15.38, 2.17.22, 3.1.1, and 5.10.54 (noting that the concept of end, *finis*, is contained in the term *definition*). Definition by genus, difference and end is also a procedure followed by Richard Wills in *De re poetica* (1573), although unlike Scott he does not make it explicit that this is what he is doing or that he is following any particular logical (or methodological) prescription. Wills lifts directly from Scaliger's first chapter, but in removing much of the detail makes the expository structure much more visible: poetry is language (genus) more ornate than that of philosophers and statesman (difference), imitating both actual and possible things (difference) with the aim of teaching pleasingly (end): Wills, 50–2. Scaliger also plays with these categories: the poem is matter, poetry is form; the poet is then the efficient cause, giving us three causes, and the final cause is either imitation or teaching (5d2–6a1). For a more recently printed analogue, though dating from the 1550s, see Benedetto Varchi's *Lezzioni* (Florence, 1590), defining poetry by 'genere, come materia' (*'genus*, as matter'), 'differenza, come forma' (*'difference*, as form'), and end (2N5^{r-v}).

6.38–41 genus . . . some good end Scott is following Quintilian, who discusses at length whether rhetoric is an art at 2.17. He sticks close to Quintilian in moving on to discuss whether poetry (in Quintilian's case eloquence) owes most to art or to nature (2.19); see **8.36–7n.** Cf. also Cicero's discussion of whether oratory is an art in *De oratore*, esp. 1.22.102–24.110 and 2.7.30–8.33, and Scott on the limits of rules, **29.37–40**. For 'art' and 'instrument of reason' see **6.1–4n.** and **7.10–14n.**

7.1 quintessence . . . conceits (i) *Quintessence*: 'the most essential part or feature of some non-material thing' (*OED*, *quintessence*, n., 3a); (ii) *nice*: precise, pedantic; (iii) *conceit*: mind or thought.

7.2–6 high treason . . . meanest handmaids Scott's personifications draw generally on the iconographic tradition of representing the various arts and may be prompted by Sidney's reference to Boethius' dialogue between himself and 'mistress Philosophy' (*DP*, 24) in *Consolation of philosophy*, which itself made 'Dame Philosophy' proverbial. The *free* or *liberal arts* were the subjects of study thought worthy of a free man, numbering seven in the medieval university: the *trivium* (grammar, logic, rhetoric) and the more advanced *quadrivium* (arithmetic, geometry, music, and astronomy). A grounding in all was thought essential to further, more specialised study. The *liberal sciences* were often a synonym for the liberal arts (*OED*, *science*, n., 3a), though the phrase was in Scott's day being used of kinds of learning more generally. The use of *science* to denote Aristotle's *epistēmē*, scientific knowledge (*Nicomachean ethics*, 1139b) as opposed to *technē*, art (see **6.1–4** and **7.10–14**) is first recorded by *OED* as late as 1678 (*OED*, *science*, n., 3b) but something like that sense may also be implicit in Scott's jest, from what follows.

7.10–14 if by art . . . civil life Referring to the definition of art (Greek *technē*) in *Nicomachean ethics* as 'a state [*hexis*] concerned with making, involving a true course of reasoning' (1140a; see also **6.1–4n.**), but also eliding it with the definition of practical wisdom (*phronēsis*) as 'a true and reasoned state of capacity to act with regard to the things that are good or bad for man' that immediately follows (1140b). And cf. also Quintilian, citing the Stoic philosopher Cleanthes: 'Art is a power reaching its ends by a definite path, that is, by ordered methods' (2.17.41). Aristotle's *Rhetoric* was one work to use the term *technē* in its customary Greek title (*Technē rhētorikē*; *Ars rhetorica* in Latin versions of the title), and the 'stream' that follow Aristotle include those especially who contribute to the art of rhetoric, with its obligations to 'civil life'. In poetics, Horace's 'Epistle to the Pisos' came to be known as the *Ars poetica*, and variations on that title were also given to Latin translations of and commentaries on Aristotle's *Poetics*. Scott might have been reminded of these backgrounds by Quintilian, 2.17.14, who points out that Aristotle 'wrote three books on the art of rhetoric [*de arte rhetorica tris libros scripsit*], in the first of which he not merely admits that rhetoric is an art, but treats it as a department of politics and also of logic'. For a contemporary association of *art/technē* with the word *frame* (**7.12**) see Alexander Richardson, *The logicians schoolmaster* (1629), 13 and 15. That an art should have an end, and that the end should be good, was commonplace: see Aristotle, *Nicomachean ethics*, 1.1 (1094a), as well as the discussion of *ars* in one of Scott's sources, Vives' *De disciplinis*, which shares Scott's Aristotelian emphasis on 'experience' and civic utility (*Vives on education*, 22–7; on Scott's use of Vives see **70.29–71.7n.**). For art and *praxis* see further **20.24–5n.** and **70.15–16n.**

7.16–18 they who . . . inspired force   The doctrine of the *furor poeticus* was influentially stated by the Florentine Platonist Cristoforo Landino in the preface to his 1481 commentary on Dante's *Divine comedy*, to which Sidney refers in passing at the end of the *Defence* (*DP*, 53). See Landino, *Comento sopra la Comedia*, ed. Paolo Procaccioli, 4 vols. (Rome, 2001), I, 259–60. Sidney himself had rejected this idea: Plato, he says, 'attributeth unto poesy more than myself do, namely to be a very inspiring of a divine force far above men's wit' (*DP*, 40). Viperano is another to reject it (10). Plato describes the madness by which the poet is possessed by the Muses in *Phaedrus* (245a), but the main line of Neoplatonic thought about poetic inspiration derives from the *Ion*, a misreading as Scott is aware, insofar as that dialogue aims at discrediting the claims to knowledge of the rhapsode, a professional reciter of poetry, and its arguments are created almost entirely for that aim. Homer, Socrates argues, was possessed by the Muses, and Ion the rhapsode, like a link in a magnetised metal chain, is possessed at second hand by the same inspiration (*Ion*, 533d–536d). Plato's criticisms of poetry in Book 10 of the *Republic* depend upon a different view of it: far from being 'only a divine fury, or inspired force' it is a merely imitative art that cannot therefore tell the truth about things. Cicero's passing mentions of the *furor poeticus* in *De oratore* (2.46.194) and the *Tusculan disputations* (1.26.64), the latter picked up by Webbe (*ECE*, I, 231–2) and thence by Meres (*ECE*, II, 313), added to its authority even for those suspicious of the idea (e.g. Wills, 72–6). The most convinced Elizabethan account is Thomas Lodge's in his reply to Gosson of 1579: for Lodge, fury means inspiration by God, and that means that all poetry has a good purpose, even if large amounts of allegoresis are required to render it ('A defence of poetry', *ECE*, II, esp. 71–2). Horace's ridicule of those poets who wish to be thought mad (*Ars poetica*, 295–301; see **8.18–23n.**) persuaded most, but the idea of the *furor* could still be eloquently opposed to a perceived excess of art, as in Chapman's judgement: '*Homers* Poems were writ from a free furie, an absolute and full soule: *Virgils* out of a courtly, laborious, and altogether imitatorie spirit' (*Achilles shield* (1598), A2ᵛ).

7.24–7 poesy is a thing . . . I know not when   The views about poetry that Scott parodies here are first found in the earliest Greek poets, predating the first prose writing about poetry. For poetic inspiration see Homer, *Iliad*, 2.484–93 and *Odyssey*,

8.477–99, and Hesiod, *Theogony*, esp. 22–34. For poetry as teacher see Aristophanes' *Frogs*.

7.27–32 I will deal Plato-like . . . our art   Scott here parodies the Socratic method of Platonic dialogue, with its questions and answers representing open discussion even as it moves towards its prejudged conclusions. Scott's use of 'Platonic' as a noun predates the first recorded usage in *OED* (from 1605: *OED*, *Platonic*, adj. and n., B1), but cf. Puttenham, 1.1 (93) and Haydocke (e.g. 2M4ʳ) for other examples.

7.34–9 divine seed . . . midwifery of reason   The imagery possibly alludes to Plato's model of learning as the bringing to light of latent (even innate) knowledge through a process of dialectical questioning that Socrates compares to an art of midwifery (*technē tēs maieutikēs*): *Theaetetus*, 161e, with the major part of the discussion at 148e–151c. For the 'divine seed', however, cf. the lines from Ovid that Scott quotes and translates at **15.8–11**.

7.38 disposed   Arranged (as by rhetorical art, *dispositio*).

8.2–6 the matter or substance . . . suitable and decent   This recapitulation of the question-and-answer of **7.32–8.1** makes clear that the three stages of rhetorical composition, invention, arrangement, and elocution (*inventio, dispositio, elocutio*), lie behind this passage (on these cf. **33.17–20n.**). *Decent* (8.6) means in accordance with the rules of decorum; on this technical usage cf. Puttenham, especially 3.23 (*Art*, 347–60). Although Scott elsewhere applies decorum to the matter of a poem (**33.31–36.33**) here the 'habiliments' (**8.5**) and 'apparel' (**7.39**) are only verbal, as at **57.16–58.13**.

8.6–8 I grant . . . a poet?   On poets 'born so' see **8.38–9.1n.**

8.9–13 in every art . . . poesy especially   See Viperano, 1.3 ('Concerning the poet'), concluding: 'We therefore seek this kind of poet and artist: one prepared by nature, educated by art, perfected by experience and imitation of the greatest geniuses, and finally one endowed with some divine and heavenly impulse. Such a one will be distinguished among all not only by human ability but by divinity' (11). Scott borrows from this passage in his conclusion, **83.1–2**.

8.11–12 habit . . . into being   The older senses of *habit* meaning dress or appearance, as in Scott's 'livery or habit' (see **12.22**, **13.22**, and **63.30n.**), were in Scott's day being supplemented by senses derived from scholastic philosophy: bodily condition or constitution (*OED*, *habit*, n., 5a, first recorded usage 1576); mental constitution or character (8, *c.*1385); custom or settled tendency to act in a certain way (9a, 1581); etc. The sense of Latin *habitus* as an acquired state or condition of mind or body is explained by Cicero (*De inventione*, 1.25.36), and that Latin term was the usual translation after Aquinas of Aristotle's *hexis*, a condition or disposition which is distinguished from others by being acquired or by involving activity. The word features in Aristotle's definitions of *technē* and *phronēsis*, which Scott glances at above (see **7.10–14n.**), and Scott's contrast between natural 'disposition' and active 'habit' derives from Aristotle's between *diathesis* and *hexis* (*Metaphysics*, 1022b).

8.18–23 Horace saith . . . docebo   Scott quotes and translates *Ars poetica*, 306. This passage follows Horace's satirical discussion of the *furor poeticus*, 295–301: because Democritus believes native talent more important than art, Horace says, and excludes sane poets from Helicon (i.e. from inspiration by the Muses), many act mad and keep themselves unkempt in order to win a reputation as a poet. Horace then continues: 'Yet it's not worth while. So I'll play a whetstone's part, which makes steel sharp, but of itself cannot cut. Though I write naught myself, I will teach the poet's office and duty; whence he draws his stores; what nurtures and fashions him; what befits him and what not; whither the right course leads and whither the wrong' (303–9).

8.26–9 as Amyntas . . . Amore   From Torquato Tasso's pastoral drama, *Aminta* (1580/1), 1.2 (ll. 437–8). In Abraham Fraunce's translation into quantitative metre: 'And [I] was a lover afore that I knew what t'was to be loving' (*The Countesse of Pembrokes Yvychurch* (1591), B4ᵛ). See further **18.4–5n.**, as well as a second quotation at **17.4–7.**

8.31–3 It is enough . . . perfited by art   Cf. Horace, *Ars poetica*, 408–11, quoted and translated by Scott at **10.27–36**. Lines 409–11 are quoted by Viperano (1.3, 10) in the short chapter from which Scott draws immediately above (**8.9–13n.**).

8.33 perfited   This is the form found in the manuscript. *OED* records it only in the spelling history of *perfect* (*OED*, *perfect*, adj., n., and adv., Forms; Etymology), observing that the Anglo-Norman form *parfit*, *perfit* was 'in later use remodelled after classical Latin *perfectus*' and that '*perfect* became the usual spelling from the late 16th cent. (although it took longer for pronunciations with /k/ to become fully established)'. This would indicate that both in pronunciation and etymology Scott's word was as given here, and should be distinguished from *perfected*, the obvious modernisation.

8.36–7 as Quintilian . . . peremptory terms   Quintilian, 2.19.1. Scott has this section of the *Institutio oratoria* open in front of him, since he continues to refer to and borrow from it in this and the following paragraph. It is worth quoting the whole section:

I quite realise that there is a further question as to whether eloquence derives most from nature or from education. This question really lies outside the scope of our inquiry, since the ideal orator must necessarily be the result of a blend of both. But I do regard it as of great importance that we should decide how far there is any real question on this point. For if we make an absolute divorce between the two, nature will still be able to accomplish much without the aid of education, while the latter is valueless without the aid of nature. If, on the other hand, they are blended in equal proportions, I think we shall find that the average orator owes most to nature, while the perfect orator owes more to education.

We may take a parallel from agriculture. A thoroughly barren soil will not be improved even by the best cultivation, while good land will yield some useful produce without any cultivation; but in the case of really rich land cultivation will do more for it than its own natural fertility. Had Praxiteles attempted to carve a statue out of a millstone, I should have preferred a rough block of Parian marble to any such statue. On the other hand, if the same artist had produced a finished statue from such a block of Parian marble, its artistic value would owe more to his skill than to the material. To conclude, nature is the raw material for education: the one forms, the other is formed. Without material art can do nothing, material without art does possess a certain value, while the perfection of art is better than the best material.   (2.19.1–3)

The relation between natural capacity and art in oratory had also been a key concern of Cicero's *De oratore*: see, e.g., 1.25.113–15, 2.20.85–9.

8.38–9.1 *orator fit* . . . poet born so   Compare Sidney in his digression on the state of poetry in England towards the end of the *Defence* (*DP*, 43): 'A poet no industry can make, if his own genius be not carried into it, and therefore is it an old proverb – *orator fit, poeta nascitur*' (*DP*, 43). On the proverb in Elizabethan literary criticism and elsewhere see William Ringler, '*Poeta nascitur non fit*: some notes on the history of an aphorism', *JHI*, 2 (1941), 497–504. Ringler traces it back to Pseudo-Acro's commentary on Horace's *Ars poetica*, 295–8 (on this passage in Horace see **8.18–23n.**).

9.3–4 I say, with Horace . . . in spite of nature   *Ars poetica*, 385: 'Tu nihil invita dices faciesve Minerva' ('But *you* will say nothing and do nothing against Minerva's will'). Cicero explains in *De officiis*, a text Scott would doubtless have read at school, that *invita Minerva* means 'in direct opposition to one's natural genius' (1.31.110). For a lengthier gloss see Erasmus, *Adagia*, 1.1.42. Cf. Viperano, 1.18 (62), and Sidney: 'taking upon us to be poets in despite of Pallas' (*DP*, 43).

9.5–6 Praxiteles . . . never be polished   A misreading of Quintilian 2.19.3 (see **8.36–7n.**). Quintilian is only putting a hypothetical, and it concerns a millstone (*molaris lapis*), not 'slate or chalk'.

9.8–15 Consider then . . . meetly well relished   Paraphrasing Quintilian 2.19.2 (see **8.36–7n.**); *beachy mould*: stony soil.

9.22–4 Sir Philip Sidney . . . professors of learning   Referring to Sidney's discussion of the stylistic shortcomings of his contemporaries, part of the *Defence*'s digression on English literature: 'Undoubtedly (at least to my opinion undoubtedly), I have found in divers smally learned courtiers a more sound style than in some professors of learning, of which I can guess no other cause but that the courtier, following that which by practice he findeth fittest to nature, therein (though he know it not) doth according to art, though not by art; where the other, using art to show art and not to hide art (as in these cases he should do), flieth from nature and indeed abuseth art' (*DP*, 51).

9.28 all in all   See *OED*, *all*, phrases, P11b, 'all in all': 'All things in all respects; all things altogether in one; everything.'

9.28–33 since the time . . . Eden   See Genesis 2:8–3:24. For the relation of learning to the Fall see **5.34–6n.**

9.33–8 Philosophers prove . . . fighting men in it   Aristotle discusses growth as a combination of internal and external factors in *On generation and corruption*, e.g. 321b–322a; cf. *Generation of animals*, 735a. He discusses the long life of elephants in, e.g., *On length and shortness of life*, 466a, and *History of animals*, 546b and 578a. A more important source here is probably Pliny, 8.1.1–13.35 (castles: 8.7.22 and 8.9.27; adult life begins at 60: 8.10.28), perhaps mediated or supplemented by Conrad Gessner, *Historiae animalium* (Zürich, 1551–8) or Albertus Magnus (*On animals*, 22.50–1). A *castle* is a 'tower borne on the back of an elephant' (*OED*, *castle*, n., 6a).

9.41–10.1 certain creatures . . . moulded in heaven first   Untraced. The middle region of the air is equivalent to the upper atmosphere, between the heavens on the one hand and the lower region on the other.

10.2 prince of poets   A phrase popular for references to preeminent classical and modern poets including (i) Homer: e.g. Webbe (*ECE*, I, 235), Harvey (*ECE*, II, 264), and Chapman, in *Seaven bookes of the Iliades of Homere, prince of poets* (1598); (ii) Virgil: Scaliger (see **30.34–8n.**); and (iii) Petrarch: *Songes and sonettes* (1557), 74ᵛ, and Meres (*ECE*, II, 314). Scott calls Du Bartas 'Prince of Poets' in the dedicatory epistle to his partial translation of *La sepmaine* (see Appendix 1, 248).

10.2–5 it is said . . . art and industry   See the 'Life of Virgil' by Donatus (*fl.* 350), 25 ('Aeneida XI perfecit annos') and 23–4 on the gradual process of composition (Colin Hardie (ed.), *Vitae Vergilianae antiquae* (Oxford, 1966), 11–12). The *Vita Donati* was incorporated (often with additions and interpolations) in Renaissance editions of Virgil: for an example printed in Britain see *Opera P. Virgilii Maronis* (1583), B1ᵛ. Scott personifies the *Aeneid* as 'he', making good on the metaphor of authorship as childbirth, and because the work is so closely identified with its titular hero. For translation see Russell, 187.

10.6–8 What if . . . instinct in the poet   Scott in this passage sets nature and inspiration – two different potential sources of poetry – against art. It is not clear here if 'instinct' means 'Innate impulse' (*OED*, *instinct*, n., 2) or 'Instigation; impulse; prompting' (†1, illustrated in quotations referring clearly to divine inspiration), or both. Plato does not discuss innate poetic ability; for his discussions of inspiration see **7.16–18n.** Aristotle shows that imitation as well as harmony and rhythm are natural to humans (*Poetics*, 1448b) and briefly sets the *furor poeticus* alongside the alternative of genius (1455a32–4), but he is little interested in these questions.

10.9–10 Bezaleel ... working in metals   On Bezaleel's divinely inspired crafts-
manship see Exodus 31:2–5 and 35:30–36:2.

10.12–15 Natalis Comes ... above ordinary men   The *Mythologiae* (Venice,
1567) of Natale Conti, also known by the Latin name Natalis Comes. See Natalis
Comes, II, 760 (Book 8, ch. 15): 'Amphion was supposed to be Jupiter's and Antiope's
son, because of his superb musical talent, and also because the ancients always claimed
that superior men were Jupiter's sons, as we remarked earlier'. Cf. I, 178 (Book 3,
ch. 7); and II, 597 (Book 7, ch. 1): 'For neither Hercules nor any other man can become
famous without Jupiter's assistance, since all power and excellence ultimately derive
from God. In fact the benefits we derive from parents seem minimal when compared
with the divine goodness. That's why Hercules is known more as the son of Jupiter
than the son of Amphitryon.' For Scott's use of Natalis Comes' account of Amphion,
cf. **25.32–6n.**

10.15–21 the painter ... poetical fury   The 'painter', here and at **35.19**, is Gian
Paolo Lomazzo (1538–92), Milanese painter and influential art theorist. Scott quotes
from and cites his *Trattato dell'arte della pittura, scoltura et architettura* (Milan, 1584) a
number of times (see Introduction, l–li). He read it in the Italian, although a translation
by Richard Haydocke of the first five of its seven books had been recently printed: *A
tracte containing the artes of curious paintinge carvinge and buildinge* (Oxford, 1598). The
whole of Scott's sentence, and a part of the following one, paraphrases parts of 2.2, 'Of
the necessitie of motion [*Della necessità del moto*]':

And herein consisteth the whole *spirite* and *life* of the Arte; which the Painters call sometimes
the *Fury* [*furia*], sometimes the *Grace* [*grazia*], and sometimes the *Excellency* [*eccellenza*]
of the arte. For hereby they ... discover all the severall passions and gestures which mans
bodie is able to performe: which heere we tearme by the name of *motions* [*moto*], for the
more significant expressing of the inward affections of the minde, by an outward and bodily
Demonstration [*una certa espressione e dimostrazione estrinseca nel corpo di quelle cose che
patisce internamente l'animo*]; that so by this meanes, mens inward motions and affections
[*i moti interni*], may be aswell, (or rather better) signified; as by their speech ... Now the
perfect knowledge of this *motion*, is (as hath beene shewed) accounted the most difficult
part of the arte, and reputed as a divine gift [*un dono divino*]: insomuch as herein alone
consisteth the comparison betweene *Painting* and *Poetrie*. For as it is required in a Poet,
that besides the excellencie of his witte, he shoulde moreover be furnished with a certaine
propension and inclination of will [*certo desiderio et una inclinazione di volontà*], inciting
and mooving him to versifie, (which the ancient called the *Furie* [*furor*] of *Apollo* and
the *Muses*.) So likewise a Painter ought, togither with those naturall partes which are
required at his handes, to be furnished with a naturall dexteritie and inborne sleight of
expressing the *principall motions*, even from his cradle [*abbi cognizione e forza d'esprimere
i moti principali, quasi come ingenerata seco e accresciuta con lui sino dalle fascie*]. Otherwise
it is a very harde (if not impossible) matter, to attaine unto the absolute perfection of this
arte.   (97–8; Haydocke, 2A2ᵛ–3ʳ)

10.23 propenseness   Inclination, propensity (*OED*, †*propenseness*, n., 1).

10.25–6 skilfulliest and most naturally sweet   Scott clearly means 'sweet both most skilfully and most naturally', i.e. Horace is himself the optimum combination of art and nature. *OED* attests to *fullyest* (*c.*1400 and *c.*1503, in illustrations of other words); to *fullyer* and *fullier* (1505 and 1653, in the entries for †*fully*, adj. and *fully*, adv. respectively); and to *fullily* and *fulliness* (1380 and *c.*1300, both obsolete forms derived from †*fully*, adj). Since the last two are the only forms recognised as such (and therefore given an authoritative modern spelling), I have modernised the manuscript spelling *skilfullyest* on that analogy.

10.27–30 Natura fieret ... coniurat amice   *Ars poetica*, 408–11: 'Often it is asked whether a praiseworthy poem be due to Nature or to art. For my part, I do not see of what avail is either study, when not enriched by Nature's vein, or native wit, if untrained; so truly does each claim the other's aid, and make with it a friendly league.' All early witnesses to Horace's text read *possit* (present subjunctive of *possum*, to be able) in the third line of the quotation (410); this is usually emended to *prosit* (present subjunctive of *prosum*, to be useful, to benefit), and all sixteenth-century texts that I have consulted share that reading. I have not traced Scott's reading *prodest* (present indicative of *prosum*), so it may be that he was relying on memory here. Since it does not appear to be a scribal error, I have preserved it.

10.38–9 Sir Philip Sidney ... artificial rules   In the *Defence*, following directly on Sidney's quotation of the proverb *orator fit, poeta nascitur*:

> Yet confess I always, that as the fertilest ground must be manured, so must the highest-flying wit have a Daedalus to guide him. That Daedalus, they say, both in this and in other, hath three wings to bear itself up into the air of due commendation: that is, art, imitation, and exercise. But these, neither artificial rules nor imitative patterns, we much cumber ourselves withal. Exercise indeed we do, but that very fore-backwardly, for where we should exercise to know, we exercise as having known.   (*DP*, 43)

11.2 as that knight ... poet-apes   *OED* (*poet*, n., compounds, C1C) agrees in giving this as Sidney's coinage, in the peroration to the *Defence*, where Sidney claims that 'the cause why [poetry] is not esteemed in England is the fault of poet-apes, not poets' (*DP*, 53). Cf. '*Pindare's* Apes' (*Astrophil and Stella*, 3.3). Scott's point is that art without nature is worse than nature without art.

11.6–7 By the *difference* ... stamp the matter   The matter of the *genus* (poetry is an art) needs to be stamped by a particular form that shows what kind of art it is: one of imitating or representing in words. This form is also a 'signet' (from Latin *signum*, seal), a small seal, often worn as a finger-ring, used to authenticate or *sign* (the same etymology) documents by making an impression (or form) in wax. The conceit derives from the equation of *genus* with matter and *difference* with form (see **6.32–7**), the relation between form and matter commonly being represented by the figure of pressing a seal or signet-ring into wax, the wax recording the form but not the matter of the metal ring: see Aristotle, *De anima*, 424a. Compare Du Bartas, *La sepmaine*, day 2,

193–7, as translated by Scott: 'The waxe that Matter of this worlde, without forme quight, | ... | The greate seale is the forme, and the Eternall mynde, | Is the high Chaunceler, which doth continually signe | With greate and litle stamps this bodye variable' (Add. MS 81083, 69ʳ).

11.8–11 we sequester poesy ... and the like   Cf. Viperano, 1.1: 'The imitation of human actions thus separates poetry from those arts which do not portray anything. The verse distinguishes poetry from those arts which, although they portray, nevertheless do not express what they portray in verse' (3–4). For the distinctness of neighbouring arts from each other see **30.8–11n.**

11.9 faculties   A *faculty* was a branch of knowledge and specifically one of the departments of learning at a university (medieval Latin *facultas*), as well as an art (*OED*, *faculty*, n., †6, 7, 8).

11.10–11 feign not style   Scott probably wrote 'feign not *in* style' (cf. **6.3**, **11.8**), but since the manuscript reading is not an impossible one I have not emended it.

11.14–21 an example or pattern ... reasonable apprehensions   For the sense of *notion* (**11.16**) here see *OED*, *notion*, n., 4a: 'an idea in a person's mind', first recorded usage Jonson, 1607 (also 'general notions' as here). Cicero gives the Latin *notio* this sense. See, for example, *Topica*, 7.31, defining *genus* and *species* as types of concept: 'By concept [*notio*] I mean what the Greeks call now *ennoia*, now *prolepsis*. This is an innate knowledge of anything, which has been previously apprehended, and needs to be unfolded.' (For *ennoia* cf. Plato, *Phaedo*, 73c.) The term is connected to the 'schoolmen' because the question of innate or acquired knowledge was a familiar talking point in the scholastic tradition and within the universities. The idea of innate notions was also important to the neo-Aristotelian and theologically reformed theory of mind articulated by Philip Melanchthon, for whom *notitiae* were innate notions implanted in the mind by God. Melanchthon was an important influence on Sidney; on this see Robert Stillman, *Philip Sidney and the poetics of Renaissance cosmopolitanism* (Aldershot, 2008), esp. 115–16, 161. And cf. Sidney's usages of *notion* (*DP*, 8 and 16). The question of whether a poetic idea can originate in the poet's mind or is only a version, innate or acquired, of some external standard or essence is central to Neoplatonic art theory and is further touched on by Scott below (see **15.29–33n.**). The word *feign*, much used by Sidney also as a synonym for *imitate* or *represent*, acquires centrality in English Renaissance poetics, relating as it does to the Latin *fingere* (to form, fashion, shape, make) and thus to the word *fiction*.

11.21–4 Aristotle saith ... succeed unto   *Poetics*, 1451a36–b11:

the poet's job is saying not what did happen but the sort of thing that would happen, that is, what can happen in a strictly probable or necessary sequence. The difference between the historian and the poet ... is that the one tells us what happened and the other the sort of thing that would happen. That is why poetry is at once more like philosophy and more worth while than history, since poetry tends to make general statements, while those of history are particular. A 'general statement' means one that tells us what sort of man would, probably or necessarily, say or do what sort of thing, and this is what poetry aims at, though it attached proper names; a particular statement on the other hand tells us what Alcibiades, for instance, did or what happened to him.

For Aristotelian universals and particulars see also **5.6–16n**. Sidney attends to this passage in the *Poetics* closely (*DP*, 18–19), as does Viperano (1.8, 24).

11.25–8 Euripides ... as they be   *Poetics*, 1460b33–4. On Euripides' female characters cf. Viperano, 2.9 (96), and Scaliger, 145c1. Euripides' interest in representing women in his plays led even in his own day to a reputation for misogyny, witnessed for example in Aristophanes' *Thesmophoriazusae*. For this aspect of his reputation see for example Gellius, *Attic nights* (15.20): 'He is said to have had an exceeding antipathy towards almost all women, either because he had a natural disinclination to their society, or because he had had two wives at the same time ... and they had made wedlock hateful to him'; Athenaeus, *Deipnosophists* (13.557e): 'Hieronymus in *Historical Notes* puts it as follows: "When somebody remarked to Sophocles that Euripides was a woman-hater [*misogunēs*], Sophocles answered: 'Yes, in his tragedies; for certainly when he is in bed he is a woman-lover'"'; and also the *Suda*, which calls Euripides a *misogunēs*, and reports the legend that he met his death, like his character Pentheus in the *Bacchae*, by being torn apart by women (*Suidae lexicon*, ed. Ada Adler, 5 vols. (Leipzig, 1928–38), E 3695). No sources, to my knowledge, suggest that Euripides earned a nickname for this supposed misogyny ('surnamed' in the sense not of family name but of additional name, title, or epithet: *OED*, *surname*, v., 1), so Scott may be misreporting one of the above sources, or a related one. Alternatively, he may merely be saying that Euripides was *known as* a misogynist (*OED*, *surname*, v., †3).

11.29–32 If the poet ... follows truth   Scaliger: the poet 'either adds a fictitious element to the truth, or imitates the truth by fiction, of course with more elaboration [*aut addit ficta veris, aut fictis vera imitatur, maiore sane apparatu*]' (1a2; Padelford, 2). Cf., immediately below: poetry 'narrated not only actual events, but also fictitious events as if they were actual, and represented them as they might be or ought to be' (1b2; Padelford, 2). For 'freedom of spirit' compare Sidney's 'that high-flying liberty of conceit proper to the poet' (*DP*, 7).

11.30–1 Theseus his ship   Alluding to the philosophical paradox of the point at which one thing becomes another, as described in Plutarch's *Life of Theseus* (23.1):

The vessell in which *Theseus* went and returned, was a galliot of thirtie owers, which the ATHENIANS kept untill the time of *Demetrius* the *Phalerian*, always taking away the olde peeces of wodde that were rotten, and ever renewing them with new in their places. So that ever since, in the disputations of the Philosophers, touching things that increase, to wit, whether they remaine always one, or else they be made others: this galliot was always brought in for an example of doubt. For some mainteined, that it was still one vessell: others to the contrarie defended it was not so.   (North, 12)

11.34–5 pictoribus . . . aequa potestas   Horace, *Ars poetica*, 9–10. Scott returns to this passage at **71.16**.

11.38–12.4 (saith Aristotle) . . . of deformity   There is in Scott's 'as pictures, so poems' a conscious echo of Horace's *ut pictura poesis* (see **6.16–18n.**). Scott brings together the passage from the *Poetics* that he had earlier paraphrased, and which discusses plot (1451a–b; see **11.21–4n.**) with an earlier passage in which Aristotle, discussing character, makes the comparison with painters:

The objects of this *mimēsis* are people doing things, and these people must necessarily be either good or bad, this being, generally speaking, the only line of divergence between characters, since differences of character just are differences in goodness and badness, or else they must be better than are found in the world or worse or just the same, as they are represented by the painters, Polygnotus portraying them as better, Pauson as worse, and Dionysius as they are.   (1448a1–6)

In doing this Scott recognises that Aristotle's discussion of how things 'should or may be' can include the representation of things as worse than they are in reality, a point Sidney does not as fully articulate. For 'worsing' see *OED*, *worse*, v. ('*Obs.* exc. in nonce-use'). Viperano, discussing epic (2.4), rather trips up in making a similar point: the poet must represent virtue as praiseworthy and vice as blameworthy, preserving decorum in each case 'in a manner dedicated to recommending well-doing and censuring wrongdoing'; and yet he must touch lightly on, conceal, or obscure anything base or shameful (75). This is to follow a troubling passage, *Poetics* 1454b8–15, where Aristotle appears to say that just as portrait painters represent people as more beautiful than they are, so the poet should represent such characters as they are (e.g. 'irascible and lazy and morally deficient in other ways'), and yet also as good. Scott may be trying to reinterpret this awkward passage in a manner more consistent with his theory of exemplarity. An important reference point for Scott's discussion of the exemplarity of evil is Plutarch, *De audiendis poetis*, especially his report that 'Euripides . . . is said to have answered critics who attacked his Ixion as impious and vile by saying: "But I didn't take him off the stage until he was nailed to the wheel"' (*Moralia*, 19e), referred to also by Sidney (*DP*, 21). Horace insists that morally compromised characters should be shown just as they are, in the interests of decorum and self-consistency (*Ars poetica*, 119–27). Sidney's discussion (*DP*, 21 and 27) shows him happier to contemplate exemplary evil on the tragic and comic stage than in heroic poetry.

12.4–10 Alexander . . . hateful things   For the general tradition of Alexander's love of Homer, without these details, see Sidney (*DP*, 37–8). The story that Alexander would rather be Homer's Thersites than an Achilles written by Choerilus of Iasus is preserved in the Horatian commentaries of Pomponius Porphyrio and Pseudo-Acro, commenting on *Ars poetica*, 357. These are reproduced in various sixteenth-century editions of Horace's works and of the *Ars* alone. Choerilus was an epic poet who travelled with Alexander on his campaigns and, according to Horace, was paid for flattering him (*Epistles*, 2.1.232–4; cf. Puttenham, *Art*, 1.8, 106). On the decorum of representing Thersites cf. Plutarch, *De audiendis poetis*: 'when we see a picture of... Thersites' face we feel pleasure and admiration not because it is beautiful but because it is *like*' (*Moralia*, 18a). Scott's witty parenthesis borrows from Sidney's description of Miso in the *Arcadia*: 'only one good point she hath, that she observes *decorum*, having a froward minde in a wretched body' (*NA*, A6^r; Skretkowicz, 18). The tradition of Richard III's physical deformity, popularised by Shakespeare, dates back to descriptions of Richard written not long after his death in 1485. See, e.g., Thomas More's *History of King Richard III* (*c*.1513–18): 'Richarde... was... little of stature, ill fetured of limmes, croke backed, his left shoulder much higher then his right, hard favoured of visage' (*The complete works of St. Thomas More*, II, ed. Richard S. Sylvester (New Haven, 1963), 7). For Scott's use of Sidney's term *poet-ape* see **11.2n**. On 'proportion' (**12.6**) as decorum see **33.31–4n**.

12.10–15 They that lay... but verse   See Sidney on the three types of poets: religious poets, including pagans; philosophical, scientific, and historical poets; and 'right poets': 'For these third be they which most properly do imitate to teach and delight, and to imitate borrow nothing of what is, hath been, or shall be, but range, only reined with learned discretion, into the divine consideration of what may be and should be' (*DP*, 10–11). Cf. Viperano, who like Scott gives the example of Empedocles (*c*.492–432 BC), the Greek philosopher-poet of the generation before Socrates (1.1, 4). The common source is Aristotle, whom Scott paraphrases: 'But as Homer and Empedocles have nothing in common except their metre the latter had better be called a scientific writer, not a poet, if we are to use "poet" of the former' (*Poetics*, 1447b17–20). Though Sidney fudges things in the passage quoted above, the rest of the *Defence*, like the *Poetics*, is committed to a definition of poetry not as versifying but as fiction-making.

12.12 story   History.

12.12–13 Lucan, Daniel's *Lancaster and York*   Samuel Daniel's *The first fowre bookes of the civile warres betweene the two houses of Lancaster and Yorke* (1595) was modelled on Lucan's epic poem of the civil war between Caesar and Pompey, *Pharsalia*. See further **19.25–6** and **72.18–20n**.

12.15–20 The other... *poets* or makers   Scott echoes a celebrated passage in Sidney's *Defence*: 'There is no art delivered to mankind that hath not the works of nature for his principal object... Only the poet, disdaining to be tied to any such subjection, lifted up with the vigour of his own invention, doth grow in effect into another nature, in making things either better than nature bringeth forth or, quite anew, forms such as never were in nature, as the heroes, demigods, cyclopes, chimeras, furies, and such like' (*DP*, 8–9). On poets as makers (the meaning of the Greek *poiētēs*, poet, from *poiein*, to make) see for example Sidney (*DP*, 8); Puttenham, 1.1 (*Art*, 93–4); Scaliger, 1.1 and 1.2 (3d1–a2); and Viperano, 1.1 (3–4).

12.18 the silkworm … own bowels The silkworm is the larva of the silkmoth (*Bombyx mori*); when it enters the pupa state it spins a cocoon made of hundreds of metres of silk thread. A long descriptive poem by the entomologist and Sidney-family client Thomas Moffett, *The silkewormes, and their flies*, was printed in 1599, against the background of efforts to start an English silk industry. Cf. John Case's commendatory epistle to Haydocke's translation of Lomazzo: 'You have … with the Silke-worme as it were woven out of your owne bowels, the finest silke' (Haydocke, *1ʳ).

12.22 verse (which is the poet's livery or habit) See **13.22** and **63.30n**.

12.25–30 true picture of Lucretia … imagined beauty Scott's use of Lucretia as an example is informed by his admiration for Shakespeare's *Lucrece*, although it owes most to Sidney's *Defence*: between historical or philosophical poets and those 'right poets' who create fictions

is such a kind of difference as betwixt the meaner sort of painters, who counterfeit only such faces as are set before them, and the more excellent, who having no law but wit bestow that in colours upon you which is fittest for the eye to see – as the constant though lamenting look of Lucretia, when she punished in herself another's fault, wherein he painteth not Lucretia, whom he never saw, but painteth the outward beauty of such a virtue. (*DP*, 11)

Scott is also thinking of a later passage in Sidney where, following on from his discussion of universal versus particular characters and again using portraits to focus his thoughts, he compares the exemplary to the faithful portrait of the (reputedly ugly) Roman emperor Vespasian:

For indeed if the question were whether it were better to have a particular act truly or falsely set down, there is no doubt which is to be chosen, no more than whether you had rather have Vespasian's picture right as he was or at the painter's pleasure, nothing resembling. But if the question be for your own use and learning, whether it be better to have it set down as it should be or as it was, then certainly is more doctrinable the feigned Cyrus in Xenophon than the true Cyrus in Justin, and the feigned Aeneas in Virgil than the right Aeneas in Dares Phrygius. (*DP*, 19)

Scott's vocabulary here is Sidneian and Neoplatonic: the poet imitates a 'conceit' (Sidney's '*idea* or fore-conceit': *DP*, 9) to produce an 'image' which gives us an 'absolute form'. For Sidney, poetry is not versification but fiction-making, and fiction-making is superior to the copying of reality. Scott is far less categorical: poetry can be fiction-making or versification, and will range from the faithful copying of reality to the entirely fictive. Cf. Gentili on the difference between the poet and the painter: *poet* only applies to those who feign the verisimilar, whereas *painter* applies also to those who depict the truth (Binns, 74).

12.33–5 The copying... ornament and fiction   A *descant* (from Latin *dis*- apart + *cantus* singing) is a melody set or extemporised against the ground of a bass-line or plainsong ('plain ground'). Cf. *Richard III*, 3.7.49: 'For on that ground I'll make a holy descant'. In Scott's metaphor, the plainsong is what is received, grounded in actuality; the descant is what is created. Comparisons of poetry to music were common, and were based in the fact that it was the metrical regularity of versification that suited poetry to musical setting. Scott's comparison may, therefore, be grounded in a view of poetry as verse ('ornament'); but it also extends the sense of *ornament*, and the reach of this common analogy, to include the fictional embellishing of reality. See **81.33** for another musical metaphor.

12.38 objected... sense   Brought before (*OED, object*, v., 7) the eyes or other senses, offered to the understanding (*OED, sense*, n., 7). Cf. **81.35**.

12.39–40 Tully could never... describe   Cicero, *Orator*, 2.7: 'in delineating the perfect orator I shall be portraying such a one as perhaps has never existed. Indeed I am not inquiring who was the perfect orator, but what is that unsurpassable ideal.' This immediately precedes Cicero's important Neoplatonic modification of Plato's account of the relation between artists and the ideal forms (see **15.29–33n.**), suggesting that that passage was in Scott's thoughts here too. Cicero returns to the point at *Orator*, 28.100–29.101 (and cf. 5.18–19). Cf. Quintilian, 1.10.4. The 'bar' is 'The barrier or wooden rail marking off the immediate precinct of the judge's seat, at which prisoners are stationed for arraignment, trial, or sentence' (*OED, bar*, n.¹, 22a) and by extension the courts (23a), as well as a barrier in the halls of the Inns of Court separating benchers from more junior students (†24), and by extension the community of lawyers or barristers.

13.2–3 LACUNA   On the evidence for the missing pages see Textual Introduction, lxxiv. On their likely contents see Introduction, lxx.

13.3 noisomest affects   Most harmful or disagreeable (*OED, noisome*, adj., †1, 3) passions, emotions, or evil desires (*OED, affect*, n., †1, †3).

13.3 before the eye as it were   On *enargeia*, the ability of words to give the impression of sights, see **38.38–9n.**, **43.35–40n.**, and **45.5–7n.**

13.5–14 the sensible beholding... thorough-digested knowledge   See Aristotle, *Poetics*, 1448b5–19:

Mimēsis is innate in human beings from childhood – indeed we differ from the other animals in being most given to *mimēsis* and in making our first steps in learning through it – and pleasure in instances of *mimēsis* is equally general... we enjoy looking at the most exact portrayals of things we do not like to see in real life, the lowest animals, for instance, or corpses. This is because not only philosophers, but all men, enjoy getting to understand something... therefore they like to see these pictures, because in looking at them they come to understand something and can infer what each thing is, can say, for instance, 'This man in the picture is so-and-so'. If you happen not to have seen the original, the picture will not produce its pleasure *qua* instance of *mimēsis*, but because of its technical finish or colour or some such other reason.

Aristotle's thoughts about the pleasure of learning involved in the recognition of the object of an imitation are further developed in *Rhetoric*, 1371a–b. Scott's account, in synthesising the two, is heavily dependent on Viperano, 1.2 (7). Scott returns to this material: see **28.12–17n**.

13.6 reflex   Reflection or, by extension, 'image, reproduction' (*OED, reflex,* n., 3b., first recorded usage 1608). Cf. **28.11**.

13.15–16 delight of harmony … man's nature   Scott stays close to Viperano and/or their source in *Poetics*, 1448b, which continues: 'As well as *mimēsis*, harmony and rhythm are natural to us, and verses are obviously definite sections of rhythm' (1448b20–2). Cf. Viperano, 1.2: 'Aristotle thinks that poetry arose from two natural causes: the inclination towards imitating and the charm of harmony, which are implanted in man by nature and perfect the poetic faculty' (7).

13.17–19 that musical kind … our metre or verse   This is a condensed, specific, and accurate description of English versification, and a thoughtful adaptation of Viperano: 'Then follows harmony [*harmonia*], and from it flowed verse [*carmen*], which consists of certain fixed rhythms [*certis… numeris*] and quantities of time [*temporum spatiis*]' (13/7). For Scott's account of versification see **59.5–64.29**.

13.17 number   Harmony, regularity, rhythm, metre (*OED, number,* †14).

13.20–2 the one the soul … livery or habit   Imitation is the soul, and versification the body. Compare *Poetics*, 1450a38–9, where plot is the soul of tragedy, and Viperano, 1.1: 'Just as the soul is the form of the body so the story is the form of a poem' (4). See also Scaliger, for whom verse is matter (*hulē,* the title of his second book, on versification) and plot is *idea* (the title of his third book), an apparent reversal of the common Ciceronian/Erasmian distinction of matter and words; and cf. Scott's 'the matter of words… which answers to the brass or marble in the carver's work' (**11.11–13**). For 'livery or habit' see **12.22** and **63.30n**. For 'soul' cf. **59.11** and **64.1–2**.

13.23–8 with Viperanus … to an art   Scott continues to follow Viperano, 1.2, closely here:

Harmony is so natural and proper to man that there is never a human being so uncivilized and savage that he cannot be charmed by song. For these reasons I think that we cannot give any definite parent and originator of poetry unless it be nature, who has fashioned us with an inclination for poetry; nor has there ever been a time when this inclination for poetry was not cultivated … The beginnings of poetry were clumsy, just as other arts, nurtured by the observation and perception of nature, were at first somewhat rough and were only refined by men of outstanding talent over a long period of time (for nothing was ever invented and perfected at the same time). So poetry was subsequently perfected and brought to fulfillment by the practice and care of sages.   (7–8)

13.29–31 they err not...poesy as the porter   *Ethnics*: heathens, pagans (*OED*, *ethnic*, adj. and n., B†1). For the commonplace that poetry had helped form men into societies see Horace, *Ars poetica*, 391–6, instancing Orpheus and Amphion. The same point was made about rhetoric: see, e.g., Isocrates, *Nicocles*, 5–9; Cicero, *De oratore*, 1.8.33. The argument about poetry's role in early society was often developed alongside a related one, that poetry was the first philosophy a young child might learn, as in Cicero, *Pro Archia poeta*, 6.13–14; Strabo, *Geography*, 1.2.3–8; Sir Thomas Elyot, *The boke named the governour* (1531), 1.10 (30^r–35^v); and the section of Sidney's *Defence* on poetry as 'the first light-giver to ignorance, and first nurse whose milk by little and little enabled them to feed afterwards of tougher knowledges' (*DP*, 4) that underpins this whole passage.

14.2–3 no human writers...Homer   *Orpheus* was the most celebrated bard in Greek myth; he was supposed to be the son of Apollo and a Muse, and his song had extraordinary powers. *Musaeus* is neither of the two later historical poets but the mythical poet closely connected with Orpheus, and sometimes his son. *Homer* was the figure to which the ancient world attributed the *Iliad* and the *Odyssey*, now dated to the second half of the eighth century BC. The three poets stand at the start of standard classically-derived canonical lists of the ancient poets, and are name-checked by Sidney in the corresponding passage of the *Defence* (*DP*, 4–5).

14.3–4 neither any...Greek poets   The 'sciences' are branches of knowledge: see 7.2–6n. Empedocles (see **12.10–15n.**) and Parmenides are examples of philosophical poets of the fifth century BC whose writings predate philosophical or scientific prose writings in Greek (though there are earlier teachers, such as Pythagoras, from whom no works survive).

14.8 the furious   That is, those who believe that poetry proceeds from the *furor poeticus* (see **7.16–18n.**); Scott also punningly implies that the advocates of that theory are themselves foolish or mad (*OED*, *furious*, adj., 3 and †4).

14.12–19 no more than Quintilian...on her wings   Paraphrasing Quintilian, 1.1.1–2, discussing education more generally (a point he makes at 1.pr.4–5) rather than only rhetoric:

there is absolutely no foundation for the complaint that but few men have the power to take in the knowledge that is imparted to them, and that the majority are so slow of understanding that education is a waste of time and labour. On the contrary you will find that most are quick to reason and ready to learn. Reasoning comes as naturally to man as flying to birds, speed to horses and ferocity to beasts of prey: our minds are endowed by nature with such activity and sagacity that the soul is believed to proceed from heaven. Those who are dull and unteachable are as abnormal as prodigious births and monstrosities, and are but few in number. A proof of what I say is to be found in the fact that boys commonly show promise of many accomplishments.

14.16 uncapable   Incapable (*OED*, †*uncapable*, adj.).

14.19–21 there be some *struthiocameli* . . . **eagle's place**   According to Pliny (10.1.2), the ostrich (*struthiocamelus*), a flightless bird, will hide its head and believe its body invisible, and can digest anything; the popular ancient notion, not in Pliny, that it could eat iron is mentioned and challenged by Albertus Magnus (*On animals*, 23.139). Both characteristics became proverbial (*ODEP*, 600 and Tilley, o 83; *ODEP*, 776 and Tilley, I 97, citing Lyly and Shakespeare, *2 Hen. VI*, 4.10.28). The eagle was believed to be able to look at the sun, and tested its young by forcing them to do this (e.g. Pliny, 10.3.10), qualities that Shakespeare refers to in several places (e.g. *3 Hen. VI*, 2.1.91–2; *Love's labour's lost*, 4.3.222–4); for the detail that when old it would fly above the clouds, burning its eyes and feathers in the sun, plunging into the water, and being renewed, see the second–fourth century AD *Physiologus*, which presents it as an explicit Christian allegory (*Physiologus*, 12). All of these details about ostriches and eagles were elaborated in the medieval bestiary tradition and Scott could have come across them in any number of places. For a brief summary of both the eagle's high flight and the ostrich's iron-eating see, e.g., William Caxton's translation of Gautier de Metz, *L'image du monde*: *The myrrour of the worlde* (1481), g6ʳ.

14.32–3 that polypus . . . **transform himself**   *Polypus* (or polyp) was the name given to what are now distinguished as different species of cephalopod (including octopus, squid, etc.); the polypus was characterised by the ability to change colour (see *OED*, *polyp*, n., 2†a and *polypus*, n., 2†a). It is conflated here with Proteus, the sea-god who could change shape; the two are also brought together in Erasmus, *Adagia*, 1.1.93 (and cf. 2.2.74, 'As many shapes as Proteus', and 2.3.91, 'Polyps').

14.34–6 as the eye . . . **altogether uncoloured**   The 'crystal humour' is the crystalline humour or lens of the eye, so called because of its transparency. See Guy de Chauliac, *The questyonary of cyrurgyens*, trans. R. Copland (1542), E3ᵛ. Scott uses *species* here in its etymologically primary sense of appearance or outward form (*OED*, *species*, n., †1a) or more particularly 'outward appearance or aspect, the visible form or image, *of* something, as constituting the immediate object of vision' (†3a, first instanced from Haydocke's Lomazzo, 1598). From that root sense developed particular philosophical and logical uses, translating Greek *idea* (form, appearance, kind, sort, class) and *eidos* (form, shape, kind, class) and so encompassing abstract forms intelligible to the mind, Platonic ideal forms, and particular classes of thing belonging to a larger *genus*. Scott rarely uses *species* in the logical senses outlined at **5.24–31n.** and **6.32–7n.** (see **79.35** for the only instance, and **5.28** for the adjective *special*). Cf. 'true idea, species, or image' (**57.40**), showing how the different senses overlap.

14.40–15.4 Scaliger discovers . . . lose himself   A close paraphrase of Scaliger, 325d1–a2. For this view of Lucan cf. Quintilian, 10.1.90.

15.5–7 Aristotle . . . edge to art   *Poetics*, 1455a32–4: 'Hence poetry is the work of a gifted person, or [or 'rather than', a suggested emendation] of a manic: of these types, the former have versatile imaginations, the latter get carried away'; cf. **10.6–8n**. See also *Poetics*, 1459a30, where Aristotle calls Homer *thespesios* (oracular, divinely sweet, divinely inspired); and the discussion of poetic and oracular frenzy and inspiration in the pseudo-Aristotelian *Problems*, 954a. In returning to the earlier question of inspiration and *furor poeticus* (see **7.16–18n**.), Scott continues to follow Viperano, who states: 'certainly we do not reject but enthusiastically admire what is assuredly not an insane but rather a divine madness' (11). Viperano then quotes Ovid (as Scott, below) and cites the same point in Aristotle that Scott has referred to.

15.8–9 est deus . . . mentis habet   'There is a god within us. It is when he stirs us that our bosom warms; it is his impulse that sows the seeds of inspiration': Ovid, *Fasti*, 6.5–6, reading 'ille' (that) for 'hic' (this) in l. 6. This variant does not figure in texts of the *Fasti* that I have consulted. The passage is also quoted (with the same variant) by Viperano, 1.3 (17/11), and Scott is probably taking it from there. It also appears (l. 5 only) in Webbe (*ECE*, I, 232) and thence in Meres (*ECE*, II, 313).

15.13 David   Sidney also gives the example of the Psalmist as divinely inspired poet (*DP*, 7).

15.15–16 the hot-spirited satirist . . . versum   Juvenal, 1.79–80: 'si natura negat, facit indignatio versum | qualemcumque potest' ('If talent is lacking, then *indignation will inspire my poetry*, such as it can').

15.19–20 love is heathenishly . . . god of poesy   Possibly an allusion to Ovid, *Amores*, 1.1.

15.20–9 this affection of love . . . spiritual affections   The ultimate source for this account of love is Aquinas, *Summa theologiae*, 1.2.26, 'De amore'. Here Aquinas finds three kinds of love corresponding to three appetites: the natural (which involves no apprehension, and might be instanced by the way a heavy object is attracted to the earth), the sensitive (which involves apprehension of a perceived good but not free will), and the rational or intellectual, 'which arises both through consciousness and by free choice' (*Summa theologiae*, 1.2.26.1). That Scott makes the latter two into three is due to his use of a passage in Lomazzo's chapter 'Of the passions of the minde', 2.3: 'The passions of the minde are nothing else but certaine motions, proceeding from the apprehension of some thing, Now this *apprehension* is three-folde: *Sensitive, Rationall*, and *Intellectuall*. And from these three, there arise three passions in the minde. For sometimes we follow *sensitive apprehensions*, and then wee consider good and evill, under the shewe [*spezie*] of that which is *profitable* or *unprofitable*, *pleasant or offensive*: and these are called *Naturall affections*. Sometimes wee pursue *rationall apprehensions*; considering good and evill in maner of *vertue or vice, praise or dispraise, honestie or dishonestie*: and these are *Reasonable affections*. Sometimes we imbrace *apprehensions intellectuall*, regarding good and evill as *true* and *false*, and these are *Intellectuall apprehensions*' (102; Haydocke, 2A5ʳ).

15.29–33 the poet proceeds . . . enamoured of   Scott follows Sidney in this Neoplatonic account of love and in relating it to artistic creation. For love as the idealising formation of an image of the beloved which both recollects and can lead towards a Platonic idea of beauty (equated with the divine by Renaissance Neoplatonists) see for example Marsilio Ficino, *Commentary on Plato's 'Symposium' on love*, trans. Sears Jayne (Woodstock, Conn., 1985), esp. 114–15; Castiglione (Cox, 355–61); and their source in Plato's *Symposium* and *Phaedrus*. Sidney's theory of poetic creation as involving the formation of a Platonic idea picks up on the attempts of classical Neoplatonists to reconcile Plato's theory of the ideas with a positive account of artistic mimesis. See Cicero, *Orator*, 2.8–10; Plotinus, *Enneads*, 5.8.1; and Seneca, *Epistulae morales*, 65.7: 'it is [the idea] that the artist gazed upon when he created the work which he had decided to carry out. Now it makes no difference whether he has his pattern outside himself, that he may direct his glance to it, or within himself, conceived and placed there by himself.' For analogues within the traditions of Italian art criticism and Protestant theology that interested both Sidney and Scott see also Shepherd, 140–1, as well as Lomazzo's chapter on *idea*, 6.65 (415–19). Puttenham rejects the Platonic vocabulary but accepts the Neoplatonic position (*Art*, 1.1, 93–4).

15.32 Pygmalion   See **15.35–8n.**

15.34 blazon   (i) Describe in heraldic language, depict (heraldically; figurative senses postdate Scott); (ii) describe fitly, boast of, proclaim or trumpet (*OED*, *blazon*, v., (i) 1, 2; (ii) 4, 5, 6); for the second sense cf. 'blaze', **23.6n.**, and **26.26**, a closely related passage.

15.35–8 Sir Philip Sidney . . . by faith   Sidney: 'And may not I presume a little farther . . . and say that the holy David's Psalms are a divine poem? . . . For what else is [its various poetic features] but a heavenly poesy, wherein almost he showeth himself a passionate lover of that unspeakable and everlasting beauty, to be seen by the eyes of the mind, only cleared by faith?' (*DP*, 7); cf. **26.23–7** for a very similar passage. Sidney several times uses a Platonic commonplace (Plato, *Phaedrus*, 250d; Cicero, *De finibus*, 2.16.52 and *De officiis*, 1.5.15, citing Plato in each case), that if we could see virtue we would fall in love with it (*DP*, 24 and 29; *Astrophil and Stella*, 25.1–4). Cf. **82.33–5n.** But that artistic creation itself might be understood as involving such an act of falling in love is only implicit in the *Defence* and in fact emerges more clearly in Sidney's poetry and prose fiction, as Scott has evidently noticed. The figure of Pygmalion (**15.32**) recurs at moments in the work of Sidney and his contemporaries when love is related to the job of the artist, or vice versa: see, e.g., Sidney's *Arcadia* (*NA*, P2ᵛ; Skretkowicz, 231) and sonnet 13 in Samuel Daniel's *Delia* (1592), C3^r. The best-known account of this sculptor, who fell in love with a woman he had carved, prayed to Venus that she might come alive, and had his prayers granted, is in Ovid, *Metamorphoses*, 10.243–97.

15.38–16.2 a truly-reverend bishop . . . love of God   Not traced. Scott's respect for a bishop is interesting in view of his family's puritan sympathies (see Introduction, xxix).

16.4 zealously   *Zeal* and related words were moving towards an association first with reforming and then with Puritan religious ardour. *OED*'s first recorded usage for *zealously* is 1575. For Scott's religious position see Introduction, xxix.

16.9–11 which Musidorus saith . . . worldly and sensual   Referring to a long passage in Book 1 of the *Arcadia* in which Musidorus attempts to argue Pyrocles out of being in love with Philoclea:

And truely I thinke heere-upon it first gatte the name of Love: for indeede the true love hath that excellent nature in it, that it doth transforme the verie essence of the lover into the thing loved, uniting, and as it were incorporating it with a secret and inwarde working. And herein do these kinds of loves imitate the excellent; for as the love of heaven makes one heavenly, the love of vertue, vertuous; so doth the love of the world make one become worldly, and this effeminate love of a woman, doth so womanize a man . . .   (*NA*, D5^v; Skretkowicz, 71–2)

For other uses of this episode see **26.3–4, 70.5–6**, and **82.25–7**.

16.17–19 Plato entitle poets . . . sons of God   Scott lifts this amalgam from Viperano, 1.2: 'Hence Plato calls poets the fathers of the virtues, the leaders of wisdom, the parents of learning, and the sons and messengers of the gods [*Hinc Plato poetas virtutum genitores, sapientiae duces, eruditionis parentes, Deorum internuntios et filios appellat*]' (14/8). Viperano draws on *Symposium*, 209a ('Wisdom and the rest of virtue, which all poets beget [*gennētores*: begetters, fathers, ancestors]'), *Lysis*, 214a ('the fathers and guides of wisdom [*pateres tēs sophias . . . kai hēgemones*]'), *Republic*, 366a ('those children of the gods who have become poets and prophets'), and *Ion*, e.g. 534e ('representatives [*hermēnēs*, messengers, interpreters] of the gods'). There may be some intended analogy to Cicero, *De oratore*, 2.9.36, where history is described by Antonius as 'witness of ages, light of truth, life of memory, guide of life, and messenger of antiquity' (my translation).

16.27–8 quod non . . . acrius urit   Ovid, *Amores*, 2.19.3: 'quod licet, ingratum est; quod non licet acrius urit' ('What one may do freely has no charm; what one may not do pricks more keenly on').

16.29 intending   Intensifying (*OED*, *intend*, v., †4, first recorded usage 1603).

16.36–41 Such love I define ... be in love   Cicero, *Tusculan disputations*, 4.34.72, a discussion of lust, forming part of an extended treatment of the passions: 'The Stoics actually both say that the wise will experience love, and define love itself as the endeavour to form a friendship inspired by the semblance of beauty [*Stoici vero et sapientem amaturum esse dicunt et amorem ipsum conatum amicitiae faciendae ex pulcritudinis specie definiunt*].'

16.41–17.9 But if ... chaste-vow'd heart   The passage is impossible to punctuate satisfactorily and may be corrupt; the sense appears to be that we should respond to lust ('that lawless common changeling') as Silvia does in Tasso and in the words Scott suggests.

17.4–7 'Non mi toccar ... Amyntas   Tasso, *Aminta* (on which see **8.26–9n.** and **18.4–5n.**), 3.1 (l. 1286): '"Pastor, non mi toccar: son di Diana ..."'('"Don't touch me, shepherd: I belong to Diana"'). Scott misremembers this and either he or his scribe splits Tasso's one line into two.

17.8–9 Let not ... chaste-vow'd heart   These lines are apparently Scott's invention, though influenced by the 'lewd unhallowed eyes' of Tarquin in Shakespeare's *Lucrece*, 392, and less certainly by Wyatt's 'If thou wilt mighty be', l. 14: 'Except foule lust and vice do conquere thee'.

17.12–18 Tully saith ... heroic kind   Scott draws on the opening paragraphs of Cicero's short treatise *De optimo genere oratorum* ('On the best kind of orator'):

It is said that there are various kinds of orators as there are of poets. But the fact is otherwise, for poetry takes many forms. That is to say, every composition in verse, tragedy, comedy, epic, and also melic and dithyrambic ... has its own individuality, distinct from the others. So in tragedy a comic style is a blemish, and in comedy the tragic style is unseemly; and so with the other genres, each has its own tone and a way of speaking which the scholars recognize. But in the case of orators if one in the same way enumerates several kinds, regarding some as grand, stately or opulent, others as plain, restrained or concise, and others in an intermediate position, forming as it were a mean between the other two [the three styles: see **51.18–19n.**], he gives some information about the men but does not tell us enough about the art of oratory. For in an art we ask what is ideal perfection; in a man we describe what actually is ... There is only one kind of perfect orator ... [The various skills and styles] are but parts of a building as it were; the foundation is memory; that which gives it light is delivery. The man who is supreme in all these departments will be the most perfect orator; one who attains moderate success will be mediocre; he who has the least success will be the worst speaker. Still they will all be called orators, as painters are called painters, though they may be inferior, and will differ in ability, not in kind. Therefore, there is no orator who is unwilling to resemble Demosthenes, but Menander did not wish to write like Homer, for he was working in a different genre.   (1.1–2.6)

Menander (?344/3–292/1 BC) was the leading exponent of New Comedy. Cicero does not complete the analogy by referring to Apelles.

17.15 Apelles, or Hilliard   Apelles (late fourth century–early third century BC) was probably the most celebrated of classical painters, and certainly the most written about in the ancient world. For Nicholas Hilliard (1547?–1619) as England's Apelles, see Harington's notes at the end of Canto 33 of *Orlando furioso* (1591), discussing Ariosto's list of celebrated ancient and modern (Italian) painters. Ariosto ranks Apelles first of the ancients; Harington (278) offers Hilliard to rival the ancients as Ariosto had offered Leonardo, Michelangelo, *et al*. Hilliard is also compared favourably to modern Italian painters by Haydocke (¶6ʳ).

17.20 argument and subject   For Scott's definition of *argument* see **33.10–14n**.

17.23–6 naturally aptest . . . lyric and comic   A mere aside in the *Poetics* (1449a2–5), on the Homeric origins of the tragic and the comic: 'On the subsequent appearance of tragedy and comedy, those whose natural bent made lampooners of them turned to comedy, while those naturally inclined to epic became tragedians.' Cf. the end of Plato's *Symposium* (223d) where as dawn breaks Socrates is trying to prove to the comic dramatist Aristophanes and the tragedian Agathon 'that authors should be able to write both comedy and tragedy' while his audience nods off.

17.27–33 That famous painter . . . feared them from approaching   Pliny, 35.36.66, immediately following the anecdote about Zeuxis and Parrhasius that Scott discusses at **45.37–46.7**:

This *Zeuxis*, as it is reported, painted afterwards another table, wherein hee had made a boy carrying certaine bunches of grapes in a flasket, and seeing againe that the birds flew to the grapes, he shooke the head, and comming to his picture, with the like ingenuous mind as before, brake out into these words, and sayd, Ah, I see well ynough where I have failed, I have painted the grapes better than the boy, for if I had done him as naturally, the birds would have beene afraid and never approched the grapes.   (Holland, II, 535)

17.36–7 Aristotle . . . as Polygnotus was   *Poetics*, 1450a23–9, part of Aristotle's important discussion of the significance of plot and character:

a work could not be a tragedy if there were no action. But there could be a tragedy without *mimēsis* of character, and the tragedies of most of the moderns are in fact deficient in it; the same is true of many other poets, and of painters for that matter, of Zeuxis, for instance, in comparison with Polygnotus: the latter is good at depicting character [*agathos ēthographos*], while Zeuxis' painting has no *mimēsis* of character to speak of.

This passage is discussed by Scaliger, 7.3 (348a1; Padelford, 82). A space for the Greek text is left blank in the manuscript, but the text can readily be inferred: on this feature of transcription see Textual Introduction, lxxix–lxxxi.

18.2 Pliny . . . Zeuxis   Pliny (35.36.63–4) praises Zeuxis' portraits, including a Penelope 'wherein hee seemeth not onely to have depainted the outward personage and feature of the bodie, but also to have expressed most lively the inward affections and qualities of her mind' (Holland, II, 534, elaborating on *in qua pinxisse mores videtur*, 'in which the picture seems to portray morality'), but does report that he is criticised for a tendency to make head and joints disproportionately large (35.36.64).

18.4–5 *Gerusalemme* . . . Tasso   The Italian poet Torquato Tasso (1544–1595) was best known for his epic of the First Crusade, *Gerusalemme liberata* ('Jerusalem liberated'), printed in 1581, but shortly before its completion he had published the influential pastoral drama *Aminta* (1580/1; written 1573). A translation of this into English quantitative hexameters by Abraham Fraunce was printed in 1591 in *The Countesse of Pembrokes Yvychurch*, and in the same year the Italian text was printed in London as a companion piece (unannounced on the title page) to Guarini's *Il pastor fido*. Richard Carew's English version of the first five cantos of the *Gerusalemme liberata* was printed in 1594 (*Godfrey of Bulloigne, or the recoverie of Hierusalem*) and Edward Fairfax's complete translation (*Godfrey of Bulloigne, or the recoverie of Ierusalem*) in 1600. I have kept the manuscript's common anglicised form *Amyntas*.

18.7–9 Aristotle saith . . . (saith he)   *Poetics*, 1448b38–1449a2, immediately preceding the point about different natures suiting different kinds to which Scott has just referred (**17.23–6n.**). Scott repeats this point at **76.36–8**. The *Margites* was a humorous narrative poem, of which only fragments survive, attributed to Homer, though even in the ancient world some doubted the ascription. The Latin title, *Iliad*, for Homer's epic of the Trojan war was often used of each individual book, with the whole being referred to in the plural, as here and in the first recorded usage in *OED* (*Iliad*, n., 1: Gosson, 1579). The *OED* does not record the same of the *Odyssey*, though some of its quotations suggest it was also pluralised (*Odyssey*, n., 1). Here Scott's, or his scribe's, form is less anglicised (cf. Latin *Odyssea*). I have not regularised either form (MS: 'Iliads and Odysseas').

18.14–15 they that reckon . . . little or nothing   Cicero, *De optimo genere oratorum*, 1.2: 'Oratorum autem si quis ita numerat plura genera . . . de hominibus dicit aliquid, de re parum' ('But in the case of orators if one in the same way enumerates several kinds . . . he gives some information about the men but does not tell us enough about the art of oratory'), quoted in context, **17.12–18n.**

18.21–3 In which division . . . modern kinds   An important moment. Literary criticism of the sixteenth century can be divided broadly into two categories: on the one hand systematic treatments of, essentially, the classical canon (such as Scaliger's, although he makes room for neoclassical writings in Latin), and on the other hand more specialised attempts to theorise vernacular literature and modern kinds, such as the *Discorsi . . . dell'arte poetica, et in particolare del poema heroico* ('Discourses on the art of poetry and on the heroic poem in particular') of Tasso (composed 1560s; published 1587). The former tended to be written in Latin and the latter in the vernacular. Earlier Elizabethan literary criticism follows this pattern only to an extent: the neo-Latin writings of Dethick, Wills, and Gentili ignore vernacular literature, but the major vernacular treatises of Puttenham and Sidney are also largely concerned with classical literature and the received analysis of the classical kinds. Because Scott is so indebted to the neo-Latin tradition and to Sidney, rather than to continental theorists of modern vernacular writing, his analysis of the genres is traditional, but he recognises a need to adapt that analysis to modern practice, as he states explicitly here.

18.24–5 some represent . . . speaks mostly   The analysis of literary kinds by division according to who does the speaking goes back to Plato (*Republic*, 392d–394c) and Aristotle (*Poetics*, 1448a), whom Scott follows below (**68.32–69.1**) when he develops the analysis more schematically. The classication is threefold: poetry in a single (narrative) voice; poetry mixing narrative and direct speech; and dramatic speech without narration. It remains the clearest means of distinguishing formally between the different kinds, although it has led to confusion with the later threefold division of lyric, epic, and dramatic, on which see Gérard Genette, *Introduction à l'architexte* (Paris, 1979). Scaliger adopts the threefold division before his account of the different kinds and sub-kinds (1.3, 'Poematum per modos divisio'), and Viperano also discusses it (1.7, 19; 2.1, 67–8). See further **68.29–69.1n.**

18.25–8 the heroical . . . glorious good   The format of this definition – as of Scott's definitions of the other genres – follows the example of Aristotelian literary theory in combining matter, form, and end (for Aristotle's definition of tragedy see **6.1–4n.**). *Admiration* is a term of central importance, implying both the usefulness of *admiratio*/wonder as a fundamental aesthetic response (cf. Plotinus, *Enneads*, 1.6.4) and the possibility of romance impossibilities as an element of heroic poetry, an issue much debated in Italy. More specifically, it is a term that achieves prominence in sixteenth-century responses to and adaptations of Aristotle's *Poetics*. Wonder is found alongside pity and terror in Plato (*Ion*, 535b–c), and close to them in Aristotle: required in tragedy, wonder has more scope in epic, where credibility is not challenged by direct representation (1460a; cf. 1452a). A number of sixteenth-century Italian Aristotelians, Trissino for one (Weinberg, II, 752), brought pity, fear, and wonder into closer proximity than they are in Aristotle, and wonder also figured prominently in critical attempts to harmonise Horace and Aristotle (so that the poet would teach and delight through causing *admiratio*: see, e.g., Weinberg, I, 138–9, 149). Sidney goes further, putting *admiratio* in place of Aristotle's *phobos* (fear, terror) in his adaptation of Aristotle's celebrated definition of tragedy (1449b) as effecting through *eleos* (pity, compassion) and *phobos* the catharsis of those emotions, which Sidney transforms into 'stirring the affects of admiration and commiseration' (*DP*, 27; cf. 46, 47, 48; see also those passages from the *Arcadia* cited at **76.37–9n.** and **78.12–16n.**). Cf. Scott's later, parallel, definition of heroic poetry, **69.8–14**. For *admiratio* within the rhetorical tradition see **38.20–6n.**

18.28 difference   On *difference* in logic see **6.32–7n.**

18.33–6 secludes all the rest . . . gather the difference   Cf. **68.32–69.1**.

18.34 interlocutory and personating relation That is, dialogue, with actors play-ing roles. All major senses of the verb *personate* distinguished by *OED* are recorded for the first time between 1591 and 1616, the relevant one for Scott's usage being first recorded by *OED* in 1598 (*personate*, v., 4).

18.35 pastoral . . . mean style *Mean*: intermediate, middling, with reference to the tripartite hierarchy of styles (see **51.18–19** and **56.18–57.12**). Scott elsewhere attributes the low rather than the mean style to pastoral (**57.12** and **80.12–14**). For the source of the latter point in Donatus see **22.16–19n**.

18.37–29.30 Now this narration . . . speak somewhat apart The account of the genres that follows is typical in giving them in a hierarchical order: heroic, pastoral, tragedy, comedy, satire, and lyric. In this mode of historical account of the genres Scott follows the example of Scaliger, Viperano, and other continental critics. A sort of imaginary generic pre-history is also to be found in Aristotle and Horace, as well as in the later classical grammarians and commentators, though not elaborated to the questionable extremes found in some Renaissance writers. For a comparably derived account of the genres cf. Book 1 of Puttenham. Many of Scott's particular details, though, come from Scaliger and Viperano.

18.41–19.1 scolia . . . cross turns Greek *skolion*, from *skolios*, curved, crooked. On the origins of the name see Plutarch, *Quaestiones convivales*, 1.1: the myrtle spray would be passed round at feasts and the recipient would sing; *scolia* are therefore not so-called because the songs are intricate, but because to sing is difficult, or because the myrtle 'did not proceed from each guest to his neighbour in orderly sequence, but was passed across from couch to couch each time' (*Moralia*, 615b–c). See also Scaliger, 1.44 (47d1) and 3.116 (164b–c1), discussing *scolia* under lyric.

19.2 encomia . . . villages proclaimed Greek *enkōmion*, from *enkōmios*, in the vil-lage. Again, Scott's definition shows an understanding of the word's etymology. Cf. Puttenham, 1.20: 'So have you how the immortal gods were praised by hymns, the great princes and heroic personages by ballads of praise called *encomia*, both of them by historical reports of great gravity and majesty' (*Art*, 133).

19.3–5 The rhapsody . . . sundry occasions Cf. Scaliger, 1.41, for a consideration of the name (45b1–46a1). Scott's 'collected pieces of them and severally rehearsed them' shows that he understands the etymology: Greek *rhapsōdia*, epic recitation or composition, or a portion of an epic poem suited to recitation, from *rhaptein*, to sew together, and as performed and interpreted by a *rhapsōdos*, rhapsode (see Plato's *Ion* for a dialogue with one such).

19.5–7 In English . . . historical ditty Scott is quoting Puttenham here, whom he is unable to name ('one saith') because *The art of English poesy* was anonymous. Puttenham, 1.19, compares the use of hexameter for classical epic to the mixed metres of poems 'of such quality as became best to be sung with the voice and to some musical instrument' (*Art*, 130), such as the odes of Pindar and the hymns of Callimachus. Puttenham then seemingly makes the connection to the use of mixed metres (typically tetrameter and trimeter in alternation) in English ballads, although he does not name the ballad *per se*. He continues:

And we ourselves who compiled this treatise have written for pleasure a little brief *romance or historical ditty* in the English tongue of the Isle of Great Britain in short and long meters, and by breaches or divisions to be more commodiously sung to the harp in places of assembly, where the company shall be desirous to hear of old adventures and valiances of noble knights in times past, as are those of King Arthur and his knights of the round table, Sir Bevis of Southampton, Guy of Warwick, and others like. Such as have not premonition hereof, and consideration of the causes alleged, would peradventure reprove and disgrace every *romance or short historical ditty*, for that they be not written in long meters or verses alexandrine, according to the nature and style of large histories, wherein they should do wrong, for they be sundry forms of poems and not all one.   (131; my emphasis)

For Chaucer's use of the terms see *romance* in the 'Tale of Thopas' (*Canterbury tales*, VII(B²) 897) and *The romaunt of the rose*; and *ballad* in *The legend of good women* (F 270, 423, etc.; G 202, 224, 411, etc.) and the titles of a number of his short poems, all of which show the term meaning a shorter song rather than a longer narrative poem. Scott's account of heroic poetry shows a noticeable lack of interest in contemporary Italian romance theory.

19.8–9 that song of David . . . ten thousand   The reference is not to one of the Psalms, but to the songs sung before Saul after David's defeat of Goliath: 'When they came againe, and David returned from the slaughter of the Philistim, the women came out of all cities of Israel, singing and dauncing to meete king Saul, with timbrels, with *instruments* of joy, and with rebecks. And the women sang by course in their play, and saide, Saul hath slaine his thousand, and David his ten thousand' (I Samuel 18:6–7; cf. 21:11 and 29:5).

19.9–10 the hymns of Pindar . . . games   Pindar (*c*.518 BC–*c*.446 BC), Greek lyric poet and author of numerous *epinicia* or victory songs to celebrate victories in the four panhellenic athletic festivals. Scott quotes Pindar at **74.19**.

19.10–12 full wry imitation . . . to this day   Cf. Sidney: 'In our neighbour country Ireland, where truly learning goeth very bare, yet are their poets held in a devout reverence' (*DP*, 6). This 'full wry [i.e. completely perverted, wrong, aberrant] imitation' of the status and function of such poetry as Pindar's is described by Irenius in Edmund Spenser's dialogue *A view of the present state of Ireland*, probably completed in the summer of 1596 and not printed until 1633, though it was entered in the Stationers' Register in April 1598, shortly before Spenser's death in January 1599:

There is amongst the Irish a certaine kind of people, called Bardes, which are to them insteed of poets, whose profession is to set foorth the praises or dispraises of men in their poems or rymes . . . their verses are taken up with a generall applause, and usually sung at all feasts and meetings . . . It is most true, that such Poets as in their writings doe labour to better the manners of men, and thorough the sweete baite of their numbers, to steale into the young spirits a desire of honour and vertue, are worthy to bee had in great respect. But these Irish Bardes are for the most part of another minde, and so farre from instructing yong men in morall discipline, that they themselves doe more deserve to bee sharpely disciplined; for they seldome use to choose unto themselves the doings of good men for the arguments of their poems, but whomsoever they finde to be most licentious of life, most bolde and lawlesse in his doings, most dangerous and desperate in all parts of disobedience and rebellious disposition, him they set up and glorifie in their rithmes, him they praise to the people, and to yong men make an example to follow.   (*View*, 75–6)

Scott had access to a manuscript text of the *View*, copied into a family miscellany now Folger Shakespeare Library MS v.b.214: on this manuscript and its implications see Introduction, xxviii–xxxvi.

19.12 in Hungary . . . still   Cf. Sidney: 'In Hungary I have seen it the manner at all feasts and other such meetings to have songs of their ancestors' valour, which that right soldierlike nation think one of the chiefest kindlers of brave courage' (*DP*, 28).

19.13–15 the music . . . the lyric   *Accidental* is used in the logical sense of an incidental rather than an essential property of a thing (see **5.24–31n.**; and cf. Blundeville, 9–10): some epic poems are sung but some are only 'repeated' (recited: *OED*, *repeat*, v., 5a), so music is not essential to epic in the way it is to lyric; instead epic poems are to be categorised as such on the basis of their subject matter. Much of Scott's material in this paragraph is drawn from discussion, in Scaliger and Sidney, ranged under *lyric* rather than *epic/heroic*.

19.17–18 whether the poet . . . of his own   Cf. Horace, *Ars poetica*, 119 ('Either follow tradition or invent what is self-consistent') and see further **73.26–8n.**

19.18–19 images of the virtues . . . of these heroes   That poetry portrays images of virtue, or attempts to, is a Sidneian (and Platonic) formulation: see further **19.39–40n.**

19.22–3 *epopoeia* . . . praiseworthy things   Greek *epopoiia*, Aristotle's preferred term for epic (e.g. *Poetics*, 1449b9), given here in its Latinised form, as in both Viperano and *OED* (*epopœia*, n., first recorded English usage 1749). (Scott's scribe gives us 'Epipoia'.) Scott's definition is not as etymologically grounded as it appears to be. Cf. Viperano, 2.2: 'This Greek term, derived from *epos* and *poiein* (the former meaning word or verse, the latter to make or represent), means all fiction expressed in prose or verse' (69). The Greek *epos* means word, utterance; more generally that which is uttered in words, speech, tale; hence song. Scaliger prefers the term *epos* for epic (1.41, 45b1).

19.24–31 Homer . . . *Faerie Queene* This canon of epic poems shows the influence of Sidney's *Defence* (in its inclusion of prose works by Xenophon, Heliodorus, and More) and of Scott's concern to map theory on to modern practice (in its ranging of modern examples against the ancients). (i) *Homer*: the *Iliad* and the *Odyssey*. (ii) *Virgil*: the *Aeneid*, Scott's gold standard (see **57.36–7n.**). (iii) *Ariosto*: the *Orlando furioso* of Ludovico Ariosto (1474–1533), an epic romance with a chivalric, fantastic, and amorous content which is not at all to Scott's taste (see **35.7–10n.** and **71.34n.**); it was printed in an early version in 1516 and complete in 1532. (iv) *Tasso*: the *Gerusalemme liberata* (see **18.4–5n.**). (v) *Lucan . . . Lancaster and York*: the *Pharsalia* of Lucan and the *Civil wars* of Samuel Daniel (1562–1619); see **12.12–13n.** and **72.18–20n.** (vi) *Albion's England*: a verse history of Britain by William Warner (1558/9–1609), printed in successively expanding editions in 1586, 1589, 1592, 1596/7, 1602, and 1612; Warner was called 'our English Homer' in the comparison of ancient and modern poets in Meres's *Palladis tamia* of 1598 (*ECE*, II, 317). (vii) *Xenophon's Cyrus*: the *Cyropaedia* ('Education of Cyrus') of the Greek historian and soldier Xenophon (*c.*430–after 360 BC), a fictionalised biography of the sixth-century Persian king. (viii) *Heliodorus*: the *Aithiopika* ('An Ethiopian Story'), a third- or fourth-century AD Greek prose romance telling the story of the lovers Theagenes and Charikleia; nothing is known about its author; an English translation by Thomas Underdowne was printed in 1569, after the French of Jacques Amyot (1547). (ix) *Utopia*: a Latin dialogue on government including an account of the fictional island of Utopia by Sir Thomas More (1478–1535), printed in 1516, with an English translation by Ralph Robinson appearing in 1551. (x) *Arcadia*: *The Countess of Pembroke's Arcadia* of Sir Philip Sidney (1554–86), a prose romance with verse interludes written around 1580 and revised and expanded before his death; the incomplete revised text was printed in 1590, with a complete composite version appearing in 1593. As Scott observes, it not only mixes pastoral with epic elements but verse with prose. (xi) *Faerie Queene*: the great allegorical epic romance of Edmund Spenser (1552?–99), printed in 1590 (Books 1–3) and 1596 (adding Books 4–6), with a fragment of a later book (twelve, or possibly even twenty-four, were projected) appearing in 1609.

19.31–3 In some example . . . particular or general Whether the 'example or precedent' – the exemplary action or more usually character that will inspire us to emulate it in our own lives – should better be 'feigned or true' is a question Scott sets to one side for now, though it is one of the central points of contention in Sidney's *Defence*. Sidney argues strongly, following Aristotle (see **11.21–4n.**), that fictitious material, or fictionalised history as in the case of Xenophon, can offer more perfectly exemplary patterns for emulation than can actuality. Note that the emulation Scott imagines is 'admiring' – activating the neo-Aristotelian vocabulary of readerly wonder (see **18.25–8n.**).

19.33–9 Xenophon . . . managed love Scott is looking at the passage in Sidney's *Defence* in which Sidney contends specifically that 'poetry' should be taken to include fictions in prose: 'For Xenophon, who did imitate so excellently as to give us *effigiem* *iusti imperii* – the portraiture of a just empire – under the name of Cyrus, as Cicero saith of him, made therein an absolute heroical poem. So did Heliodorus in his sugared invention of that picture of love in Theagenes and Charikleia. And yet both these wrote in prose' (*DP*, 12). Sidney and Scott refer to Cicero's *Letter to Quintus*, 1.1.23: 'Such a one was Cyrus as described by Xenophon, not according to historical truth but as the pattern of a just ruler [*non ad historiae fidem . . . sed ad effigiem iusti imperi*]; in him that philosopher created a matchless blend of firmness and courtesy.' (I have preserved the full genitive form *imperii* used by Scott and Sidney, though modern editions of Cicero have apocopated *imperi* here.) Meres also reproduces Sidney's passage, and adds Sidney to the list: 'so Sir Philip Sidney writ his immortal poem, *The Countess of Pembrooke's Arcadia* in Prose; and yet our rarest Poet' (*ECE*, II, 315–16). A 'scantling' is a measure, pattern, outline, or sketch (*OED*, *scantling*, n., †1b and †6), a word drawn – like much of Scott's theory – from the visual arts.

19.39–40 The *Arcadia . . .* virtues and affections   Another painting metaphor. In Scott's Sidneian, and Platonic, literary theory, the virtues and passions start out as ideal forms which are embodied in the actions or even the characters of exemplary figures in the fiction. That these 'virtues and affections' have faces which are 'limned' (painted, as in a portrait: *OED*, *limn*, v., 3, first recorded usage 1593) blurs the line between personification allegory (as practised by Spenser), in which a virtue or passion is allegorically embodied in a character, and the representation, in Sidney's poetics of exemplary character, of what he calls 'notable images of virtues, vices, or what else' (*DP*, 12, the passage of the *Defence* from which Scott draws immediately above). According to Plato (and Sidney may consciously be parodying this passage), 'all poetic imitators, beginning with Homer, imitate images of virtue [*mimētas eidōlōn aretēs einai*] and all the other things they write about and have no grasp of the truth' (*Republic*, 600e). That failure in Platonic terms (an image is not reality, let alone the ideal form that lies behind it) is turned by Sidney into a Neoplatonic success (an image takes you closer to the ideal form than does actuality). See further **15.29–33n**.

19.40–1 Bartas . . . virtuously living woman   On the French Protestant poet Guillaume de Salluste, Sieur du Bartas (1544–90) see Introduction, lv–lix. *Judith* was a biblical epic in six books, printed as part of *La muse Chrestiene* (1574). It is based on the apocryphal Book of Judith, which tells of the beautiful widow who murders the Assyrian general Holofernes and thus saves Israel. As Du Bartas observes in the 'Advertissement au lecteur' in that volume (Du Bartas, II, 3): 'je n'ay pas tant suivi l'ordre ou la frase du texte de la Bible, comme j'ay taché (sans toutesfois m'esloigner de la verité de l'histoire) d'imiter Homere en son *Iliade*, Vergile en son *Æneide*, l'Arioste en son *Roland*, et autres qui nous ont laissé des ouvrages de semblable estoffe' ('I have not so much followed the order and wording of the text of the Bible as I have tried (without nevertheless going far from historical truth) to imitate Homer in his *Iliad*, Virgil in his *Aeneid*, Ariosto in his *Orlando*, and others who have left us works of similar material'). Scott perhaps recalls Du Bartas's Virgilian opening: 'Je chante les vertus d'une vaillante vefue' ('I sing the virtues of a valiant widow': Du Bartas, II, 5). Scott refers again to *Judith* at **32.28–9** and **43.5–9**. Cf. Sidney on the edifying image of Judith and Holofernes (*DP*, 36).

20.1–8 that sacred and lofty poem . . . not known perfectly   The Old Testament Book of Job tells of its godly hero's suffering at the hands of Satan, a divinely sanctioned test of whether Job's piety will survive the loss of his family, prosperity, and health. It does, to an extent, and Job is rewarded by God at the Book's end. One opinion preserved in the Babylonian Talmud ascribes the Book of Job to Moses; also recorded there is the view that 'Job never was and never existed, but is only a typical figure': Baba Bathra, 14b–15a, in *Baba Bathra*, trans. Maurice Simon and Israel W. Slotki, 2 vols. (London, 1935), I, 71 and 74. Scott's source for these details and for his response that Job is not 'a feigned thing' is probably the work he cites next, the *Bibliotheca sancta* (Venice, 1566) of Sixtus of Sienna (1520–69): Moses as author (24); and the refutation of what is called the Anabaptist heresy that Job is a tragicomic fable (1027). Scott refers directly, with a slight error, to Sixtus' suggestion that a prose narrative framework surrounds the elaborate (verse) speeches that form the main matter of Job's 42 chapters: 'ab initio autem tertii capitis usque ad initium quadragesimi secundi capitis hexametris versibus labitur' (24: 'for from the start of the third chapter through to the start of the forty-second chapter it flows in hexameters'). Scott also leans heavily on two passages in Sidney here: 'And may not I presume a little farther . . . and say that the holy David's Psalms are a divine poem? If I do, I shall not do it without the testimony of great learned men both ancient and modern. But even the name of "Psalms" will speak for me, which, being interpreted, is nothing but "songs"; then, that it is fully written in metre, as all learned Hebricians agree, although the rules be not yet fully found' (*DP*, 7); 'Such were David in his Psalms, Solomon in his Song of Songs, in his Ecclesiastes and Proverbs, Moses and Deborah in their Hymns, and the writer of Job, which, beside other, the learned Emanuel Tremellius and Franciscus Junius do entitle the poetical part of the Scripture' (10). Sidney refers to the *Biblia sacra* of Immanuel Tremellius and Franciscus Junius, a Latin Bible translated from the Hebrew and published in stages on the continent between 1569 and 1579, and in an edition printed in London in 1580; it divided the Old Testament into parts, each with a separate title page and with the third part (Job, Psalms, Proverbs, Ecclesiastes, The Song of Songs) being subtitled 'Quinque libri poetici' ('five poetic books'). Cf. Wills, 64–6; and Puttenham: 'King David also and Solomon his son and many other of the holy prophets wrote in meters and used to sing them to the harp, although to many of us ignorant of the Hebrew language and phrase, and not observing it, the same seem but a prose' (*Art*, 99). Cf. also Harington, borrowing from Sidney: 'some part of the Scripture was written in verse, as the Psalmes of *David*, and certain other songs of *Deborah*, of *Salomon*, and others, which the learnedest divines do affirme to be verse, and find that they are in meeter, though the rule of the Hebrew verse they agree not on' (*ECE*, II, 207). The tradition of describing Hebrew poetry in the terms of Greek and Latin quantitative metrics began in the first century AD with the Jewish writers Philo and Josephus and was taken up by the Church Fathers, including Origen, Eusebius, and (most influentially) Jerome. On the Renaissance background see Israel Baroway's series of articles, 'The Bible as poetry in the English Renaissance', *JEGP* 32 (1933), 447–80; 'Tremellius, Sidney, and biblical verse', *MLN*, 49 (1934), 145–9; and 'The Hebrew hexameter: a study in Renaissance sources and interpretation', *ELH*, 2 (1935), 66–91. Baroway suggests that among Sidney's 'learned Hebricians' (and therefore Scott's 'best divines') is perhaps Joannes Mercerus ('The Hebrew hexameter', 85). The extent and nature of Hebrew biblical metrics (possibly accentual, and making heavy use of patterns of repetition and parallelism) are still debated, though the comparison to classical quantitative metrics is no longer made.

20.9–11 natural knowledge . . . Palingenius   On Empedocles see **12.10–15n**. Marcellus Palingenius is thought to have been an anagrammatic pseudonym under which one Pier Angelo Manzolli published the much-reprinted Latin didactic poem *Zodiacus vitae* [1535?]. It was banned by the Inquisition, which only increased its popularity among Protestants. An English translation in fourteeners by Barnabe Googe (1540–94), *The zodyake of lyfe*, appeared in stages between 1560 and 1565, with further revised editions in 1576 and 1588. The title page of the 1565 edition summarises its contents: 'wherein are conteyned twelve bookes disclosing the haynous crymes and wicked vices of our corrupt nature: and plainlye declaring the pleasaunt and perfit pathway unto eternall lyfe, besides a numbre of digressions both pleasaunt and profitable'.

20.11–12 Ovid's *Metamorphoses* . . . moral knowledge   The great mythographic poem the *Metamorphoses* (Scott's scribe gives 'Metamorphosis') by the Roman poet Ovid (43 BC–AD 17) was in the sixteenth century still read to an extent in the allegorical terms of the medieval *Ovide moralisé* tradition. The first four books of the English translation by Arthur Golding (1535/6–1606) were printed in 1565 with a complete edition following in 1567; a prefatory poem makes clear that a moralising reading is expected of the reader. For this view of Ovid cf. Webbe (*ECE*, I, 238). Scott returns to the point at **40.36–8**, and see **40.36–8n.** for 'natural . . . knowledge'.

20.13–15 our incomparable Bartas . . . the creation   On Du Bartas see Introduction, lv–lix. The reference is to *La sepmaine, ou creation du monde* (1578), Du Bartas's verse elaboration of the account in Genesis of the first week of the Creation, part of which Scott himself, like a number of other Elizabethan poets including Sidney, translated. It was known as the *Première sepmaine* after the publication of *La seconde sepmaine* in 1584.

20.17–19 Jerome Zanchius . . . discussed and concluded   Girolamo Zanchi (1516–90), an Italian Protestant clergyman and academic theologian popular in England. Several of his works were translated into English in the 1590s, including *An excellent and learned treatise, of the spirituall mariage betweene Christ and the church, and every faithfull man* ([Cambridge?], 1592) and *H. Zanchius his confession of Christian religion* ([Cambridge], 1599), and other publications in England, in English and Latin, followed in the seventeenth century. Of his many works Scott is probably thinking in particular of Zanchius' account of the Creation, *De operibus Dei intra spatium sex dierum creatis* (Neustadt, 1591).

20.20 minced . . . tenderest stomach   This digestive metaphor runs through many of Scott's sources. See further **32.8–11n.** and **47.33–6n.**; Hebrews 5:12–14 and I Corinthians 3:2; and Sidney's *Defence*, which Scott alludes to here: 'the poet is the food for the tenderest stomachs; the poet is indeed the right popular philosopher' (*DP*, 18). Cf. Sidney on philosophical poets, 'which who mislike, the fault is in their judgement quite out of taste, and not in the sweet food of sweetly uttered knowledge' (*DP*, 11).

20.24–5 knowledge . . . action   Another Sidneian perspective in Sidneian language. Cf. *Defence*, following Aristotle, *Nicomachean ethics*, 1.1–2 (1094a–b), on 'the highest end of the mistress-knowledge, by the Greeks called *architektonikē*, which stands as I think in the knowledge of a man's self, in the ethic and politic consideration, with the end of well-doing and not of well-knowing only' and 'the ending end of all earthly learning being virtuous action' (*DP*, 13). See further **70.15–16n.**

20.29–30 thorough error . . . overthrown   Scott's prose rhythm deserves scrutiny here, since this sentence ends with a perfect pentameter. The periodic prose style modelled on the Latin of Cicero in particular made use of metrical patterning especially at a sentence's end (*clausula*). For *error* as Aristotle's *hamartia* see **77.5–11n.**

20.30–1 *Mirror of Magistrates* . . . in English   It may not be coincidental that Scott's canonical list of complaint poetry comes in chronological order of printing. *A Mirror for magistrates* inaugurated the Elizabethan vogue for complaint poems. Printed in 1559 after an earlier 1554 edition was suppressed, it was initially overseen by William Baldwin and George Ferrers, with various writers contributing complaints by unfortunate figures from English history; further, ever-expanding, editions followed regularly over the next sixty years. Sidney judges the *Mirror* 'meetly furnished of beautiful parts' (*DP*, 44). Samuel Daniel's *The complaint of Rosamond*, in the voice of Henry II's mistress Rosamund Clifford, was printed with his sonnet sequence *Delia* in 1592. Shakespeare's *Lucrece* followed in 1594, and in 1595 *Saint Peters complaint* by the Jesuit poet and martyr Robert Southwell (1561–95). The latter was based on *Le lagrime di San Pietro* by Luigi Tansillo (or Tanzillo), published first in 1560 under the name of Cardinal de Pucci, and in numerous editions under Tansillo's name thereafter: see Mario Praz, 'Robert Southwell's "Saint Peter's complaint" and its Italian source', *MLR*, 19 (1924), 273–90. Scott's recognition of this relationship was not shared by his contemporaries or by students of Southwell before the twentieth century.

20.32–3 these answer . . . of the heroical   See **19.3–5.** That is to say they are pieces of epic material that might be stitched together into longer works but are suitable for performance (or publication). In classical Latin and Hellenistic Greek, as well as the English of Scott's day, the term *rhapsody* could be used of a single book or other portion of an epic poem suitable for recitation (see *OED*, *rhapsody*, n., and **19.3–5n.**). A similar sense lies behind the modern resurrection of the rare Greek term epyllion (*epullion*, diminutive of *epos*, hence 'little epic') to describe a slightly wider range of classically modelled short narrative poems from the 1590s especially. There was no comparable attempt to label this sort of writing at the time. By 'one act of the heroical' Scott implies both a single, unified action (in the terms of Aristotelian poetics: see **35.23–5n**. and cf. 'one act' at **77.12**) and an analogy to the five-act structure of a play, by which the complaint poem might comprehend something like a fifth of the material that would make up an epic poem. Cf. **76.8–9**; and **76.33–5** for a similar point about dramatic form: 'the fables or subjects of these poems are but as certain parts, acts, or special passages of the heroic'. Cf. Viperano, 2.4, on epic containing 'more than one action [*plures actiones*]' (75/74).

20.33–4 Chaucer's *Troilus . . . Legends* Both Sidney (*DP*, 44) and Puttenham (*Art*, 1.31, 148–50) praise Chaucer and single out *Troilus and Criseyde*, but neither mentions *The legend of good women*, Chaucer's collection of narratives about celebrated women from classical myth, including Dido, Lucretia, and Philomela. Each is separately titled ('The legend of Cleopatra', 'The Legend of Thisbe', etc.: see for example *The workes of our antient and lerned English poet, Geffrey Chaucer* (1598), 200ʳ), which is why Scott refers to plural '*Legends*'.

20.35–21.3 such narrations . . . greater consequence Scott has few precursors in this discussion of mock epic; hence perhaps his resort to an authority outside the realm of literary criticism in Castiglione. (i) 'Homer's Frog-mouse-fight': a literal translation of *Batrachomyomachia*, a parody of the *Iliad* describing a battle between the frogs and the mice, written some time in the third–first centuries BC, and mistakenly believed to be by Homer in the Renaissance. It is discussed by Puttenham, not in his treatment of genre in Book 1 but in Book 3, during a preliminary discussion of the decorum of matching style to matter, in terms that Scott is clearly echoing: 'to that trifling poem of Homer: though the frog and mouse be but little and ridiculous beasts, yet to treat of war is a high subject, and a thing in every respect terrible and dangerous to them that it alights on, and therefore of learned duty asketh martial grandiloquence, if it be set forth in his kind and nature of war, even betwixt the basest creatures that can be imagined' (*Art*, 235). (ii) 'Virgil's *Gnat*': *Culex*, one of the poems in the Appendix Virgiliana, a collection of spurious works believed to be by Virgil in antiquity; it gives an account of the underworld in the voice of a gnat who appears in a dream to the shepherd whom the gnat had prevented from being bitten by a snake. (iii) 'Spenser's *Muiopotmos*': *Muiopotmos, or the fate of the butterflie* is a mock-heroic poem published in 1591 as part of *Complaints*, a volume which also included Spenser's version of *Culex*, *Virgils gnat*. *Muiopotmos* tells of the death of the butterfly Clarion in the web of the spider Aragnol, with long Ovidian back-stories of the origins of both kinds of creature. Critics still debate whether its story shadows 'some moral of greater consequence'. (iv) Balthazar: Count Baldassare Castiglione, whose *Il cortegiano* (1528), a dialogue on the ideal courtier with extended digressions on themes such as Platonic love, was essential reading for the would-be Elizabethan courtier. An English translation by Thomas

Hoby, *The courtyer*, was printed in 1561. Scott may be alluding, appositely in view of Sir Henry Lee's activities in the tiltyard (see **81.41–82.6n.**), to Castiglione's discussion of tilting and other occasions when the courtier might 'shewe feates of Chivalrie in open sightes' in Book 2 of *Il cortegiano* (Cox, 109; cf. the summary of the qualities of the courtier, 370). This would be to view mock epic as a rehearsal for real epic, and to open up the possibility of finding the business of the tiltyard – rehearsal for real battle that it was – somewhat ridiculous.

21.4–14 Now follows... Virgil's *Eclogues* Scott continues to define the kinds by mode of delivery (pastoral, like drama, has people actually speaking) and subject matter (whereas tragedy and comedy represent people doing bad things, pastoral handles 'mean', that is ordinary, lowly, or everyday, matters: see **18.35n.**). He nicely qualifies his definition to include both dialogue poems, as most eclogues are, and those in a single voice (cf. Viperano, 3.7, 145–6), and to distinguish between what is the subject on the surface ('immediately') and what might be the subtext. Elizabethan definitions of pastoral emphasise its potential for indirection, encouraged by the arguments about church and court politics under the surface of Spenser's *Shepheardes calender* (1579), and citing, as here, the precedent of Virgil, who allows the vexed politics of Roman agricultural land ownership in the first century BC (with longstanding farmers being dispossessed to make way for veteran soldiers) to darken the pastoral idyll, as in the first of his *Eclogues*. So Puttenham: 'the poet devised the eclogue long after the other dramatic poems, not of purpose to counterfeit or represent the rustical manner of loves and communication, but under the veil of homely persons and in rude speeches to insinuate and glance at greater matters, and such as perchance had not been safe to have been disclosed in any other sort, which may be perceived by the *Eclogues* of Virgil . . .' (*Art*, 1.18, 127–8). And see the passage from Sidney's *Defence* (*DP*, 26) quoted by Scott at **80.6–9**. Cf. Sidney's *Arcadia*, with its sets of eclogues performed between each of the five books, 'sometimes under hidden formes uttering such matters, as otherwise they durst not deale with' (*NA*, B2ʳ; Skretkowicz, 24; cf. *OA*, 56). Such concerns do less to ruffle the surface of the (imaginatively) historical accounts of Scaliger (1.4, 6b2–10a1), Viperano, *et al.*, but they are there: 'some think the story ought to be fashioned *allegorically*, that it ought to say one thing and understand something else . . . This can often be done properly, suitably, and aptly, but we deny that it ought always to be done' (Viperano, 3.8, 151).

21.17–18 divine... to be meant See the May, July, and September eclogues for examples of church allegory, drawn attention to in the arguments to each eclogue. For many years the authorship of *The shepheardes calender*, published in 1579 under the pseudonym 'Immerito', was unknown or an open secret. So Puttenham can only refer to 'that other gentleman who wrote the late *Shepheardes Calender*' (*Art*, 151). Sidney, to whom the work was dedicated, left Spenser's mask in place in the *Defence* (*DP*, 44), and Webbe was only prepared to attribute it uncertainly to 'Master *Sp.*' (*ECE*, I, 245, 263). Even after his death in 1599, editions omitted to attribute the work to Spenser, though he had implicitly claimed authorship in *Colin Clouts come home againe* (1595), and there is no mystery as far as Scott is concerned.

21.21 without much counterfeited action   That is to say, little happens at the level of plot, since the poem comprises staged dialogue and is therefore essentially static.

21.22–41 And this some say . . . the pastoral   Accounts consonant with those of the nameless authorities cited here can be found in Scott's usual sources. Cf. Viperano, 3.7–8, itself leaning heavily on Scaliger, 1.4 and 3.99. Scaliger asserts blithely that 'The earliest kind of poetry was of course the product of one of the earliest stages of life' (6b2; Padelford, 21). Scott is especially close to Puttenham, 1.18, in many of his details; Puttenham argues against Scaliger that although the eclogue represents a more primitive society than epic or tragedy, it does so artfully, and so was not the first genre to come into being (*Art*, 127–8). Scott's arm's-length tone indicates sympathy for this position but also the reservation of judgement against his favourite modern authority.

21.31–2 divine testimony   Many of the stories of the early books of the Old Testament have a pastoral setting; for women tending flocks see, e.g., Jacob and Rachel in Genesis 29.

22.1–2 Theocritus . . . exceed his pattern   Theocritus: early third-century BC Greek poet, whose pastoral poems – which represent the inception of the genre – became known as the *Idylls*. Virgil imitates Theocritus throughout his ten *Eclogues*; this imitative relationship was itself imitated by later pastoral poets (see the 'August' eclogue of Spenser's *Shepheardes calender*, for example), and is a dynamic of particular importance to the genre, although Scott's 'as he useth' reminds us that Virgil's other writings are imitative too – as the *Aeneid* imitates Homer – and that they too can be seen as outdoing their models.

22.3–11 *Shepheardes Calender* . . . Normans of England   Scott borrows this point from Sidney: 'The *Shepheardes Calender* hath much poetry in his eclogues, indeed worthy the reading, if I be not deceived. That same framing of his style to an old rustic language I dare not allow, since neither Theocritus in Greeke, Virgil in Latin, nor Sannazaro in Italian did affect it' (*DP*, 44). E. K. addresses the question of Spenser's deliberately archaic diction in the epistle to Harvey that opens *The shepheardes calender*, and alludes to Evander's mother (*Shorter poems*, 27), perhaps prompting what follows (see **22.5–10n.**). Scott returns to this point about Spenser at **48.16–20**.

22.5–10 Favorinus, in Agellius . . . first inhabitants of Italy   A close paraphrase from the *Attic nights* (*c*.AD 180) of Aulus Gellius, often and mistakenly known as 'Agellius' in the middle ages and even in Scott's day; the essay in question is titled 'In what terms the philosopher Favorinus rebuked a young man who used language that was too old-fashioned and archaic':

The philosopher Favorinus thus addressed a young man who was very fond of old words and made a display in his ordinary, everyday conversation of many expressions that were quite too unfamiliar and archaic: 'Curius,' said he, 'and Fabricius and Coruncanius, men of the olden days, and of a still earlier time than these those famous triplets, the Horatii, talked clearly and intelligibly with their fellows, using the language of their own day, not that of the Aurunci, the Sicani, or the Pelasgi, who are said to have been the earliest inhabitants of Italy. You, on the contrary, just as if you were talking to-day with Evander's mother, use words that have already been obsolete for many years [*Curius, inquit, et Fabricius et Coruncanius, antiquissimi viri, et his antiquiores Horatii illi trigemini, plane ac dilucide cum suis fabulati sunt neque Auruncorum aut Sicanorum aut Pelasgorum, qui primi coluisse Italiam dicuntur, sed aetatis suae verbis locuti sunt; tu autem, proinde quasi cum matre Euandri nunc loquare, sermone abhinc multis annis iam desito uteris*], because you want no one to know and comprehend what you are saying. Why not accomplish your purpose more fully, foolish fellow, and say nothing at all? ... Live by all means according to the manners of the past, but speak in the language of the present.'   (1.10)

Evander was a mythical Greek settler who fled Arcadia and landed at what would become Rome on the advice of his mother Carmentis. She was associated with childbirth and prophecy, and was said to have taught writing to the native inhabitants of Italy. This passage in Gellius was popular: cf. Thomas Wilson, *The arte of rhetorique* (1553), A2ʳ. Scott's scribe gives 'Phavorinus' and 'Corun-Canus'.

22.11–12 Sir Philip Sidney ... pastoral kind   Most of Sidney's pastoral poems were written for the eclogues in the 'old' *Arcadia*. Though many were omitted from the 1590 printing of the revised *Arcadia*, the 1593 edition rescued as many as possible from the original manuscript version (on the *Arcadia*'s texts see also **19.24–31n.**), and included one probably never intended for inclusion by Sidney, which was to be Scott's favourite: 'Lamon's Tale' (see **55.1–3n.**, **65.30–1**, and **80.16–18n.**). Sidney does not adopt a rustic or archaic diction; rather, his pastoral poems are highly wrought and formal, both prosodically and rhetorically.

22.13 eclogues ... best ones   The Greek term 'eclogue' (*eklogē*) means a selection, as Scaliger (7a1; Padelford, 22) and Viperano (149) explain.

22.14–16 howsoever some ... wrestingly   This was a common enough view (e.g. Webbe, *ECE*, I, 262), but the particular culprit in Scott's mind, or open book on his desk, may be *The shepheardes calender*, the 'generall argument' of which opens with a lengthy defence of this false etymology (*Shorter poems*, 32).

22.16–19 These are subdivided ... their name agreeable   Scott only partially depends on Scaliger and Viperano here, and goes back to a familiar passage from Donatus; Puttenham is not interested in the origins of the various terms. (i) *pastoral*: Latin *pastoralis*, from *pastor*, shepherd, an etymology therefore ignored in Scaliger's account (1.4) of the (Greek) prehistory of the genre; (ii) *bucolic*: Greek *boukolikos*, from *boukolos*, herdsman, from *bous*, cow; cf. Scaliger, 7d1 (Padelford, 23) and Viperano, 148;

(iii) *georgic*: Greek *geōrgikos*, from *geōrgos*, husbandman, from *gē*, earth, plus the root of *ergon*, work; (iv) *goatherd kinds*: Greek *aipolia*, from *aipolion*, herd of goats; cf. Scaliger, 7d1 (Padelford, 23) and Viperano, 148; no related term was coined in English. The tripartite division – (1) pastoral (Greek *poimenikos*, from *poimēn*, shepherd; again, there is no English word from the Greek), (2) bucolic, and (3) concerning goats – comes from Donatus' *Life of Virgil* (see **10.2–5n.**): Jacob Brummer (ed.), *Vitae Vergilianae* (Leipzig, 1912), 12, ll. 213–18. Petrus Ramus develops the picture in the opening remarks of his 1555 commentary on Virgil's *Eclogues*: 'Pastorum genera tria sunt . . . ait Donatus: imo etiam plura, ut sunt porcorum, equorum et animantium reliquarum custodes: per synecdochen ex specie genus appellatur *boukolikon*, tanquam diceres bubulum pro pastorali' ('There are three kinds of herdsman . . . according to Donatus. Indeed, there are more, since there are also the keepers of pigs, horses, and other animals. By synecdoche the genus is named *bucolic* from one of its species, just as if you were to say *bovine* instead of *pastoral*'): *P. Virgilii Maronis bucolica, P. Rami . . . exposita*, 2nd edn (Paris, 1558), B7ʳ. Donatus also associates the low style with pastoral (cf. **18.35n.** and **21.4–14n.**), noting that Virgil used it in the *Eclogues*, the middle style in the *Georgics*, and the grand style in the *Aeneid* (Brummer (ed.), *Vitae Vergilianae*, 14, ll. 254–9). Scott's inclusion of georgic alongside the pastoral kinds runs against these inherited views.

22.17 neatherds or creaght-keepers (i) *neatherd*: cowherd, from the Old English word for *cow*. (ii) *creaght-keeper*: not in *OED*. See *OED*, *creaght*, n., 1a: 'In *Irish Hist*. a nomadic herd of cattle driven about from place to place for pasture, or in time of war with the forces of their owners'; the first recorded usage is from Spenser's *View* (on which see **19.10–12n.**). *OED* has no compounds listed under *creaght*, although it does have a separate entry, with one instance from 1653, for *creaghter*. Scott's scribe spells the word 'Cretekeepers'.

22.19–20 Sannazar . . . (saith Scaliger) Scaliger, 3.99 (150a1), and cf. Viperano, 148. Jacopo Sannazaro (1458–1530) was an influential pastoralist, author of a short pastoral romance in Italian called the *Arcadia* (printed in 1504), divided into twelve chapters with an eclogue at each's end, and the five (Latin) *Piscatorial eclogues* (1526) referred to here.

22.20–3 Chaucer's *Canterbury Tales* . . . much after this This is an original observation: Scott's thinking is that – like pastoral – Chaucer's *Canterbury tales* deal with everyday people and are defined most readily by their setting and occasion rather than their (highly varied) content. They are 'quartered' in two senses: divided (*OED*, *quarter*, v., 1b and †2a; cf. 'subdivided', **22.16**) but also given quarters (*OED*'s sense 5) because Scott's model of poetry is a building with rooms, and Chaucer's pilgrims are to be lodged with the shepherds, goatherds, and the rest.

22.23–5 The gardener . . . *Richard the Second* Cf. Viperano, 3.7: '[Pastoral] got its name from shepherds particularly, although it also admits farmers, vinedressers, and gardeners, because all these, more suitably than others, have abundant leisure time to take pains with singing' (148). Scaliger also mentions the simpler style of the gardener (150c1). Shakespeare's *Richard II* was printed in 1597, anonymously, with two further editions following in 1598 in which Shakespeare is named on the title page. Scott does not name Shakespeare as the play's author at any point, but we cannot infer from this that he used the anonymous 1597 quarto: he also fails to name Shakespeare as the author of *Lucrece*, and Shakespeare's authorship of that work was clear from the signed dedication to the Earl of Southampton (though, again, both editions available to Scott, 1594 and 1598, name no author on their title pages). The scene (which appears in all three editions available to Scott) in which the Queen overhears and then talks with the gardener is 3.4 in modern editions (the early editions lack act and scene divisions). It is possible that Scott's reference ('brought on the stage') indicates that he saw as well as read the play; or the 'stage' may be mental. For Scott's other references to the play see **45.28–30**, **54.29–30**, and **66.33–8**.

22.26–30 those kind of interlocutory poems . . . running in action 'Drama' comes from the Greek *dran*, to do or act. See *Poetics*, 1448b1–2. Aristotle reports this etymology in a digression, with apparently less conviction about it than modern lexicographers have. Cf. Scaliger, 10b1 and Viperano, 2.12 (114). The sense of 'stir' as action or movement without including an idea of disturbance is rare (see *OED*, *stir*, n.[1], 1) and may show the influence of Puttenham, who uses the word with some frequency in Book 2 of *The art of English poesy* to describe the movement of verse lines (see, e.g., *Art*, 154, 157, 159, and 167). For Scott's usage cf. **59.13–15**.

22.27–8 as well attending . . . penniless bench That is to say, dealing with the highest level of society as well as the lowest. Chairs of estate are thrones; the *penniless bench* was 'a covered bench which formerly stood beside St Martin's Church, Carfax, Oxford; (also) any of various similar open-air seats elsewhere. Hence *allusively*: †the resort of wayfarers or destitute people; a state or condition of penury' (*OED*, *penniless*, adj. (and n.), special uses).

22.31–2 in dissembled action . . . as they seem A reverse etymology. The Greek *hupokritēs* and related words come from the verb *hupokrinomai* (reply, expound, speak in dialogue), the root of which is the same verb, *krinō* (separate, distinguish, choose) that lies behind *critic* and related words (on which see **33.22–3n.**). *Hupokrinomai* came to be used of playing a part on stage because of the use of dialogue (which was, for the Greeks, dialectical). The senses of deceitfulness and dissembling are a metaphorical extension of the sense of speaking a part, rather than vice versa.

22.33–7 Tragedy . . . (agreeable to Aristotle) Scott's account draws on and synthesises his usual sources, with Aristotle cited, but filtered in places through Scaliger and Viperano. Scaliger and Viperano both insist, for instance, that Aristotle's remarks about the early perfecting of tragedy and implication that comedy reached maturity rather later (1449a–b) should not be taken to mean that tragedy came first: Scaliger, 1.5 (10c2, 11c1; Padelford, 36, 37), Viperano, 2.8 (91).

22.37–9 First … private men   Viperano, 2.12 (113), and *Poetics*, 1449a9–14.

22.40–23.3 After … *comedy* took his name   An account Aristotelian in its outlines (and etymological concerns), but conventionally embellished. See *Poetics*, 1448a35–8, part of a digression on the Megarians' claims to have originated comedy: 'they say that while they call outlying villages *kōmai*, the Athenians call them *dēmoi*, and they take 'comedy' to be derived not from *kōmazein*, 'to revel', but from the fact that the comic actors wandered among the villages because driven in contempt from the city'. And, e.g., Evanthius (Preminger, 302); Donatus (Preminger, 305–6); Diomedes (Keil, I, 488); Scaliger, 1.5 (esp. 10b1, 10d1, 10b–c2; Padelford, 33, 34, 35); Viperano, 1.7 (20), 2.8 (89), and 2.13 (119); and Webbe (*ECE*, I, 248).

23.4 ales and May sports   *OED*, *ale*, n., 3: 'A festival or merry-meeting at which much ale was drunk'. May games or sports were performances forming part of the traditional May or springtime celebrations, on popular themes such as Robin Hood (*OED, May game*, n., 1).

23.6 blaze   See *OED*, *blaze*, v.², 2a: 'To proclaim (as with a trumpet), to publish, divulge, make known'; 2†d: 'To decry, defame, hold up to infamy'; 4†b: 'To describe pictorially, depict, portray'. Cf. 'blazon' (**15.34n.**), and 'blazing' (**26.26**).

23.10–18 Such like beginning … to their neighbours   The details here are again conventional and found in the same sources as above, **22.40–23.3n.** See, e.g., Evanthius (Preminger, 301–2), Donatus (Preminger, 306), Diomedes (Keil, I, 487–8), Viperano, 1.7 (20–1) and 2.8 (89–90); for Aristotle on the dithyrambic origins of tragedy see *Poetics*, 1449a10–11.

23.20–4 Horace … faecibus ora   *Ars poetica*, 275–7. These details from Horace are also repeated by Scaliger, 1.6 (11c–d2; Padelford, 39–40).

23.29–30 Thus, lastly … the height they are   Following Aristotle, *Poetics*, 1449a: the four main changes in the evolution of tragedy were the number of actors (Aeschylus adding the second and Sophocles the third), the scale of plot, the metre, and the increased number of episodes.

23.30–1 *tragedy* so named … (saith Horace)   *Ars poetica*, 220. *Tragedy* means 'goat-song' (*tragos*, 'goat' + *ōdē*, 'song'). The conventional point is elaborated and examined by, e.g., Evanthius (Preminger, 301–2), Donatus (Preminger, 306), Diomedes (Keil, I, 487), Scaliger, 1.6 (11c2; Padelford, 39), Viperano, 2.8 (89–90), Puttenham, 1.15 (*Art*, 124), Lodge (*ECE*, I, 80), and Webbe (*ECE*, I, 248).

23.31–4 It may be thus defined ... cruel affections   Compare the definitions in Aristotle (1449b24–8: 'a tragedy is a *mimēsis* of a high, complete action ... in speech pleasurably enhanced, the different kinds [of enhancement] occurring in separate sections, in dramatic, not narrative form, effecting through pity and fear the *catharsis* of such emotions'); Scaliger: 'A tragedy is the imitation of the adversity of a distinguished man; it employs the form of action, presents a disastrous *dénouement*, and is expressed in impressive metrical language' (1.6, 12a1; Padelford, 40); and Viperano: 'Tragedy is poetry which portrays the downfall of illustrious men by means of characters acting' (2.8, 93–4). Scott is notable for preserving Aristotle's emphasis on *catharsis*, perhaps following Sidney, who emphasises 'the affects of admiration and commiseration' in his sketch of tragedy's features (*DP*, 27; and see **18.25–8n.**), but we should note that where the end of any kind of poetry is for Sidney always didactic, for Scott here, as for Aristotle, the end of tragedy is simply *catharsis*. Compare, though, Scott's later (less explicitly cathartic, more didactic) definition: 'his end by fear and compassion to drive men into hatred of those foul affections and manners that bring forth such sad events' (**78.9–11**). The use of *purge* for *catharsis* has many precedents in Latin and Italian translations, commentaries, and treatises; for examples see the index to Weinberg, *s.v.* 'purgation'.

23.34–6 The comedy ... vicious dispositions   Compare Scaliger, 1.5: 'Comedy is a dramatic poem, which is filled with intrigue, full of action, happy in its outcome, and written in a popular style' (11d1; Padelford, 38); Viperano, 2.13: 'Comedy is poetry which for the purpose of teaching habits of life imitates private actions of citizens by means of characters acting, not without jokes and humour' (120); and Webbe (*ECE*, 1, 249). Scott's emphasis is again, in spite of his fundamentally Sidneian doctrine of poetry as teaching, on Aristotelian *catharsis* or 'purging' (Aristotle does not supply a definition of comedy, but it can be easily enough inferred along these lines). Cf. Scott's later definition, **78.33–9**.

23.37–24.8 these verses ... more lovely show   I have not found these lines elsewhere and we can only therefore speculate about who the exceptionally promising ('more than hopeful': *OED*, *hopeful*, adj., 2a) kinswoman to whom Scott addressed them might be. A likely candidate is the young Elizabeth Tanfield (1585–1639), the only child of Scott's patron and kinsman Lawrence Tanfield (see Introduction, xxxi). She was to become Elizabeth Cary in 1602 and Viscountess Falkland in 1620, and was the first woman to write original drama in English: her *The tragedy of Mariam* was printed in 1613. At some point before 1602 she dedicated a manuscript translation of Abraham Ortelius' *Le miroir du monde* (1579) to her great-uncle Sir Henry Lee. She had also attracted the attention of Michael Drayton: see **29.20–1n.**

23.39 Plautus' *Menaechmi*   See **39.30–3n.**

24.1–6 A comedy ... the vices we live in   Cf. Sidney: 'the comedy is an imitation of the common errors of our life, which he representeth in the most ridiculous and scornful sort that may be, so as it is impossible that any beholder can be content to be such a one' (*DP*, 27). For the conventional definition of comedy as a mirror (Scott's 'common error's glass'), attributed to Cicero, see **78.34–5n**.

24.9–13 The Greeks...the Greek comedian   A conventional classical canon, except for the inclusion of the neo-Latin dramatist George Buchanan (1506–82), a Scot who was a friend of Sidney and of Scaliger and a teacher of Montaigne. His neoclassical plays include two translations from Euripides, *Medea* and *Alcestis*, and two original works on biblical themes, *Baptistes* and *Jephthes*; he is twice singled out for praise in Sidney's *Defence* (*DP*, 42 and 48). Scott's listing is by language rather than country or age, but it is still an oddity to put the ancient and the modern Latin dramatist together rather than contrasting them. Sophocles (*c*.495–*c*.406 BC) and Euripides (*c*.480–*c*.406 BC), together with Aeschylus (?525/4–456/5 BC), are the three great fifth-century Athenian tragedians and the only ones whose works were preserved for us. Seneca the younger (*c*.4 BC–AD 65) was of all these writers the most influential in Scott's day, his tragedies, written in the tradition of the Greek tragedians, being widely read in Latin as well as in English translation and being imitated in numerous Elizabethan tragedies. Aristophanes (*c*.460–*c*.386 BC) and Menander (?344/3–292/1 BC) were the canonical writers of Greek Old and New Comedy respectively. Plautus (*fl. c*.205–184 BC) and Terence (died 159 BC) were Latin writers in the tradition of New Comedy.

24.14–19 which either Tacitus...(saith he)?   A close paraphrase of Tacitus, *Dialogue on orators*, 29.3, spoken by Vipstanus Messalla: 'Again, there are the peculiar and characteristic vices of this metropolis of ours [*propria et peculiaria huius urbis vitia*], taken on, as it seems to me, almost in the mother's womb – the passion for play actors, and the mania for gladiatorial shows and horse-racing; and when the mind is engrossed in such occupations, what room is left over for higher pursuits? [*quibus occupatus et obsessus animus quantulum loci bonis artibus relinquit*]'. Scott's attribution of the essay to 'either Tacitus or Quintilian' shows that he was using Justus Lipsius' great edition of Tacitus. Lipsius believed that the dialogue was Quintilian's lost book 'de causis corruptae eloquentiae' ('on the causes of the corruption of eloquence'), referred to by Quintilian at 6.pr.3, and in his edition he presents the work as 'Fabii Quinctiliani, ut videtur, Dialogus... Cor. Tacito falso inscriptus' ('The Dialogue of, it would seem, Fabius Quintilian... falsely ascribed to Cornelius Tacitus'): *Opera* (Antwerp, 1574), 609 and 755–6. In the revised *Opera omnia* (Antwerp, 1581), the contents page is less dogmatic: 'Dialogus, de causis corruptæ eloquentiæ, ambigui scriptoris' ('Dialogue of the causes of the corruption of eloquence, of ambiguous authorship').

24.20–4 Sir Philip Sidney saith...*tragicomedy*   Scott here runs together three separate passages from Sidney's *Defence*. When countering the objections of poetry's detractors Sidney runs through the genres in turn, coming to 'the comic, whom naughty play-makers and stage-keepers have justly made odious' (*DP*, 27). Later, in his digression on modern English literature, Sidney considers tragicomedy, criticising it in Aristotelian terms: 'so as neither the admiration and commiseration [of tragedy] nor the right sportfulness [of comedy] is by their mongrel tragicomedy obtained' (46). Sidney then dwells on the many problems he finds in modern drama, because no other type of poetry is 'so much used in England, and none can be more pitifully abused; which, like an unmannerly daughter showing a bad education, causeth her mother Poesy's honesty to be called in question' (48).

24.25–32 the ancient satyr and mimic ... countenance of poesy   The satyr play was a short play featuring drunken and priapic satyrs that was performed along with each entrant's trilogy of tragedies in the Athenian Dionysia. The only complete satyr play to survive is Euripides' *Cyclops*. The mime was a type of crude farce notable for its use of mimicry. Although it seems to have been formalised in Roman times, only fragments of texts survive, so any Renaissance treatment is based on references and discussion in non-dramatic classical sources. Scaliger's synoptic treatise covers mime at 1.10, 1.15, and 3.97; Viperano accords it a brief chapter, 3.6.

24.31 clowns, antics, or jigs   An *antic* was a clown or a (grotesque) entertainment performed by one; a *jig*, similarly, was a light or comical (and originally musical) performance given at the end or in the interval of a play.

24.33–6 that kind ... originally the Latins'   Most of the details here are suggested by Viperano, 3.5 (140–2); cf. Scaliger, 1.12 and 3.98, and Diomedes (Keil, I, 485–6). The connection between the satyr play and satire – rejected by modern scholars – was not questioned by most Renaissance authors, though Viperano does mention some alternative etymologies (3.5, 140), coming close to that now preferred: the full dish of mixed food (*satura*).

24.36–7 iambic ... calumniating   *Iambos* derives from *iaptein*, to assail (in words); cf. *iambizein*, to assail in iambics. On the latter term see Aristotle, *Poetics*, 1448b32, Scaliger, 20b1, and Viperano, 1.7 (20).

24.37–9 or else ... (nowadays) the *satirical epigram*   Scott's sources account for the differences between the various Latin satirists, with Scaliger proposing three methods of dividing satire (149a–b2; cf. 19b2): by (i) subject matter; (ii) mode, either narrative, personating or mixed (see **68.29–69.1n.**); or (iii) style. Scott simplifies his account to suit modern practice. He was writing at the height of a fashion for satire and satirical epigram (recently halted in its tracks by the Bishops' Ban – see **79.32–4n.**), with poets consciously modelling their work on the Roman poets Martial, Juvenal, and Persius, and in some cases combining satire and epigram in a single volume: see, for example, Everard Guilpin, *Skialetheia. Or, a shadowe of truth, in certaine epigrams and satyres* (1598). The epigram was a popular form among Elizabethan poets, writing in both English and Latin; their range was traditional, combining satirical and more benign material (on the latter, which Scott distinguishes as *lyrical* epigrams, see **29.23–30**). Contemporary writers of printed books of satires or epigrams, or both, included

Thomas Campion (1595), Joseph Hall (1597–8), John Marston (1598), Thomas Bastard (1598), Sir John Davies (1599), and, in manuscript, John Donne.

25.2 with a goad galling Vexing, mocking at, or making sore with a cattle-prod (*OED*, *gall*, v.¹; *goad*, n.¹).

25.4 I here oppose narrative to personating A nod to Scaliger (see **24.37–9n**.).

25.5 Of this kind ... the first As Viperano points out, 3.5 (140). See Quintilian, 10.1.93.

25.6–10 Juvenal ... et lacrimae Juvenal, *Satires*, 1.165–8. The early textual witnesses, and modern editors, are split equally at l. 168 between 'ira' (singular, 'rage') and 'irae' (plural, 'rages'), the reading in Scott's text.

25.16–17 surely Baal ... by the prophet I Kings 18:18–46, in which the prophet Elijah challenges the 450 Priests of Baal to call on their god to light a fire under a sacrificial bull; they fail and, before Elijah succeeds in the same task by calling on God, he 'mocked them, and said, Cry loud: for he is a god: either he talketh or pursueth *his enemies*, or is in his journey, or it may be that he sleepeth, and must be awaked' (18:27). On *Baal* cf. **43.1–3n**.

25.17 girded *OED*, *gird*, v.², 4a: 'To make "hits" at, to jest or gibe at'; 4b: '*trans*. To assail with jest or sarcasm; to sneer or scoff at'.

25.17–18 We have of our times ... in this kind See **24.37–9n**.

25.21–2 which may be all ... enlargeth the word Scaliger treats lyric at 1.44 but this point is from the opening of 3.124 (169c1): 'Mihi ita videtur. Quaecunque in breve Poema cadere possunt, ea Lyricis numeris colligere ius esse' ('It seems to me thus: whatever may be got into a short poem, it is right to gather it in lyric measures'). And cf. Viperano, 3.9, paraphrasing Scaliger closely: 'In general, whatever can be bound up with lyric measures and can be comprised in a short poem, presumably falls into the category of lyric subject matter' (154). Lyric, a term from the Library at Alexandria that displaced the earlier Greek term *melos*, was seen to be generically distinct from such neighbouring kinds as elegy: see, e.g., Sidney (*DP*, 26–9).

25.26–30 these are ... some instrument In part this emphasis on the musical context of lyric (Greek *lurikos*, from *lura*, 'lyre') is a humanist theme, but it should not be forgotten that a great deal of Elizabethan lyric poetry was indeed, in Sidney's words, 'either accompanied with or prepared for the well-enchanting skill of music' (*DP*, 23).

25.30–2 the harp ... devised by Amphion On the mythical bard Amphion as inventor of the lyre (Scott makes no technical distinction in calling it a *harp*) see, e.g., Plato, *Laws*, 677d. In some versions Amphion is given the lyre by Hermes (see, e.g., Apollodorus, *Library*, 3.5.5) or taught by him (see, e.g., Pausanias, *Description of Greece*, 9.5.8).

25.32–6 who by his harmonious . . . assemble stones   See Natalis Comes, II, 760 (Book 8, ch. 15): 'They say that Amphion was skilled in music and that he could lead the stones and wild beasts in any direction he wanted. This means that he used his sweet speech to soften hard, unsophisticated men, charming them into building cities and obeying civil laws.' (For Scott's use of Natalis Comes' account of Amphion, cf. **10.12–15n.**) For other versions of the common myth see, e.g., Horace, *Ars poetica*, 394–6; Pausanias, *Description of Greece*, 9.5.7; Sidney (*DP*, 5); Puttenham, 1.3 (*Art*, 96); Wills, 88–90.

25.37 *melic* or melodious kind   Cf. Viperano, 3.9 (153). The Greek words *melos* (limb; hence musical unit, stanza, melody) and *melikos* (lyric) in effect define lyric as musical and strophic, therefore excluding stichic forms like elegy.

26.3–4 the poet . . . (as one saith)   Although Scott here glances at a major issue in poetics, his actual source is a misread or misremembered passage in Sidney's *Arcadia*, where Pyrocles addresses Musidorus: 'I gave my selfe to sing a little, which as you knowe I ever delighted in, so now especially, whether it be the nature of this clime to stir up Poeticall fancies, or rather as I thinke, of love; whose [s]cope being plesure, wil not so much as utter his griefes, but in some form of pleasure' (*NA*, E2ʳ; Skretkowicz, 80). That the 1593 text reads 'cope' for 'scope'– the reading in both the 1590 *Arcadia* (12ᵛ) and the 1598 *Arcadia* (E1ʳ) – is only weak evidence that Scott might have been using the 1598 text, since the mistake is obvious. Cf. Scott's use of the same episode, **16.9–11, 70.5–6,** and **82.25–7.** Puttenham says something like this, but not in so few words (*Art*, 3.7, 239), and for him as for Scott the position would not be his normal, morally didactic one. Scott would have known Strabo's refutation of the contention of the Alexandrian scholar Eratosthenes that 'the aim of every poet is to entertain, not to instruct' (Strabo, *Geography*, 1.1.10; 1.2.3). For contemporary discussions of what the single aim of poetry is see, e.g., Fracastoro (1555), esp. 54–9; and Tasso's *Discorsi* of 1594 (Gilbert, esp. 467–9). Among the few but prominent voices to insist that pleasure was the main or sole aim of poetry were Castelvetro in 1570 (Weinberg, I, 506) and Riccoboni in 1591 (Weinberg, I, 234).

26.4–6 Those of anger . . . furious kind   Following Scaliger, 1.53 (53a–c1). The Latin word *dirae* (ill-boding signs, portents), from *dirus* (cf. English *dire*) was also, as Scaliger points out (53a1), the name for the Furies (hence Scott's 'the furious kind'); it is not used in classical sources as a name for a poetic kind, but is taken up on the authority of the pseudo-Virgilian *Dirae*, a set of curses in the voice of a dispossessed farmer. On *dirae* cf. Puttenham, 1.29 (*Art*, 145).

26.12 exagitate   Harass, persecute, attack violently, rail at (*OED*, †*exagitate*, v., 2b and 3).

26.15 as the Italians ... desperate poems   Scaliger, 53a1: 'Itali vocant *Desperatum carmen*' ('the Italians call it the desperate song').

26.16–17 the 137 Psalm ... in Babylon   Psalm 137 ('By the rivers of Babylon'), verses 7–9: 'Remember the children of Edom, O Lord, in the day of Jerusalem, which said, Rase it, rase it to the foundation thereof. O daughter of Babel, worthie to be destroied, blessed *shall he be* that rewardeth thee, as thou hast served us. Blessed *shall he be* that taketh and dasheth thy children against the stones.' Scott's scribe mistakenly writes '132' for '137'.

26.23–7 when by the clear-seeing ... unutterable glory   Echoing Sidney's reference to the Psalmist as 'a passionate lover of that unspeakable and everlasting beauty, to be seen by the eyes of the mind, only cleared by faith' (*DP*, 7); cf. **15.35–8** for a closely related use of this passage, and for 'blazing' (**26.26**) cf. **15.34n.** and **23.6n.**

26.25 prevent   Anticipate.

26.31–2 David ... many hymns   The Psalms (cf. **15.35–8n.** and **20.1–8n.**).

26.32–4 this stirred up Mary ... their redemption   Scott refers to two of the biblical hymns or canticles, both taken from Luke 1: that of Mary (the 'Magnificat', Luke 1:46–55) and that of John the Baptist's father and Mary's kinsman Zacharias (Zechariah, Zachary: the 'Benedictus', Luke 1:68–79). They both featured in the Anglican forms of service in the 1549 and 1559 *Book of common prayer*, the 'Benedictus' at morning prayer and the 'Magnificat' at evening prayer (see *BCP*, 11–12 and 15; 109 and 112).

26.37–27.2 expressed in divers forms ... *hymns of solemnity*   Cf. Viperano, 3.12 (160), and Puttenham, 1.23 ('The form of poetical rejoicings'): 'And as these rejoicings tend to diverse effects, so do they also carry diverse forms and nominations, for those of victory and peace are called triumphal ...', etc. (*Art*, 135). All three authors are following the example of Scaliger in this taxonomy of kinds of lyric. See 1.44, esp. 47a2 (*epipompeutica*) and 48a1 (*epinicia*). The *epinicion* (Greek *epi* + *nikē* = on victory) is a victory ode. The term *epipompeuticon* may have been coined by Scaliger (from Greek *pompē*, triumph, procession).

27.4–5 the proto-hymn of Moses and Miriam   In Exodus 15:20–1 Miriam takes up the song of praise Moses has sung (15:1–19). Cf. Viperano, 1.2 (6). 'Proto-hymn' is Scott's coinage; it is not in *OED*.

27.5 the heathen paeans   For example the thirty-three ancient Greek hymns known as the Homeric Hymns. Cf. Scaliger's brief separate chapter on hymns (1.45) and the earlier discussion of hymns and paeans (1.44, 48b1–b2).

27.6 *genethliaca* **or natal songs**   Cf. Scaliger, 3.102 (155–6) and Puttenham, 1.23 and 1.25 (*Art*, 135 and 138). Greek *genethliakon*, birthday ode, from *genethliakos*, belonging to a birthday, from *genethlē*, race, stock, birth.

27.6–7 *epithalamia* . . . **bride chamber**   Cf. Scaliger, 3.101 (150–5) and Puttenham, 1.26 (*Art*, 138–41), both extensive treatments. Scaliger points out the etymology (from Greek *epi*, upon + *thalamos*, bride chamber), 150b2.

27.8 Dido's entertaining of Aeneas   *Aeneid*, starting 1.637 (and including Aeneas' narration in Books 2 and 3).

27.10–11 as I have seen . . . some such thing   The Christmas boar's head feast, preceded by the carrying in of a roasted boar's head to the accompaniment of a sung carol, appears to have originated in medieval Oxford, and was practised in Scott's day in both Oxford and Cambridge colleges and the Inns of Court. The carol begins 'The boar's head in hand bring I'. For text and discussion see James E. Spears, 'The "Boar's head carol" and folk tradition', *Folklore*, 85 (1974), 194–8. A version of the carol was printed by Wynkyn de Worde in 1521 (*STC* 5204, a fragment).

27.11–12 Virgil . . . Iopas his songs   *Aeneid*, 1.740–6, at the feast Scott has just mentioned: 'Long-haired Iopas . . . makes the hall ring with his golden lyre. He sings of the wandering moon and the sun's toils; whence sprang man and beast, whence rain and fire; of Arcturus, the rainy Hyades and the twin Bears; why wintry suns make such haste to dip themselves in Ocean, or what delay stays the slowly passing nights.' Scott's great-grandfather Sir Thomas Wyatt wrote an unfinished version of what the song might have been like, printed in *Songes and sonettes* (1557), M1^v–2^v ('When Dido feasted first the wanderyng Troian knight'). For Iopas as an example of the union of poetry, music, and philosophy, see Quintilian, 1.10.10.

27.13–15 this kind . . . abominably lascivious   Scott is probably thinking of popular broadside ballads. The lack of an 'ingenious conceit' goes against Sidney's stress on the primacy of the 'fore-conceit' (*DP*, 9), an emphasis shared by Gascoigne (*SRLC*, 237–9); *ingenious* was sometimes used mistakenly for *ingenuous* (*OED*, *ingenious*, adj., †4), so the judgement may be of moral as well as poetic shortcomings.

27.14 crowed   The word is ambiguous. The manuscript reads 'Crow'd'. This is probably not, therefore, to be modernised as 'crude', an unlikely spelling even at one scribal remove from an author aware of its Latin etymology (*crudus*). 'Crowed' might refer to the *crowd* or Celtic fiddle, a traditional minstrel's accompanying instrument for popular ballads, as in Sidney's reference to the ballad of Percy and Douglas 'sung by some blind crowder' (*DP*, 28). But more likely it refers to a 'crowing' voice (see *MED*, *crouen*, 2; *OED*, *crow*, v.^{1}), in which case the meaning is probably 'badly sung'.

27.18–20 Those lyrics . . . grace of his countenance   Sidney licenses Scott's connection between love poetry and devotional poetry: what else are the Psalms of David, he asks, 'but a heavenly poesy, wherein almost he showeth himself a passionate lover of that unspeakable and everlasting beauty, to be seen by the eyes of the mind, only cleared by faith? But, truly, now having named him, I fear me I seem to profane that holy name, applying it to poetry, which is among us thrown down to so ridiculous an estimation. But they that with quiet judgements will look a little deeper into it shall find the end and working of it such as, being rightly applied, deserveth not to be scourged out of the Church of God' (*DP*, 7–8). On biblical poetry cf. **20.1–8n.**

27.21–3 the Song of Songs . . . his spouse the Church   The traditional allegorical reading of The Song of Solomon.

27.23–9 Or otherwise this desire . . . only discern   For objects presented to our 'sense and appetite' cf. Scott's paraphrase of Vives at **70.29–71.7** and a related discussion at **31.27–30**. For beauty as an accord of proportion and colour see **32.35–41n**. For the Platonic and Stoic models of love as an intellectual apprehension of an idea of beauty, alluded to in 'that beauty reason's eye can only discern', see **16.20–17.11**.

27.29–35 Now because desire . . . *elegiac* or plaintive   It is not entirely clear which came first, the name of the metre or the kind of poem to which that metre was suited. The Greek *elegos* appears to mean 'song' before it develops the more specialised sense of 'lament, song of mourning'; from this word comes *elegeia* – a lament for the dead – and *elegeion*, the distich consisting of a hexameter and a pentameter that is now known as the elegiac couplet. Although the original elegiac poets wrote in that metre on a range of topics, the term *elegeia* early acquired the more specialised meaning of 'lament', so that later Latin love elegists appear to be so called not because of their content but only because of their use of elegiac metre. Scott's ingenious explanation may lack historical validity, but it does suggest why a metre associated with funeral lament could be felt to suit a broader range of topics. Scaliger suggests the outlines of Scott's points, 1.50 (esp. 52d1) and 3.125 (169).

27.36–8 divers of David's psalms . . . the fresh waters   Scott alludes to Psalm 42:1–2: 'As the Hart braieth for the rivers of water, so panteth my soule after thee, O God. My soule thirsteth for God, *even* for the living God: when shall I come and appeare *before* the presence of God?'

27.38–40 the complaints . . . refiner of our vulgar kinds   The unconscious bridge from the Psalms to Petrarch may be the connection between Psalm 42 and Petrarch's allusion to it in *Rime* 190, 'Una candida cerva', itself the source for Wyatt's 'Who so list to hunt' (in both poems the deer has become the metaphorical object of the poet's desire rather than a figure for the desire itself). On Petrarch's influence on English literature see Puttenham, 1.31: 'In the latter end of [Henry VIII's] reign sprung up a new company of courtly makers, of whom Sir Thomas Wyatt the elder and Henry,

Earl of Surrey, were the two chieftains, who, having traveled into Italy and there tasted the sweet and stately measures and style of the Italian poesy, as novices newly crept out of the schools of Dante, Ariosto, and Petrarch, they greatly polished our rude and homely manner of vulgar poesy from that it had been before, and for that cause may justly be said the first reformers of our English meter and style' (*Art*, 148). See also **29.14–16n.**

28.2–3 English admirers . . . that follow him   Scott refers to the many minor sonneteers of the 1590s, who had crowded a marketplace initiated by the sequences of Sidney, Daniel, and Constable. The 'English admirers of their sundry stars' are of course led by Sidney, whose lover and beloved are named Astrophil (star-lover) and Stella (star); many subsequent sonnet mistresses had similarly celestial names.

28.12–17 not unlike that . . . monstrous creatures themselves   *Poetics*, 1448b9–12: 'we enjoy looking at the most exact portrayals of things we see with pain [*lupērōs*] in real life, the lowest animals, for instance, or corpses'. See **13.5–14n.** Sidney also fixes on this passage: 'as Aristotle saith, those things which in themselves are horrible, as cruel battles, unnatural monsters, are made in poetical imitation delightful' (*DP*, 23). See also *Astrophil and Stella*, 34.4: 'Oft cruell fights well pictured forth do please.' And Meres (*ECE*, II, 309), with no attribution to Aristotle.

28.20 For sorrow . . . wind of words   Shakespeare, *Lucrece*, 1330 (reading 'For' for 'And'). Quoted rather out of context, since in the poem Lucrece has written only a short note to her husband Collatine asking him to come to her and has avoided expressing her misery: 'the life and feeling of her passion | She hoards, to spend when he is by to hear her' (1317–18).

28.24–9 Ma ben veggio . . . breve sogno   The sestet (ll. 9–14) of *Rime*, 1; Durling's translation: 'But now I see well how for a long time I was the talk of the crowd, for which often I am ashamed of myself within; and of my raving, shame is the fruit, and repentance, and the clear knowledge that whatever pleases in the world is a brief dream.'

28.30–5 Lo now . . . dream is vain   Scott translates Petrarch's hendecasyllables into hexameter and varies the rhyme pattern in the sestet from Petrarch's cdecde to cddcee, a variant not used by Petrarch but preferred by Wyatt; so the translation also effects a subtle Englishing in form.

29.2–4 those moral precepts . . . some odes   Most of the biblical Book of Proverbs is attributed within the text to Solomon. The writings of Cato Censorius (234–149 BC) include various didactic works in prose but Scott is thinking of the later, falsely attributed, collection of maxims, the *Distichs of Cato*, a popular school textbook throughout the Middle Ages and into the early modern period, which probably dates from the fourth century AD. It was frequently reprinted in Britain, both in Latin and in English translation and especially in the edition of Erasmus, most recently in 1592. A number of Horace's *Epistles*, philosophical in tone, could be called works of instruction, including most obviously the Epistle to the Pisos better known as the *Ars poetica*. The *Odes* are mostly not didactic, but a number are philosophical meditations, some addressed to particular friends, on such themes as the inevitability of death, the simple life, steadfastness, and the meaninglessness of riches.

29.5–6 and him doth Sir Thomas Wyatt . . . so happily follow   Three of Wyatt's verse epistles were printed in *Songes and sonettes* (1557), with Horace an important model: 'Of the meane and sure estate written to John Poins' ('My mothers maides . . .'), 'Myne owne John Poyns', and 'How to use the court and him selfe therin, written to syr Fraunces Bryan' ('A Spendyng hand . . .'). They are also found in manuscript, and Scott may have had access to Wyatt's poetry in manuscript through his uncle George Wyatt (see Introduction, xxxiii, and **55.25–30n.**).

29.10–11 sweetness and fullness   Virtues of poetic style, derived from Scaliger, discussed at **55.31–56.17** and **55.4–10** (and see **54.18–20n.**).

29.11–12 my Lord of Surrey . . . linked in love   Henry Howard, Earl of Surrey (1516/17–47) was the other star of Richard Tottel's *Songes and sonettes* (1557). He and Wyatt seem to have been friends, in spite of the gap of years (and religion, and politics) between them, and both translated or imitated Petrarch as well as translating psalms. Surrey pushed English metre decisively towards a regular iambic pattern, where Wyatt's verse was more irregular. Tottel's edition, however, smoothed out his metre and gave a decided impression that the two poets together had reformed English versification. Wyatt addressed a psalm translation to Surrey (poem 239 in Muir and Thomson) and Surrey wrote a prefatory sonnet for Wyatt's translation of the Penitential Psalms, as well as another sonnet on his death and a longer elegy ('Wyatt resteth here that quick could never rest'), the last three all included in Tottel (D2^{r-v}) after the elegy had been separately printed in 1542 as *An excellent epitaffe*.

29.14–16 one saith . . . upon English poesy   An accurate quotation from Puttenham, 1.31 (*Art*, 150):

Henry Earl of Surrey and Sir Thomas Wyatt, between whom I find very little difference, I repute them (as before) for the two chief lanterns of light to all others that have since employed their pens upon English poesy. Their conceits were lofty, their styles stately, their conveyance cleanly, their terms proper, their meter sweet and well-proportioned, in all imitating very naturally and studiously their master Francis Petrarch.

See also **27.38–40n.**

29.17–18 Sir Philip Sidney . . . noble mind   A close quotation again: Sidney finds 'in the Earl of Surrey's lyrics many things tasting of a noble birth, and worthy of a noble mind' (*DP*, 44). Sidney does not mention Wyatt; Webbe sidelines Surrey and omits Wyatt altogether (*ECE*, I, 242–3). As Wyatt's great-grandson, Scott has clear motive for adjusting this emphasis.

29.18–19 the *Heroical Epistles* of Ovid   Ovid's *Heroides* ('Heroines'), a set of poems in the form of letters, mostly from loving women to their absent beloveds, though the last six poems are paired letters including the voices of the men concerned.

29.20–1 one of our age... honestly   Michael Drayton (1563–1631), in *Englands heroicall epistles* (1597), which comprises nine pairs of letters (twelve in later editions) between famous lovers from English history. One pair is dedicated to Scott's kinswoman Elizabeth Tanfield, later Cary (on whom see **23.37–24.8n.**). The work was frequently reprinted, starting with enlarged editions in 1598 and 1599.

29.21–6 those that are merrily... banner, shield, etc.   *Epigram* comes from the Greek *epigramma*, inscription (from *epigraphein*, to mark the surface, inscribe, write upon), the conditions of inscription establishing the form's brevity. Scott draws on Puttenham, 1.27: 'Therefore the poet devised a pretty fashioned poem short and sweet... For this epigram is but an inscription or writing made as it were upon a table, or in a window, or upon the wall or mantle of a chimney' (*Art*, 142). The senses of *table* (**29.26**) include board, (writing) tablet, picture (*OED*, *table*, n., 1, 2, 3). Cf. **24.37–9n.**, on the satirical epigram.

29.28–9 epitaphs; poesies... and the like   Puttenham devotes a brief chapter, 1.28, to epitaph ('but a kind of epigram': *Art*, 144) and includes another, 1.30, 'Of short epigrams called posies': 'We call them posies and do paint them nowadays upon the backsides of our fruit trenchers of wood, or use them as devices in rings and arms and about such courtly purposes' (*Art*, 146). *Posy* is merely an alternative spelling for *poesy*, though *OED* gives separate (parallel) definitions (*OED*, *posy*, n., 1; *poesy*, n., 3).

29.29 mots... and impresses   See **81.28–9n.** for Scott's discussion of emblems and *imprese*, and **37.32n.** for the form *impress*; the 'mot' was the verbal part of such a device.

29.37–40 It is neither possible... grow infinite   For the infinitude of poetics cf. George Gascoigne, in *Certayne notes of instruction concerning the making of verse or ryme in English* (first published in his *Posies* of 1575), discussing *inventio*: 'To deliver unto you general examples it were almost unpossible, sithence the occasions of inventions are (as it were) infinite' (*SRLC*, 238).

29.38 institution   Training, instruction, education (*OED*, *institution*, n., †4), with a nod to the title of Quintilian's *Institutio oratoria*.

29.41–30.1 Quintilian... Scaliger in our faculty   The longest and most comprehensive treatises available to Scott on rhetoric and poetics respectively, and two of his most important sources.

30.2–3 prudence and discretion ... of the poet's   *Prudentia* (decorum; also *proportion* elsewhere in the *Model*) is Scaliger's, and Scott's, first virtue of poetic composition, and therefore governs the rest. See below, esp. **33.1–8n.** and **33.31–4n.**, and cf. Hoskyns: 'but let Discrecion bee the greatest and generall figure of figures' (*Directions*, 129).

30.4 read   Lecture on, teach (*OED, read*, v., †18).

30.6–7 a general good scholar ... a rhetorician   Rhetoric was a fundamental of classical and Renaissance humanist education, and one of the three lower arts, along with grammar and logic, that formed the basis of schooling (see **7.2–6n.**). Anyone educated would therefore be 'a rhetorician'. But rhetorical theory (and especially Cicero: e.g. *De oratore*, 2.2.5) also idealised the orator as a complete scholar, and this dogma was reflected in poetics, most memorably in Horace's 'Scribendi recte sapere est et principium et fons' (*Ars poetica*, 309), which Scott quotes and translates at **58.11–13**. Scott may glance at this tradition in requiring that any poet be 'a general good scholar in all kinds of learning'. Plato had turned this on its head: poets claim to know about many things, but are authoritative about none – if you want to know about generalship, ask a general, not Homer (*Republic*, 598d–600e; cf. *Ion*, 536e–542a).

30.8–11 those rules only ... strange and bordering rules   Scott distinguishes between the rules of poetry and the 'rules of other sciences', which are 'strange and bordering' (i.e. foreign and neighbouring). The contemporary importance of the idea that each art was discrete, homogeneous, and self-sufficient was due in no small part to Petrus Ramus, who had extracted from Aristotle's *Posterior analytics* three 'laws', originally meant by Aristotle to govern the handling of terms in syllogistic inference, but taken by Ramus to mean that (i) within each methodically expressed art every proposition should be universally and necessarily true (the *lex veritatis* or law of truth); (ii) no art should trespass on another, since each art is directed to its own particular end (the *lex iustitiae* or law of justice); and (iii) within an art all propositions should be arranged in a strict hierarchy of generality (the *lex sapientiae* or law of wisdom). Among the practical consequences of Ramistic method were the splitting of the traditional five parts of rhetoric (on which see **8.2–6n.** and **33.17–20n.**) between logic (*inventio*, *dispositio*, and *memoria*) and rhetoric (*elocutio* and *pronuntiatio*) in works such as the Ramistic *Rhetorica* of Talaeus used by Scott (see **67.32–4n.**). On the distinctness of the art of poetry cf. **11.8–11**.

30.13–14 every work ... the end   On the 'end' (*telos* or final cause) and its importance to the definition of an art see **6.32–7n.**

30.15–25 as they that would build an house ... beautiful and uniform   Scott returns to the image of poetry, or poetics, as a house (introduced at **5.23–33**), distinguishing various kinds of end, analogous to the three ends of poetry: move, teach, delight. For the house as a topos in Aristotelian logic see **5.24–31n.** Scott's scribe omitted 'the house . . . to this end' (**30.16–17**) through eyeskip, and the missing words were inserted in another hand, probably Scott's (see Textual Introduction, lxxvii–lxxix).

30.25–8 what we proposed . . . knowledge and virtue   See **6.1–4**.

30.27–8 as in a pleasant alley   See *OED*, *alley*, n., 2a: 'A walk in a garden, park, shrubbery, maze, or wood . . .'. Cf. Sidney's image of the reading of poetry as a similarly delightful journey: 'For he doth not only show the way, but giveth so sweet a prospect into the way as will entice any man to enter into it; nay, he doth as if your journey should lie through a fair vineyard – at the very first give you a cluster of grapes that, full of that taste, you may long to pass further' (*DP*, 22–3).

30.32 inartificialness   The word may be Scott's coinage (I have found no earlier usage), and caused some trouble to the scribe, who wrote 'martifialnes'. *Inartificialness* is not in *OED*, which gives 1609 as the first recorded usage of the adjective *inartificial* in this sense (*OED*, *inartificial*, adj., 2: 'Not in accordance with the principles of art; constructed without art or skill . . .'). Scott's source is probably Quintilian, who gives *artificialis* and *inartificialis* as Latin equivalents of the Aristotelian *entechnos* and *atechnos* (*Rhetoric*, 1355b35; and see **38.6n.**). That usage had been adopted into Ramistic logic, giving *inartificial* a precise currency in English in translations of Ramus from the 1570s on. Sidney uses the adverb *inartificially* (*DP*, 45; see **77.23–8n.**).

30.34–8 Scaliger saith . . . unpleasant or disgraceful   Scaliger, 5.2 (214c2), introducing an extensive comparison of Homer and Virgil; Scaliger also praises Virgil's sense of decorum in 3.26 (114c1). Since Scaliger does not say that Virgil knows only what indecorum is (and not what decorum is), the sense must be that Virgil only knows and never practises indecorum. On the phrase 'prince of poets' see **10.2n.** Scaliger calls Virgil 'poetarum princeps' (prince of poets) at, e.g., 255c1 and 278c2.

30.39–40 Horace . . . reason and discretion   *Ars poetica*, 140 (literally 'he toils at/undertakes/devises nothing improperly/absurdly'). Horace is sending up the belated epic poet who goes over old ground, and is embarking on his point about Homer not trying to tell the whole story of the Trojan war, but beginning *in medias res* (140–9). In adding that Horace praises Homer 'for less reason' Scott shows that he is following Scaliger, for whom Virgil's restraint is the opposite of Homer's excess (see especially 5.2, the chapter from which Scott has just borrowed).

30.40–1 the common saying . . . *index et obliqui*   The Latin tag (correctly reading *iudex*, 'judge' and not *index*, 'sign', 'one who discovers', though it is found in both forms) appears to come ultimately from Aquinas: 'Now goodness discovers more good than evil, which after all is known only through good: as Aristotle observes, *The straight is rule both for itself and the crooked* [*rectum enim est iudex sui ipsius, et obliqui*]' (*Summa theologiae*, 2.2.9.4). Aquinas is paraphrasing Aristotle, *De anima*, 411a3–7: 'one element in each pair of contraries will suffice to enable it to discern both that element itself and its contrary. By means of the straight line we know both itself and the curved – the carpenter's rule enables us to test both – but what is curved does not enable us to distinguish either itself or the straight.' The medieval and Renaissance translations of Aristotle printed in the sixteenth century do not repeat Aquinas' wording, but his tag is found alongside the passage in the margins of certain editions, e.g. *Libri tres de anima* (Venice, 1540), 25.

31.5–6 he that aims ... at a landmark   Scott is developing a commonplace from some of his favourite authors. Cf. the opening of Aristotle, *Nicomachaean ethics*, 1.2 (1094a24–6): 'Shall we not, like archers who have a mark to aim at, be more likely to hit upon what we should?'; the opening of Quintilian, 1.pr.20: 'Perfect eloquence is assuredly a reality, which is not beyond the reach of human intellect. Even if we fail to reach it, those whose aspirations are highest will attain to greater heights than those who abandon themselves to premature despair of ever reaching the goal and halt at the very foot of the ascent' (and 12.11.30); and principally Sidney: 'Who shootes at the midde day Sunne, though he bee sure he shall never hit the marke; yet as sure hee is, he shall shoote higher, then who aimes but at a bushe' (*NA*, L2ᵛ; Skretkowicz, 158). Sidney's version is the first instance given in *ODEP* for this proverb (*ODEP*, 726; Tilley, M 1115).

31.8–12 as divines say ... (there described)   Chapters 1–2 of the New Testament epistle of James concern the need for works and not faith only: 'And be ye doers of the worde, and not hearers onely' (James 1:22). Scott also alludes to James 1:27: 'Pure religion and undefiled before God, even the Father, is this, to visite the fatherlesse and widowes in their adversitie, *and* to keepe him selfe unspotted of the world.' These verses (and cf. James 2:24: 'of workes a man is justified, and not of faith onely') are strong arguments against the reformed doctrine of justification by faith alone, as expressed in Article 11 of the *Thirty-nine articles* (*Articles* (1571), A4ᵛ–B1ʳ). Scott quotes from James again at **72.28**.

31.8 *sic parvis ... solebam*   'Thus I used to compare great things with small': Virgil, *Eclogues*, 1.23. The idea was a commonplace: see, e.g., Cicero, *Orator*, 4.14.

31.13–14 Quintilian ... clear from faults   Quintilian, 8.3.41: 'But, before I discuss ornament, I must first touch upon its opposite, since the first of all virtues is the avoidance of faults [*nam prima virtus est vitio carere*]'.

31.18 Aristotle saith ... beautifies   This seems to be not a reference to a particular passage but a summary of Aristotle's position; for various comments on Homer's merits and superiority to other poets see, e.g., *Poetics*, 1451a22–4, 1459a30–1, 1459b12–16, and especially 1460a5–1460b5.

31.19–20 those two parts ... device itself   The standard Ciceronian and Erasmian *res/verba* distinction from rhetoric, as observed by Sidney (*DP*, 9: 'for any understanding knoweth the skill of each artificer standeth in that *idea* or fore-conceit of the work, and not in the work itself'). Aristotle's division of the elements of tragedy (1447a and 1449b–50a) is not built on this binary, but rather on the three categories of mode (spectacle), media (verbal expression and song writing), and object (the representation of plot, character, and intellect); see further **68.29–69.1n**. For subject/ground/argument see further **33.10–14n**.

31.27–30 That pleasure . . . sense-objects   Cf. Scott's discussion from Vives of two kinds of 'affections', the second of which is concerned with sensual pleasures (**70.29–71.7**).

31.34–8 Quintilian will say . . . neatly-cut myrtle   As part of an argument that 'true beauty and usefulness always go hand in hand' (Quintilian, 8.3.11): 'Shall I regard a farm as a model of good cultivation because its owner shows me lilies and violets and anemones and fountains of living water in place of rich crops and vines bowed beneath their clusters? Shall I prefer the barren plane and myrtles trimly clipped, to the fruitful olive and the elm that weds the vine?' (8.3.8).

31.39–32.8 a true saying . . . outward sense   On Lomazzo see **10.15–21n**. Scott draws on and quotes the short opening chapter of Book 7 of Lomazzo's *Trattato* (459–60). I have preferred Scott's reading 'si sente' ('one hears'), the reading in the 1584 text, over Ciardi's 'risente', a variant that appears to be without authority.

32.8–11 that sauce . . . progress in good   A traditional topos in poetics. Cf. Harington, translating Tasso (*ECE*, II, 198–9), and Sidney:

Even as the child is often brought to take most wholesome things by hiding them in such other as have a pleasant taste, which if one should begin to tell them the nature of the aloes or rhabarbarum they should receive, would sooner take their physic at their ears than at their mouth, so is it in men (most of which are childish in the best things till they be cradled in their graves): glad they will be to hear the tales of Hercules, Achilles, Cyrus, Aeneas, and hearing them must needs hear the right description of wisdom, valour, and justice, which if they had been barely (that is to say, philosophically) set out, they would swear they be brought to school again.   (*DP*, 23)

Cf. **20.20n**. and **47.33–6n**.

32.11–12 they that under . . . golden goblet   Scott seems to be thinking of the long line of romance enchantresses with their golden cups of poisoned drink, from Homer's Circe (*Odyssey*, 10) via Ariosto's Alcina and Tasso's Armida to Spenser's Acrasia; with allegorical transparency the men they ensnare tend to be turned into beasts. However, there may also be a specific reference to the whore of Babylon, who 'had a cup of gold in her hand, full of abominations, and filthinesse of her fornication' (Revelation 17:4). In Spenser it is one of Acrasia's gate-keepers, Excesse, who offers Guyon a drink from her 'Cup of gold' (*FQ*, 2.12.56.1), in the celebrated Bower of Bliss episode. That episode seems to inform Scott's thinking here, since it makes a clear equation between deceptively beautiful surfaces and the delights of poetry: in each case something less salubrious may lurk below. A final source is Du Bartas, *La sepmaine*, day 2, 15–18, on the misuse of poetic eloquence, as translated by Scott: 'But in the hony-baytes of their best furnisht writts, | They hyde a murdringe poyson, which yonge hungry witts | Doe greedily suck in . . .' (Add. MS 81083, 66ʳ).

32.13 soul-murderers   See *OED*, *soul*, n., C1b(a) for this compound noun, possibly derived from 1 John 3:15, and which seems to have been a popular term with reformers. Examples include William Tyndale's 'Prologue into the fourth boke of Moses', where the priest who turns communion into a financial transaction 'is a theef, and a soule murtherer' (*The whole workes* (1573), 20); John Bale, in *The apology of Iohan Bale* (1550), F3ʳ; and more recently for Scott the first part of Martin Marprelate's *Oh read over D. John Bridges* [1588; *STC* 17453], again on the abuses of priests: 'Som men are theeves and soul murtherers before God' (51).

32.15–19 Sabina Poppaea . . . exquisite strumpet   Poppaea Sabina became mistress to the emperor Nero during her second marriage, to the future emperor Otho, and the couple subsequently married; she died in AD 65. Scott quotes Tacitus, *Annales*, 13.45: 'Huic mulieri cuncta alia fuere praeter honestum animum' ('She was a woman possessed of all advantages but a character'). A *check-roll* (originally *checker-roll*) is a list of names, specifically those in service to be paid by the (royal) exchequer; the first recorded usage in this figurative sense is 1599 (*OED*, †*check-roll*, n.).

32.21–3 being now but burnished dross . . . purified   Scott's extended metaphor is clever. Poetry that hides vice under a pleasing veneer is like polished base metal: it might appear fair, but just as a touchstone (used to assay the quality of precious metal alloys) will show that the metal is not precious, so virtue can see through the surface to reveal the vice beneath; and just as purer metals can be got from alloys by smelting, so these poems (or their poets) should be burnt. On the burning of books of satire in 1599 see **79.32–4n.**

32.26–9 out of this argument . . . men to affect her   This metaphorical body is first of all Aristotelian (plot is the soul of tragedy: *Poetics*, 1450a38–9; cf. **13.20–2n.**) and then Sidneian: 'if the saying of Plato and Tully be true, that who could see virtue would be wonderfully ravished with the love of her beauty – [the heroic poet] sets her out to make her more lovely in her holiday apparel to the eye of any that will deign not to disdain until they understand' (*DP*, 29).

32.28–9 Judith-like temptation   In the apocryphal Book of Judith, the Jewish widow ingratiates herself with the Assyrian general Holofernes and then beheads him. Cf. Scott's discussion of Du Bartas's *Judith*, **19.40–1n.**

32.30–1 delight . . . appetite or will   Cf. **31.27–30n.**

32.33–4 the beauty . . . constant Argalus   The idealised lovers of Sidney's revised *Arcadia*. That Argalus loves the substance and not the surface is proved when in Book 1 a jealous rival destroys the beauty of Parthenia's face with poison, she vanishes, and when a beautiful look-alike appears, reporting Parthenia's dying wish that Argalus take her in Parthenia's place, Argalus refuses. The look-alike then reveals herself to be Parthenia, her beauty magically restored (Skretkowicz, 28–32, 43–5).

32.35–41 We describe *beauty* **. . . to our sight**   This is the traditional Stoic definition of beauty, as repeated for instance by Cicero (*Tusculan disputations*, 4.13.30–1) and the Neoplatonist Plotinus (*Enneads*, 1.6.1): 'Almost everyone declares that the symmetry of parts towards each other and towards a whole, with, besides, a certain charm of colour, constitutes the beauty recognized by the eye' (46). Scott follows Viperano's chapter 'On the beauty of a poem' closely: 'Aristotle . . . says that beauty consists of two things: magnitude, which is the proper quantity and measure of the parts; and symmetry, which is the necessary arrangement of the members with each other. But Plato also insists on a pleasantness of color, without which a poem cannot be beautiful' (1.19, 63). Cf. Aristotle: 'It is not enough for beauty that a thing, whether an animal or anything else composed of parts, should have those parts well-ordered; since beauty consists in amplitude as well as in order, the thing must also have amplitude . . . but no more than can be taken in at one view; and similarly a plot must have extension, but no more than can be easily remembered' (*Poetics*, 1450b34–1451a6); and 'The chief forms of beauty are order and symmetry and definiteness' (*Metaphysics*, 1078a36–b1). The attribution of the last point to Plato is a simplification: passages which discuss colour include *Meno*, 76d (in relation to sight); and *Phaedo*, 100d, *Philebus*, 51b–d, and *Republic*, 601a (in relation to beauty).

33.1 Great Julius Scaliger . . . Bartas calls him   Du Bartas, 'Babylone' (the second part of the second day of *La seconde sepmaine*), 329. Du Bartas uses the epithet in the context of praising Scaliger's son, the philologist Joseph Justus Scaliger (1540–1609): 'Scaliger, merveille de nostre age | . . . | Digne fils du grand Jule, et digne frere encore | De Sylve . . .' (Du Bartas, III, 130); in Sylvester's translation: '*Scaliger*, our ages wonder | . . . | Great *Julius* sonne, and *Sylvius* worthy brother' (Snyder, I, 430). Joseph Justus Scaliger's older brother Sylvius Aeneas Scaliger, to whom Scaliger's *Poetices libri septem* was dedicated, was a friend and neighbour of Du Bartas, and he contributed commendatory verses to the 1579 edition of Du Bartas's *Oeuvres poétiques* (see Du Bartas, I, 13). Cf. Alberico Gentili on 'magnum Scaligerum' (Binns, 80).

33.1–8 Scaliger . . . persuasion and motion   In his chapter 'De quatuor virtutibus poetae' ('On the four virtues of the poet', 3.25) Scaliger reiterates the Horatian desire for beauty and utility and then introduces his four poetic virtues: *prudentia*, *varietas*, *efficacia*, *suavitas* (113d1–a2; Padelford, 53). Note that the first and last, as Scott understands them, correspond to the Platonic–Aristotelian elements of beauty just discussed (**32.35–41n.**). Scott reorders them and even in this initial outline is already looking ahead to their more detailed definitions in the chapters of Scaliger that follow:

efficacia is only glossed as the Greek *energeia* at the opening of 3.27, for example (116b2). Analysis of 'virtues' (Greek *aretai*) of style goes back to Aristotle on the four virtues of prose style (correctness, clarity, dignity, propriety): *Rhetoric*, 1407a–1408b, and 1414a23 for 'virtue' (*aretē*); cf. Cicero, *De oratore*, 3.10.37.

33.8–9 all of these... device or style   Scott takes a cue from the opening of Scaliger's chapter on *efficacia*: 'Intelligo nunc non verborum virtutem, sed Idaearum, quae rerum species sunt' (116b2, 'I believe [*efficacia*] to be a virtue not only of style but also of ideas, which are the models of matter'). Scott returns to this point in his discussion of these four stylistic virtues at the level of *verba* (**57.15–16n.**).

33.10–14 a difference... accomplishing it   Referring to **31.19–20**, where Scott first distinguishes the ground/subject/argument of the fiction from 'the device itself'. Cf. Aristotle, *Poetics*, 1450a–b, on plot (*muthos*) standing in relation to tragedy as soul to body, and character being there in order to realise plot. But note that Scott's scheme replaces plot with the moral argument of a fiction, which must come first. No exact source in Scaliger is referred to. The dichotomy that runs through Scaliger and Scott, variously configured as thing/word (Plato), matter/form (Aristotle), res/verba (Cicero), inventio/dispositio (rhetoric), fore-conceit/work itself (Sidney), form/content, and (here) argument/device, is discussed at the start of Scaliger's Book 3 (80a–c1).

33.14–17 the argument... express the other by   Referring to Sidney's *Arcadia* and its two heroes, the princes Pyrocles and Musidorus. The 'argument' of the *Arcadia* as Scott defines it corresponds to Sidney's '*idea* or fore-conceit' (*DP*, 9), and is what ideally the reader should be left with after reading. This enables Scott to ignore the obstacles to a Sidneian reading of Sidney's own works presented by the many morally questionable episodes in the *Arcadia*: we start and end with 'the valour and virtue of the two princes'.

33.17–20 the orators say... persuasive conceits   That is, 'invention' (*inventio*), the discovery of the arguments 'whereby we labour to persuade', is the first stage of rhetorical composition, followed by their arrangement (*dispositio*), and only then do we move from matter to words, with the third stage, *elocutio* or style ('the clothing and adorning of our persuasive conceits'). See for example Cicero, *De partitione oratoria*, 1.3–7.24, or *De oratore*, 2.19.79 (where that *inventio* must come first is something anyone will realise instinctively).

33.22–3 the dignity of a *critic*... our best writers   The use of *critic* to mean 'literary critic' (rather than someone more generally, and often satirically, censorious) was new in English. *OED*'s first recorded usage (*OED*, *critic*, n.¹, 2: Bacon in 1605) postdates Scott. This seems appropriate enough, since Scott is 'well near without any precedent' (**4.7–8**). However, the word is there in Scott's sources in this particular sense: e.g. in Horace, *Epistles*, 2.1.51, Quintilian, 2.1.4, and in Scaliger, much of whose fifth book, titled 'Criticus', is devoted to the activity of selecting and comparing passages in Homer and Virgil. *OED* shows usages in English of the Latin form in this specific sense predating Scott (*OED*, *critic*, etymology). But it misses one notable use of *critic* in the new sense just before Scott: John Marston, *The metamorphosis of Pigmalions image. And certaine satyres* (1598), 'Reactio', where Joseph Hall, the author of *Virgidemiarum* (1597), is 'our moderne *Crittick*' (E5^r).

33.25–7 with Scaliger . . . which is the art   Scaliger, 1.5: 'Adhaec, non omnia ad Homerum referenda, tanquam ad normam, censeo: sed et ipsum ad normam' (10d2; Padelford, 36: 'Furthermore I do not think that all writing should be referred to Homer as a standard, for he ought to be judged by a standard himself').

33.27–8 if Homer sometime sleep . . . offended with that   *Ars poetica*, 358–9: 'and yet I also feel aggrieved, whenever good Homer nods [*dormitat Homerus*]'.

33.31–4 The *proportionableness* **. . . convenient whole**   Scaliger, 113d1 (' . . . et res vero propiores, ac sibiipsis semper convenientes exequuti fuerint'), and cf. 113c2 ('vel in re, vel in verbis'): the *argument* should accord with truth, and the *device* should be self-consistent. *Proportion* and cognate terms are used by Scott as synonyms for *decorum*, in preference to Scaliger's *prudentia*, although forms of the latter surface occasionally (**9.16, 30.2, 53.13, 71.19**).

33.35–8 our apprehension . . . proper being and nature's   On *idea* see Scaliger, 80a–c1, and **11.14–21n., 12.25–30n., 15.29–33n.,** and **19.39–40n.**

34.1–2 describe an elephant . . . in his feet   Scott, if he is thinking of any particular source here, may be remembering Aristotle, *History of animals*, 494a (human body, including foot) and 497b–498a (legs and feet of various quadripeds, with differences of elephants noted). Note, however, that the *Physiologus* describes the elephant as having 'no knee joints enabling him to sleep lying down' (*Physiologus*, 30), a point challenged by Albertus Magnus (*On animals*, 22.51). For a contemporary description of the elephant in English see Edward Topsell's *The historie of foure-footed beasts* (1607), 190–211. Scott may have known its major source, vol. 1 of Conrad Gessner's *Historiae animalium* (Zürich, 1551).

34.2–4 Some herein will blame . . . temperate woman   Viperano, 2.3: 'Virgil has not avoided censure in that he made Dido out to be impure, immodest, and captivated by love for Aeneas, when she was a virtuous and chaste woman, who also had lived long before Aeneas' (71).

34.5–7 tied not himself . . . virtue of Aeneas   See Viperano, 2.3, for Virgil's fictional licence in the interests of creating an exemplary image (71–2), and cf. Scott's discussion of the real or imagined exemplary characters of heroic poetry, **19.16–20.3**.

34.8–10 with more reason . . . place affords none   A common criticism of *Aeneid*, 1.184–93, going back to Servius. See Viperano, 1.4 (14), perhaps Scott's direct source.

34.10–11 Scaliger blames Sannazar . . . out of the east   Scaliger, 314a2, referring to the *De partu virginis* (1526) of Jacopo Sannazaro (on whom see **22.19–20n.**), 1.244; cf. Matthew 2:1–12.

34.12–17 Master Spenser . . . wonders of the world   *The ruines of time*, 414–15, describing the vanity of attempts to defy time with monuments: 'Such one *Mausolus* made, the worlds great wonder, | But now no remnant doth thereof remaine'; cf. *Ruines of Rome* (a translation from Du Bellay), sonnet 2 (line 21), which refers to '*Mausolus* worke'. Both works were printed in *Complaints* (1591); the former was an extended meditation on Sidney's death. The Mausoleum, one of the seven wonders of the ancient world, was in fact begun during the lifetime of Mausolus, ruler of Caria from 377–53 BC, and finished after the death of his sister, wife, and fellow-ruler Artemisia in 351 BC. Pliny (36.4.30–1) does indeed record the details that the Mausoleum was 'built by Artemisia' and that the sculptor Scopas was joined by Bryaxis, Timotheus, and Leochares ('together with him they worked on the carvings of the Mausoleum'). The architect, however, was Pythius of Priene. Scott may be recalling Aulus Gellius' account of how the grief-stricken Artemisia drank her brother-husband's ashes and built the Mausoleum (*Attic nights*, 10.18). See also Cicero, *Tusculan disputations*, 3.31.75.

34.18–19 if you stand . . . necessary or probable or possible   The scribe omitted, through eyeskip, the key words 'necessary or probable or possible' here, and Scott inserted them himself. Scott depends on Aristotle: 'the poet's job is saying not what did happen but the sort of thing that would happen, that is, what can happen in a strictly probable or necessary sequence' (*Poetics*, 1451a36–8); 'it is what is possible that arouses conviction' (1451b16); 'In the representation of character as well as in the chain of actions one ought always to look for the necessary or probable, so that it is necessary or probable that a person like this speaks or acts as he does, and necessary or probable that this happens after that' (1454a33–6); and 'One ought to prefer likely impossibilities to unconvincing possibilities' (1460a26–7). Cf. Viperano's account (1.9, 25–6).

34.19–21 Necessary . . . provide for after-times   Probably from Cicero, *De officiis*, 2.9.33: 'we have confidence in those who we think have more understanding than ourselves, who, we believe, have better insight into the future [*futura prospicere*]'. Scott's meaning is that a fictitious sequence of events that is in Aristotle's terms 'necessary' – that is, one thing follows another because it would have to; no alternative could be imagined, and therefore it is entirely lifelike – will because of its proximity to reality be as useful a guide to what might happen in the future as a historical sequence of events.

34.24–7 Aeneas . . . ex aliis   Virgil, *Aeneid*, 12.435–6: "'Learn valour from me, my son, and true toil; fortune from others.'"

34.30 Aristotle . . . verisimile   Scott is likely to have read Aristotle in Latin. That he quotes him both in Greek and, here, in Latin, may suggest that Scott has access to a parallel Greek–Latin edition, such as Casaubon's beautifully printed two-volume *Operum Aristotelis . . . nova editio* (Lyon, 1590), on which cf. **77.5–11n**. However, any or all quotations may equally be taken from a secondary source, such as Viperano (see **34.36–8n**.). *Verisimile* (translating Greek *eikos*) is perhaps given in Latin by Scott because the term has such wide currency in the commentaries on Horace's *Ars poetica* (see Weinberg, I, 77–8) as well as in Cicero (e.g. *De inventione*, 1.7.9) and the rhetorical tradition (e.g. *Ad Herennium*, 1.2.3; Quintilian, 2.4.2), and in contemporary English neo-Latin writings, e.g. Gentili (Binns, esp. 72–6); it is also found in Pliny (e.g. 35.36.103).

34.30–3 Horace . . . fabula credi   *Ars poetica*, 338–9: 'Fictions meant to please should be close to the real, and your tale must not ask for belief in anything it chooses.' Scott's text includes variant readings from the early manuscript tradition in line 339 that are not preferred by modern editors (*nec*, 'neither', for *ne*, 'so that not'; *volet*, 'will wish', for *velit*, 'should wish'). Scott's text also reads singular 'sit' for plural 'sint' (both third person present subjunctives of *sum*, 'to be'), but as this does not agree I have emended it.

34.36–8 Aristotle saith Agathon . . . may fall out   *Poetics*, 1456a24–5, also quoted by Viperano (1.13, 38). All sixteenth-century printed Latin versions that I have consulted, including the standard medieval translation of William of Moerbeke, agree in using the term *verisimile* in this passage, as does Viperano's Latin (43). Cf. *Rhetoric*, 1402a, for the same remark of Agathon, in verse.

34.38–35.2 the poet hath liberty . . . must be extraordinary   Possibly drawn from Viperano's chapter on the marvellous (1.14, 42).

35.2–6 It is very reprovable . . . without a guide   *Poetics*, 1460a26–32: 'One ought to prefer likely impossibilities to unconvincing possibilities and not compose one's argument of irrational parts. Preferably there should be no irrationality at all, and if there is it should be outside the plot . . . It should not be inside the plot like . . . the man who went speechless from Tegea to Mysia in the *Mysians*.' The reference is to a lost play by Aeschylus or Sophocles. Scott is clearly leaning on the parallel discussion in Viperano here (1.13, 38); Viperano names Sophocles as the author and adds the other details not in Aristotle.

35.7–10 Ariosto . . . he reports   Ariosto, *Orlando furioso*, 9.68. Scott of course disapproves of Ariosto's over-sexed and for the most part morally unexemplary romance, although this disapproval has to be limited by the good use Sidney and Spenser make of it. A few of Ariosto's many characters (Orlando, Ruggiero, Rodomont) are superhuman in a way that greatly exceeds the abilities of most of the rest, however exaggerated these nevertheless are, as befits the genre. Scott ought perhaps to allow for this. The episode in question sees Orlando ambushed outside the gates of Dordrecht by the King of Frisia. Orlando charges and 'on his lance he impaled first one, then a second, then a third and fourth, as though they were made of dough; six he impaled, carrying them all on his lance; and the seventh, for lack of room, he did not impale – nevertheless he inflicted on him a wound from which he died' (89). One might, then, argue, that Ariosto has a strong regard for verisimilitude in his careful calculation of how many bodies could fit on a lance. The simile 'like so many gloves' is Scott's (it is not found in Harington's translation (*Orlando furioso* (1591), 9.62). This passage may betray the influence of Giovanni Giorgio Trissino's *La quinta e la sesta divisione della poetica* (Venice, 1562; the first four parts having appeared in 1529); Trissino gives as an example of likely impossibility 'that a knight had killed three or four armed men, one after the other with a single lance' (Weinberg, II, 754).

35.11 Horace 'incredulus odi'   *Ars poetica*, 188, describing not so much incredible sights as ones better narrated than staged.

35.12–13 but ... into particulars   *But* is perhaps used here in the sense 'except', 'unless' (*OED, but*, prep., etc., C. II), although the 'not' is then redundant; i.e. 'as long as they descend not ...'.

35.16–19 Horace ... concluded in a fish   *Ars poetica*, 1–4.

35.19–21 It is, saith the excellent painter ... mind of the beholder   Scott is perhaps conflating various passages in Lomazzo: 1.3 – 'Such is the importance and vertue of *Proportion*, that nothing can any way satisfie the eie, without the helpe thereof ... And hence it is, that when wee beholde a well proportioned thing, wee call it *beautifull*; as if wee shoulde saie, indued with that exact and comely grace, whereby all the perfection of sweete delightes belonging to the sight, are communicated to the eye, and so conveyed to the understanding' (38; Haydocke, C1$^{r–v}$); 1.4 – the ancient view 'that whatsoever was made without measure and proportion, could never carry with it such congruity, as might represent either *beauty* or *grace* to the judicious beholder' and the conclusion that 'it is impossible, to make any decent or well proportioned thing [*ch'abbia in sé armonia o convenevolezza*], without this symmetricall measure of the partes orderly united' (40; C2$^{r–v}$); 6.3 – 'The limbs must be symmetrical, measured and harmoniously [*armonicamente*] proportioned in relation to each other, so that there is no figure in which one sees a large head, a small chest, a wide hand, one leg longer than the other, and similar unsuitable things' (248; my translation).

35.23–5 The poem must be ... upon another   *Poetics*, 1450b–1451a, esp.: 'a plot ... should be a *mimēsis* of one action and that a whole one, with the different sections so arranged that the whole is disturbed by the transposition and destroyed by the removal of any of them; for if it makes no visible difference whether a thing is there or not, that thing is no part of the whole' (1451a31–5). Cf. Viperano, 1.9 (25).

35.25–7 Horace . . . hermaphrodite or mongrel   *Ars poetica*, 23: 'In short, be the work what you will, let it at least be simple [*simplex*: simple, single, unmixed] and uniform [*unum* (accusative): one].' For the 'hermaphrodite or mongrel' (Horace doesn't use these terms), see *Ars poetica*, 1–4 and 12–13. Scott may be thinking of Sidney's 'mongrel tragicomedy' (*DP*, 46; see **24.20–24n.**). Cf. also Viperano, 1.9, for this line of argument and the same passages from Horace (25–6).

35.27–9 Scaliger . . . constancy the imitation   In the chapter on *prudentia* (3.26): 'imitatio rem sequatur: constantia imitationem comitetur' (113c2).

35.30–36.1 You must make . . . his own unsitting authority   This whole passage shows the influence of Hoskyns's account of 'Illustracion': 'hee that will truely set downe a man in a figured storie, must first learn truely to set downe an humour a passion, a virtue, a vice, and therein keeping decent proporcion add but names . . . [Hoskyns digresses on Sidney's use of Aristotle's *Rhetoric*] . . . I thinke alsoe that he had much help out of *Theophrasti imagines* [see **35.31–2n.**] . . . But to owr purpose what personages and affeccions are sett forth in *Arcadia* . . . [long list includes] proud vallour in *Anaxius* . . . feare and rudenes with ill affected civillitie in Dametas . . . wise courage in *Pamela*, mylde discrecion in *Philoclea* . . . nowe in these persons is ever a stedfast decencie and uniforme difference of manners observed whereever yow finde them' (*Directions*, 155–6). On consistency in characterisation cf. *Poetics*, 1454a16–36, Horace, *Ars poetica*, 119–27, and Viperano, 1.15 (46–8).

35.31–2 describing notes . . . may be called   These terms are complex and considered. First of all, 'describing note' is borrowed from Sidney: 'it is that feigning notable images of virtues, vices, or what else, with that delightful teaching, which must be the right describing note to know a poet by' (*DP*, 12). It means 'distinguishing feature'. The Greek word *character* originally meant an engraving instrument, and so was used to mean 'A distinctive mark impressed, engraved, or otherwise formed' (*OED*, *character*, n., 1a), including that of someone's handwriting or speech (relating to style, the equivalent term in Latin: for this usage cf. **51.1n.**). Metaphorical uses in Scott's day did not extend to the sense we now attach to the word: 'The sum of the moral and mental qualities which distinguish an individual' (*OED*, *character*, n., 11, first recorded usage 1660), let alone such a character as a fictive creation (17a, first recorded usage 1664). However, Shakespeare was using the word to mean the outward appearance as indicative of the inward nature at this time (*OED*, *character*, n., 10). Scott is to an extent, as he indicates, using the term in the sense in which it figures in the title of the *Characters* (Greek *Charaktēres*) of Aristotle's successor Theophrastus, a set of sketches of moral types first imitated in English in Joseph Hall's *Characters of vertues and vices* (1608). Scott could be talking about the distinguishing features of all aspects of a literary work ('the describing notes or *characters . . .* of every particular'), but that he goes on to discuss what we would call *characters* shows that the word is moving towards its modern usage here.

35.33–4 Aeneas . . . Achates faithful   The hero of Virgil's *Aeneid* and his loyal companion, whom Virgil tends to call *fidus*, faithful: e.g. 1.188; 6.158; 8.521, 586. Cf. **52.35–6**.

35.34–7 Pamela . . . honourable regard   The two princesses in the *Arcadia*; Pamela is the older (and heir to the throne of *Arcadia*), Philoclea the younger, and Sidney distinguishes their characters in the way Scott describes.

35.38–36.1 Anaxius . . . unsitting authority   More characters from the *Arcadia*. Anaxius becomes central to the peripheries of the revised *Arcadia* and develops an ongoing feud with Pyrocles, which is still being settled when the incomplete work breaks off. Dametas is a shepherd with whose family Pamela is obliged to lodge when her father Basilius decides to live among the shepherds.

36.1 unsitting   Unbecoming, unfitting (*OED*, †*unsitting*, adj.).

36.3 exigents   *OED*, *exigent*, adj. and n.[1], B†1a: 'A state of pressing need; a time of extreme necessity; a critical occasion, or one that requires immediate action or remedy'.

36.3 conveyances   *OED*, *conveyance*, n., †9a: 'The conveying of meaning by words; expression, or clothing of thought in language; disposition of material in a poem, etc.'; and hence †9b: 'Manner of expressing thought, form of expression or utterance, style.'

36.3–4 and shuffling . . . contrary   Omitted by the scribe through eyeskip and inserted in a neat hand that may be Scott's. See Textual Introduction, lxxix.

36.4–9 Chariclea's excellent conceit . . . many circumstances   After many adventures Theagenes and Charikleia are captured by King Hydaspes at the end of the ninth book (of ten) of Heliodorus' *Aithiopika* (on which see **19.24–31n.**). Hydaspes does not know that Charikleia is his daughter. Since the stakes are high, Charikleia is not prepared to tell her story until recognition tokens, witnesses, and all concerned are in one place; and so the denouement is delayed for a book. Scott is not quoting Underdowne's 1569 translation (as he appears to later, **43.15–16**), but he may be looking at it: 'My deere, great businesse must be donne with great circumspection. For it is necessary that the endes of those thinges must be donne with many circumstances . . . [margin: 'Great matters may not be sleightly handled']' (*An Æthiopian historie*, 129ᵛ).

36.10–11 Our tragedies . . . in one hour   This remark derives from Aristotle: *Poetics*, 1449b, on 'tragedy attempting so far as possible to keep to the limit of one revolution of the sun . . . while epic is unfixed in time'; 1451a, on the limit of length of tragedy (leading with the previous passage to the doctrine of the unity of time) and the need for a singleness of action, observed even in Homer; and 1456a, on how one should not 'make an epic [that is, episodic] body of material into a tragedy . . . , as if, for instance, one were to compose a play on the whole story of the *Iliad*'. Cf. Sidney for an extended discussion of the issue, referring more directly to the Aristotelian unities of time and action (*DP*, 45–6), and see further **76.41–77.28n**.

36.12–14 second persons . . . first and chief   Normally *partes* [rather than *personae*] *secundae*. Horace does not discuss them in *Ars poetica*; the reference is possibly to *Epistles*, 1.18, on the imitative flatterer who 'so echoes [the rich man's] speeches, and picks up his words as they fall, that you would think a schoolboy was repeating his lessons to a stern master or a mime-player acting a second part [*partis . . . secundas*]' (12–14). Cf. Cicero, *In Q. Caecilium*, 15.48, on precedence among teams of lawyers: 'We know how Greek actors behave on the stage; very commonly the man who has the second or third part [*secundarum aut tertiarum partium*] could speak a good deal more loudly and clearly than the man who has the first part, but lowers his voice considerably, in order that the superiority of the chief actor may be as pronounced as possible.'

36.14–21 an excellent painter in Milan . . . disciples above their master   From the opening of Lomazzo 1.10, an otherwise technical chapter about the relative proportions of the parts of the body of a man of eight heads in height: 'in every worke there is some one entire figure, whereunto all the particulars of the whole History ought to be principally referred', and yet this will prove a source of criticism for the painter, 'For it is most certaine, that the worke will proove offensive, where some inferiour and bye matter, is more curiously handled then the *principall*: and the rather, because the other partes cannot but loose their grace.' He gives two classical examples,

Not unlike unto which was that of *Leon: Vincent* of late daies; who being to paint *Christ* at his last supper in the middest of his disciples in the *Refectory of S. Maria de gratia in Milane*; and having finished the other *Apostles*, he represented the two *Jameses* with such perfection of grace and majesty, that indevoring afterwards to expresse *Christ*, hee was not able to perfite and accomplish that sacred countenance, notwithstanding his incomparable skill in the arte. Whence being in a desperate case, hee was enforced to advise with *Bernard Zenale* concerning his faulte, who used these words to comfort him . . . Wherefore content thy selfe, and leave *Christ* unperfitte, for thou maist not set *Christ* neere those *Apostles*. Which advise *Leonard* observed, as may appeare by the picture at this day, though it bee much defaced.   (52–3; Haydocke, D4ᵛ–5ʳ)

Cf. Vasari's life of Leonardo, with no mention of the Jameses (Giorgio Vasari, *The lives of the artists*, trans. Julia Conaway Bondanella and Peter Bondanella (Oxford, 1991), 289).

36.22–6 Was it not a fault . . . not have so erred   In Book 5 of the original manuscript *Arcadia*, a portion of the work that appeared in print in 1593 to complete a narrative which in its revised form had been printed incomplete in three books in 1590. Modern scholars continue to debate the extent of Sidney's hand or that of his editors in the differences between the 'old' *Arcadia* and the corresponding parts of the 1593 text. The 1593 editors made clear that the ending provided was 'the conclusion, not the perfection of *Arcadia*: and that no further then the Authours own writings, or known determinations could direct' but also suggested that Sidney's sister, the Countess of Pembroke, who had overseen this edition, though she 'begonne in correcting the faults, ended in supplying the defectes; by the view of what was ill done guided to the consideration of what was not done' (*NA*, ¶4^r). Scott would therefore have been encouraged to think that any inconsistencies in the later parts of the text might be the fault of Sidney's editors, though in this case the manuscript evidence is clear that the details are Sidney's own. Scott refers to *NA*, 2P1^r (a messenger reports to Philanax that Euarchus 'was nowe come within halfe a mile of the Lodges'; = *OA*, 351) and 2P2^r (Philanax reports to the assembly that Euarchus 'is this day come . . . within two miles of this place'; = *OA*, 353). Since 'this place' is probably not 'the Lodges', there may be no inconsistency at all.

36.28–31 Aristotle . . . out of the memory   *Poetics*, 1450b–1451a:

> Though a very small creature could not be beautiful, since our view loses all distinctness when it comes near to taking no perceptible time, an enormously ample one could not be beautiful either, since our view of it is not simultaneous, so that we lose the sense of its unity and wholeness as we look it over; imagine, for instance, an animal a thousand miles long.

36.36 quatted   Satiated, satisfied, filled up (*OED*, *quat*, v.^{1}, 3).

36.37 conveyance   See 36.3n.; in this case the word means *dispositio*, arrangement.

36.37–9 wrapping and inverting . . . knot of a garden   Scott's analogy between the interweaving of narrative strands and an Elizabethan knot garden is original, but related analogies between kinds of what was often called *interlacing* (of verse lines, decorative elements, plot strands, etc.) were familiar in literature and writing about it.

36.41 additaments   Additional elements, appendages (*OED*, *additament*, n.).

36.41–37.8 In the first, of *order* . . . precepts with narration   Scott moves from the interlaced plot (exemplified in Ariosto's *Orlando furioso* and imitated in Spenser's *Faerie queene*), in which many different strands can be in play at once, to another kind of mixing: of mode or genre. For the former, cf. Harington, defending Ariosto from the charge 'that he breaks off narrations verie abruptly, so as indeed a loose unattentive reader will hardly carrie away any part of the storie' (*ECE*, II, 216–17). Sidney had reported that 'Some, in the manner, have mingled prose and verse, as Sannazaro and Boethius. Some have mingled matters heroical and pastoral. But that cometh all to one in this question, for if severed they be good, the conjunction cannot be hurtful' (*DP*, 25). But later in the *Defence* he is critical of 'mongrel tragicomedy' (*DP*, 46) for its mixing of high and low social classes, and serious and humorous material. Scott may, however, simply be recommending less systematic mixtures, akin to comic relief.

37.8–9 Scaliger . . . as a pattern   Scaliger, 3.96, on heroic poetry, manipulations of sequence, interruptions, and the control of suspense: 'This principle of arrangement has a most admirable realization in the *Aethiopica* of Heliodorus, a book, I take it, that should be most carefully conned by the epic poet, as furnishing him the best model' (144d1; Padelford, 55). Scott's remarks throughout this paragraph are indebted to this chapter in Scaliger.

37.10–11 Sir Philip Sidney . . . did imitate him   Sidney's debt to Heliodorus was also observed by Hoskyns and Markham, though the latter apparently was criticised for it. See Gervase Markham, *The English Arcadia* (1607), A2^v, and *The second and last part of the first booke of the English Arcadia* (1613), A4^{r-v}; and Hoskyns: 'for the webb (as it were) of his storie hee followed three[:] *Heliodorus* in greeke, *Sanazarus Arcadia* in Itallian, and *Diana* de montemajor in spanish' (*Directions*, 155). Scott's emphasis on narrative form is distinct, however (he is not saying anything about Sidney's imitation of particular episodes from Heliodorus, such as in the revised *Arcadia*'s opening), and underscores how much more Aristotelian his approach is in comparison to his contemporaries. On Scott's use of Hoskyns see **68.1–4n**.

37.10 gate of conveyance   Method of arrangement (*OED*, *gate*, n.², 9).

37.21–5 those supplies and additaments . . . main stream of your work   *Poetics*, 1455b; the similes are Scott's own. Cf. *Poetics*, 1451b33–5, for criticism of episodic plots in tragedy; and 1452b20–1, for the narrow and earlier sense of episodes as the portions of dialogue between choric songs in tragedy. Scaliger, 3.97, explicitly prefers the broader definition in his brief discussion (148d1; Padelford, 69). Scott draws more in this case from Viperano's chapter on episodes and digressions (1.10, 29–32), including the neo-Latin form *episodia*, where Scaliger prefers the Greek form *epeisodia*.

37.29–32 as in painting . . . or the like   These details correspond to the styles of portrait being commissioned in the 1590s by Scott's patron Sir Henry Lee, and are a notable expansion on the source of the thought in Viperano, 1.10, where epic digressions are compared to 'the pictures of painters which are embellished with rivers, forests, birds, and other such ornaments' (31). On Scott and the visual arts see Introduction, lxiii–lxvi.

37.32 impress   Impresa (*OED*, *impress*, n.³). Cf. **29.29** and see **81.28–9n**.

37.33–5 he that Horace speaks of . . . part thereof   *Ars poetica*, 19–21. The painter of cypress trees had become proverbial (see Erasmus, *Adagia*, 1.5.19), but while Viperano refers only to 'the common proverb' (1.10, 31) Scott returns this to its source in Horace.

37.38 schoolpoint   Something taught or debated in the universities (*OED*, *school-point*, n.).

37.40 as the dog at Nilus   *ODEP*, 194, first citation from Erasmus, *Adagia*, 1.9.80 (*Ut canis e Nilo*): the dog drinks and runs, for fear of crocodiles.

37.40–38.1 which rule Lucan…high, and abstruse   Viperano, 1.10: 'Those digressions which do not fit into the context not only do not embellish the matter but also disfigure and obscure it. Of this sort are those carefully exquisite reasonings about abstruse and obscure matters existing for the sake of some juvenile display of learning (a thing which most condemn in Lucan)' (31). *Impertinent*: unrelated; irrelevant; inappropriate, out of place (*OED*, *impertinent*, †1, 2, 3a).

38.2–5 in that commended tragedy…rash aspiring   An exaggeration: the two instances are four leaves apart in *The tragedie of Gorboduc* (1565) and are hardly closer in later printings. The play (which was 'commended' by Sidney for one: *DP*, 44–5) concerns King Gorboduc's rebellious sons Ferrex and Porrex. The chorus at the end of Act 1 argues that too much parental love can harm children: 'This doth the proude sonne of *Appollo* prove…' (B3^r). At the end of the next scene (2.1) Dordan refers to the rebellious princes: 'Lo suche are they nowe in the Royall throne | As was rashe *Phaeton* in *Phebus* Carre' (B7^r). Phaeton (the usual spelling in Scott's day, though the more correct transliterated form is *Phaethon*) was the son of Helios, the sun-god (identified with Apollo). Helios lets him drive the chariot of the sun for a day, but he cannot manage its horses, and only a fatal thunderbolt aimed at him by Zeus stops him setting the world alight. See Ovid, *Metamorphoses*, 1.750–2.400.

38.6 proved…but by example   Scott is thinking of the different types of proof in Aristotelian rhetoric. Example (*paradeigma*) is one of the two kinds of logical proof (common to all kinds of rhetoric); logical proof (*logos*) is one of the three kinds of artificial proof (as opposed to inartificial proofs: witnesses, contracts, etc.). See Aristotle, *Rhetoric*, 1356b and 1393a–1394a.

38.9–11 Quintilian…competent plenty   Possibly Quintilian, 8.pr.24, prefacing a book which includes discussion of various kinds of rhetorical excess (8.3.53–8) and of amplification (8.4).

38.13–15 principally in those apt conceits…shadowed in the style   That is, sweetness in *res* (matter) or the Sidneian '*idea* or fore-conceit' is more important than sweetness in *verba* (words).

38.15–20 Aristotle's opinion…creature or story   *Poetics*, 1450a–b, on the primacy of plot over *mimēsis* of character, 'a relation similar to one we find in painting, where the most beautiful colours, if smeared on at random, would give less pleasure than an uncoloured outline that was a picture of something. A tragedy, I repeat, is a *mimēsis* of an action, and it is only because of the action that it is a *mimēsis* of the people engaged in it' (1450a39–1450b4). There is a significant difference between Aristotle's imagining of random colours and Scott's of colours 'disposed [i.e. arranged, perhaps patterned] to please the sight'. Scott's 'images . . . barely lineated in white' translates (probably via a Latin translation) Aristotle's *leukographēsas eikona* (1450b2–3), i.e. 'likeness drawn in white'. Liddell and Scott have only this example for their definition of *leukographeō* as 'paint in white on a coloured ground', so the meaning is far from clear, though Scott coincides with modern translations in clarifying the meaning by adding in a sense of outline ('lineated').

38.20–6 The orators . . . swinge of admiration   Alluding to Quintilian, 6.2, and influenced by Viperano. Quintilian several times in 6.2 argues for the pre-eminence of appeals to emotions over other methods of argument (e.g. 6.2.2, 4, 7). Scott follows Quintilian closely at 6.2.9, where he redescribes Aristotle's *ēthos* and *pathos* as two types of emotion (*affectus*): '*pathos* as describing the more violent emotions and *ēthos* as designating those which are calm and gentle: in the one case the passions are violent, in the other subdued, the former command and disturb, the latter persuade and induce a feeling of goodwill'. This is something of a distortion of Aristotle's account, in the *Poetics* and the *Rhetoric*, of *ēthos* as the representation of (good) moral character, and is symptomatic of a tendency in Roman oratory to dissociate Aristotle's three means of persuasion (*logos*, *ēthos*, and *pathos*) from their offshoot, the proverbial three aims of rhetoric, to teach, delight, and move (*docere*, *delectare*, *movere*). Scott avoids the problem by avoiding the terminology. Cf. Cicero's division of *ēthos* and *pathos* at *Orator*, 37.128 and his extended discussion in *De oratore*, 2.43.182–53.216. For the two triads temporarily reconnected see Quintilian, 8.pr.7. For 'admiration' as the result of eloquence see Quintilian, 8.3.6; on *admiratio* see **18.25–8n.** and **69.9–10n.**

38.25 swinge   Sway, power, rule, influence; impetus, impulse (*OED*, *swinge*, n.[1], †1 and †3).

38.26–9 The poet . . . both their faculties   On the kinship of poetry and oratory see **46.26n.**

38.29–34 those graces . . . other virtue of *efficacy*   Scott now relates Quintilian's *ēthos* and *pathos* to each of his last two virtues, sweetness and *energeia*. He is perhaps influenced by Viperano, who, following Quintilian 6.2.20, associates *ēthos* with comedy and *pathos* with tragedy (1.11, 34–5). For *pathos*, tragedy, and *energeia* see **43.25–6n.**

38.34–6 Scaliger acknowledgeth . . . intended and powerful   Quintilian in fact says that '*pathos* and *ēthos* are sometimes of the same nature, differing only in degree . . . sometimes however they differ' (6.2.12). Scaliger: '[sweetness] tempers the ardency of [*energeia*], of itself inclined to be harsh' (113a2; Padelford, 53). Scaliger omits to give *suavitas* (sweetness) a separate chapter.

38.35 remissness   *OED*, *remissness*, n., †1: 'Reduction or lack of force or intensity; diminution; weakness.'

38.38–9 ever possessing... with evidency   *Evidency* is 'The quality or state of being evident or clear' (*OED*, †*evidency*, n., 1). But Scott is also thinking of *evidentia*, a Latin term for *enargeia* or vivid description, the rhetorical ability to set something before the mental eyes of the listener or reader (Quintilian, 6.2.32–6 and 8.3.61–71), which he calls *evidency* at **45.5**. See further **43.35–40n.** and **45.5–7n.** In the tradition of the stylistic virtues, *evidentia* follows *perspicuitas* or clearness (Quintilian, 8.2) – Scott pairs them at **39.4** – and is followed by *suavitas* (Scott's 'sweetness'), as in Cicero, *De partitione oratoria*, 6.19–22.

39.6–8 smooth and cleanly alterations... always delightful   Quintilian, 8.6.51, on allegory: 'for it is novelty and change that please in oratory, and what is unexpected always gives special delight'. And cf. Quintilian, 6.3.84 and 9.2.22–4, for figurative deceivings of expectation.

39.8–10 either with gladness... sad and unworthy events   The equation of sweetness with comedy and *energeia* with tragedy (see **38.29–34n.** and **43.25–6n.**) lies behind this. For 'astonishing admiration' and tragedy cf. **43.36n.** and **78.12–16n.**

39.11–16 those *peripeteiae*... reader or beholder   The manuscript consistently gives the word in the form 'peripetia(e)', the spelling used also by Viperano (and Harington: *ECE*, II, 216). Scaliger keeps the term in Greek (146b1). I have regularised the spelling to reflect its Greek origins, though maintaining the Latin (-*ae*) rather than Greek (-*ai*) plural form. Aristotle discusses *peripeteia* at *Poetics*, 1452a22–4: 'A *peripeteia* occurs when the course of events takes a turn to the opposite..., the change being also probable or necessary in the way I said.' Viperano discusses it at 1.11 (39/33).

39.19–24 when the two friends... joy than wonder   An episode in Book 1 of the *Arcadia*; Scott as usual follows the text closely. Pyrocles and Musidorus have been separated and are travelling under the names Daiphantus and Palladius. They end up at the heads of opposing armies and fight until Pyrocles strikes off Musidorus' helmet and recognises him, at which point he speaks and Musidorus recognises his voice: 'By that watche worde *Palladius* knew that it was his onely friend *Pyrocles* whom he had lost upon the Sea, and therefore both most full of wonder, so to be met, if they had not bene fuller of joye then wonder, caused the retraite to bee sounded' (*NA*, B6ᵛ; Skretkowicz, 38). Scott is following Aristotle, who treats recognition (*anagnorisis*) alongside *peripeteia*: 'The best sort of recognition is that accompanied by *peripeteia*' (1452a32–3). On *wonder* see **18.25–8n.** Scott recognises that the reactions Sidney describes within the fiction are formulated in the terms of poetics, and so transfer readily to 'the readers' (**39.22**).

39.27–30 Terence . . . with a plaudite   An example also used by Viperano (1.11, 34), in his discussion of recognition and *peripeteia*. Terence's comedies were printed with their *didascaliae* (production notices), giving details of their date, among other things, and were presented in date order. So Scott is right to talk of *Andria* ('The girl from Andros') as Terence's 'first comedy'. The plot is too intricate to summarise, but for its resolution requires the arrival from Andros of an old man, Crito, who shows that Glycerium is Chremes' daughter, enabling her marriage to Pamphilus. The last word of the *Andria* is 'plaudite' ('Give us your applause') and all of Terence's plays end with this formula or a variation on it; cf. Horace, *Ars poetica*, 155. The word entered English in the mid-sixteenth century via neoclassical comedy and Horatian translation (*OED*, *plaudite*, n., 1: 'An appeal for applause at the end of a play, etc.'). For Terence see **1.5–7n**. and **24.9–13n**.

39.29 compassion of joy   Since Scott's scribe repeatedly misread Scott's ampersand as *of*, the correct reading may be 'compassion and joy' (see Textual Introduction, lxxix). Cf. the pairing of *joy* and *wonder* at **39.23–4**, which serves, as would 'compassion and joy', to provide a comic equivalent to tragic pity and fear.

39.30–3 that comedy . . . acknowledging one another   The comedies of Plautus (*fl. c*.205–184 BC) are the earliest Latin works to survive complete. They are adaptations from Greek New Comedy. The *Menaechmi* ('The two Menaechmuses') was itself adapted as Shakespeare's early *The comedy of errors*, and although Scott is referring explicitly to William Warner's 1595 translation, *Menaecmi. A pleasant and fine conceited comædie*, Shakespeare's play may be recalled in 'delightful errors' (**39.31**). In Plautus' play Menaechmus and Sosicles (who has been renamed Menaechmus in memory of the long-lost twin brother he is searching for) are finally reunited after the necessary comedy caused by their identical appearances and names.

39.33–5 intruding merry matters . . . solvere affectus   Quintilian, 6.3.1, on the orator's use of humour, 'which dispels the graver emotions [*tristes solvit affectus*] of the judge by exciting his laughter'; Scott changes third-person singular *solvit* to infinitive *solvere*.

39.36–8 in Virgil's fifth book . . . end of Dido   Book 5 of the *Aeneid* describes the funeral games for Aeneas' father Anchises, which follow Aeneas' flight from Carthage and Dido's suicide in Book 4.

39.38–41 that change in Heliodorus . . . nimble activity   In the final Book of the *Aithiopika* (on which see **19.24–31n**. and **36.4–9n**.) Theagenes is lined up for human sacrifice but first captures and wrestles to the ground the bull that had taken fright (Reardon, 578–80) and is then made to wrestle a man (581–2). Perhaps Scott conflates the two episodes, each of which includes precise descriptions of wrestling technique.

39.41–40.2 bringing-in Dametas . . . grave matters   Characters in Sidney's *Arcadia*. For Dametas see **35.38–36.1n**. Mopsa is his daughter, who forms a comical attachment to Dorus the shepherd (Musidorus in disguise). Along with Dametas' wife Miso, this grotesque family features prominently alongside the 'noble personages' of the main plot.

40.5–6 goodly plots of lilies . . . new-springing meadows   Stanley Wells (Wells, 238–9) considers this an adaptation of Shakespeare, *Richard II*, 5.2.46–7 (spoken by the Duchess of York): 'Who are the violets now | That strew the green lap of the new-come spring?' Scott's words may have been influenced by Shakespeare's, but this is not an allusion by Scott's standards. Scott exploits the old analogy between rhetorical and poetic ornaments and flowers, and the language is no closer to Shakespeare than to the passage from Pierre Matthieu's *Vasthi* translated at **45.12–25**, or to that from Quintilian cited at **31.36**. For other stylistic or mental meadows see, e.g., Dionysius, *Demosthenes*, 5 (*ALC*, 309); Plutarch, *Moralia*, 854c; Sidney's poem 'Like divers flowers' (Ringler, OA 50); and Jonson, *Discoveries* (*CWBJ*, VII, 564).

40.8–9 those pretty turnings . . . models of the *peripeteiae*   In figurative terms, such figures as *anacoluthon*, whereby the sentence concludes in a way different from the expectations created by the grammar of its beginning; *hyperbaton*, whereby normal word order is disrupted; *aposiopesis*, whereby the sentence is broken off incomplete; or *parenthesis*, whereby an additional syntactical unit is interpolated. Cf. the figures briefly discussed at **68.14–22**. The analogy between sentence structure and plot structure is not unprecedented in the period, but is unusual. It is encouraged by the tradition of using metaphors to explain the classical sentence: e.g. Aristotle (*Rhetoric*, 1409a32–4), Demetrius (*On style*, 11), and cf. **75.2–5n**.

40.10 *facetiae . . . lepores*   (i) *facetiae* (plural): a witty or clever thing, witticisms, humour; (ii) *sales* (plural of *sal*, salt): witticisms; (iii) *lepores* (plural): witticisms. The three Latin words are synonyms and often travel together: e.g. Cicero, *De oratore*, 1.57.243. The 'and' here is an ampersand in the manuscript, and might alternatively be construed as Latin *et* were this a quotation.

40.12–13 discerning judgement . . . decorum   Scott discusses decorum at length at **33.31–36.33** and **57.16–58.13**.

40.16–18 that kind of invention . . . sensible thing   Similes and metaphors, but also (since Scott is still discussing sweetness in *res* rather than *verba*) extended metaphors, what are now called metaphysical conceits, and allegories.

40.19–22 this pleaseth . . . 'old age is stubble'   Aristotle discusses metaphor in detail in the *Poetics*, 1457b and 1459a, concluding that a flair for metaphor 'is a sign of natural genius, as to be good at metaphor is to perceive resemblances' (1459a7–8). But Scott is referring here to the discussion of metaphor in Book 3 of the *Rhetoric*. Aristotle turns to the question of how to generate clever and popular remarks, and the role of learning in the pleasure we feel in such cases: 'Easy learning is naturally pleasant to all, and words mean something, so that all words which make us learn something are most pleasant. Now we do not know the meaning of strange words, and proper terms we know already. It is metaphor, therefore, that above all produces this effect; for when Homer calls old age stubble, he teaches and informs us through the genus; for both have lost their bloom' (1410b). Aristotle refers to *Odyssey*, 14.213–15. Cf. Hoskyns on metaphor: 'a *Metaphor* is pleasant because it enricheth owr knowledge with two things at once[,] with the truth and with simillitude' (*Directions*, 122).

40.24–7 Philosophy tells us ... reference to other things   For Scott's account of definition see **5.24–31n.** and **6.32–7n.** For the shift from the thing itself to contiguous things in developing arguments cf. Cicero, *Topica*, 2.8–3.11. From metaphor Scott moves on to the broader rhetorical category of similitude (the word he uses overleaf at **41.1** and **41.15**) or comparison (Greek terms include *paradeigma* and *parabole*), the many ways of using analogy or comparison, including fable, historical example, and simile. See, e.g., Quintilian, 5.11, *Ad Herennium*, 4.46.59–49.62, Scaliger, 3.50–3.

40.31 apologi   Plural of Latin *apologus*, from Greek *apologos*, account, story, fable. On this term see Quintilian, 5.11.20.

40.31–2 those of Aesop   The first references to Aesop as a fabulist are from the end of the fifth century BC; there is as little historical basis to his identity as there is to Homer's. The first collection of Aesopic fables was compiled around 300 BC and surviving collections, in Greek and Latin prose and verse, derived from it and date from the first to fifth centuries AD. For Scott's use of Aesop see **46.40–1n.**

40.33–6 that one effect ... prophets   II Samuel 12:1–15, Nathan's fable of the rich man with the flock and the poor man with one lamb, told to convey God's anger at David's affair with Bathsheba and his murder of her husband Uriah (on which see **71.40–1n.**). Sidney also gives this example (*DP*, 25) and in a later mention puts it alongside Aesop's fables (*DP*, 34).

40.36 suit   Kind, sort, class (*OED*, *suit*, n., †15).

40.36–8 those fabulous narrations of Ovid ... instructions   Cf. **20.11–12n.** on 'Ovid's *Metamorphoses*, in narration clouding much natural and moral knowledge'. The *Metamorphoses* is an epic gathering of legends of transformation that are 'fabulous', i.e. mythical. Many of the myths describe the origins of flora, fauna, and natural features of the landscape (hence Scott's 'natural instructions'). The tradition of allegorising the individual narratives exemplified by the fourteenth-century *Ovide moralisé* continued to Scott's day; as well as enabling tales of lust to deliver edifying morals ('moral ... instructions', and hence 'fabulous' in a sense closer to the Aesopic and biblical fables Scott has just discussed) it enabled a pagan author to be respectable reading within a Christian society.

40.38–40 all allegories . . . to be a woman   By 'the feigning of persons' Scott means both *prosopopoeia* (Latin *fictio personae*) and related figures (cf. **68.14–22n.**), by which a voice (and even body) is attributed to an absent person, mute animal, inanimate thing, or abstraction (in the biblical example, throughout Proverbs 1–9, Wisdom is a woman who speaks and is to be courted) as well as the more extended personification allegory of Spenser, whereby ideas are made into persons within a narrative setting.

41.1–5 The rules . . . clear and confirm   *Rhetoric*, 1405a:

we must make use of metaphors and epithets that are appropriate. This will be secured by observing due proportion; otherwise there will be a lack of propriety, because it is when placed in juxtaposition that contraries are most evident . . . And if we wish to ornament our subject, we must derive our metaphor from the better species under the same genus; if to depreciate it, from the worse.

41.6–8 Neither . . . that you would prove   *Rhetoric*, 1405a30–1, for a word that 'exceeds the dignity of the subject', and 1405a–b for obscurity: 'metaphors must not be far-fetched, but we must give names to things that have none by deriving the metaphor from that which is akin and of the same kind, so that, as soon as it is uttered, it is clearly seen to be akin'.

41.8–11 as he that would show . . . authority of the pulpit   Apparently a reference to a contemporary sermon, which I have not been able to trace. For the popular tradition of the Man in the Moon and his bush of thorns cf. Shakespeare, *A Midsummer Night's Dream*, 3.1.59–60 and 5.1.257–9. The allusion may not have been that inappropriate, since the thorns already had allegorical value: Dante, for example, alludes to the tradition of seeing the moon with his thorns as the accursed Cain (*Inferno*, 20.124–7).

41.12–13 phoenix her contempt of the world   The phoenix was not traditionally associated with a contempt for the world. Scott in fact elides a traditional identification of the (unique, reborn) phoenix with Christ (see, e.g., Laurence Andrew, *The noble lyfe and natures of man of bestes, serpentys, fowles and fisshes* [1527], M4^v) and the popular medieval Christian *contemptus mundi* tradition, itself figured as the imitation of Christ (as in Thomas à Kempis's early fifteenth-century work known both as *Contemptus mundi* and *The imitation of Christ*).

41.13–14 swan's . . . embracing her death   *ODEP*, 791; Tilley, s 1028. See, e.g., Shakespeare, *Lucrece*: 'And now this pale swan in her wat'ry nest | Begins the sad dirge of her certain ending' (1611–12).

41.14–16 Quintilian and Scaliger . . . more than instruct   Quintilian, 8.6.14–15; Scaliger, 3.51 (129a2).

41.17–18 that which by religion ... resemble to anything   Referring to the first two or three (depending on how they were counted) of the Ten Commandments, in Exodus 20:3–5 ('Thou shalt have no other Gods before me. Thou shalt not make thee no graven image ... Thou shalt not bow downe to them, neither serve them: for I the Lord thy God, a jelous God ...') and Deuteronomy 5:7–9.

41.30 *sic itur ad astra*   Virgil, *Aeneid*, 9.641: 'So man scales the stars'. Common out of its context: Iulus, Aeneas' son, has just invoked Jupiter's help in killing Remulus with his bow, and Apollo looks down approvingly.

41.37 shipwreck of our true worship   For the allusion to I Timothy 1:19 see **48.30–2n.**

41.38 Shall I say ... rise against us?   Echoing Psalm 2:1 and Obadiah 1:1.

42.1–2 Sir Philip Sidney ... to praise him   In the *Defence*, discussing lyric: 'Other sort of poetry almost have we none, but that lyrical kind of songs and sonnets, which, Lord, if He gave us so good minds, how well it might be employed, and with how heavenly fruits, both private and public, in singing the praises of the immortal beauty, the immortal goodness of that God who giveth us hands to write and wits to conceive; of which we might well want words, but never matter, of which we could turn our eyes to nothing, but we should ever have new-budding occasions' (*DP*, 48–9).

42.5 that exacteth ... of our lips   Hosea 14:3: 'so will we render the calves of our lippes'.

42.5–9 the first fruits ... sons of men   The language here, and throughout this paragraph, with its vague echoes and rhythms of scripture, shows Scott's immersion in scripture but also his affinity with the puritan tradition (see Introduction, xxix).

42.10–13 The *Courtier* ... affect that withal   Book 1 of Castiglione's *Il cortegiano* (on which see **3.20–1n.** and **20.35–21.3n.**). In Thomas Hoby's translation:

And even as the bee in the greene medowes fleeth alwayes aboute the grasse chousynge out flowres: so shall our Courtyer steale thys grace from them that to hys seming have it, and from ech one that percell that shal be most worthy praise. And not do, as a frende of ours, whom you al know, that thought he resembled much kyng Ferdinande the yonger of Aragon, and regarded not to resemble hym in anye other poynt but in the often lyftyng up hys head, wrying therewythall a part of hys mouth, the whych custome the king had gotten by infymitye. And manye such there are that thynke they doe much, so they resemble a great man in somewhat, and take many tymes the thynge in hym that woorst becommeth hym.   (*The courtyer* (1561), E2^r; Cox, 52–3)

Cf. Cicero, *De oratore*, 2.22.90–2. Castiglione sets up Scott's comparison of literary imitation to the imitation of behaviour by his use of the image of bees taking nectar from different flowers, which was commonly used of literary imitation (see Seneca, *Epistulae morales*, 84.3–5).

42.15–19 those superstitious conceits... Deity among us Paraphrasing and quoting Sidney on the argument against poets that 'Plato banished them out of his commonwealth' (*DP*, 33) in the *Republic*. Plato, Sidney argues, 'only meant to drive out those wrong opinions of the Deity (whereof now, without further law, Christianity hath taken away all the hurtful belief), perchance, as he thought, nourished by the then esteemed poets' (*DP*, 40).

42.19–21 why it should not... with divine Bartas Scott may be referring to Du Bartas's *L'Uranie*, a verse prosopopoeia in the voice of Urania, the Muse of religious poetry, printed in *La muse Chrestiene* (1574): Urania advises writers to shun heathen stories and turn to Christian subjects and biblical themes (e.g. 105–12, 189–96; Du Bartas, II, 178, 182).

42.20–1 confession of the mouth... companion of our belief 'Confession of the mouth' is a common phrase in sixteenth-century religious writing, juxtaposing what is believed in the heart with what is said; it occurs often in theological consideration of whether salvation depends on one only or on both, and is derived from Romans 10:8–10. See, for example, *Twelve sermons of Saynt Augustine* (1553): 'For the beliefe of the hearte justifieth and the confession of the mouth maketh a manne safe. And therefore he that hathe the worde of confession in hys mouth, and not in hys hearte is other crafty, or elles false. And he that hathe it in hys hearte, and not in hys mouth is other prowde or fearefull' (E5ᵛ).

42.22–3 a reverend ancient father... grown an Arian Arians (named after the early Christian heretic Arius, *c*.AD 260–336) believed the Son of God to be a subsequently created being. The controversy divided the church in the fourth century, and councils convened to resolve it failed. The Council of Rimini of 359 resulted in a creed that avoided saying that Christ was *consubstantialem Patri* (of one substance with the Father), and it was in reference to this that St Jerome (*c*.AD 347–420), in the 'Dialogue against the Luciferians', famously wrote 'Ingemuit totus orbis, et Arianum se esse miratus est' ('the whole world groaned and was amazed to find itself Arian'): *Opera*, ed. Desiderius Erasmus, 9 vols. (Basle, 1524–6), II, 145.

42.27 Ovid's gross fables For a more tolerant view of Ovid's *Metamorphoses* see 20.11–12 and 40.36–8.

42.29–30 Scaliger justly taxeth... of their swine Scaliger, 5.2 (216a1): 'nam quae ille de suis diis infamia, infandaque prodidit?' ('for what shames and abominations does he report of his gods?').

42.30 unreverend Irreverent (*OED*, *unreverend*, adj., †1).

42.32–9 Tully ... entitle themselves unto   A complete paraphrase, with some quotation, of the following from Cicero, *Orator*, 51.171, on the imitation of the older Greek orators: 'Ego autem illos ipsos laudo idque merito quorum se isti imitatores esse dicunt, etsi in eis aliquid desidero, hos vero minime qui nihil illorum nisi vitium secuntur, cum a bonis absint longissime' ('I, on the other hand, praise precisely those whom they profess to imitate, and I am quite right in doing so, although I find something lacking in them; but I have scant praise for these moderns who imitate only the weak points of the ancients while they are far from attaining to their real merits'). Scott inserts 'laudo' ('I praise') into his quotation from earlier in the sentence; the 'etc.' may be a note to himself or his scribe to complete the quotation, which breaks off abruptly without the verb *secuntur*, 'imitate'.

42.40 Babylonish garments   Alluding to Joshua 7:21: Achan's looting of gold, silver, and 'a goodly Babylonish garment' from Jericho leads to him being stoned to death.

42.41 that Law   Mosaic Law; see **41.17–18n.**

43.1–3 the almighty Maker ... attributed to idols   The Semitic word *Baal* means simply 'Lord' but in the Old Testament is used of a number of local deities regarded as false gods: e.g. Judges 8:33, I Kings 18:21–40 (for this episode see **25.16–17n.**), II Kings 10:26. The reference here is to the episode of the golden calf (II Kings 17), set in relation to the Commandments on graven images and false gods that Scott has earlier discussed (**41.17–18**): 'Finally they left all the commandements of the Lord their God, and made them molten images, even two calves, and made a grove, and worshipped all the hoste of heaven, and served Baal' (II Kings 17:16).

43.3–5 to have His uncommunicable name ... Herod   Agrippa I (10 BC–AD 44), grandson of Herod the Great, and King of the Jews; known as Herod in Acts: 'And upon a day appointed, Herod arayed himselfe in royall apparell, and sate on the judgement seate, and made an oration unto them. And the people gave a shoute, *saying*, The voyce of God, and not of man. But immediatly the Angel of the Lorde smote him, because he gave not glory unto God, so that he was eaten of wormes, and gave up the ghost' (Acts 12:21–3).

43.5–9 Bartas ... *Judith*   Cf. **42.19–21n.**; for *Judith*, see **19.40–1n.**

43.9–12 he craves pardon ... our corrupted faculties   Scott's reference is to the preface to *La muse Chrestienne*: 'Tant y a que comme estant le premier de la France, qui par un juste poeme ay en nostre langue illustré la sainte Escriture, j'espere recevoir de ta grace quelque excuse: veu que les choses de si grand pois ne peuvent estre et commencées et parfaites tout-ensemble' ('being the first in France to illustrate Holy Scripture in a true poem, I hope to receive some excuse, seeing that matters of such great weight cannot be both begun and perfected in one go': Du Bartas, II, 3). In that preface Du Bartas in fact claims explicitly to be imitating Homer, Virgil, and Ariosto rather than following the order or wording of the Bible (*ibid.*, and see **19.40–1n.**).

43.14–16 Heliodorus... custom among them   As before (**36.4–9** and **39.38–41**), Scott returns to the climax of the *Aithiopika*, in which Theagenes is only just saved from being a human sacrifice. He seems to be using Underdowne's translation here. Hydaspes resists Charikleia's pleas to spare Theagenes: 'But he cannot be delivered from this offeringe. For neither pitie, nor Religion will admitte that the custome of our Country be al broken as concerning the makinge of sacrifice for victory: beside this the people wil not be content, which scant was moved by the goodnes of the Gods to pitie thee' (*An Æthiopian historie* (1569), 140ᵛ).

43.20–4 that forcibleness or *energeia*... reader and beholder   Cf. Sidney, on convincing love poetry requiring 'forcibleness or *energeia* (as the Greeks call it)' (*DP*, 49). The word 'forcibleness' is otherwise rare. *Energeia* (meaning 'activity', 'vigour') is discussed by Aristotle (*Rhetoric*, 1411b–1412a) and Quintilian (8.3.89), but features little in the sixteenth-century rhetoric books because it is not a figure as such (as Scott recognises with his distinction here). Puttenham, 3.3, pairs it with *enargeia* as terms governing a binary classification of figures – those that are ornamental and those that give language 'efficacy by sense' (*Art*, 227). For Scaliger's point (116b2) see **33.8–9n.**; his Latin term for *energeia* is *efficacia*.

43.24–5 It is not... *poematibus*   Scaliger, 116d2: 'varietas omni generi poematum est necessaria: efficacia nonnisi operosioribus' ('variety is necessary to all kinds of poems; *energeia* only to the more active/difficult/elaborate kinds').

43.25–6 as which... tragedy   As discussed above (**38.20–6n.**), Scott's division of sweetness and *energeia* derives with some misunderstanding from Quintilian's discussion of *ēthos* and *pathos*. There, Quintilian suggests that 'I cannot better indicate the nature of the difference than by saying that *ethos* rather resembles comedy and *pathos* tragedy' (6.2.20).

43.29–30 in the comedy... (according to Horace)   *Ars poetica*, 92–4: 'Let each style keep the becoming place allotted to it. Yet at times even Comedy raises her voice, and an angry Chremes storms in swelling tones.'

43.30 the very shepherd   Even the shepherd (*OED*, *very*, adj., adv., and n.¹, 8a).

43.32–5 We showed... degree from it   See **38.34–6n.**

43.35–40 this worketh... his own case   *Energeia* figures in Aristotle and Quintilian in close proximity to discussions of vivid description, more firmly established in the rhetorical taxonomy as *enargeia*, and so Scott does nothing new in conflating the two terms. Most of his discussion refers to extended passages on *enargeia* and the performance and evocation of strong emotions in Quintilian: 6.2.20–36, 8.3.61–71, and 9.2.40–4. The reference to judges here may derive from Quintilian, 6.2.28: 'the first essential is that those feelings should prevail with us that we wish to prevail with the judge'.

43.36 a stonishing admiration   See *OED*, †*stonish*, v. Cf. 'astonishing admiration' at **78.16**, and on *admiratio* see **18.25–8n.** and **69.9–10n.**

43.39 interested   Involved, concerned, given a share (*OED*, †*interess*, v.).

44.1–2 this efficacy . . . liveliness of expressing   Perhaps Quintilian, 6.2.32 (see **45.5–7n.** and **66.1–3n.**).

44.5–12 as you describe fear . . . devouring another   This list is modelled on those in Quintilian at 6.2.31 and 8.3.67–70.

44.15–19 in the lowest estate . . . rock of despair   In raiding his store of commonplaces Scott echoes Sidney in particular: e.g. 'even when the Sunne (like a noble harte) began to shew his greatest countenaunce in his lowest estate' (*NA*, F2ᵛ; Skretkowicz, 100), or, for the rock of despair, Ringler, OA 71.50–1.

44.19 Statius . . . timor   Statius, *Thebaid*, 10.493 ('Sometimes excess of fear lends strength').

44.21–9 Was Aeneas . . . in mortem   *Aeneid*, 2.353, 354 (the only complete line), 358–9. Scott's manuscript reads 'hostes' for 'hostis' at 358; either is a possible form of the accusative plural.

44.32–6 In the most desperate . . . immortally blessed   Leonidas, the King of Sparta who with his 300 men led an advance guard of combined Greek forces against the Persians at Thermopylae in 480 BC, is reported as saying this in Plutarch's *Apophthegmata Laconica* (*Moralia*, 225d: 'He bade his soldiers eat their breakfast as if they were to eat their dinner in the other world') and *Parallela Graeca et Romana* (*Moralia*, 306d); it is also found – among other places – as what is now considered a spurious insertion in Cicero, *Tusculan disputations*, 1.42.101.

44.37–9 that noble general's answer . . . (said he)   This seems likely to be a remark – not otherwise known – attributed to Robert Devereux, 2nd Earl of Essex (on whom see Introduction, xxxiv–xxxvi, and cf. **52.41–53.4n.**). Paul E. J. Hammer (personal communication) believes it may be a reference to the abortive departure of Essex's fleet to attack Spain in July 1597, when a storm blew most of the ships straight back to England; Essex criticised Sir Walter Ralegh's hasty return to port when the storm first hit. The remark refers to Revelation 20:13 ('And the sea gave up her dead, which were in her'). These words must already have had some currency for those at sea, and were perhaps used in burial ceremonies, as was formally recognised in the 1662 *Book of common prayer*. It included a variant on the normal service for the burial of the dead as part of a set of 'Forms of Prayer to be used at Sea'. Instead of the usual form of words ('we therefore commit his body to the ground; earth to earth, ashes to ashes', etc.) is suggested the form: 'We therefore commit his body to the Deep, to be turned into corruption, looking for the resurrection of the body, (when the sea shall give up her dead,) . . .' (*BCP*, 621; and cf. 455).

44.38 aggravated   Exaggerated (*OED*, *aggravate*, v., 8).

44.40–45.1 The Lacedaemonians . . . their enemies be   Plutarch, *Apophthegmata Laconica* (*Moralia*, 215d: 'He said that the Spartans did not ask "how many are the enemy," but "where are they?"') and 'Sayings of Kings and Commanders' (*Regum et imperatorum apophthegmata*, *Moralia*, 190c), attributed in both cases to Agis (either Agis II, King of Sparta *c.*427–400 BC or Agis III, King of Sparta 338–*c.*330 BC).

45.4 glass   Reflect (*OED*, *glass*, v., 4a, with Sidney the first recorded usage in that sense).

45.5–7 Quintilian . . . (saith he)   Quintilian, 6.2.32: 'From such impressions arises that *enargeia* which Cicero calls *illumination* and *actuality* [*illustratio et evidentia*], which makes us seem not so much to narrate as to exhibit the actual scene, while our emotions will be no less actively stirred than if we were present at the actual occurrence'. Quintilian draws on Cicero, *Academica*, 2.6.17 [= *Academica Priora / Lucullus*]: '*enargeia* (as the Greeks call it: let us term it perspicuousness [*perspicuitatem*] or evidentness [*evidentiam*]'; a revision of *perspicuitas* to *illustratio* in the now lost second version of this book of the *Academica* is possible, and would account for Quintilian's apparent misquotation. Cf. Quintilian, 8.3.61–2, on '*enargeia* . . . vivid illustration [*evidentia*], or, as some prefer to call it, representation [*repraesentatio*] . . . oratory fails of its full effect . . . if its appeal is merely to the hearing, and if the judge merely feels that the facts on which he has to give his decision are being narrated to him, and not displayed in their living truth to the eyes of the mind'. On Scott's use of Quintilian, 6.2.32, see **66.1–3n.**

45.8–25 Vasthi's passionate delivering . . . her former clear   'Peter Matthew' is Pierre Matthieu (1563–1621), a French Catholic whose five tragedies mostly on biblical or classical subjects glanced at the French Wars of Religion. *Vasthi* concerns Vashti, the wife of King Ahasuerus in the Old Testament Book of Esther. She refuses her husband's summons to appear before him, 'that he might shew the people and the princes her beautie' (Esther 1:11), and is banished and replaced as queen by Esther. Scott translates, preserving the original's alexandrine couplets, a portion of the final speech of the short fifth act, spoken by Vasthi, and ending 15 lines from the play's end: 'Come celuy qui voit en la saison de Flore, | Un jardin qui de fleurs se bigarre et colore. | Qui tient le Lis, le Thim, le Muguet et L'œillet, | Et qui nourrit la Rose en son tain vermeillet: | Quant le souffle frilleux du despité Boree | Sur l'hiver mal plaisant revient d'Hyperboree, | Desrobant la perrucque à l'arbre printanier | A grand peine peut-il plaire à son jardinier, | Qui ne le recognoit: car par l'aspre froidure, | Pauvre il est despouillé de grace et de verdure. | Ainsi ceux qui verront le malheur de Vasthi, | Vasthi qui de la gloire eslevoit le parti, | Ne la recognoistront, car la belle lumiere | N'aura plus les rayons de sa clarté premiere' (*Vasthi* (Lyon, 1589), E4ʳ). I have preserved Matthieu's form of the name, since this seems intended in the manuscript's 'Vasties' at **45.8** and **45.22**.

45.14 flower delice   Manuscript: 'flowere delice'. Scott, or his scribe, presumably shared one current view of the etymology of fleur-de-lis linking it to the Latin for delight (*deliciae*). It therefore seems preferable to keep this form than to modernise to either of the two forms rather arbitrarily preferred by *OED*: *fleur-de-lis* and *flower-de-luce*.

45.18 ball   Bald: either apocope *per licentiam poeticam* (see **49.13–14n**. and **64.24–9n**.) for the sake of rhyme, and justifiable in view of etymology (see *OED*, *bald*, adj., from *balled*, 'made ball-like'), or possibly a regional or archaic form.

45.20 nap   Nip. There is no entry for this sense of *nap* in *OED* but it is clearly there in related Germanic forms: see etymology of *nap*, v.[3]

45.28–30 very well-penned tragedy ... with their woes   Adapting Shakespeare, *Richard II*, 3.3.164: 'Or shall we play the wantons with our woes | And make some pretty match with shedding tears?' (164–5). Richard is talking to and about his cousin Aumerle, and not the Queen, who begins the next scene, relatedly, with 'What sport shall we devise here in this garden | To drive away the heavy thought of care?' (3.4.1–2).

45.31–2 David seems ... clap their hands   Cf. Sidney on the Psalmist's 'telling of the beasts' joyfulness and hills' leaping' (*DP*, 7). See, e.g., Psalm 98:8 ('Let the floods clap their handes, *and* let the mountaines rejoyce together'); 114:4 ('The mountaines leaped like rammes, *and* the hilles as lambes').

45.31 insulting   Possibly 'boasting', 'triumphing', but more likely a sense not recorded in *OED*, 'rejoicing', 'leaping for joy', on the analogy of a contemporary sense of the French *insulter* recorded in 1611 by Cotgrave (*OED*, *insult*, v., etymology). The etymological sense of leaping in *insult* (probably from Latin *salire*, to leap) suggests that the word may have been prompted by thought of the leaping and skipping hills.

45.32–5 All those *peripeteiae* ... virtue of *sweetness*   See **39.11–24**.

45.37–46.7 Pliny reports ... beyond that is expressed   Scott has already reported one of Pliny's famous anecdotes about Zeuxis (**17.27–33n**.). Immediately preceding that in Pliny is the anecdote alluded to here (35.36.65), in which, in a contest between Zeuxis and Parrhasius, Zeuxis paints some grapes which deceive birds into thinking them real, whereas Parrhasius paints a curtain which deceives Zeuxis into thinking it a real curtain covering a painting. Zeuxis 'yeelded the victory unto his adversary, saying withall, *Zeuxis* hath beguiled poore birds, but *Parrhasius* hath deceived *Zeuxis*, a professed artisane' (Holland, II, 535). Scott translates much of the paragraph that follows the two Zeuxis anecdotes verbatim: 'primus symmetrian picturae dedit, primus argutias voltus, elegantiam capilli, venustatem oris, confessione artificum in liniis extremis palmam adeptus. haec est picturae summa subtilitas ... extrema corporum facere et desinentis picturae modum includere rarum in successu artis invenitur. ambire enim se ipsa debet extremitas et sic desinere, ut promittat alia et post se ostendatque etiam quae occultat' (35.36.67–8: 'Parrhasius ... was the first to give proportions to painting and the first to give vivacity to the expression of the countenance, elegance of the hair and beauty of the mouth; indeed it is admitted that he won the palm in the drawing of outlines. This in painting is the high-water mark of refinement ... to give the contour of the figures, and make a satisfactory boundary where the painting within finishes, is rarely attained in artistry. For the contour ought to round itself off and so terminate as to suggest the presence of other parts behind it also, and disclose even what it hides'). Scott misunderstands Pliny's point about outline, taking *extremum* and *extremitas* to mean *finishing touch*, understandably since this is a Ciceronian usage (e.g. *Brutus*, 33.126).

46.12–14 Quintilian saith ... parts of oratory   Quintilian, 8.pr.13: 'For I have now to discuss the theory of style, a subject which, as all orators agree, presents the greatest difficulty.'

46.14–16 the invention and disposition ... properly the orator's   In fact taken from the same passage of Quintilian, who alludes to Cicero, *Orator*, 14.44: 'Et Marcus Tullius inventionem quidem ac dispositionem prudentis hominis putat, eloquentiam oratoris' ('Again, Cicero holds that, while invention and arrangement are within the reach of any man of good sense, eloquence belongs to the orator alone': Quintilian, 8.pr.14).

46.16–21 Quintilian will perhaps ... polished arms   Scott paraphrases Quintilian, 8.3.2, adjusting the sense to emphasise 'learned judgements':

Even the untrained often possess the gift of invention, and no great learning need be assumed for the satisfactory arrangement of our matter ... On the other hand, by the employment of skilful ornament the orator commends himself at the same time, and whereas his other accomplishments appeal to the considered judgement of the learned, this gift appeals to the enthusiastic approval of the world at large, and the speaker who possesses it fights not merely with effective [*fortibus*], but with flashing weapons [*fulgentibus armis*].

46.22–3 the same end ... teach and move   See 6.3–4.

46.26 Tully saith . . . nearest affinity   Cicero, *De oratore*, 3.7.27: 'poets being the next of kin to orators'. Or 1.16.70: 'The truth is that the poet is a very near kinsman of the orator, rather more heavily fettered as regards rhythm, but with ampler freedom in his choice of words, while in the use of many sorts of ornament he is his ally and almost his counterpart.' See also *Orator*, 20.66–8 for an important discussion of the relations between oratory and poetry.

46.26–7 in the wordish consideration . . . they agree   During Sidney's digression on the state of current English writing towards the end of the *Defence*: 'Methinks I deserve to be pounded for straying from poetry to oratory. But both have such an affinity in the wordish consideration, that I think this digression will make my meaning receive the fuller understanding' (*DP*, 51).

46.28–9 (according to Quintilian) . . . ornament of style   Quintilian discusses the connections of poetry to oratory at 10.1.27–30 and 10.5.4, but Scott must be referring to the passage he has already quoted (8.3.2), where poets are unmentioned.

46.35–8 one instructing parents . . . loving them too much   A possible allusion to Plutarch's essay on the education of children, here in Sir Thomas Elyot's translation: 'But beware gyve them not to many prayses, leste they take therby to moche courage and presumption: and with to moche cockenayenge be spylled and lost. I have knowen many faders, whom to moche love hath caused, that they loved not their children' (*The education or bringinge up of children* (1532), D4ʳ; *Moralia*, 9b). Cf. Proverbs 13:24: 'He that spareth his rod, hateth his sonne: but he that loveth him, chasteneth him betime.' For the common analogy between parenting and authorship, which follows, cf. Plato, *Phaedrus*, 275d–e; Montaigne's essay 'On the affection of fathers for their children' (2.8, in Michel de Montaigne, *The complete essays*, trans. M. A. Screech (London, 1991), esp. 449–52); Sidney's preface to the *Arcadia* (*OA*, 3); and Bacon's Essay 'On parents and children' (*Francis Bacon*, ed. Brian Vickers (Oxford, 1996), 352).

46.40–1 catch at shadows . . . the substance   For the Aesopic fable of the dog with the piece of meat who sees its reflection in a stream, drops the meat, and tries to snatch the reflection, see Babrius, 79 and Phaedrus, 1.4. The word for reflection is often 'shadow' (Greek *skia*, Latin *umbra*) in versions of the fable: see, e.g., 'De cane et umbra' ('On the dog and the shadow') in *Aesopi . . . fabellae* (1535), A1ᵛ.

47.4 complement   Manuscript spelling: 'complement'. The older spelling was supplanted by the form *compliment* for many senses, but not for all of those in play here. Since the modern form suppresses the relation between still-current senses of *complement* as completion (*OED*, complement, 3, 4, 5) and obsolete senses of gentlemanly quality, civility, formality, politeness, ceremony (*OED*, complement, †7, †8, †9), I have preferred the older spelling here.

47.8 piece out   *OED*, *piece*, v., phrasal verbs, *to piece out*: 'To enlarge or complete by the addition of a piece; to eke out or extend with extra pieces.'

47.9 fustian   Bombast: fustian was a type of coarse cloth, as bombast was rough cotton used for padding, so the meaning is sense stuffed or padded out with ornamental nonsense.

47.10–11 Tully said ... steps of his virtue   Cicero, *De officiis*, 1.39.140, referring to Lucius Licinius Lucullus (died 57/6 BC), consul and sucessful general in the east (whence his immense wealth), and senior figure in the political generation before Cicero's.

47.15 they are loath ... wet their foot   *ODEP*, 109 (The cat would eat fish and would not wet her feet) and Tilley, C 144; cf. 'Letting "I dare not" wait upon "I would", | Like the poor cat i' th' adage' (*Macbeth*, 1.7.44–5).

47.17–18 *quod supra* ... leap not at   'What is above us is nothing to us'. A common saying, attributed to Socrates, and usually in the form *quae supra* ('those things that are above us...'), as in Erasmus, *Adagia*, 1.6.69.

47.18 paste-arms   Not in *OED*. Shields for heraldic display or for hanging in the tiltyard were made of paste (*OED*, *paste*, n. and adj., 3†b), more usually known as pasteboard (*OED*, *pasteboard*, n., 3 and 4). This allusion connects to Sir Henry Lee's determining influence on the rituals of Elizabethan courtly tilting, on which cf. **81.41–82.6n.**, and Introduction, xxxii. Cf. 'the orator fights not only in strong but in polished arms' (**46.21** and **46.16–21n.**).

47.20–2 a Lacedaemonian ... nought else   Plutarch, *Apophthegmata Laconica* (*Moralia*, 233a). Cf. Rainolds (*Oratio*, 53).

47.29–32 that golden rule ... meekly and easily   Castiglione's celebrated *sprezzatura*, the aim being for the courtier 'To do his feates with a slight, as though they were rather naturally in him, then learned with studye: and use a Reckelesnes to cover art, without minding greatly what he hath in hand, to a mans seeminge' (Cox, 367; cf. 53).

47.33–9 careless art ... art that conceals art   This is a Renaissance commonplace, with perhaps its most famous expression in the story of the sculptor Pygmalion in Ovid's Metamorphoses, 10.252: 'ars adeo latet arte sua' ('So does his art conceal his art'). For an extended essay on the theme cf. the penultimate chapter of Puttenham (3.25). Cf. Sidney on Zelmane's hair, 'in locks, some curled, and some as it were forgotten, with such a carelesse care, and an arte so hiding arte, that shee seemed she would lay them for a paterne, whether nature simply, or nature helped by cunning, be the more excellent' (*NA*, D4ᵛ; Skretkowicz, 68).

47.33–6 Plutarch . . . no fish   Plutarch, *De audiendis poetis* (*Moralia*, 14d–e). Plutarch probably means Philoxenus of Leucas, fifth–fourth century BC author of at least one mostly lost gastronomic poem. For this image cf. **20.20n.** and **32.8–11.**

48.2 it is no more . . . nothing is learned   Possibly suggested by the passage from Aulus Gellius Scott discusses in detail above (see **22.5–10n.**): 'You . . . use words that have already been obsolete for many years, because you want no one to know and comprehend what you are saying. Why not accomplish your purpose more fully, foolish fellow, and say nothing at all?' (*Attic nights*, 1.10.2).

48.3–4 Horace . . . norma loquendi   *Ars poetica*, 70–2: 'Many terms that have fallen out of use shall be born again, and those shall fall that are now in repute, if Usage so will it, *in whose hands lies the judgement, the power and the rule of speech.*' The more recent and philologically exacting texts in Scott's day read 'ius' (authority, right) at l. 72 but Scott's reading of 'vis' (power) was still widespread, and it is preserved here.

48.7–9 with Tully and Quintilian . . . rude and faulty   Cicero, *De oratore*, 3.10.37–9; Quintilian, 1.6.43–5: 'we must make up our minds what we mean by usage. If it be defined merely as the practice of the majority, we shall have a very dangerous rule affecting not merely style but life as well . . . I will therefore define usage in speech as the agreed practice of educated men, just as where our way of life is concerned I should define it as the agreed practice of all good men' (cf. 1.6.1–3; 8.pr.25; 8.1.1–2; etc.). Cf. Puttenham, 3.4 ('Of language').

48.10–11 warned out and unbilled   Put on notice and dismissed from service (*OED*, *warn*, v.¹, †8.: 'To give (a person) notice to leave his employment or tenancy. Also to *warn out*.'; *OED*, *unbilled*, adj.: 'Not enrolled' [of soldiers]).

48.16–19 Master Spenser . . . in his rhymes   *DP*, 44; see **22.3–11n.**

48.17 whilst   *OED*, *while*, adv. (and adj.) and conj. (and prep.), B1†c: 'Without necessarily implying duration: At the time that; when'; cf. *OED*, *whilst*, adv. and conj. (and prep.), 1b.

48.22 cashiering   *OED*, *cashier*, v., 1†a.: '*Mil.* To discharge, break up, disband (troops)'.

48.23 servitors   *OED*, *servitor*, n., 3: 'One who serves in war; a soldier'.

48.25 *procerity*   Height, tallness (from Latin *proceritas*). *OED*'s first two examples are from 1550 (Hugh Latimer) and 1604, the latter concerning trees; I have found no other instances between them, and many throughout the seventeenth century: the word was just coming into fashion.

48.25 *summity*   Summit, highest part, highest degree (from Latin *summitas*); first recorded in this figurative sense in 1588 and 1600 (*OED*, †*summity*, n., 3), and more common after 1600.

48.26 *amass*   A less good example, since *amass* had entered English from the French in the fifteenth century, if not earlier, and would not have seemed an inkhorn term to most (*OED*, *amass*, v., first recorded usage 1481, in sense 3).

48.27–8 Be ye as azyms . . . Rhemists   The 'Rhemists' are those exiled Catholics at the English College at Douai in France (established in about 1561) responsible for the translation of the Bible from the Latin Vulgate into English, the New Testament of which was published at Rheims in 1582 (hence the 'Douay-Rheims Bible'). The easiest access to this text for English Protestants was in the form of a parallel text edition confronting the Douay-Rheims text with that of the Bishops' Bible, produced by William Fulke in 1589: *The text of the New Testament . . . translated out of the vulgar Latine by the papists of the traiterous seminarie at Rhemes . . . Whereunto is added the translation out of the original Greeke, commonly used in the Church of England* (1589; *STC* 2888). This followed a refutation Fulke had published in 1583 (*A defense of the sincere and true translations of the holie scriptures*); see **50.2–5n**. The text here is II Corinthians 5:7. As Fulke gives them, the two texts read (Bishops') 'Purge out therfore the olde leaven, that ye may be a new lumpe, as ye are unleavened. For even Christ our Passeover is offered up for us'; and (Douay-Rheims) 'Purge the old leaven, that you may be a new paste, as you are azymes. For our Pasche, Christ, is immolated' (*The text*, 269ʳ). Fulke's prefatory glossary explains that 'azymes' are 'unleavened bread' and 'Pasche' means 'Easter, and the paschal lambe' (*4ʳ). Scott's form 'immolate' seems also to have a Catholic pedigree (*OED*, *immolate*, adj., illustrated from Thomas More and Stephen Gardiner). 'Be ye' was inserted in the manuscript by Scott, the scribe having left rather more space than needed between 'like' and 'As' (**48.27**), suggesting some confusion as to the reading in the scribe's copy, which was perhaps closer to the Douay-Rheims text; Scott may then have made his correction without checking his own original manuscript or its source.

48.29 embondaged   *OED*, †*embondage*, v.: 'To bring into a state of bondage or slavery; *lit.* and *fig.*' (first recorded usage 1607).

48.30–2 by putting away truth . . . to another purpose   John Rainolds, *Th'overthrow of stage-playes, by the way of controversie betwixt D. Gager and D. Rainoldes* ([Middelburg], 1599), P3ʳ: 'as *some by putting away a good conscience, made shipwracke of their faith*: so it may bee feared that you, by putting trueth and singlenes away, will hazard the shipwracke of common sense and reason' (Rainolds's italics). Rainolds is addressing William Gager and alluding to I Timothy 1:19: 'Having faith and a good conscience, which some have put away, and as concerning faith, have made ship-wracke'. On the implications of this quotation for dating the *Model*, see Introduction, xxxvii.

48.34–6 some ancient words... sparingly and modestly *Ars poetica*, 46–72, esp. 48–53 (for neologisms coined *pudenter*, 'modestly', l. 51, and *parce*, 'sparingly', l. 53) and 58–9 (for the coin-stamping metaphor); on the use of old and new terms cf. Horace, *Epistles*, 2.2.115–19 and Aulus Gellius, *Attic nights*, 11.7, as well as the rhetorical sources, including Quintilian, 1.6 and 8.3.24–37.

48.37–8 The certainest direction... the oldest Quintilian, 1.6.41: 'Ergo, ut novorum optima erunt maxime vetera, ita veterum maxime nova' ('Consequently in the case of old words the best will be those that are newest, just as in the case of new words the best will be the oldest'). The manuscript reading is 'of newe and usuall the oldest'; since the *new* is the opposite of the *usual* (cf. 'unacquainted newness', **49.1**), this has to be wrong. Part of the scribe's problem, and Scott's point, may lie in the fact that *unusual* is itself a 'new and unusual' word at this date, though it is 'In common use from c1630' according to *OED* (*unusual*, adj.); the first recorded usage is from Stanyhurst's lexically eccentric translation of the *Aeneid*, which Scott mines below (see **52.16–19n.**).

49.3 circumstance and ambage of speech (i) *circumstance*: circumlocution (*OED*, *circumstance*, n., 6); (ii) *ambage*: roundabout, indirect, or obscure modes of speech (*OED*, *ambage*, n., 1, †2, †4). *Ambage* is a term liked by Puttenham (e.g. *Art*, 98) and used by him as the English equivalent for the figure *periphrasis* (*Art*, 277–8). Cf. also 'by long ambage and circumstance of words' (*Art*, 271).

49.6–7 tongue and pen... of the mind That the tongue is the ambassador of the heart or mind seems to have become proverbial (see, e.g., Giacomo Affinati, *The dumbe divine speaker* (1605), 41). The origin (in English at least) may be John Lyly, *Euphues and his England* (1580): 'the tongue the Ambassador of the heart' (2B3ʳ). But Scott seems to have read John Hoskyns's *Directions for speech and style* (see **35.30–6.1n.** and **68.1– 4n.**), which opens with an extended take on the idea: 'The Conceipts of the minde are pictures of things and the Tongue is Interpreter of those pictures... Were it an honor to a Prince to have the majestie of his Embassage spoyled by a carelesse Embassadour? And is it not as great an indignity that an excellent Conceipt and Capacitie, by the indilligence of an idle tongue should be defaced?' (*Directions*, 116).

49.9–12 Will we take... we might have corn Cicero, *Orator*, 9.31.

49.13–14 the poet... especial privilege The rhetoric books codified various ways of manipulating the forms of words and the term 'poetic licence' properly applied to a greater freedom in this regard that poets were perceived as having, as is explained, for example, by Quintilian (1.8.14), and Viperano, 1.17 (54). See Gascoigne for the clearest statement of this in English (*SRLC*, 244), and cf. his preface to *Posies* ('To the reverende divines') where he admits to being 'sometimes constreyned for the cadence of rimes, or *per licentiam Poeticam*, to use an ynkehorne terme, or a straunge word' (Pigman, 361–2). Puttenham, 3.11, gives a comprehensive English listing of the grammatical figures, from which Scott derives his shorter list below, **64.22–9**.

Cf. Cicero, *De oratore*, 3.38.153, Quintilian, 1.6.2 and 10.1.28–9, and Vida, *De arte poetica*, 3.267–84.

49.14 denizing   *OED*, †*denize*, v., 2: '*fig*. To admit into recognized use (as a word, a custom, etc.); to naturalize.' A very common metaphor in discussion of the English language: see, e.g., Hart, *Orthographie*, D4ᵛ–E1ʳ.

49.15 naturals   Natives (*OED*, *natural*, n.¹, 19).

49.21 addition... imitation   Latin *imitatio*. Here the 'n' belongs to the word as it declines in Latin (*imitationem*, etc.) and is found, e.g., in the French *imitation*, from which the English word is perhaps directly taken (*OED*, *imitation*, n., etymology).

49.22 taking away... galliard, cavalier   The endings that most obviously identify words as non-English are usually dropped in such cases. Here, Italian *gagliardo* becomes *galliard*, though Scott likely means the French dance (in which case the French form, already *galliarde*, is more relevant), rather than the older sense of a courageous, hardy, spirited, lively, or spruce man and related adjectival senses (see *OED*, *galliard*, adj. and n.¹, A1, 2, †3, and B1 for the older senses; B2 and †3 for the dance). The form *cavalier* (literally 'horseman') comes from the Italian *cavaliere*, though, again, probably via French *cavalier* (cf. *chevalier*); cf. Spanish *caballero*, the form in which the word was originally adopted into English; the source is late Latin *caballarius* (see *OED*, *cavalier*, n. and adj.).

49.23 exchange... extremity   Exchanging 'y' for 'as' and thus naturalising the Latin '-itas' suffix in *extremitas*. Again, a French form intervenes in which the change has already been made: *extrémité* (see *OED*, *extremity*, n.).

49.23–4 exchange and contracting... patience   Again, the word entered English from French and in this form; the source is Latin *patientia* (adj. *patiens*). This is a common paradigm, where the Latin 't' is softened in Romance languages (Spanish *paciencia*, Italian *pazienza*) and the final vowel(s) silent in the anglicised form.

49.29 Dutch   'In the 15th and 16th c. "Dutch" was used in England in the general sense in which we now use "German", and in this sense it included the language and people of the Netherlands as part of the "Low Dutch" or Low German domain' (*OED*, *Dutch*, adj., n., and adv.).

49.30–1 changing the harsher letter... father   The distinction between the *aspirate* – the *th* in English *father* – and the *media* – a voiced stop with an intermediate degree of aspiration (in this example the *d* in Dutch *vader* or possibly the *t* in German *Vater*) – derives from the *Institutes* of the sixth-century Latin grammarian Priscian: see Keil, II, 18–21. *Media* is not attested in English before 1841 in *OED*. On *aspirate* see further **51.40n**. The form *father* has older roots than Scott realises: e.g. Old English *fæder*.

49.31–3 taking away... God   Scott is thinking of German *Gott*: a weaker point when Scott made it than it looks now, since the English spelling could still be *Godd* (though this was now less common) and the German spelling could be *Got* (cf. Dutch *God*; see *OED*, *god*, n.).

49.33–4 in our enfranchising... proportion and derivation   The likely source is Quintilian, 1.6.3–27 (*analogia/proportio*) and 1.6.28–38 (*etymologia*), but cf. Viperano, 1.17, on inventing words by (i) analogy, (ii) derivation, (iii) combination, and (iv) onomatopoeia (53–4), and Mulcaster, whose principles for the correct writing of English words are: proportion, enfranchisement, composition, derivation, distinction, and prerogative (Mulcaster, 106–7).

49.34–5 if one make *similitude... aptitudo*   In both cases from Latin words with identical suffixes: *similitudo*, from *similis*, 'like'; medieval Latin *aptitudo* from *aptus*, 'suitable'. The manuscript has 'apitude... apitudo'; there is no evidence for either form. Scott's sense of precedence is backed up by *OED*'s first recorded usages: *c.*1374 (*similitude*, n., 3†a) and 1548 (*aptitude*, n., 3c).

49.35–6 if one say *potent... clement*   From the Latin *potens*, 'powerful', and *clemens*, 'mild' (both third declension adjectives declining with a -*t*- ending to the stem, and with related noun forms *potentia* and *clementia*).

49.37–8 it cannot well beseem... *powerful* may supply there   In fact *mightful* is well-attested in the *OED* from Old English onwards, with several thirteenth- to fourteenth-century examples being given (*OED*, *mightful*, adj. and n.); for a contemporary example cf. Shakespeare, *Titus Andronicus*, 4.4.5. *Spiteful* is not seen, according to *OED*, before the fifteenth century (*OED*, *spiteful*, adj. and adv.). Both *spiteful* and *mightful* combine Germanic stem and suffix (cf. German *machtvoll*), whereas *powerful* (*OED*, *powerful*, adj., n., and adv., first recorded usage fifteenth century) brings together a Romance stem and a Germanic suffix, and might just as well be criticised before the other two.

49.40 primitive   *OED*, *primitive*, n. and adj., A6a: 'A word, base, or root from which another develops or is derived; a root-word'.

49.40–1 because an envious... *incendiary*   A confusing example. The literal meaning of the verb *incense* is 'set on fire' (*OED*, *incense*, v.², from Latin *incendo*); that should therefore be the 'sense the original and primitive imparts to it'. But the Latin verb was also used figuratively, and the evidence of *OED* suggests that figurative senses (inflame, excite, anger, incite, etc.) for the English verb *incense* were similarly well-established. The same was not yet true of the form *incendiary*. The Latin equivalent (*incendiarius*, noun and adjective) is limited to literal senses of fire-setting, as are the earliest recorded usages of *incendiary* (*OED*, *incendiary*, a. and n.: A1a, 1611; B1a, 1606), with the first recorded usage in Scott's sense being 1631 (B2a; A2a, 1614 for the equivalent adjectival sense). However, the only usage of *incendiary* that I have found before Scott is figurative, although not in Scott's exact sense: Gabriel Harvey, apparently coining the word, in *Foure letters* (1592), H2ᵛ; cf. Thomas Nashe's ridiculing of this usage in a list of Harvey's inkhorn terms in *Strange newes* (1592), I4ᵛ. It is unclear, therefore, whether Scott is (i) simply saying that the noun is a possible word by extension from the verb, and ignoring the root sense, or (ii) arguing that since a figurative sense is established for the verb, so the sense of the noun can be extended.

50.2–5 priest in English... opposition to the former　　*Priest* derives from the Greek *presbuteros*, 'elder', via the post-classical Latin *presbyter*. It is one of William Fulke's complaints in *A defense of the sincere and true translations of the holie scriptures* (1583) that the Rhemists translate both *sacerdos* (a sacrificing priest) and *presbyter* (the leader and instructor of a congregation) with the single word *priest*, and so make no distinction 'betwene the Priesthoode of the Newe Testament, and the Olde' (A8ʳ; on Fulke and the Rhemists see **48.27–8n.**). Scott's related complaint ('we use it for a sacrificing and massing priest') is that the word priest is now associated with the performance of Mass (by what was often known as a 'mass-priest': see *OED*, *mass-priest*, n.; *massing*, n.¹, C2), and specifically with a Catholic understanding that the words of the priest have transformed Eucharistic bread and wine into the body and blood of Christ. *Sacrificing* means literally 'making sacred', but it has inevitable associations of animal slaughter, related by Scott (and Fulke, A8ʳ) to the idea of real presence.

50.3 acception　　Accepted meaning (*OED*, *acception*, n., 3).

50.5–9 Marcus Caelius... moderate sparing　　Quintilian, 1.6.29, referring to Marcus Caelius Rufus (88/87–48 BC), extravagant and dissolute sometime protégé of Cicero: 'Etymology is sometimes of the utmost use, whenever the word under discussion needs interpretation. For instance, Marcus Caelius wishes to prove that he is *homo frugi*, not because he is abstemious (for he could not even pretend to be that), but because he is useful to many, that is *fructuosus*, from which *frugalitas* is derived.'

50.11–12 adding a particle... enforceth the signification　　The addition of a letter or syllable to the start of a word was known as *prothesis*. For the grammatical figures see further **49.13–14n.** and **64.24–9n.** Scott may, however, be following Quintilian, 1.5.65, where a discussion of compounds begins with words formed by the addition of a prefix.

50.11 intendeth　　*OED*, *intend*, v., †4a: 'To increase the intensity of, to intensify' (first recorded in this sense, 1603).

50.12 *engrieve*   Cause grief or pain; make grievous (*OED*, †*engrieve*, v.).

50.13–18 that coupling of words . . . almost equal us   Quintilian's discussion of compounds (1.5.65–70) includes the observation that they 'are better suited to Greek than to Latin' (1.5.70). But Scott's main source here is Sidney: English 'is particularly happy in compositions of two or three words together, near the Greek, far beyond the Latin, which is one of the greatest beauties can be in a language' (*DP*, 52). Sidney was recognised for his use of compounds. See, e.g., Joseph Hall's *Virgidemiarum. The last three bookes* (1598), 6.1, on 'that new elegance, | Which sweet *Philisides* fetch't of late from *France*, | That well beseem'd his high-stil'd *Arcady*, | Tho others marre it with much liberty, | In Epithets to joyne two wordes in one, | Forsooth for Adjectives cannot stand alone' (93). See also *Poetics*, 1457a–b; *Rhetoric*, 1405b–1406a, on the pitfalls of using compounds; Demetrius, *On style*, 91–3, cautioning against overuse; and Puttenham, 3.9 (*Art*, 241).

50.22–7 *swift-sure . . . never-enough-praised*   Of Scott's various compounds, those that are common enough to be given entries in the *OED* are *star-gazer* (noun, first recorded usage 1560); *handfast* (noun, adjective, and verb, from around 1200 onwards); *rose-coloured* (adjective, 1526, in Tyndale's translation of the scarlet-coloured beast of Revelation 17:3); and *never-ending* (adjective, 1592), for which cf. Shakespeare's usage quoted at **53.9**. *Never-enough-praised* (not in *OED*) is a special case, as it originates in Sidney's *Arcadia* ('the never-inough praised *Philoclea*': *NA*, E3ᵛ; Skretkowicz, 84) but was later used to refer to Sidney himself. See, e.g., the 'HEXAMETERS, *Upon the never-enough praised Sir Phillip Sidney*' contributed to Francis Davison *et al.*, *A poetical rapsody* (1602), 18ᵛ. Scott uses *swift-sure* of angels in his Du Bartas translation (Add. MS 81083, 64ᵛ), translating *vite*, fast (*La sepmaine*, day 1, 687).

50.25 Homer . . . *rose-fingered morn*   A well-known Homeric epithet (*rhododaktulos ēōs*); see, e.g., *Odyssey*, 23.241.

50.28–9 *between-kingdom . . . interregnum*   *Between-kingdom* is neither in *OED* nor in Sidney. Scott has probably confused Sidney's word 'under-kingdoms' (*DP*, 45) with the phrase in the *Arcadia* by which Sidney very clearly refers to an interregnum: 'those betweene times of raigning' (*NA*, L3ʳ; Skretkowicz, 159). *OED* cites this as the first recorded usage of the noun *between-time* (*OED*, *between*, prep., adv., and n., compounds), which Scott uses in a similar context in his letter to Cecil, Appendix 2, 251.

50.38 favour   Appearance, aspect, look, countenance, face (*OED*, *favour*, n., 9a–b).

50.39 constant and [. . .] sentences   Some text appears to be missing here. A cross has been marked, probably by Scott, in the margin by this passage in the manuscript, presumably to indicate that it needs checking. Elsewhere Scott's scribe skips a line in copying by slipping from an *and* in one line of his/her copy to one in the next (see

57.32–3n.); on this feature see further Textual Introduction, lxxvii–lxxix. This passage is full of paired terms and therefore of conjunctions ('sentences and clauses', 'tenor and agreeableness', 'figure and form', etc.) as is its analogue or source in Puttenham, 3.5: 'Style is a constant and continual phrase or tenor of speaking and writing, extending to the whole tale or process of the poem or history, and not properly to any piece or member of a tale, but is of words, speeches, and sentences together a certain contrived form and quality . . .' (*Art*, 233). It seems likely, therefore, that a line somewhat like the following has been lost in this way: 'arising of the constant *and continual joining and disposing of our words* and sentences'. That *words* should be paired with 'sentences' here seems likely, from the opening of the paragraph (50.31–3) and the precedents for this straightforward pairing (cf., e.g., Cicero, *De oratore*, 3.37.149).

51.1 *character*   Scaliger's word for style (4.1, esp. 174a–d1), from the Greek *charaktēr*, engraving instrument and hence impress, stamp, distinctive nature. On its meaning see further **35.31–2n.** Among Greek sources to use the term is Demetrius, *On style* (e.g. 36, the four styles). Puttenham also uses the term, 3.5 (*Art*, 233). For *character* as descriptive of particular (rather than abstract) styles, cf. Cicero, *Orator*, 39.134. For the analogy between the type of style and the type of person (a double meaning always available in *character*), cf. **51.20–2n.**

51.4–9 **every motion of the mind . . . countenance and gesture**   See Cicero, *Orator*, 17.55 ('delivery is a sort of language of the body, since it consists of movement or gesture as well as of voice or speech. There are as many variations in the tones of the voice as there are in feelings . . . I might also speak about gestures, which include facial expression'), and, for the relation of style to personality, *De oratore*, 3.7.25–9.34, esp. 9.34 ('as many styles of oratory as orators').

51.9–17 **It is not seen . . . answerable to his nature**   Cf. Puttenham, 3.5 on the analogy between physiognomy, behaviour, and style: 'For if the man be grave, his speech and style is grave; if light-headed, his style and language also light; if the mind be haughty and hot, the speech and style is also vehement and stirring', etc. (*Art*, 233).

51.13 gate   Manner of going (*OED*, *gate*, n.², 7a). I have not modernised the manuscript's 'gate' to *gait*, since that form only subsequently supplanted *gate* for the specialised sense of 'manner of walking, pace' (*OED*, *gait*, n.¹), and would exclude such possible senses as 'going, course' (*gate*, 6).

51.14 furious, like Jehu in his march   Jehu was a king of Israel described in II Kings 9–10, who acted swiftly and ruthlessly to take power from his predecessor Joram. As he approaches Jezreel to confront Joram, the watchman observes: 'the marching *is* like the marching of Jehu the sonne of Nimshi: for he marcheth furiously' (II Kings 9:20). The translation is 'driving . . . driving . . . driveth' in the Great Bible and the Bishops' Bible.

51.15 hot-mettled   Fiery. *OED*'s first recorded usage for this compound is 1648 (*OED*, *hot*, adj. and n.¹, s3; and cf. *mettled*, adj., 1).

51.15 'stare loco nescit'   'He is unable to stand in one place'. Virgil, *Georgics*, 3.84, describing 'the foal of a noble breed': 'should he but hear afar the clash of arms, he cannot keep his place; he pricks up his ears, quivers in his limbs, and snorting rolls beneath his nostrils the gathered fire' (75–88). Quintilian cites this passage (8.2.15), as does Seneca (*Epistulae morales*, 95.67–9), who finds that the passage 'might perfectly well be the portrayal of a brave man' (69).

51.18–19 all forms of style… *mean* or indifferent   The doctrine of the three styles (though they are sometimes elaborated or expanded to four or more) is almost universal in rhetorical theory. For classic statements see Cicero, *De oratore*, 3.52.199, and *Orator*, 20.69. See further Quintilian, 12.10.58–72; *Ad Herennium*, 4.8.11; Scaliger, 4.1 (esp. 174d1–a2). Scott gives the three styles here in the order grand (= '*high* or noble'), plain (= '*low* or base'), middle (= '*mean* or indifferent'), as do Scaliger (*ibid.* and 183c2) and Puttenham (*Art*, 234 and 237). See *OED*, *mean*, adj.²; and *indifferent*, adj.¹, n., and adv., A†6.

51.20–2 the complexions of our speech… animate our style   As a person's character and behaviour is determined by the make-up of the four humours (so that a melancholic has an excess of black bile) so style is determined by content. As usual Scott pursues bodily and biological metaphors for poetic and rhetorical structures with singular persistence. There was a tradition of personifying the three styles that may lie behind these and related thoughts. See for example Gellius, *Attic nights*, 6.14, exemplifying the three styles in three different writers, showing that Homer exemplifies them in three different characters, and giving an anecdote about three Athenian envoys sent to Rome, one per style. For the point about Homer cf. Quintilian, 12.10.64–5. Dionysius offers an exemplar in each literary genre for each style (*On literary composition*, 21–4).

51.23–5 (as Tully saith)… properties of the other   See Cicero, *De oratore*, 3.7.25–9.36 (esp. 7.26–8 and 9.34) and cf. Quintilian, 12.10.66–72.

51.29–52.5 in words there are degrees… voluble and easy   Scott's terms and general analysis are imported from Latin grammars, and Latin translations of Greek grammars, with some possible attention to English works on the English language or on Latin, and to classical critics and rhetoricians. The discussion is inspired by Scaliger's chapter on the qualities of vowels and consonants in Latin words, 4.47 (207–10), and perhaps indirectly by Quintilian, to whom Scaliger refers (209a1): see for example Quintilian, 8.3.16–17 and 9.4.37–43. The most important and extensive classical treatment, though it is unclear if Scott has access to it, is in Dionysius' *On literary composition*, 14–16: 'The most elegant writers of poetry or prose have understood these facts well, and both arrange their words by weaving them together with deliberate care, and with elaborate artistic skill adapt the syllables and the letters to the emotions which they wish to portray' (15). Relatedly, Demetrius, *On style* 173–8, offers a brief fourfold classification of word qualities (implicitly analogous to his fourfold classification of styles) – smooth, rough, well-proportioned, weighty – but 'leave[s] this theorising as rather an irrelevance' (178). Hermogenes, *On types*, in enumerating aspects of each type of style, including diction, shows how word sound contributes to stylistic effect (e.g. 247–8, in *ALC*, 569). And Plato's *Cratylus* includes a discussion of the meanings of individual letters (426c–427c; resumed at 434b–435a) that may have been in Scott's mind. Although there were classical and neo-Latin analogues, then, the details of Scott's treatment are unprecedented in the discussion of English. Those who wrote about the English language in English tended to be concerned with spelling reform – 'orthoepists' such as Sir Thomas Smith, in *De recta et emendata linguae Anglicae scriptione* (1568); John Hart, in *An orthographie* (1569); William Bullokar in several books printed in the 1580s; and Richard Mulcaster in the *Elementarie* (1582). Such texts of course use the terms *vowel, consonant, diphthong, liquid,* and even *aspirate* (though only the first two were well-established in English). But they do not use the terms *media* or *tenuis* (on these see the separate notes, **49.30–1n., 51.41n.,** and **51.39n.**). More importantly, they do not have any reason to think about the stylistic qualities of the sounds of English words: the concern of the orthoepists is for the correct spelling of words and the understanding of their etymology and grammatical function. Well after Scott was writing, Alexander Gill published an extensive treatise on the English language, *Logonomia Anglica* (1619), in Latin. More sophisticated than its predecessors, and showing some concern for poetic language, it does not repeat Scott's analysis of certain letters as *tenues* and *mediae* or venture anything like his analysis of sound. Where English grammarians come closest to Scott is in discussing the length and quality of vowels; see, for example, Mulcaster: 'The vowells generallie sound either long as, *compāring, revēnged, endīting, enclōsure, presūming*: or short as *ransăking, revĕlling, penĭtent, omnipŏtent, fortŭnat*: either sharp, as máte, méte, rípe, hópe, dúke. or flat as: màt, mèt, rìp, hòp, dùk' (110; note the use of *penitent* as an example). This classically derived analysis of vowel length belongs alongside quantitative prosody, and indeed it is in the Elizabethan poets' experimentation with classical metres (and with theorising them) that we find a tradition of thinking about English words purely as sound (see **61.30–3n.**). The *prosodia* sections of the Latin grammars, with their discussions of which syllables of words to stress in pronunciation, also related to this tradition, and informed early metrical analysis (see **60.25–31n.**).

51.33 *ou* **and** *oa* **(dipthongs)**   Although the ultimate sources of Scott's terms are the chapters on letters in the Latin grammarians (e.g. Priscian, *Institutes*, in Keil, II, 6–37; Diomedes, in Keil, I, 421–6) there were already several treatments of the English language along the same lines. The diphthong *oa* is not commonly found in English lists of diphthongs (e.g. Mulcaster, 118–19; Leech, A4ʳ), but *aw* (which is possibly the same) and *ou* are. Hart, *Methode* has both *oa* and *ou* (B4ʳ).

51.34 (diphthongs) *ai, ei, eu, ie*   Mulcaster (118) has *ai, ei, ew*; Leech (A4ʳ) has *ai, ei, ew, ie* (as alternative to *ee*) and lists *eu* among the five Latin diphthongs. Smith

(14^v–18^r) has *ai, ei, eu, ie*, though he is writing in Latin and making a direct comparison between Latin and English. Hart (*A methode*, $B4^r$) has all four, though his table simply lists every possible combination of the five vowels. It is therefore unclear whether this is Scott's own analysis by analogy with traditional analysis of Latin, or he has consulted English grammarians.

51.39 tenues   Plural of *tenuis*, a term from Greek grammars in Latin, translating Greek *psilon* (bare, smooth) and distinguishing the Greek letters κ, τ, π (corresponding as Scott sees to *k, t, p* in Latin and English) from the related aspirates. *OED*'s first recorded usage in English is 1650 (*OED*, *tenuis*, n.).

51.39 liquids   The *liquids* are the letters *l, m, n, r* (as in Leech, $A3^r$).

51.40 aspirates   From the Latin *aspiratus*, 'breathed'. An aspirate is 'A consonantal sound in which the action of the breath is prominently marked; one which is followed by or blended with the sound of H' (*OED*, *aspirate*, adj and n., B1). *OED*'s first recorded usages are 1669 for the adjective, 1728 for the noun. Scott's 'go for the aspirates' shows that he is thinking about the extent to which terms for Greek letters can be applied to English ones. The Greek aspirates are χ, θ, φ, so Scott gives *ch, th*, and *f* (= *ph*). See also **49.30–1n.**

51.41 mediae   For Priscian these are intermediate in their degree of aspiration between the tenues and the aspirates (see **49.30–1n.**). He gives three (*b, g, d*) corresponding to Greek β, γ, δ.

51.41 *u*-consonant   The alphabet in Scott's day had 24 letters. Instead of *u* and *v* there was only *u*, which could be vocalic or consonantal and was usually represented in print at this point by a *u*-graph if positioned in the middle or end of a word and by a *v*-graph if in the initial position. There was no *j* but only *i* as vowel or consonant.

52.1 *x* and *z*   These are the two double consonants in Leech ($A3^r$).

52.1–2 *n* hath a tingling sound, *r* a rough and rattling   Scaliger (208c–d2): 'Vibratio et asperitas in R. Tinnitus in N'.

52.6–7 Scaliger notes . . . great difference   Scaliger, 4.16, on dignity, one of the two stylistic virtues required constantly in the grand style (see **56.22–8n.**): 'dignity may be in gravity of sentences [or thoughts] and grandeur of words [*dignitas sit in sententiarum gravitate et in verborum granditate*]' (187b–c1); and 187c1 for Virgil.

52.10–11 Scaliger notes . . . 'incedo regina'   Scaliger, 187c2. Juno's self-description in Virgil, *Aeneid*, 1.46: 'Yet I, who move as queen of gods, sister at once and wife of Jove, with one people [the Trojans] am warring these many years' (1.46–8).

52.13–15 The grammarians...*femina* Paraphrasing Scaliger, 187c–d1. *Mulier* is the more everyday Latin word for 'woman'; *femina* is also used of gender in biology and grammar.

52.16–19 Was it not unworthy...'scurvy love' Scott follows others such as Thomas Nashe (preface to *Menaphon* (1589), in *ECE*, I, 315–16) and Joseph Hall (*Virgidemiarum* (1597), 1.6) in criticising Richard Stanyhurst (1547–1618), *Thee first foure bookes of Virgil his Aeneis translated intoo English heroical verse* (Leiden, 1582), a translation into English quantitative hexameters, and using an eccentric diction that represents Stanyhurst's attempt to demonstrate the variety of the English lexicon. Puttenham, in his chapter on decorum (3.23), also criticises Stanyhurst for saying 'that Aeneas was fain to trudge out of Troy, which term became better to be spoken of a beggar, or of a rogue, or a lackey' (358). (i) *squeezed*: *Aeneid*, 3.2 (1–3: 'Postquam res Asiae Priamique evertere gentem | immeritam visum superis, *cecidit*que superbum | Ilium...'; 'After it pleased the gods above to overthrow the power of Asia and Priam's guiltless race, after proud Ilium *fell*...'), which Stanyhurst translates 'When giltlesse Asian kingdoom sterne destenye quasshed, | With Priamus country when squysd was the Ilian empyre' (H1ʳ); (ii) *trudged*: *Aeneid*, 1.2 (1–3: 'Arma virumque cano, Troiae qui primus ab oris | Italiam fato profugus Laviniaque *venit* | litora'; 'Arms I sing and the man who first from the coasts of Troy, exiled by fate, *came* to Italy and Lavinian shores'), which Stanyhurst translates '...too famosed Italie trudging' (B3ʳ); (iii) *improbe amor*: *Aeneid*, 4.412 ('wicked Love'), which Stanyhurst translates 'Scurvye loove' (L4ᵛ).

52.22 *epithetons* Adjectives (*OED*, *epitheton*, n., 2 = *epithet*, n., 1a).

52.23–30 being as pages...how ridiculous the wearer was The personifications and anecdote show the general influence of Puttenham at this point.

52.32–4 he that says...servant's duty It is not clear if Scott is imagining something that might be said or quoting a source (which I have not found). The phrase 'faithful diligence' is a common one, well attested in discussion of the parable of the talents in Matthew 25:14–30, and so applying also to a Christian's duty.

52.35–6 *heroical* Aeneas, *devout* Aeneas (i) *magnanimus Aeneas*, e.g. *Aeneid*, 1.260; 5.17; 9.204; (ii) *pius Aeneas*, e.g. *Aeneid*, 1.220, 305, 378; 4.393; 5.26, 286, 685; 6.9, 176, 232; 7.5; 8.84; 9.255; 10.591, 783, 826; 11.170; 12.175, 311.

52.36 Achates *faithful* On 'faithful' Achates see **35.33–4n.**

52.37–40 Homer, is by Scaliger...his great mind The opening of Scaliger, 5.3, in which parallel *loci* in Homer and Virgil are directly compared: 'The epithets of Homer are often cold, puerile, or pointless. Thus, what point is there in calling tearful Achilles "fleet-footed?"' (216c2; Padelford, 73). Achilles is repeatedly referred to as *podas ōkus Achilleus* (e.g. *Iliad*, 1.58, 84, 148, 215, etc.) at the end of a hexameter line. It was only in the twentieth century that a proper understanding was developed of the genesis of stock epithets in the metrical demands of oral-formulaic composition.

52.39 diminishing Disparaging, depreciative (*OED*, *diminishing*, adj., †2; first recorded usage 1675, with first recorded usage in any sense, 1660).

52.41–53.4 What honour . . . particular active quality? On Robert Devereux, second Earl of Essex (1565–1601), and the dating implications of this passage, see Introduction, xxxiv–xxxvii. Paul E. J. Hammer (personal communication) suggests '*swift-footed Essex*' may be an ironic allusion either to the slow pace of Essex's Irish campaign between May and August 1599 or, as Stanley Wells has also suggested (Wells, 235), to the extraordinary speed of Essex's return from Ireland in September of that year, against orders, to answer criticisms of his handling of the campaign. However, Scott's other comments weigh against the latter. Rushing straight to court and into the Queen's chamber, Essex found her still being dressed and ended the day under house arrest and no longer 'general of the army of the most famous prince' (i.e. Earl Marshal), at least *de facto* (official proceedings were delayed until June 1600). Scott's remark therefore probably predates Essex's return from Ireland. Hoskyns also uses Essex's Irish campaign as an illustration, in this case of the synecdoche that exchanges 'the speciall for the perticuler, as the Earle is gone into Ireland for E: E:' (*Directions*, 124), immediately following the passage cited at **58.25–6n.**). Cf. also Shakespeare, *Henry V*: 'Were now the general of our gracious Empress, | As in good time he may, from Ireland coming, | Bringing rebellion broached on his sword . . .' (Act 5 Chorus, 30–2). On Essex cf. **44.37–9n.**

53.1–2 one says . . . Achillean virtues George Chapman, in the dedication of *Seaven bookes of the Iliades of Homere, prince of poets* (1598) 'To the most honored now living Instance of the Achilleian vertues eternized by divine HOMERE, the Earle of ESSEXE, Earle Marshall etc.' (A3ʳ), and again in the dedication of *Achilles shield. Translated as the other seven bookes of Homer, out of his eighteenth booke of Iliades* (1598), 'humbly presenting your Achilleian vertues with *Achilles* Shield' (B1ʳ).

53.5–7 when Achilles' great heart . . . 'swift-footed Achilles wept' Probably a misreading of Scaliger's 'Quid enim convenit Achilli flenti, *podas ōkus*' (216c2; literally, 'for how does "swift-footed" suit a weeping Achilles?'). Homer does not say 'swift-footed Achilles wept', but on two occasions when Achilles does weep, he is then immediately introduced in dialogue as 'swift-footed': *Iliad*, 1.364 (after 357–63) and 18.78 (after 73–7). Chapman omits the epithet and avoids the indecorum in translating the former passage (*Seaven bookes of the Iliades of Homere* (1598), C2ᵛ).

53.7–8 you must not . . . (saith Scaliger) Scaliger, 213a1.

53.8–10 The endless date . . . Lucrece her rape Shakespeare, *Lucrece*, 935, in Lucrece's apostrophe to Time: 'Why hath thy servant Opportunity | Betray'd the hours thou gav'st me to repose? | Cancell'd my fortunes, and enchained me | To endless date of never-ending woes?' (932–5). For *never-ending* cf. **50.22–7n.**

53.16–21 though the propriety . . . no words are natural Not Aristotle, but Plato, in the *Cratylus*, an examination of the conflicting views that 'there is a correctness of name for each thing, one that belongs to it by nature' (Cratylus' position, 383a) and that 'No name belongs to a particular thing by nature, but only because of the rules and usage of those who establish the usage and call it by that name' (Hermogenes' view, 384d).

53.16 propriety *OED*, *propriety*, n. †1 ('Particular or individual character, nature, or disposition . . . properly characteristic state or condition') shading into 5†b ('Strictness of meaning, literalness; the proper, strict, or literal sense of a word'; first recorded usage 1648).

53.21–6 (with Tully) . . . rooms of the former *De oratore*, 3.37.149: 'The words we employ then are either the proper and definite designations of things, which were almost born at the same time as the things themselves; or terms used metaphorically and placed in a connexion not really belonging to them; or new coinages invented by ourselves.' The point is elaborated in *De partitione oratoria*, 5.16–17.

53.26–7 Tully saith . . . penury *De oratore*, 3.38.155: 'the use of metaphor . . . sprang from necessity due to the pressure of poverty and deficiency, but it has subsequently been made popular by its agreeable and entertaining quality'. The point is developed, 3.38.155–40.161.

53.31–3 used as ornament . . . sweet indirectness See **58.20–3n.**

53.38–9 the difference . . . words and sentences Scott's vocabulary of 'texture' and 'coherence' may be drawn from Quintilian's discussion of style as connected or loose (see 9.4.19–20 for *contextus*, 'woven together', and *cohaereo*, 'to cohere').

53.39–40 The poet . . . divers forms On poetic licence see **49.13–14n.** and **64.24–9n.**

53.41–54.1 forthright Dunstable tenor of speech The 'Dunstable way', the road (now the A5/A5183) from London to Dunstable, 35 miles away in Bedfordshire, was proverbial for plainness or straightforwardness (the road was essentially the old Watling Street Roman road, and so very straight for long stretches). See *OED*, *Dunstable*, adj. and n., †1c: 'in phr. *plain* (or *downright*) *Dunstable*: plain speaking or language' (first recorded usage 1597).

54.3 *they had not left many trees behind them*   Cf. Sidney's *Arcadia*, from Pyrocles'
encounter with Pamphilus and Dido upon entering a wood: 'I left not many trees
behinde me, before I sawe at the bottome of one of them a gentle-man . . .' (*NA*, 2P4ᵛ;
Skretkowicz, 236).

54.6–9 The incomparable excellencies . . . bold and fearful   The words, a few
pages earlier in Book 2 of the *Arcadia*, with which the Amazon Zelmane begins the
process of explaining to Philoclea that she is in fact Pyrocles, with one omission: 'many
circumstances in the uttering *my speech*, both . . .' (*NA*, 2P2ᵛ; Skretkowicz, 230). Scott's
text preserves the parentheses common to all three printed texts available to him: the
editions of 1590, 1593, and 1598. Scott, or perhaps his scribe, has mistakenly crossed
through *both* in 'doth require ~~both~~ many ceremonies . . .', believing it to be dittography
because of the *both* in 'both bold and fearful'. Since the text was clearly copied with
intentional correctness in the first place, I have privileged that original intention.

54.11–13 that phrase . . . one unto the other   A brief allusion to the periodic style
of intricate sentence construction, on which see Puttenham, 2.5; Cicero, *De oratore*,
3.43.171–2; Scaliger, 4.25; and cf. **63.22–3n.**

54.14–15 Sir Philip Sidney . . . matchable to him   Sidney was as influential as a
prose stylist as he was as a versifier. See, e.g., Richard Carew in *c.*1595–6 ('Will yow
have all in all for prose and verse? take the miracle of our age Sir *Philip Sydney*': *ECE*,
II, 293); Meres in 1598 (*ECE*, II, 315–16); Drayton in 1627 (*SRLC*, 293–4).

54.18–20 (after Scaliger) . . . in every kind   The list of six stylistic virtues that
follows selects from the longer list of virtues given in Scaliger, 4.3–15. These are
'affectus communes' (183c2, 184a1), aspects shared by all three styles or as Scott says
'*common* graces' and '*affections* . . . found in every kind'; Scaliger also lists other virtues
particular to the three styles, grand, middle, and low, in chapters 16–22 (see **56.22–
8n.**, **56.35–57.3n.**, and **57.4–12n.**). Scott selects, in order, perspicuity (*perspicuitas*,
4.3), purity (*puritas*, 4.13), fullness or completeness (*plenitudo*, 4.8), plentifulness or
fluency (*floridum*, 4.9), smoothness or softness (*mollitia* or *molle*, 4.10), and sweetness
(*suavitas*, 4.11). He omits refinement (*cultus*, 4.4), propriety (*proprietas*, 4.5), elegance
(*venustas*, 4.6), rhythmicity (*numerositas*, 4.7), ardour (*incitatio*, 4.12), acuteness (*acu-
men*, 4.14), and sharpness (*acre*, 4.15). Scaliger's main classical source is Hermogenes,
On types (Scaliger, 4.1–2, *passim*). Scott may show Cicero's influence in beginning with
perspicuity and ending with sweetness. Compare the five stylistic virtues in *De partitione oratoria*, 6.19: lucidity (*dilucidum*), brevity, acceptability, brilliance, and sweetness
(*suave*).

54.20–7 The first . . . understand what is delivered   Scaliger, 4.3 (184) and also
4.1 (176d1–177a1), making the point that obscurity is the opposite of clarity. See also
Cicero, *De partitione oratoria* (6.19), and especially Quintilian (8.2.1–24), who, like
Scott, finds it easier to give examples of obscurity.

54.21 thorough Thoroughly, from beginning to end (*OED, thorough*, prep. and adv., 9).

54.23 *medium* A new word in English, especially in this sense (*OED, medium*, n. and adj., 5a, first recorded usage 1595), though the Latin usage was more established (hence it is a 'school term').

54.24 (as we showed before) See esp. **47.40–49.17**.

54.29–30 That when . . . lower world Shakespeare, *Richard II*, 3.2.37–8. This type of grammatical ambiguity was labelled *amphibologia* in the rhetoricians' lists of stylistic vices (see, e.g., Puttenham, 3.22: *Art*, 345–6). Q1 (1597) punctuates with a comma after 'hid' and none after 'globe', Q2–5 (1598–1615) with no commas, and F (1623) with a comma after 'globe' and none after 'hid', suggesting that the sense of the line caused Shakespeare's printers some trouble too.

54.33–6 The next is *purity* . . . **tegmine fagi, etc.** Scaliger, 4.13: 'Est enim Puritas nuditas, cum nihil ornamenti admiscetur' (186d1). Scaliger gives the opening two lines of Virgil, *Eclogues*, 1, where Scott only gives the first, and an 'etc.' (l. 2: 'silvestrem tenui musam meditaris avena', 'wooing the woodland Muse on slender reed').

55.1–3 Sir Philip Sidney . . . same purity The 544-line eclogue, first printed in the 1593 *Arcadia* and attributed by its editors to the shepherd Lamon, was probably written by Sidney after completing the 'old' *Arcadia* (Ringler, 494). It begins 'A Shepheard's tale no height of stile desires | To raise in words what in effect is lowe: | A plaining songe plaine-singing voice requires . . .' (Ringler, OP 4.1–3). Strephon and Klaius feature within the *Arcadia* as friendly rivals in their love of Urania. However, the poem was probably not intended by Sidney for inclusion, since its subject matter is too clearly English (a game of barley-break), and the characterisation of the two shepherds does not match that within the revised *Arcadia*. On this poem as a 'pattern of pastorals' cf. **65.30–1**.

55.4–8 A third grace . . . permisit agresti Again, Scott's definition and example are taken from Scaliger's chapter on *plenitudo*, 4.8 (185c1): 'Plenum est . . . cum nihil desit quod desideres, nihil redundat.' The example is again from Virgil, *Eclogues*, 1.9–10: '[it is a god who wrought for us this peace] . . . Of his grace my kine roam, as you see, and I, their master, play what I will on my rustic pipe.'

55.11–15 Another is *plentifulness* . . . **describes sleep** Scaliger's chapter on *floridum* follows directly after *plenitudo*; it differs from *plenitudo*, he says, not essentially, but in accident: both are full, but *floridum* is so by the addition of something pleasant and delightful that could be taken away without loss (185d1–a2). The final one of Scaliger's three examples is the description alluded to by Scott of a night in which all sleep except Dido (Virgil, *Aeneid*, 4.522–8).

55.15–23 Sir Philip Sidney . . . did reign   As Scaliger milks Virgil's first Eclogue, so Scott mines Lamon's 'tale' (Ringler, OP 4.57–64). The manuscript orthography is close in places to that of the 1593 and 1598 printed texts, but there are substantive differences, suggesting that Scott rather than his scribe was copying from the printed text. I have therefore preserved the manuscript's *whilst* (for Sidney's *while*) in each of the first two lines (the duplication of this variant suggests that it may have been deliberate, and *whilst* is the preferred form in the rest of the *Model*), but have restored Sidney's 'ran' in the first line (the manuscript reads 'runne', which is clearly a scribal error).

55.24–5 Likewise *softness* . . . enter the ears   Scaliger, 4.10 (185c2).

55.25–30 that virtuous sonnet . . . least surmise, etc.   On George Wyatt (1553–1624), see Introduction, xxxiii. The poem is preserved in a group of four sonnets (possibly autograph) in a collection of Wyatt family papers, Add. MS 62135, 263^v, varying only from Scott's text in the final line: 'Must once retorne and fale as we did rise.' See further my 'William Scott and the dating of George Wyatt's sonnets', *Notes and queries*, 59.1 (2012), 58–60.

55.31–5 the last and perfectest . . . leave reading it   Scaliger, 4.11: 'Est igitur suavis oratio, quae allicit auditorem ad legendum vel invitum. Qualis illa Herodo[tus] cuius libros mihi difficilius est deponere, quam cyathum' (186b1). Scott elaborates Scaliger's bare reference: Herodotus' books are more difficult for him to put down than a *cyathus* (a ladle used for serving wine).

55.34 ale-knight   *OED*, †*ale-knight*, n.: 'A votary of the ale-house, a tippler'.

55.36–56.7 Bartas his description . . . douce nuit, etc.   Du Bartas, *La sepmaine*, day 1, 499–507 (Du Bartas, ii, 212). On Scott and Du Bartas see Introduction, lv–lix; for the evidence in this passage of the editions of Du Bartas that Scott used see Textual Introduction, lxxxi–lxxxii.

56.8–16 The night . . . Sweet night, etc.   Scott's translation here varies from that in his incomplete translation of Du Bartas (Add. MS 81083, 61^{r-v}): 1 doth] should; 2 Doth] Should; 4 cares] care; 4 gives our mind free peace] setts our myndes at ease; 6 earth] worlde; 7 calmly . . . soft] softely . . . calme. These signs of revision might suggest that a further stage of work on the Du Bartas intervened between the scribal copying of the *Model* and that of the Du Bartas.

56.17 Can anything . . . and sweet?   Recapitulating the six virtues of style just treated.

56.18–19 all style . . . affection   Scott glances at the question of whether (rhetorical) style is expressive of genuine passions or merely simulates them. Cf. Puttenham's chapter on style, 3.5 (*Art*, esp. 233–4) and the rhetorical theory of *ēthos* or performed character, on which see **38.20–6n.**

56.22–8 We say then, with Scaliger . . . appropriate unto itself   A free synthesis of what Scaliger says at various points in Book 4 of *Poetices libri septem*, with Scott perhaps drawing here and in the two succeeding paragraphs on *Ad Herennium*, 4.8.11 or an early modern derivative: 'The grand type consists of a smooth and ornate arrangement of impressive words. The middle type consists of words of a lower, yet not of the lowest and most colloquial, class of words. The simple type is brought down even to the most current idiom of standard speech.' Scaliger, 4.1, is on *character* (style), a term reflected in Scott's 'that character of speech'. Scaliger defines the grand style in 4.2: 'The grand style is that which portrays eminent characters and notable events. The sentiments are correspondingly choice, and they are couched in choice and euphonious diction' (183d2; Padelford, 71). He lists there two stylistic virtues that are invariably present in the grand style alone – dignity (*dignitas*) and sonorousness (*sonus*) (183c2; Padelford, 70). These are reflected in Scott's 'well-sounding words . . . perpetual dignity in words and phrase', with Scott also looking at their separate treatments later in the book (4.16–17), where *dignitas* resides 'in phrases and in words [*in sententiarum . . . et in verborum*]' (4.16, 187b–c1). Scaliger also lists two other virtues – *gravitas* and *vehementia* – that may be used as required (183c2; Padelford, 70; discussed further, 4.18). The phrase 'well-raised admiration' comes from Sidney (*DP*, 47, quoted at **78.39–79.9n.**).

56.24 embossed   Carved in relief; Scott uses the word in translating from Lomazzo (**65.7**, and see **65.1–7n.**).

56.28–33 *Grave* speech . . . hot repetitions   Both definitions paraphrase and elaborate Scaliger, 4.18 (193c–d1).

56.33–4 the courtier's . . . garment   On clothing metaphors see **63.30n.**, and cf. Puttenham, 3.20, on the figure of final polish, *exergasia*, as equivalent to dressing a naked body 'in rich and gorgeous apparel' and therefore named by Puttenham 'the Gorgeous' (*Art*, 333).

56.34 Scaliger . . . generous form   Scaliger uses the term *forma* for the styles (e.g. 174b–d1, 183c2), and lists synonyms for the grand style, which 'I also call the Generous [*ego etiam Generosum voco*]', in 4.1 (174a2).

56.35–57.3 The *indifferent* . . . frugal form   Again, freely adapting and elaborating Scaliger, 4.21 (193c2) and 4.22 (193d2–194a1), including the two virtues particular to this style: *volubilitas* (volubility, fluency) and *rotunditas* (smoothness, roundedness). For the 'frugal form' see 193d2.

56.38 Helen   Helen of Troy, in Homer's *Iliad* and subsequent literature.

57.4–12 The lowest and basest . . . shepherd and ploughman Freely adapting Scaliger, 4.2 (183d2) and 4.19–20 (193d1–c2): the style of comedy and pastoral, the particular qualities of the low style are constant *tenuitas* (fineness, slightness) plus *simplicitas* (simplicity) and *securitas* (carelessness) as required.

57.5 like Lalus Lalus is a name used twice by Sidney in separate pastoral works. He is one of the shepherds of the eclogues in the *Arcadia*; he is paired in dialogue with Musidorus, in his disguise as Dorus the shepherd, and cannot match him (Ringler, OA 7). In the 1590 *Arcadia* Scott might also have read of Lalus' 'wit full of prety simplicitie' (κ8ᵛ). However, Lalus becomes Thyrsis in the 1593 *Arcadia*, though there remain traces of him through poor editing, including the 'prety simplicitie' (F2ʳ; Skretkowicz, 100). Scott may therefore have been using the 1590 text in this case. It is also possible that Scott is thinking of 'Lalus the old shepherd', a minor character in Sidney's brief entertainment known as 'The Lady of May' (see *Prose*, 22–3), but since this Lalus likes inkhorn terms, this is unlikely.

57.15–16 first four conditions . . . clothing of the conceit Having examined style in relation to a list of stylistic virtues selected from Book 4 of Scaliger (**54.17–56.17** and see **54.18–20n.**), Scott now returns to the four virtues from Book 3 of Scaliger discussed at length above (**33.1–45.35** and see **33.1–8n.**), which concern *res* or matter ('the conceit'), and relates them to *verba*, words ('the clothing of the conceit'). Scaliger does not himself make this connection, but *suavitas* (sweetness) figures in both of his lists (see **59.7–8n.**), and this may have encouraged Scott to do so.

57.17–22 *proportionableness* in the style . . . low or base *Decorum* (Greek *to prepon*) is a key concept in Aristotle's *Rhetoric*, central to Horace's *Ars poetica*, and discussed at length by the rhetoricians (see, e.g., Cicero, *Orator*, 21.70–22.74, 35.123; Quintilian, 11.1.1–93; Puttenham, 3.23–4). Neither Scaliger nor Scott uses the term *decorum* with much regularity. See also **33.31–4n.**

57.27–36 observe with Tully . . . and so of the rest Scott is following a section of *De oratore* supposedly concerned with rhetorical delivery ('nature has assigned to every emotion a particular look and tone of voice and bearing of its own', 3.57.216) rather than style, but Scott's adaptation of the material is encouraged by Cicero's exemplifying each emotion with a literary quotation. Scott follows Cicero's characterisations of the performance of each emotion closely, adding 'pride' and 'courage' to Cicero's anger, sorrow, fear, and pleasure (3.58.217–19), whilst omitting forcefulness (or possibly transforming it into pride and courage) and dejection.

57.29 cutted *OED*, †*cutted*, adj., 3a: 'Contracted in expression; abbreviated, concise.'

57.32–3 and uncertain . . . careless remissness This entire phrase was inserted in the manuscript in another hand, almost certainly Scott's, the scribe having skipped a line in copying. See Textual Introduction, lxxvii–lxxix.

57.32–3 remissness Translating Cicero's *remissus*, 'relaxed, cheerful' (*De oratore*, 3.58.219). Cf. *OED, remissness*, †3: 'Relaxation; ease' (first recorded usage 1624); earlier senses are of weakness or laxity.

57.36–7 Examples ... patterns of decorum An adaptation of Scaliger's finding of examples ('exempla') of the various kinds of person ('varia genera personarum') in Virgil (83c1).

57.39–40 the true idea ... image thereof Although *idea* and *image* are key terms for Sidney (see **12.25–30n.**), Scott's terminology here owes most to Scaliger, who discusses the term *idea* at length, as applying both to poetic *res* – character, situation, etc., e.g. 3.1 (80c1), 3.25 (113a–b1) – and to the types or kinds or forms of style: e.g. 4.1 (174c1). For the meaning of *species*, cf. **14.34–6n.**

57.40–58.2 Scaliger notes ... beast Virgil, *Aeneid*, 5.481, when a sacrificial bull is felled at a blow from the boxer Entellus: 'sternitur exanimisque tremens procumbit humi bos' ('Outstretched and lifeless, the bull falls quivering on the ground'). The line achieves its effect with a rare monosyllabic line ending, a detail Scaliger comments on briefly in 2.29 (73a1), and at greater length in the passage Scott refers to in 4.48 (210b2–211a1). Although Servius, as Scaliger points out, disapproved of this line, it is an 'incomparable verse' (210b2) for Scaliger and has since been almost universally admired (cf. John N. Hough, 'Monosyllabic verse endings in the *Aeneid*', *Classical journal*, 71 (1975), 16–24 (22): 'Usually considered Virgil's best; the thud of falling is all but audible').

58.3–4 una Eurusque ... litora fluctus *Aeneid*, 1.85–6 ('East and South winds together, and the South-wester, thick with tempests – and shoreward roll vast billows'). The lines figure in the preceding chapter of Scaliger, 4.47, on the qualities of words (208c1, 208d2–209a1), from which Scott has already drawn his hints about the sounds of different vowels and consonants (**51.29–52.5**), as well as in a comparative chapter on the description of storms, 5.12 (266a1). The classic treatment of the way poetic sound imitates sense is Dionysius of Halicarnassus, *On literary composition*, 15–16, though he was little used in Scott's day, and his examples are from Homer. Another possible source is Vida, *De arte poetica*, 2.367–71: 'when the poet ... attempts to compose a work in which his words will emulate the thing itself ... Perhaps he will tell of a fearful storm on the savage sea, or the roar of winds ...'.

58.11 Scribendi ... fons Horace, *Ars poetica*, 309.

58.20–3 describe *figure* ... direct use See Quintilian: 'A *figure* ... is the term employed when we give our language a conformation other than the obvious and ordinary' (9.1.4; cf. 9.1.11). Cf., almost identically, Diomedes (Keil, I, 443), Scaliger (120a2), and, in English, Puttenham, 3.7: 'As figures be the instruments of ornament in every language, so be they also in a sort abuses, or rather trespasses, in speech, because they pass the ordinary limits of common utterance, and be occupied of purpose to deceive the ear and also the mind, drawing it from plainness and simplicity to a certain doubleness, whereby our talk is the more guileful and abusing' (*Art*, 238). Cf. **53.26–35**.

58.23 I will not . . . *eternal being*   An example of the rhetorical figure *periphrasis*.

58.23–4 I will not still say *Tully* . . . *the orator*   Although Scott consistently fails to do this, he does refer to Lomazzo as 'the painter' (**10.15, 35.19**), and Aristotle as 'the philosopher' (**13.9**).

58.25–6 I will not say *sword* . . . general *iron*   Synecdoche (*weapon*) and metonymy (*iron*). Cf. Hoskyns on the synecdochic exchange of genus for species: 'Soe the generall name for the speciall put upp yowr weapon, for yowr dagger' (*Directions*, 124).

58.29–34 give the general description . . . enlightened by examples   Many sixteenth-century rhetoric books, in English and in Latin, were treatments of *elocutio* either alone (e.g. Susenbrotus, Peacham) or almost exclusively (Talaeus and his English imitators, Puttenham). Although Scott shows a deep familiarity with Cicero and Quintilian, he also seems to have used a Ramistic rhetoric – Talaeus' *Rhetorica* or an English version of it – for quick reference to the figures (see esp. **67.32–4n.**). Scaliger deals with figures of thought in Book 3 of *Poetices libri septem* and figures of speech in Book 4. On Scott's treatment of the rhetorical figures see Introduction, lxviii.

58.35–6 a variation . . . without figure   The plain style was relatively devoid of figuration, and although *aschematiston* (a lack of figures) was listed as a stylistic vice (e.g. Quintilian, 8.3.59; cf. 9.1.13), there were also terms for a more deliberate and virtuous stylistic simplicity, such as *apheleia* (Quintilian, 8.3.87), which could be treated as figures themselves.

58.36 coloured   Full of rhetorical ornament (*OED*, *coloured*, adj. and n., 5, from *colour*, n.¹, 15). The term *colour* (Latin *color*) is common in classical and Renaissance rhetoric books.

58.38 the ground or field . . . heralds speak   The *field* is the surface of an escutcheon or shield on which the heraldic devices (known as the *charge*) are displayed (*OED*, *field*, n.¹, 17a); in effect a background colour (or 'ground').

59.2–4 heaped one upon another . . . measure or order   Equivalent to various stylistic vices, such as *periergia* ('Over-Labor' or 'the Curious' in Puttenham, *Art*, 344).

59.3 over-riotous   Not in *OED*, but see *OED*, *riotous*, adj., 2, 3a, and 6 for relevant senses of extravagance, excess, and over-exuberant growth.

59.4 guards   *OED, guard*, n., 11a: 'An ornamental border or trimming on a garment.'

59.7–8 (that we repeat not... affections of style advertised)   Referring to the discussion of sweetness as one of the 'common graces of our speech and affections... that may be found in every kind' (**54.19–20**) at **55.31–56.17**; see **54.18–20n.** and **57.15–16n.**

59.8–10 we, with Tully... the other *sound*   Cicero, *Orator*, 49.163: 'Duae sunt igitur res quae permulceant ['permulcent' in some texts] auris ['aures' in some texts], sonus et numerus'. *Number* is often a synonym for *metre* but Scott uses it in the more general sense of 'Harmony; conformity; in verse or music, to a certain regular beat or measure; rhythm' (*OED, number*, n., †14a).

59.10–11 though sound... soul of number   Scaliger's remark is found in the opening of the chapter on the qualities of words from which Scott has already drawn (**51.29–52.5**): 'videtur enim Numeri anima, sonus' (4.47, 207c2); *dictio* – speech or diction – is the body. In his brief chapter on the stylistic virtue of *numerositas* (see **54.18–20n.** for its place in the full list of virtues), Scaliger also says that *numerus* or rhythm is the soul of poetry (4.7, 185b1). For sources and analogues of the *soul* image see **13.20–2n.** and **64.1–2n.**

59.11–12 we may consider... figure and rhyme   That is, *sound* may be considered apart from *number*, as a component of *figure* (the brief discussion of the grammarians' figures at **64.22–9** and of the figures of speech at **64.30–7**) and of *rhyme* (**62.16–35**).

59.12–14 there is no speech... number   Cf. the extended discussion of prose rhythm in Cicero, *Orator*, 49.162–71.236, on which Scott draws throughout this passage (56.190: 'there are rhythms [*numeros*] even in prose, and... those used in oratory are the same as those of poetry'). And cf. Viperano, 1.16 (esp. 50–1).

59.13–15 stirring... stir   For this meaning of *stir*, see **22.26–30n.**

59.14 discrete quantity   A distinction was commonly made between continuous quantity (= magnitude) and discrete quantity (= number, comprising separable units); see, e.g., Aristotle, *Metaphysics*, 1020a, Quintilian, 7.4.16, Campion (*ECE*, II, 328).

59.14 numbrous   Cf. Sidney: 'that numbrous kind of writing which is called verse' (*DP*, 12). See *OED, numbrous*, adj., †2, equivalent to *OED, numerous*, adj., †5, Puttenham's preferred form.

59.15–20 of this time and motion... less sensibly   Conflating two passages from Cicero's *Orator*: 'in the choice of sounds and rhythms the ear is the judge' (49.162); and 'For the ear, or rather the mind which receives the message of the ear, contains in itself a natural capacity for measuring all sounds. Accordingly it distinguishes between long and short, and always looks for what is complete and well proportioned' (53.177–8). Because Scott is following Latin and neo-Latin sources, he is content for now to talk in terms of quantities, by which every syllable was either long or short, with a long syllable taking twice as long to say as a short one; but see **60.11–16n.** and **60.25–31n.**

59.19 currentness   *OED*, *currentness*, n., †1: 'Fluency, easy flow (of language, etc.)'. Both Webbe (*ECE*, I, 262) and Puttenham (*Art*, 165, 171) use this word.

59.25–7 this kind . . . a *sentence*   Cicero, *Orator*, 51.170: 'numerus nihil affert aliud nisi ut sit apte verbis comprehensa sententia' ('rhythm does nothing except to form the words into a well-knit sentence').

59.30–1 as, often times, the sense . . . due extent   Cicero, *Orator*, 53.178: 'certain phrases [the ear] feels to be shortened, mutilated as it were, and is offended by these as if it were cheated of its just due; others are too long and run beyond reasonable bounds'. Scott and Cicero both use the word sentence/*sententia* ambiguously. It can mean a unit of syntax, or rather prose rhythm (comma, colon, or period, on which see **63.22–3n.**), or a verbalised thought (our modern sense of *sententia*); see further **67.32–4n.**

59.32–3 concinnity . . . in the orator   *Concinnity* is harmony or formal symmetry, Cicero's *concinnitas* (*Orator*, esp. 12.38, 24.81, 25.83–4, 44.149, 49.164–5, 60.201–2, 65.219–20; cf. *Brutus*, e.g., 9.38, 95.325).

59.33–6 saith the orators . . . delight and willingness   *Orator*, 52.174, examining the claim that the Greek orator Isocrates (436–338 BC) was 'the first to introduce rhythm into prose. For when he observed that people listened to orators with solemn attention [*oratores cum severitate audiri*], but to poets with pleasure, he is said to have sought for rhythms to use in prose as well'.

59.37–8 order or disposition . . . proportion or compass   (i) *disposition*: arrangement; (ii) *proportion*: relation of parts to whole, used of poetic form by Puttenham (*Art*, Book 2: 'Of proportion poetical'); (iii) *compass*: measure, regularity (*OED*, *compass*, n.[1], adj., and adv., A †1), circuit, extent.

59.39 comprehension   *OED*, *comprehension*, n., †3: 'A comprehensive arrangement, summation, summary of any matter' (first recorded usage 1659).

60.1–6 Grecians and Latins . . . apt for   In Scott's view Greek and Latin words tend to be longer than English words; this view is of course affected by the kind of words – often complex and technical – that were being borrowed from these languages into English in the early modern period. Cf. Puttenham, 2.3: 'The Greeks and Latins, because their words happened to be of many syllables and very few of one syllable, it fell out right with them to conceive and also to perceive a notable diversity of motion and times in the pronunciation of their words' (*Art*, 158). Greek and Latin prosody was quantitative, and both languages synthetic where modern European languages (and especially English) are more analytic. Word-stems were extended in complex ways according to grammatical relation by the addition of inflectional elements through the declension of nouns, adjectives, and pronouns, and the conjugation of verbs; whereas in English word form is less variable and word order more important in determining grammatical relation. The quantitative, highly inflected nature of the Greek and Latin languages, Scott argues, suited them to quantitative prosody.

60.2 stinted   Fixed, limited, set (*OED*, *stinted*, adj., †1).

60.6–16 But our modern languages . . . still certain   Highly confusing, perhaps corrupt, and impossible to punctuate smoothly. *We* slides between meaning modern European languages and meaning just the English; Scott might therefore appear to believe that French and Italian poetry is written in disyllabic feet, though this is unlikely.

60.6–8 our modern languages . . . Babylon's curse   Just before his discussion of prosody in the *Defence*, Sidney defends the English language:

I know some will say it is a mingled language. And why not so much the better, taking the best of both the other? Another will say it wanteth grammar. Nay, truly, it hath that praise that it wants not grammar: for grammar it might have, but it needs it not, being so easy in itself, and so void of those cumbersome differences of cases, genders, moods, and tenses, which I think was a piece of the Tower of Babylon's curse, that a man should be put to school to learn his mother tongue.   (*DP*, 51)

Sidney, and Scott, refer to Genesis 11:1–9: 'Then the whole earth was of one language, and one speach' (11:1), often believed to be Hebrew, but when men built a great tower, God made them unable to understand each other; 'Therefore the name of it was called Babel [margin: '*Or, confusion*'], because the Lorde did there confound the language of all the earth' (11:9). Babel is the Hebrew (and Akkadian) for Babylon.

60.8 the Hebrew hath them not   In fact Hebrew is only partly analytic, using inflection, though to a lesser extent than Greek or Latin.

60.9 particles   Particles are indeclinable function words such as prepositions, as well as prefixes and suffixes.

60.10–11 the English . . . appellatives   *Appellative* is an ironically Latinate, poly-syllabic word for *noun*. Cf. Puttenham, 2.3:

Now because our natural and primitive language of the Saxon English bears not any words (at least very few) of more syllables than one (for whatsoever we see exceed cometh to us by the alterations of our language grown upon many conquests and otherwise), there could be no such observation of times in the sound of our words, and for that cause we could not have the feet which the Greeks and Latins have in their meters.   (*Art*, 158)

60.11–16 we are not capable … still certain   There was some reluctance, as Scott expresses here, to confuse classical and modern prosody by adopting the terminology of feet. Cf. Puttenham, 2.3: 'This quantity with them consisteth in the number of their feet, and with us in the number of syllables which are comprehended in every verse, not regarding his feet otherwise than that we allow in scanning our verse: two syllables to make one short portion (suppose it a foot) in every verse. And after that sort ye may say we have feet in our vulgar rhymes, but that is improperly' (*Art*, 157). Puttenham prefers to describe English metres in more syllabic terms, though both Gascoigne (1575) and Webbe (1586) had talked in terms of feet. James VI, in 'Ane schort treatise, conteining some reulis and cautelis to be observit and eschewit in Scottis poesie' (1584; *ECE*, I, 208–25), uses 'foot' to mean 'syllable'. Scott's clarity is admirable: he finds a way to theorise accentual-syllabic prosody whilst recognising the limitations of the borrowed terminology.

60.16–20 that grace of tuneableness … we call *rhyme*   Cf. Sidney, *Defence*: 'Now, of versifying there are two sorts, the one ancient, the other modern. The ancient marked the quantity of each syllable, and according to that framed his verse. The modern observing only number, with some regard of the accent, the chief life of it standeth in that like sounding of the words which we call rhyme' (*DP*, 52).

60.17 currentness   Movement, running; fluency, flow: see **59.19n**.

60.22 *caesure*   Scott's scribe spells the word 'Cæsure' (twice), 'caesure' (twice), and 'cesure' (once). Clearly, Scott understands the word as an anglicised form of the Latin *caesura* and/or French *césure*; *cesure* is the preferred form in Puttenham (2.5). *OED* (*caesura*, n.), however, presents the spelling *caesure*, along with *cesure* and *ceasure*, as merely a variant form of *caesura*. Because the older forms are no longer current, *caesure* is not given a separate entry (compare *OED*'s treatment of *through*, prep. and adv., and *thorough*, prep. and adv., which are treated as distinct words rather than merely variant forms). But the verse examples cited in *OED* from Spenser (3b) and Drayton (2, rhyming with 'measure') show that the Anglicised form of the word was sufficiently separate to justify its preservation in modernised form here.

60.24–5 Sir Philip Sidney saith … in our verse   A slight and significant rephrasing of 'observing only number, with some regard of the accent' (*DP*, 52, quoted at **60.16–20n.**).

60.25–31 our foot is restrained … short-timed syllable   Both in his combination of the terminologies of pitch and syllable-length and in his slight complaint about the limitations of disyllabic feet, Scott appears to be following Gascoigne (*SRLC*, 239–41) here. Gascoigne's thoughts about metrical accent clarify as much about vernacular versification as they confuse, since they are based on the *prosodia* sections of the Latin grammars (e.g. Diomedes, in Keil, I, 430–6), where the rules on quantitative metrics are complemented by rules on how to pronounce Latin, and three degrees of (pitch) accent are set out – grave (Latin *gravis*, 'heavy'), acute (Latin *acutus*, 'sharp'), and circumflex, 'the which I would English thus: the long accent, the short accent, and that which is indifferent' (*SRLC*, 239). For a contemporary example see the posthumously published *Brevissima institutio seu ratio grammatices cognoscendae* (1549) of William Lily (1468?–1522/3), which was sold with numerous editions of Lily's *A short introduction of grammar* (e.g. the 1596 edition, 15ᵛ–6ʳ, printed with the 1597 *Short introduction*); or George Buchanan's posthumously printed *De prosodia* (Edinburgh, [1595]), B7ᵛ. But where Gascoigne confounds length and accent Scott rightly sees accent as corresponding to (or taking the place of) quantity. This is a significant development. Puttenham's account of accent in 2.7 (*Art*, 167–8) is also based on the Latin *prosodias*' three degrees of accent, as is James VI's (*ECE*, I, 213). But Scott anticipates Samuel Daniel, who in *A defence of rhyme* (1603) preserves Gascoigne's terminology but ignores the three degrees of accent and instead posits a direct analogy, as Scott does here, between (binary) quantity and (binary) accent: 'For as Greek and Latin verse consists of the number and quantity of syllables, so doth the English verse of measure and accent. And though it doth not strictly observe long and short syllables, yet it most religiously respects the accent, and as the short and long make number, so the acute [Scott's 'sharp'] and grave [Scott's 'depressed'] accent yield harmony' (*SRLC*, 211). These origins also explain the prosodic notation used by Gascoigne, Scott, and others. Mulcaster, in his *Elementarie* (1582), explains: 'The *sharp accent* is a streight line rising toward the right hand, which sheweth that the vowell or diphthong, over which it is, must be sounded sharp and high, as *ráge, crépe, míne, hóme, púre*. The *flat accent*, is a streight line rising towards the left hand, which sheweth that the vowell or diphthong over which it is must be sounded flat and quik, as *ràg, stèp, thìn, fòr, stùr*' (151).

60.31–3 we may be said . . . if they be odd   That is to say, given that length is not an issue, all syllables may be deemed to have equal length (hence spondees). But insofar as accent replaces length, then feet are iambic or trochaic because one syllable in each pair will be accented relative to the other. Scott's point about even-footed and odd-footed verses assumes masculine endings, as becomes clearer at **61.6–23**. In a trochaic line the last foot will be a half-foot and the syllable count will be an odd number (this is known as catalexis), whereas in an iambic line all feet will have two syllables and the syllable count will be even. Of course, trochaic lines need not be odd-footed/catalectic.

61.3 Whose senses . . . Nature lays   The opening of Sidney, *Astrophil and Stella*, song 7 (Ringler, AS vii.1). Scott's scribe gives 'ill', preserved here, instead of the usual 'evil'. The printed texts available to Scott – the 1591 *Astrophel and Stella* (H4ʳ); its revised reprinting, also 1591 (H1ʳ); the 1597 reprinting (G4ᵛ); the 1598 *Arcadia* (3A2ʳ); and the 1599 Edinburgh *Arcadia* (2Z3ᵛ) – read 'evil', with the exception of Abraham Fraunce's *The Arcadian rhetorike* (1588), which gives the poem in full (Fraunce, D4ᵛ) and reads 'ill'. Scott may, then, have been quoting the line from this source. However, although it is clear (see **67.32–4n.**) that Scott used Fraunce's key source, Talaeus' *Rhetorica* (or an English version of it), and thus was interested in Ramistic rhetoric, there is no other evidence to suggest that he might also have looked at Fraunce. Less likely is that he was using a manuscript source, either Fraunce's (also used in the 1598 printing: Ringler, 562) or another. Likeliest of all is that he intelligently adjusted the spelling of 'evil' to reflect its metrics. *Evil* is often found as a monosyllable in verse and we must therefore assume it to have been pronounced *ill*. *OED* (*ill*, adj. and n., etymology) states that the two words are unrelated, but this was not the perception at the time: Puttenham gives the contraction of *evil* to *ill* as an example of *aphaeresis* (*Art*, 245; see **64.24–9n.**).

61.5 Now was … the light   Ringler, OA 73.1; the poem was originally assigned to Sidney's persona Philisides within the fourth eclogues of the 'old' *Arcadia*, but was given by Sidney to Amphialus in Book 3 of the revised *Arcadia* as printed in 1590 and thereafter.

61.8 the last   That is, the second syllable of each complete trochaic foot, ignoring the terminal 'odd syllable' in a catalectic line such as this, which is also accented.

61.9–10 Sigh they did … much care   Two separate lines from song 8 of *Astrophil and Stella* (Ringler, AS viii.17, 9). The poem is in trochaic tetrameter couplets, alternating between catalectic and full couplets (i.e. a pair of rhyming seven-syllable trochaic lines followed by a pair of rhyming eight-syllable trochaic lines), grouped into stanzas of four lines; these are both catalectic lines from the openings of stanzas.

61.16–18 Neither can … due place   Cf. Gascoigne on the importance of maintaining 'natural emphasis' (*SRLC*, 239), and Webbe (*ECE*, 1, 268). *Misrank(ing)* is not in the *OED*.

61.20–2 Interchangeably reflected … Reflected interchangeably   Also from song 8 of *Astrophil and Stella* (Ringler, AS viii.16). As the only line in the poem with just two words, this is a good example of the natural pattern of accents in polysyllabic words. What Scott does not say is that this line is not, in his terminology, 'odd-footed' (**61.19**), since it is a full (i.e. 8-syllable) trochaic line, or that the second version is, necessarily, perfect iambic tetrameter. For a similar example where word order is adjusted to show the dependence of metre on natural accent, see Gascoigne (*SRLC*, 241). Compare Puttenham's confusion over poems that alternate seven- and eight-syllable lines, 2.4 (*Art*, 161).

61.26–7 volubly … volubility   'Volubility' – meaning 'ready flow of speech' and 'Smooth, easy, or copious flow of verse or poetic utterance' (*OED*, *volubility*, n., 5a and b) – and the related terms 'volubly' and 'voluble' are possibly borrowed from Puttenham's Book 2; see, e.g., 2.6: 'which flowing of words with much volubility smoothly proceeding from the mouth is in some sort harmonical' (*Art*, 166).

61.27–8 distinguishing the volubility . . . our consonants Scott seems to imply that the rules for accent might in fact be similar to those for quantity in Latin; that is, that doubled consonants and long vowels might make a syllable metrically accented, whereas single consonants and short vowels might make the syllable unaccented. This is an intelligent casual hypothesis.

61.29 our hexameter . . . Latin heroic Scott's view that the English hexameter is the best vehicle to match the classical hexameter is tested in his translation of Du Bartas (where the French alexandrine makes the same attempt). Others shared his view but the result of the various Elizabethan experiments with pentameter, hexameter, and heptameter in the translation of Greek and Latin hexameters was a seventeenth-century preference for pentameter in both translated and original works of epic, as well as in drama. Scott returns to this point at **75.36–9**.

61.30–3 Sir Philip Sidney . . . affliction holdeth Scott quotes the opening line of an epistolary complaint in elegiac couplets assigned to Philisides in the 'old' *Arcadia* (Ringler, OA 74.1, reading 'Unto *the* caitiff. . . .') and to Dorus in the revised *Arcadia*. Sidney wrote some thirteen poems in quantitative metres, though, as Scott recognises, he strove to make metrical length and ictus coincide with natural speech stress, so that the metres are often accentual–quantitative. On the quantitative movement in England see further Ringler, 389–93, and Derek Attridge, *Well-weighed syllables: Elizabethan verse in classical metres* (Cambridge, 1974). Given Scott's devotion to Sidney, it might seem odd that he does not give further credence to the quantitative movement, but whereas it was a live topic for Puttenham (2.13–18) and Webbe (*ECE*, i, 278–90), as for others in the 1570s and 80s like Spenser and Harvey, and found new practitioners such as Abraham Fraunce and John Dickenson in the early 1590s, by the late 1590s interest had largely fizzled out, so that Campion's effort to revive it in 1601 seemed belated. Cf. Scott's earlier scorn for Stanyhurst, **52.16–19n**.

62.1–3 This goes marvellous . . . no accent is missounded In a hexameter line (elegiac couplets alternate hexameter and pentameter) the penultimate foot must be a dactyl and the final foot a spondee or trochee, but the first four feet can be spondees or dactyls, and here only the first foot is dactylic. Scott has already observed (**60.31–2**) that all feet in English metre can be viewed as spondees, since quantity is not an issue.

62.3–7 Contract the two last . . . lines unfoldeth The second line is of Scott's composition. Scott has not learned to theorise what his quantitative scansion of the first line should have shown him – that if Sidney's line is viewed as accentual-syllabic, the first foot is reversed; otherwise, the analysis is faultless. Scott again anticipates Daniel's *Defence of rhyme* (1603), in this case the latter's demonstration that Campion's quantitative poems can be scanned as accentual-syllabic (*SRLC*, 226–7).

62.4 female rhyme Scott here uses Sidney's word *female*; see further **62.24–35n**.

62.8–10 The next . . . his anguish   Line 3 of the same poem (line 2 being a line of pentameter), in which the high incidence of dactyls means that there are too many syllables for the line to be scanned as accentual-syllabic hexameter. The other problem for Scott ('displaceth the accent') is 'monument', where accent should fall on the first syllable but as scanned by Sidney the last is long and also bears metrical ictus.

62.12 unproper   See *OED*, *unproper*, adj., †1a (= *improper*, adj., 1: irregular, incorrect); †1b: '*spec*. Of language'; and 2 (= *improper*, adj., 2: unsuitable, unfit, inappropriate).

62.13–15 those kinds of measures . . . saith Sir Philip Sidney   Cf. Sidney: 'Now, of versifying there are two sorts, the one ancient, the other modern . . . Truly, the English, before any vulgar language I know, is fit for both sorts' (*DP*, 52). *Vulgar*, here and elsewhere, means 'ordinary', 'vernacular', or 'common', without the modern pejorative sense.

62.18–19 the like sounding . . . we call *rhyme*   Clarifying Sidney: 'that like sounding of the words which we call rhyme' (*DP*, 52).

62.19–22 Tully saith . . . (saith he)   Cicero, *Orator*, 59.199: 'Therefore, since the ear is always awaiting the end [*extremum*] and takes pleasure in it, this should not be without rhythm [*numero*].'

62.24–35 this rhyme is of three sorts . . . admits not the male   Scott draws heavily on Sidney: 'Lastly, even the very rhyme itself, the Italian cannot put it in the last syllable, by the French named the masculine rhyme, but still in the next to the last, which the French call the female, or the next before that, which the Italian term *sdrucciola*: the example of the former is "buono" / "suono", of the *sdrucciola* is "femina" / "semina". The French, of the other side, hath both the male, as "bon" / "son", and the female, as "plaise" / "taise", but the *sdrucciola* he hath not; where the English hath all three, as "due" / "true", "father" / "rather", "motion" / "potion"' (*DP*, 52–3). Scott departs from Sidney with 'feminine' (**62.28**). The *OED*'s first recorded usage in this sense is in a translation from the French from 1578 (*OED*, *feminine*, adj. and n., s1, *feminine rhyme*), and cf. Harington in 1591: 'the French call them the feminine rime . . . and the one syllable the masculin' (*ECE*, II, 221). On the three types of rhyme cf. Puttenham, 2.8 (*Art*, 169).

62.29 *sdrucciola*   The Italian literally means 'slippery': see *OED*, *sdrucciola*, adj. (first recorded usage is Sidney's).

62.30–3 For the first . . . *blamed is*   Scott assiduously, and perhaps unnecessarily, finds all these examples in Sidney's own poems. 'Show', 'know', 'low' are found in that order in AS 63, ll. 1, 4, 5. 'Treasure', 'pleasure', 'measure' are found in other orders in OA 7 (the dialogue between Lalus and Dorus – see **57.5n.**), ll. 73, 71, 75;

OA 69, ll. 5, 1, 4; OA 75, ll. 47, 51, 49; and also CS 29 and AS v; but the likeliest source is OA 28. Here Scott found 'pleasure doth', 'treasure doth', and 'measure doth' at ll. 56, 58, 60, interlocking with 'framed is', 'named is', 'blamed is' at ll. 53, 55, 57, and 'carefulness', 'warefulness', 'sparefulness' at ll. 41, 43, 45. OA 28 is an apt source, since it is an eclogue in which Dicus and Dorus compete to outdo each other in virtuoso rhyming. Cf. Harington's defence of his use of feminine and triple rhymes in his *Orlando furioso* (1591), using OA 7: 'Sir *Philip Sidney*, not only useth them, but affecteth them – *signifie, dignifie, shamed is, named is, blamed is, hide away, bide away*' (*ECE*, II, 221). Sidney had introduced systematic feminine and triple rhymes into English versification, and they were still not standard practice in 1591. Daniel clarified rules for their use in the *Defence of rhyme* (1603), responding to their vogue in the 1590s (*SRLC*, 232).

62.35–63.4 by the varying . . . by observation only   This brief but dense discussion of stanzaic form – at the same time as it argues for practical observation over theoretical analysis – shows in its vocabulary and perspective that Scott has studied previous theoretical treatments of English verse form. In a detailed discussion of the aesthetics of verse form in Book 2 of the *Art* Puttenham offers a dizzying array of stanzaic forms (a theoretical compendium which finds its practical analogue in Sidney's verse practice) and emphasises the separate variables of rhyme scheme and varying line length, as Scott does here. Puttenham, 2.2 is a chapter 'Of proportion in staff' that opens with a discussion of the English and Italian terms *staff* and *stanza*. *Staff* was the usual term, used by Gascoigne too (see *OED*, *staff*, n.¹, 19†b). In his briefer but also highly intelligent account in *A discourse of English poetry*, Webbe shows that: 'There are nowe wythin this compasse as many sortes of verses as may be devised differences of numbers: whereof some consist of equall proportions, some of long and short together, some of many rymes in one staffe (as they call it), some of cross ryme, some of counter ryme, some ryming with one worde farre distant from another, some ryming every thyrd or fourth word' (*ECE*, I, 269).

63.5–29 The third thing . . . unadvised speed   The rules for caesura in English verse developed by Gascoigne and Puttenham were influenced by both Latin and French versification, especially the latter. For a grammarian's discussion of the Latin rules see, e.g., Diomedes, in Keil, I, 497–8. For the rules developed by sixteenth-century French writers see, e.g., Peletier (1555) and Ronsard (1565). In the Latin hexameter, caesura might commonly fall halfway through the third foot (penthemimeral, explained as dividing the line into five and seven half-feet), or halfway through the fourth foot (hephthemimeral, dividing the line into seven and five half-feet); important here is that word-end and foot-end do not coincide. The French rules, based on the Latin, require caesura after the fourth syllable in a ten-syllable line, and after the sixth in a twelve-syllable line, with only these longer line lengths requiring caesura (contra Puttenham, *Art*, 162 and 164): see Peletier, 2.2 (Goyet, 267) and Ronsard (Goyet, 443). Peletier notes, additionally, that caesura need not always coincide with word end (Goyet, 267). The rules in Scott's discussion are essentially those of the French, as copied by

Gascoigne (*SRLC*, 244) and Puttenham (*Art*, 162 and 164) and require word-end and
foot-end to coincide, subject to Peletier's qualification about mid-word caesura, which
Scott follows (**63.24–9**). Although the 4:6 division in pentameter/decasyllables clearly
resembles penthemimeral caesura in the Latin hexameter, the difference from Latin
practice is stark: there seems no possibility in these Anglo-French rules of caesura in
the middle of a foot. Gascoigne is less dogmatic than Scott in what is a deliberately
brief discussion since 'it is at discretion of the writer, and they have been first devised
(as should seem) by the musicians' (*SRLC*, 244). Insofar as caesura is an achieved
affect, which is doubtful in much pentameter, its placement is clearly more variable in
verse of Scott's period (including Scott's own), as later theory acknowledges. Webbe's
intelligent discussion (*ECE*, I, 268–9) of how long lines can divide in two is a better
realised justification for the more predictable caesural placement in lines of three, four,
six, seven, and eight feet. All Scott's examples continue to be found in Sidney, with
the exception of his final example.

63.12 Can Reason . . . counted be?   A dialogue poem opening the second eclogues
of the *Arcadia* in all versions (Ringler, OA 27.3).

63.15 Now was . . . the light   Ringler, OA 73.1, quoted above, **61.5**.

63.16–17 seven feet . . . tongue admits   A theoretical mistake (though a fair observation of most practice) which again shows that Scott should have read Webbe: 'The
longest verse in length which I have seene used in English consisteth of sixteene
syllables' (*ECE*, I, 268).

63.19 Whose senses . . . Nature lays   Ringler, AS vii.1, quoted above, **61.3**.

63.22–3 if the sense rest . . . shortest rest of a comma   Possibly following Puttenham (*Art*, 163–5), Scott equates caesura with the smallest rhythmic or syntactic
division in the classical period, the comma, and also perhaps (as is explicit in Puttenham) with the modern punctuation mark that takes its name from that periodic unit.
See, e.g., Quintilian, 9.4.121–2, Diomedes (Keil, I, 465–6), and Mulcaster (148) for the
comma in relation to the period, and the latter for the association of the punctuation
mark with the rhythmic/syntactic unit. For Diomedes, the same word – *incisio* ('cut') –
serves as an alternative term for both comma and caesura (Keil, I, 497), since the sense
of cutting is there in both Greek *komma* and Latin *caesura*.

63.24–9 sometimes for variety . . . unadvised speed   This time Scott uses his
own verse, from the end of the first day of his Du Bartas, and appropriately enough
about pausing between one 'journey' (French *journée*, 'day') and a second (Add. MS
81083, 65ᵛ). Scott's (French-influenced) thoughts about caesuras splitting words show
how shaky the theory of caesura was and is. Perhaps the second line of his couplet
has a caesura after 'hasty', or perhaps it has none at all; the first line may be less
successful precisely because of its clunking mid-line pause, but it is also unsettled by

the disruption 'at first' creates in the metrical pattern. That Scott attempts to explain theory in relation to the practicalities of English monosyllables and polysyllables is nevertheless striking.

63.30 habit or livery   Metaphors of style or verse as clothing are ubiquitous. See, for an extended instance, Puttenham's introductory discussion of 'ornament poetical' (*Art*, 3.1, 221–2); and cf. the discussion immediately below of Sidney, Aristotle, and the 'complemental cut' of verse (**63.32–64.7**). Scott repeats this pair of terms from **12.22** and **13.22**.

63.32–6 Sir Philip Sidney . . . scholar's gown

For indeed the greatest part of poets have apparelled their poetical inventions in that numbrous kind of writing which is called verse – indeed but apparelled, verse being but an ornament and no cause to poetry . . . it is not rhyming and versing that maketh a poet (no more than a long gown maketh an advocate, who though he pleaded in armour should be an advocate and no soldier), but it is that feigning notable images of virtues, vices, or what else, with that delightful teaching, which must be the right describing note to know a poet by; although indeed the senate of poets hath chosen verse as their fittest raiment.   (*DP*, 11–12; and cf. 32, where Sidney returns to the question)

64.1–2 Aristotle . . . soul of the poem   *Poetics*, 1450a38–9 (see **13.20–2n.**).

64.6–7 in purple . . . complemental cut   Both verse and prose are imagined as garments dressing the plot or imitation, but they are of different cuts (*OED*, *cut*, n.², 17a, first recorded usage 1578) and equally good colours. The associations of both purple and scarlet are with high status, and are mostly good, the exception being the whore of Babylon in Revelation 17:4 ('And the woman was arayed in purple and skarlet . . .'). Purple in the ancient world meant royalty or high office (the senator's toga had a broad, purple stripe); scarlet was associated in the modern world with the robes of bishops and cardinals and the gowns of academic doctors. Scott has mentioned academic gowns ('a scholar's gown') and in the passage which he has open in front of him Sidney has talked of the 'senate of poets' (see **63.32–6n.**); this may have set Scott's mind on this track. *Complemental* is a new word, which *OED* has not found before 1602. The sense may be close to *OED*, *complemental*, adj and n., 1: 'Of the nature of a complement; completing' (first recorded usage 1602); or †3: 'Additional, accessory' (1634, the Dodo's wings, and so with a strong sense of inessential); or †4: 'Of the nature of an accessory ceremony; formal; ceremonial, ceremonious' (1637). The latter two senses seem closer to Scott's intention.

64.12–14 some kinds . . . as the comedy   See **79.30–1**.

64.15–16 as Pindar's number . . . in his lyrics   On Pindar see **19.9–10n**. With one exception no two of his poems are identical metrically, which perhaps occasioned Horace's comment (in an ode which praises him) that he wrote 'in measures freed from rule' (*Odes*, 4.2.11–12); this passage, however, is explained by Viperano as only meaning that 'he, a pioneer, could put as many meters as he wanted together just as it pleased him to combine them' (1.16, 51), and not that his verse was unmetrical.

64.17–22 Rules of verse... discretion and modesty   Scott gives a rule for each of the three components of versification that he has considered – foot, rhyme, and caesura (**60.21–2**) – plus a grammarians' rule about 'orthography or congruity'. The closest analogues for this brief summary of rules are found in Gascoigne and Webbe and help to explicate Scott's rather elliptical remarks. His first rule, 'that no accent be altered in your measures', is ambiguous, corresponding either to the important rule in Gascoigne and Webbe 'that you hold the just measure wherewith you begin your verse' (Gascoigne, *SRLC*, 239; cf. Webbe, *ECE*, I, 268) or – more likely – to the need 'to place every word in his natural emphasis or sound' (Gascoigne, *SRLC*, 239; cf. Webbe, *ECE*, I, 268, 273), a point about the importance of not subjugating natural speech stress to metrical accent that Scott has already glanced at (**61.16–18**). What it might mean for a caesura to 'fall natural' is also unclear: natural for the phrase or word boundary, or natural for the rhythmic/musical structure of the verse line? The points about rhyme are misleading, because they are an apparent compression of Puttenham's strictures:

> But though we have said that to make good concord your several verses should have their cadences like, yet must there be some difference in their orthography, though not in their sound, as if one cadence be *constrain*, the next *restrain*, or one *aspire*, another *respire*, this maketh no good concord, because they are all one, but if ye will exchange both these [initial] consonants of the accented syllable, or void but one of them away, then will your cadences be good and your concord too, as to say: *restrain, refrain, remain; aspire, desire, retire* ... And this may suffice to show the use and nature of your cadences, which are in effect all the sweetness and cunning in our vulgar poesy.   (*Art*, 170)

This use of Puttenham is confirmed by what follows, for having thus ended 2.8 Puttenham commences 2.9, '*How the good maker will not wrench his word to help his rhyme, either by falsifying his accent or by untrue orthography*'. Puttenham's treatment is hamstrung by his preference for visible rhymes: *door* can rhyme with *poor* but *restore* is more of a stretch, so that 'it is better to rhyme *dore* with *restore* than in his truer orthography' (*Art*, 170–1). Scott's briefer remarks are in this case less problematic, and his addition of a point about maintaining 'congruity' – that is, grammatical agreement or (more loosely) correctness of speech (*OED*, *congruity*, n., †4) – is judicious. Scott's allowance for writerly discretion recalls Gascoigne's pragmatism (*SRLC*, 243–4).

64.23 *euphoniae gratia*.   For the sake of good sound; a term from grammar. Cf. Leech, A3ᵛ.

64.24–9 the poet is allowed... *morn* for *morning*, etc.   See **49.13–14n**. Scott follows Puttenham, 3.11 closely, and all his examples are found there (*Art*, 245–6),

Scott selecting one example in each category from the two or three that Puttenham provides. The grammatical figures described here are, respectively, *prothesis*, *epenthesis*, *paragoge*, *aphaeresis*, *syncope*, and *apocope*, and their order is conventional (cf. Diomedes, in Keil, I, 440), but the typical lists are twice as long, so Scott's 'etc.' may imply more than usual.

64.26 *ydone*   Adding a standard Middle English prefix (which was usually *i-*) adopted as a deliberate poetic archaism (often *y-*) by Spenser and his followers (see *OED*, †*i-*, prefix).

64.27 *goldilocks*   See *OED*, *goldilocks*, n., and *goldy*, adj.; the illustrations in *OED* (though there is always a literary bias to these) seem to suggest that both forms are more commonly poetic.

64.27 *spoken*   Not past participle *spoken* but *spoken* as one of the earlier Middle English simple past tense plural forms, which became *spoke* (*OED*, *speak*, v., forms, 3bδ).

64.28 *twixt*   The aphetic form *twixt* is indeed most found in verse texts.

64.28 *ta'en*   Scott's scribe spells it *tane*, a common Elizabethan form.

64.29 *morn*   The derivation of this form (*OED*, *morn*, n.) is more complex than Scott suggests: it is not simply a matter of repeated conscious rhetorical acts of *apocope*. Nevertheless its use is almost exclusively poetic.

64.30–7 To this virtue of sweetness ... rhetoricians' observations   This point follows Puttenham down the page from 3.11, 'Of auricular figures appertaining to single words ...', to 3.12, 'Of auricular figures pertaining to clauses of speech ...':

As your single words may be many ways transfigured to make the meter or verse more tunable and melodious, so also may your whole and entire clauses be in such sort contrived by the order of their construction as the ear may receive a certain recreation, although the mind for any novelty of sense be little or nothing affected. And therefore all your figures of grammatical construction, I account them but merely auricular, in that they reach no further than the ear. To which there will appear some sweet or unsavory point to offer you dolor or delight, either by some evident defect, or surplusage, or disorder, or immutation in the same speeches, notably altering either the congruity grammatical, or the sense, or both.   (*Art*, 246–7)

This rhetorical usage of *auricular* is Puttenham's – he justifies it in the chapter just before the two Scott has used (*Art*, 3.10, 244–5) – and is not found in other English treatments of the figures of speech. On the rhetorical figures see **67.32–4n**.

65.1–7 The painter ... (as they speak)   This is drawn from various parts of Lomazzo, and especially the opening chapter, in which the initial definition of painting is examined point by point (a parallel to Scott's method: see **5.2–36n.**). The italics in the following quotations are Haydocke's. Painting is an art that *'representeth upon a plaine [in piano], the thickenesse and roundenesse of bodily thinges'* (27; Haydocke, B1ᵛ). Lomazzo continues: 'by meere arte, uppon a flat, where it findeth onelie length, and breadth, it representeth to the eie the third Dimension [*la terza dimensione*], which is *roundenesse* and *thicknesse [il rilievo e la grossezza]*: and so maketh the bodie to appeare uppon a flatte, where naturally it is not' (27; B2ʳ). Further on in the same chapter, Lomazzo continues the definition: 'in all this the Painter observeth the *Perspective light [il lume perspettivo]*, without which he can doe nothing'. He then discusses 'raysed, bowed, convexed, and arched lines', 'straight lines', 'hollowe and circular lines', and so on (32; B4ʳ). The discussion of light and shadow is taken up later in the treatise. Book 4 is on light, and its opening states that correct disposition of light and shade 'doth not only adde perfection to the draught, but so *sets it off from the flat*, that it seemes to be imbossed [*come se fosse di rilievo*]' (186; 2M2ʳ). Haydocke customarily translates Lomazzo's 'rilievo' ('relief') with 'emboss-', as Scott does.

65.7 embowed   curved.

65.11–18 Tully saith ... that faculty   A close paraphrase of Cicero, *De optimo genere oratorum*, 3.8. Those who only avoid error 'may be compared to athletes who are fit to promenade in the gymnasium [*in xysto*], but not to seek the prize at Olympia. The prizewinners, though free from all diseases, are not content with merely good health, but seek strength, muscles, blood, and even as it were an attractive tan.'

65.23–6 as we said before ... passionate apprehensions   See **43.24–32**, where *energeia* is examined at the level of matter ('conceit').

65.30–1 that excellentest pattern ... Lamon   Ringler, OP 4 (see **55.1–3n.** and **80.16–18n.**).

65.34–8 the principal force ... as it were unborn   Referring to his earlier discussion (**43.20–4**) and to Cicero, *De oratore*, 3.5.19: 'Every speech consists of matter and words, and the words cannot fall into place if you remove the matter, nor can the matter have clarity if you withdraw the words'; cf. 3.6.24.

66.1–3 Quintilian (tracing Tully) ... before the eye   Scott conflates Quintilian's treatments of *energeia* and amplification, which come in adjacent sections of the *Institutio oratoria*, as well as adding material from an earlier discussion of *energeia*, in which the concept is referred to Cicero (6.2.32, part of Quintilian's discussion of *pathos*: see **45.5–7n.**). Quintilian's discussion of rhetorical ornament begins at 8.3.61 with an extensive discussion of *energeia*, moves on to treat other ornaments that add light to descriptions (including simile), and then turns (in 8.4) to discuss amplification. As well as using Quintilian throughout this passage (**66.1–67.11**), Scott may also be drawing on Hoskyns's extensive treatment of amplification (*Directions*, 131–43; on Scott and Hoskyns see **68.1–4n.**).

66.5–8 then speech . . . wrapped up and straitened   Plutarch, 'Life of Themistocles', 29.3, which Scott is using in North's translation. Themistocles (*c*.524–459 BC) had fled Athens and voluntarily entered the service of the Persian king Artaxerxes I. Themistocles' point is made at their first meeting, when he has not yet mastered Persian, and is about the limitations to his ability to express himself: '*Themistocles* then aunswered him. That mens wordes did properly resemble the stories and imagery in a pece of arras: for both in the one and in the other, the goodly images of either of them are seene, when they are unfolded and layed open. Contrariwise they appeare not, but are lost, when they are shut up, and close folded' (North, 139).

66.9–21 he that saith a city was sacked . . . imagination to work out   A loose and expansive paraphrase of Quintilian, 8.3.67–9. Cf. Hoskyns (*Directions*, 136), on amplification by division.

66.24–5 he pitieth . . . tempers his words   A direct quotation from a manuscript source of Richard Hooker's *A learned discourse of justification* (first printed in 1612), a tractate that 'comprises several sermons . . . delivered shortly before March 1586' (Laetitia Yeandle and Egil Grislis (eds.), *Tractates and sermons*, The Folger Library edition of the works of Richard Hooker, v (Cambridge, Mass., 1990), 83; and 143 for the quoted passage). Hooker alludes to Mark 10:16 ('And he tooke them up in his armes, and put his hands upon them, and blessed them'), and is describing St Paul's attitude to repentant heretics.

66.29–32 heaping our words . . . mind of the reader   Cf. Quintilian, 8.4.1–3 and Hoskyns, *Directions*, 138–9.

66.33–8 Shorten my days . . . my breath   John of Gaunt, in Shakespeare, *Richard II*, 1.3.227–32, with no variants between this and any of the printed texts then available.

67.2–3 a gradation . . . by scale   Scott's terms show that he is thinking in part of the figure *climax* or *gradatio* (Greek and Latin for 'ladder' and 'staircase' respectively, for either of which Scott's 'scale' is a synonym: *OED*, *scale*, n.³, †1 and †3), although Quintilian in the analogous passages of 8.4 (3–9; 26–7) is not thinking in explicitly figurative terms, even in using the word *gradus* (8.4.3, 7, 9; 8.4.26), as he is when he returns to the figure *climax* at 9.3.54–7. Cf. Hoskyns on '*Progression* . . . which by stepps of comparison stores everie degree, till it come to the topp' (*Directions*, 140–1) and Puttenham on 'the Climbing Figure' (*Art*, 292–3).

67.4–5 He lost . . . and life   An example taken from Puttenham's account of the figure *auxesis*, 'or the Advancer', when 'to urge and enforce the matter we speak of, we go still mounting by degrees and increasing our speech with words or with sentences of more weight one than another' (*Art*, 303). Puttenham indicates that the lines are the work of another author; they have not as yet been attributed.

67.6–8 Bartas . . . il tonne   Du Bartas, *La sepmaine*, day 2, 661–2 ('Continually it swirls, it hums, it trembles, it bellows, it buzzes, it roars': Du Bartas, II, 247). The damaged manuscript of Scott's Du Bartas translation breaks off just a few lines before this passage, but clearly these lines come from that project.

67.12–13 a contrary way . . . pithy terms   Cf. Quintilian, 8.3.81–2.

67.13–16 (as Plutarch says) . . . by few words   Plutarch, *Life of Phocion*, 5.3: 'For, as a valuable coin has greatest worth in smallest bulk, so effective speech would seem to indicate much with few words.' Scott returns to this passage immediately below (**67.18–25**). The analogy between words and coins is ubiquitous (cf. **48.34–5n.**): both operate as tokens and the relation between them and the value or thing they represent may be merely conventional. We therefore talk of coining words (e.g. Puttenham, *Art*, 338, on those who like to be seen to 'coin fine words out of the Latin'). Plutarch's analogy is more straightforward than Scott realises, because he is familiar with a different system of coinage. Compare North's Plutarch, Scott's direct source here: 'For like as coynes of gold or silver, the lighter they waye, the finer they be of goodnes: even so the excellencie of speeche consisteth in signifying much, by fewe wordes' (North, 799). It is in North's source, Amyot's French translation of 1559, that Plutarch's 'coin' [*nomismatos*] becomes gold or silver: 'Car tout ainsi comme les pieces d'or ou d'argent sont les meilleures, qui soubz moins de masse ont plus de pris et plus de valeur . . .' (*Les vies des hommes illustres Grecs et Romains* (Paris, 1559), 516ᵛ: 'For just as those gold or silver coins are the best that with less weight have more price and more value . . .'). Plutarch's point is that more precious metals tend to be used for higher-value coins, and they are therefore smaller than coins of lower value, which are made from non-precious metals. But neither Scott nor North (nor Amyot, for that matter) was familiar with coins made without precious metal, and so the point mutates into one about the proportion of silver or gold (fineness) in coins. Plutarch was familiar with coinage both at Rome and in the Greek provinces where the system was recognisably based on that at Rome. Lower-value coins (sestertius, dupondius) were made of bronze and were larger in size and weight than the more valuable silver denarius and gold aureus. In sixteenth-century England, coins were made of gold or silver; there was no bronze, let alone copper or alloys of nickel, tin, zinc, and so forth. Copper coinage was considered but never introduced, although some shopkeepers issued their own lead or tin tokens to allow transactions in small change. When Thomas North (1535–1603?) translated this passage he would have remembered the legacy of the debasement of the coinage under Henry, the issuing of shillings of varying weights and fineness (but constant diameter) under Edward, and the improvements under Elizabeth, with base Edwardian shillings being devalued and countermarked with their new value. This might explain his quite technical emphasis ('the finer they be of goodnes'). Scott would have been better placed than North to notice that a large silver coin might be of lower value than a smaller gold coin of more precious metal, since the gold and silver coinages only overlapped with the introduction in Elizabeth's third coinage of 1583 of large silver crowns and half-crowns, twice the size of their gold equivalents. But in this case he clearly wasn't looking at the Greek; and perhaps had little call for or experience of gold coins. See Andrew Burnett *et al.*, *Roman provincial coinage*, 2 vols. (London and Paris, 1992–9), IIi, 20, 55; R. A. G. Carson, *Coins of the Roman empire* (London, 1990), chs. 15–16, esp. 228–32; and J. J. North, *English hammered coinage, volume II: Edward I to Charles II, 1272–1662* (London, 1991), 16–19 and 130.

67.16–18 Chaucer . . . (saith he)   From the description of the Clerk of Oxford in the General Prologue to Chaucer's *Canterbury tales* (I (A) 306). As printed in *The workes of our antient and lerned English poet, Geffrey Chaucer* (1598), the line reads 'And short and quick, and of full hie sentence' (A3ᵛ).

67.18–25 Phocion . . . mincer of my words   Plutarch, 'Life of Phocion', 5.2–4, in North's translation (continuing the passage Scott has quoted above, **67.13–16**): '. . . by fewe wordes. And touching this matter, it is reported, that the Theater being full of people, *Phocion* walked all alone upon the scaffold where the players played, and was in a great muse with him selfe: whereuppon, one of his friendes seeing him so in his muses, said unto him, Surely *Phocion*, thy minde is occupied about somewhat. In deede so is it, sayd he: for I am thinking with my selfe, if I could abridge any thing of that I have to say to the people. For *Demosthenes* selfe litle esteeming all other Orators, when *Phocion* rose up to speake, he would round his friendes in their eares, and told them: See, the cutter [*kopis*, 'cleaver'] of my wordes riseth' (North, 799). The anecdote is repeated in Plutarch's 'Life of Demosthenes', 10.2–3.

67.25 mincer   See *OED*, *mince*, v., 4d: 'to moderate or restrain (one's language) so as to keep within the bounds of prudence, politeness, or decorum, esp. in phrase *to mince words*, and variants.'

67.26 Veni, vidi . . . Caesar   According to Suetonius (*The lives of the Caesars*, 1.37) the words were displayed at the head of the Triumph for Julius Caesar's victories in Pontus; according to Plutarch ('Caesar', 50) Caesar sent the words as a message to a friend at Rome to announce his success in the same campaign. Puttenham (*Art*, 259) gives Caesar's famous phrase as an example of *asyndeton* (lack of conjunctions). Scott quotes the famous phrase again in his 1605 letter to Cecil (see Appendix 2, 251).

67.27–8 Sallust . . . compactedness of phrase   *Compactedness*: *OED* (*compactedness*, n.) records no usage before 1622. Sallust (86–35 BC), was a Roman historian and contemporary of Caesar, admired by Scott's contemporaries for his concise style (in an age when Roman history was generally popular: there was a similar vogue for Tacitus in Scott's day).

67.29 coloured   Rhetorically ornamented; see **58.36n**.

67.29–30 bold metaphors, presumptuous hyperboles   At the end of the section of
Quintilian that Scott has been following, Quintilian turns to hyperbole briefly (8.4.29),
returning to it at the very end of the book (8.6.67–76), and there considering its relation
to metaphor (8.6.69). Cf. Talaeus on metaphor (in Fraunce's translation): 'But hyperbolicall amplifications and allegories have singular excellencie in a Metaphore, and
therefore commonly they are here most usuall: and by these hyperbolicall metaphores
the speach is made very loftie and full of majestie' (Fraunce, B3^{r–v}).

67.30 *pitchy night*   Scott may be deliberately quoting Shakespeare, who uses 'pitchy
night' in *Venus and Adonis*, l. 821 (also in *All's well that ends well*, 4.4.24, though this was
first printed in 1623). But the phrase was becoming common enough to be proverbial
in the 1590s. Drayton uses it twice, in his set of pastorals, *Idea the shepheards garland
fashioned in nine eglogs* (1593), 30, and in sonnet 45, 'Blacke pytchy Night, companyon
of my woe', in *Ideas mirrour* (1594), G3^{r}. Spenser uses it in *The faerie queene*, 6.7.43.7.
And Scott could have read it in works by Farrant, Middleton, Rous, and Sabie. The
likeliest source, however, may be one of the portions of Sylvester's translation of Du
Bartas already printed by 1599: *The triumph of faith. The sacrifice of Isaac. The ship-
wracke of Ionas* (1592), ₂C2^{r}, ll. 29–30 of 'The ship-wracke of Ionas': 'Or if some beams
break through their pitchy night, | Tis nought but lightnings flashes ful of fright'
(Snyder, II, 728, ll. 913–14). The *Venus and Adonis* and Sylvester examples both occur
in *Englands Parnassus* (1600), 362 and 451.

67.31–2 *frozen heart . . . a flood*   Both now seem so common as to be proverbial,
though there are fewer instances of each pre-1599 than of 'pitchy night'. For 'frozen
heart' see, e.g., Gascoigne's *Jocasta*, 5.4.32 (Pigman, 132), and his 'Dan Bartholmews
dolorous discourses', l. 58 (Pigman, 339), both printed in *A hundreth sundrie flowres*
(1573). A *flood* of tears is of course also a metaphor, albeit one more dead in 1599 than
an *ocean*, for which see, e.g., William Fulbecke, *A booke of Christian ethicks or moral
philosophie* (1587), B3^{r}.

67.32–4 the habit or form . . . very powerful   Having flirted at **64.22–37** with the
first category of Puttenham's idiosyncratic tripartite division of the rhetorical figures
(into 'auricular' figures, 'sensable' figures, and 'sententious figures'), Scott returns to
a more conventional model. *Ad movendum et pervincendum,* 'for moving and completely
conquering', is a quotation from Talaeus, ch. 27 (55), also found in Charles Butler's
adaptations of Talaeus, *Rameae rhetoricae libri duo* (Oxford, 1597) and *Rhetoricae libri
duo* (Oxford, 1598): Butler1, D1^{r}; Butler2, E4^{r}. Cf. Fraunce's translation in *The Arcadian
rhetorike* (Fraunce, E4^{v}–5^{r}): 'These are more forcible and apt to perswade'. Scott follows
Talaeus (probably via Butler) throughout this section on rhetorical ornament. Talaeus
presents a relatively standard division of the figures into (i) tropes (including metaphor,
which Scott has just mentioned, **67.29–30**); (ii) schemes or figures of speech (equivalent
to Puttenham's auricular figures); and (iii) figures of thought, or what Scott calls here

'the habit or form of figurative phrase which the rhetoricians call of the sense or sentence'. Cf. Quintilian, 9.1.17 on figures of thought, 'that is of the mind, feeling or conceptions' (*mentis vel sensus vel sententiarum*). For *sententia*/sentence see further **59.30–1n.**, and an essay on the meanings of the word from Quintilian, 8.5.1–3.

67.35–68.1 passionate exclamations . . . *Oh* or *Alas*   Ch. 28 of Talaeus, following on immediately from the passage quoted above, is on exclamations ('De exclamatione'), and Scott's details are taken from there (Talaeus, esp. 56–8) or from either Butler1 (D1ᵛ–D2ʳ) or Butler2 (E4ʳ–5ʳ). Cf. Fraunce, ch. 27.

68.1–4 interrogations . . . doubted of   Talaeus and Butler do not draw attention to questions, although some of their examples include them. Scott here crosses from Talaeus to John Hoskyns's *Directions for speech and style*, probably written a matter of months before the *Model* (see Introduction, xxxi): 'There are other figures that fitly come in after *Amplificacion*, or any great heate justly inflamed. *Interogation* and *Exclamacion*, *Interogation* is but a warme proposicion, and therefore often times serves more fitlie then a bare affirmacion' (*Directions*, 146). Exclamation and questioning are often neighbours in lists of figures: see, e.g., Puttenham (*Art*, 3.19, 296–8). I have not found the phrase 'warm proposition' in any other English rhetoric book before Hoskyns.

68.5 Pro deum . . . non est?   Terence, *Andria*, 1.5.3, reading 'si haec contumelia non est' for 'si non haec contumelia est', and followed immediately by Scott's English translation. The line is given as an example by Talaeus (57), without that variant. The only English printing also lacks the variant (*Audomari Talaei rhetorica* (Cambridge, 1592), 33) but Scott's reading is shared by Butler1 (D1ᵛ) and Butler2 (E4ᵛ). This suggests strongly that one of Butler's two versions of Talaeus was Scott's direct source.

68.7 tantaene . . . irae?   'Can resentment so fierce dwell in heavenly breasts': Virgil, *Aeneid*, 1.11, given as an example of *apostrophe* by Talaeus (64), Butler1 (D3ʳ), and Butler2 (E6ʳ).

68.8–10 And is there . . . that of Virgil   From the opening, closely modelled on Virgil, of Spenser's mock-epic *Muiopotmos* (on which see **20.35–21.3n.**), ll. 15–16.

68.10–13 The *epiphonema* . . . high state to rear   Talaeus supplements his account of exclamations with a brief point about *epiphonema* (58–9), which is 'a kinde of exclamation when after the discourse ended, we adde some short acclamation, as a conclusion or shutting up of all in wondring wise' (Fraunce, F3ᵛ); he uses this example from Virgil, *Aeneid*, 1.33, as does Puttenham (*Art*, 302), both deriving it from Quintilian, 8.5.11. Cf. Butler1, D2ʳ, and Butler2, E5ʳ. The translation is Scott's.

68.14–22 Likewise, those forms . . . as the rhetoricians show you   Scott briefly summarises the first five of the remaining nine figures of thought dealt with in Talaeus' stripped-down taxonomy in the chapters following that on exclamations: *epanorthosis* (ch. 29), *aposiopesis* (ch. 30), *apostrophe* (ch. 31), *addubitatio* (ch. 33), and *prosopopoeia* (ch. 32). He follows Talaeus' definitions, for the most part closely: (i) 'Epanorthosis correctio est, quando antecedens aliquid revocatur' (Talaeus, 61; '*Epanorthosis* correction, is, when any thing passed is called backe', Fraunce, F6ʳ); (ii) 'Aposiopesis reticentia est, qua sententiae inchoatae cursus ita revocatur, ut inde pars eius aliqua deinceps non dicta intelligatur' (Talaeus, 62; '*Aposiopesis, Reticentia*, concealing, is when the course of a speach begun is in such sort staid, that some part thereof not uttred, is nevertheless perceived', Fraunce, F6ᵛ); conventional accounts emphasise the emotions involved, as Scott does; (iii) 'Apostrophe aversio est, quando oratio ad alienam personam convertitur, quam instituta oratio requirit' (Talaeus, 62; '*Apostrophe* turning away, is when the speach is turned to some such person to whom it was not first prepared', Fraunce, F7ᵛ); (iv) 'Addubitatio ... est deliberatio nobiscum' (Talaeus, 72; 'Addubitation or doubting is a kinde of deliberation with our selves', Fraunce, G7ʳ); (v) 'Prosopopoeia fictio personae, qua velut alienam personam oratione nostra loquentem fingimus', 'Eadem figura, licet mutis et inanimatis rebus sermonem dare' (Talaeus, 65–6, 70; '*Prosopopoia* is a fayning of any person, when in our speach we represent the person of anie, and make it speake as though he were there present', 'By this figure wee sometimes make dumme and senceles things speake', Fraunce, G2ʳ, G5ʳ). All of Talaeus' material is reproduced, in the same order and with only subtle changes of wording, in Butler1 (D2ʳ–5ᵛ) and Butler2 (E5ʳ–8ᵛ). Scott's way of describing in passing a set of figures that are to be found elsewhere in a more detailed taxonomy resembles Cicero's, for example in *De oratore*, 3.53.202–54.208, and Viperano's chapter 'On the embellishment of poetic style' (1.17).

68.25–6 Quintilian saith ... stateliness of it   Paraphrasing Quintilian on the reading of Homer and Virgil by children in order to add knowledge of 'what is morally excellent' to that of 'what is eloquent' (1.8.4): 'It is therefore an admirable practice which now prevails, to begin by reading Homer and Vergil ... let his mind be lifted by the sublimity of heroic verse, inspired by the greatness of its theme and imbued with the loftiest sentiments' (1.8.5).

68.29–69.1 what we made above ... bodily motions   See **17.12–18.36**, esp. **18.16–36**. For 'differences and properties' see **5.24–31n.**, and cf. **78.7**. Scott refers to the very opening of the *Poetics*, 1447a–1448a. Scott's three categories are Aristotle's objects, mode, and media, though he changes Aristotle's order, which is to divide the *genus* poetry by the three *differentia* of media, objects, and mode (1447a16–18). Compare Viperano, 2.1 (67), where the order is as in Aristotle. The *media* might be colours and shapes for the visual arts, or harmony and rhythm for instrumental music; for poetry they are, at least, speech or verse, plus rhythm (including bodily movement) and song (1447a18–b29). The *objects* 'are people doing things, and these people must necessarily be either good or bad' (1448a1–2). The *mode* 'in which one represents each of these objects' might be '(i) sometimes in narration and sometimes becoming something else, as Homer does, or (ii) speaking in one's own person without change, or (iii) with all the people engaged in the *mimēsis* actually doing things' (1448a19–24). Aristotle continues: 'So, if we use one of them, Sophocles will be in the same class as Homer, since both represent people as good, and if we use another, he will be in the same class as Aristophanes, since they both represent people as actively doing things' (1448a25–8). Scaliger, 1.3 (6), and Viperano, 1.7 and 2.1 (19, 67–8), outline the three modes, but they were also familiar from Book 3 of Diomedes' *Ars grammatica* (Keil, I, 482), reordered for clarity: (i) narrative; (ii) dramatic / mimetic / dialogistic; (iii) mixed. See also **18.24–5n.**, where Scott first introduces the distinction. Viperano, 1.7, emphasises the binary Aristotelian division of poetry by whether it represents good or bad actions (20).

69.1–3 we may now for our memory . . . before your eye This sort of chart – though its use in an English work of poetics is unprecedented – was popular in sixteenth-century scholarship and has come to be associated in particular with Ramism, especially when using the kind of binary logic that Scott employs. The chart in fact ignores the Aristotelian *difference* of *media* (since these are all poems), Scott having made the reasonable point ('lastly (which we comprised under this last if it belong to the poet)', **68.35–6**) that as far as poetry is concerned the category of *media* is collapsed into the category of *mode*. Scott also introduces the *accidents* (see **5.24–31n.**) of 'solemnly' and 'vulgarly'. A further simplification in the interests of binary division is of the three modes into two, by conflating the poem in narrative that includes direct speech (Diomedes' mixed mode; e.g. epic and lyric) with the poem in a single narrated voice (the examples in Diomedes are mostly historical or didactic, including Hesiod, Lucretius, and Virgil's *Georgics*). This makes some sense, since lyric clearly crosses between the narrative and mixed categories (it can be in a single voice; it can include more than one voice). It is also a possible reading of Aristotle's Greek (see *ALC*, 93n.1), one apparently supported by Aristotle's binary distinction between tragedy and (narrative) epic at 1449b9–12. Scott's six kinds come close to the six of Diomedes (Keil, I, 502), as reported by Viperano, 1.7 (18): heroic, tragic, comic, melic, satiric, and dithyrambic (Viperano gives choriambic). Cf. Sidney's 'special denominations . . . heroic, lyric, tragic, comic, satiric, iambic, elegiac, pastoral and certain others' (*DP*, 11); and for Scott's enlarging of the lyric category (to absorb elegy and related subgenres), see **25.21–2n.**

69.5–7 the heroical . . . most eminently Aristotle (*Poetics*, 1459b–60a) considers some respects in which epic has the advantage over tragedy, including size (1459b22–31) and greater scope for the marvellous (1460a11–17), but at 1462a14–b15 he argues clearly that tragedy has everything that epic has, and more, and so is superior (and cf. 1449b9–20).

69.9 or as high Some text may be missing, or the scribe may have misread.

69.9–10 His particular . . . admiration (saith Aristotle) Aristotle nowhere gives a definition of epic, as he does for tragedy (1449b), though he does see epic as better suited to the production of wonder, or admiration, than tragedy (1460a). Many Renaissance Aristotelian critics promoted wonder in their definitions of poetry, tragedy, or the aesthetic effect, including Sidney. See further **18.25–8n.**

69.10–12 (according to Sir Philip Sidney)... most excellent truth From Sidney's account of 'the heroical' in the *Defence*: 'who doth not only teach and move to a truth, but teacheth and moveth to the most high and excellent truth' (*DP*, 29).

69.12–14 drawing the portraiture... worthiest good Following the same passage in Sidney more loosely, and copying Scott's own earlier definition (see **18.25–8n.**).

69.17–18 under-kind Subgenre (*OED*, †*under-kind*, n.: 'A subspecies; an inferior or lower kind', first recorded usage 1571). Scott returns to the question of the heroic subgenres at **76.3–13.**

69.22–5 Horace shows in Homer... monstravit Homerus Horace, *Ars poetica*, 73–4, reading present indicative *possunt* for imperfect subjunctive *possent*. Scott's prose translation, immediately following (69.26–7), is accurate.

69.29 Arma... cano *Aeneid*, 1.1: 'Arms I sing and the man'. An imitation of Homer, *Iliad*, 1.1 ('The wrath sing, goddess, of Peleus' son, Achilles').

70.2 Canto... capitano 'I sing of holy war and the captain...': the opening line of Tasso's *Gerusalemme liberata* (1581), on which see **18.4–5n.**

70.3 Spenser another Tasso The proem to Book 1 of *The faerie queene* begins with an imitation of the opening of the *Aeneid*, including the spurious lines surveying the poet's pastoral and georgic career, building to: 'And sing of Knights and Ladies gentle deeds' (1.pr.1.5). See **73.4–5n.** and **73.5–7n.**

70.5–6 that passion... saith Musidorus Scott alludes to Musidorus' moral lecture in Book 1 of the *Arcadia* on the evils of amorous love, delivered to Pyrocles just before Musidorus himself falls in love: 'as the love of heaven makes one heavenly, the love of vertue, vertuous... this effeminate love of a woman, doth so womanize a man, that (if hee yeeld to it) it will not onely make him an *Amazon*; but a launder, a distaff-spinner; or what so ever other vile occupation their idle heads can imagin and their weake hands performe' (*NA*, D5ᵛ; Skretkowicz, 72). For Scott's other uses of this episode see **16.9–11, 26.3–4,** and **82.25–7.** Sidney deals less bluntly than Scott with the problem that much heroic poetry is concerned with amorous matters (*DP*, 35).

70.10–11 carpet poets Modelled on *carpet-knight*, 'a contemptuous term for a knight whose achievements belong to "the carpet" (i.e. the lady's boudoir, or carpeted chamber) instead of to the field of battle; a stay-at-home soldier' (*OED*, *carpet-knight*, n.). *OED*'s first and only recorded usage of *carpet poet* is from 1854 (*OED*, *carpet*, n., C2a(c)).

70.13 unbilled   Dismissed: see **48.10–11n**.

70.14 *Amadis de Gaule*   A chivalric prose romance, Spanish originally (and first printed in 1508), *Amadis* and its many sequels were known in England principally through a series of French translations printed from 1540 onwards, and amounting to twenty-four books.

70.15–17 Monsieur de la Noue . . . Machiavel for the aged   François de la Noue (1531–91) was a Huguenot military leader in the French religious wars of the later sixteenth century, who also fought in the Low Countries. He wrote his *Discours politiques et militaires* (Basle, 1587) in captivity and it appeared almost immediately after its publication in an English translation by Edward Aggas. The sixth discourse is entitled: 'Que la lecture des livres d'Amadis n'est moins pernicieuse aux jeunes gens, que celle des livres de Machiavel aux vieux', translated as 'That the reading of the bookes of Amadis de Gaule, and such like is no lesse hurtful to youth, than the works of Machiavel to age' (*The politicke and militarie discourses of the Lord de La Nowe* ('1587' [i.e. 1588]), G4ʳ). Scott probably used the French text. Francis Meres, *Palladis tamia* (1598), in the section headed 'A choice is to be had in reading of bookes' cites Noue's essay from the title of the Aggas translation, and follows it with a long list of proscribed romances (268ʳ⁻ᵛ).

70.15–16 he so well both knew and did   That is, he represented an Aristotelian ideal combination of knowledge and action. See *Nicomachean ethics*, 1.1–3 on politics as the 'master art' (1094a27) and how 'the end aimed at [in political science] is not knowledge but action' (1095a5–6); cf. Sidney on 'the end of well-doing and not of well-knowing only' (*DP*, 13) and 'as Aristotle saith, it is not *gnōsis* but *praxis* must be the fruit' (*DP*, 22). Cf. **20.24–5n**.

70.17–19 Sir Philip Sidney . . . that effeminate invention   *Diminishing*: disparaging; see **52.39n**. What Sidney says is more equivocal: 'Truly, I have known men that even with reading *Amadis de Gaule*, which God knoweth wanteth much of a perfect poesy, have found their hearts moved to the exercise of courtesy, liberality, and especially courage' (*DP*, 23).

70.21–5 the heroical poet . . . triumph upon his head   Cf. Sidney, on comedy: 'who seeth not the filthiness of evil wanteth a great foil to perceive the beauty of virtue' (*DP*, 27). This point, rather marginal to Sidney's *Defence*, is crucial to a Sidneian account of the practice of Sidney and Spenser.

70.29–71.7 we will with Vives distinguish . . . to succeed after   The whole passage is a close translation, with some elaboration, of a discussion of the teaching of moral philosophy to the young in the *De disciplinis* (Antwerp, 1531) of Juan Luis Vives (1493–1540), Spanish humanist and sometime tutor to the future Queen Mary. Vives remained a popular writer in England and lies behind some celebrated passages in Ben

Jonson's *Discoveries*. Scott quotes from the second part of *De disciplinis, De tradendis disciplinis* ('On the transmission of knowledge'). See *De disciplinis* (Cologne, 1536), 2B3ᵛ; English text: *Vives: On education*, trans. Foster Watson (Cambridge, 1913), 254–5.

70.30 noughty   Bad, immoral, wicked (*OED, noughty*, adj., †1, †2).

71.13–14 Apelles drew . . . want of one eye   Apparently paraphrasing Quintilian, 2.13.12 ('Apelles painted Antigonus in profile, to conceal the blemish caused by the loss of one eye [*ut amissi oculi deformitas lateret*]'); though the anecdote is also in Pliny, 35.36.90. Antigonus I (*c*.382–301 BC) was a Macedonian nobleman who governed Greater Phrygia for Alexander the Great. For Apelles see **17.15n.**

71.14–16 our Italian painters . . . better hidden shames   Scott is thinking of the newly unrestrained representation of violence, nudity, and eroticism in the historical and mythological paintings of such artists as Titian (e.g. Titian's *The rape of Lucretia*).

71.16 Pictoribus atque poetis   Horace, *Ars poetica*, 9–10. Scott's irony is Horace's too to an extent: '"Painters and poets," you say, "have always had an equal right in hazarding anything." We know it: this licence we poets claim and in our turn we grant the like; but not so far that savage should mate with tame, or serpents couple with birds, lambs with tigers' (9–13). Scott uses this passage earlier: see **11.34–5.**

71.18–20 Virgil is esteemed . . . this distinction   Cf. Viperano's chapter, 2.4., 'On the nature or form of the epic': 'if the disposition of the story should incidentally include anything disgraceful, the poet will either touch on it lightly, intelligently conceal it, or discreetly obscure it – so that, while he censures vice, he should not use indecent expressions . . . And so he certainly understood little who described Virgil as being too pure [*castum*]' (77/75–6).

71.20–4 in expressing the love . . . end and issue   Book 4 of the *Aeneid* concerns the love of Dido for Aeneas. Dido keeps this hidden too (*Aeneid*, 4.1–2), and when she and Aeneas seek refuge from a storm in a cave while hunting, Virgil draws a veil of euphemism over what happens (166–72). The book ends, after Aeneas leaves to pursue his imperial destiny, with Dido's suicide.

71.25 a posteriori . . . by the effects   Reasoning from effects to causes or inductively (literally 'from what comes after') rather than *a priori* ('from what is before') or deductively. *OED* first recorded usage 1624, but cf. Euclid, *The elements of geometrie* (1570), 9ʳ: 'A demonstration *a posteriori*, or resolution is, when . . . we passe from the last conclusion made by the premisses, and by the premisses of the premisses, continually ascending, til we come to the first principles and grounds, which are indemonstrable, and for theyr simplicity can suffer no farther resolution.'

71.25–9 If Tasso . . . disgrace and reproach   The Syrian sorceress Armida is sent by her uncle to seduce the Christian camp in cantos 4 and 5 of Tasso's *Gerusalemme liberata* (on which see **18.4–5n.**). Tasso's lavish description of her charms is periodically undercut by comment on her motives and supplemented by some detailed analysis of her methods (e.g. 4.85–96).

71.29–33 If Heliodorus . . . high or hardy attempt   In Heliodorus' *Aithiopika* (see **19.24–31n.** and **36.4–9n.**). Theagenes and Charikleia are notable in romance for their continence (the conclusion even features a test of virginity that both pass).

71.34 that of Ariosto . . . chaste ears?   On Ariosto's *Orlando furioso* see **19.24–31n.** and **35.7–10n.** Ariosto's knights and ladies are all motivated by love, and it is the love of Angelica and Medoro (Ariosto describes its consummation if not graphically then plainly) that causes Orlando's madness.

71.35–6 self-convinced Ovid . . . 'teneros ne tange poetas!'   'Touch not the poets of love [literally, 'the soft poets']': Ovid, *Remedia amoris* ('The remedies for love'), 757.

71.36–7 as Bartas saith . . . wanton argument   Urania's advice to Du Bartas in *L'Uranie*. See, e.g., 165–6 (Du Bartas, II, 181; in James VI's translation: 'Let not your art so rare then be defylde, | In singing *Venus* and her fethred chylde', in *The essayes of a prentise, in the divine art of poesie* (Edinburgh, 1584), F1ʳ). See further **42.19–21n.** Scott may also be thinking of the proem to Day 2 of *La sepmaine*, the passage he quotes at **72.3–6.**

71.37–9 Ovid was banished . . . just exile?   Ovid (43 BC–AD 17) was banished by Augustus in AD 8 to Tomis on the Black Sea, living in exile there until his death. Scott refers to *Tristia*, 2, in which Ovid speaks of 'two crimes, a poem and a blunder [*carmen et error*]' (207), on only one of which he may elaborate: that he has been punished for writing the *Ars amatoria* ('Art of love'). The explanation popular in Scott's day – though Scott seems not to be thinking of this – was that the 'error' was an affair with the Emperor's granddaughter Julia. See, for example, the depiction of the affair and Ovid's punishment in Ben Jonson's play *Poetaster* (performed 1601, printed 1602).

71.40–1 Uriah's letters . . . to the bearer   Uriah was a soldier in King David's army and the husband of Bathsheba, who was pregnant by David; David had Uriah murdered in battle by ordering Joab, in a letter given to Uriah himself to deliver: 'Put ye Uriah in the forefront of the strength of the battell, and recule [recoil] yee backe from him, that he may be smitten, and die' (II Samuel 11:15). Scott has earlier referred to the next episode in II Samuel, in which Nathan uses a fable to tell David of God's displeasure (**40.33–6**).

71.41–72.6 divine Bartas . . . la vierge puisse lire   Day 2 of *La sepmaine*, 27–30 (Du Bartas, II, 223). Scott inserted 'j'ai' above the line after the scribe had omitted it.

In this case, the scribe may have been copying faithfully, since some editions of Du Bartas share that omission. See Textual Introduction, lxxxii.

72.7–10 For me ... therein delight The version in Scott's incomplete translation of Days 1 and 2 reads 'virgins *may* therein delight' and 'The poet's resolution' in the margin (Add. MS 81083, 66ʳ).

72.12–14 we showed the heroical kind ... the *narration* itself Scaliger analyses tragedy and comedy into their parts (1.9), but not epic. Scott here follows the medieval, rhetorical scheme for narrative form, divided into the three parts of *propositio*, *invocatio*, and *narratio*, as outlined in Viperano's chapter, 2.5, on the parts of epic (77). The scheme is of limited use: in Virgil, for example, the three parts cover, respectively, 7 lines, 4 lines, and 9,885 lines. Quintilian, in considering Homer's eloquence, asks: 'in the few lines with which he introduces both of his epics, has he not, I will not say observed, but actually established the law which should govern the composition of the exordium?' (10.1.48).

72.14–15 The proposition ... in the history The *Methodus* (1566) of Jean Bodin (1530–96) is in fact a reaction against the rhetorical approach to the writing of history. Scott is remembering a passing remark (pp. 70–1 in the 1566 edition) in a passage in which Bodin is questioning the right of the Greek historian Diodorus Siculus to be ranked with the major historians: 'Correctly and in order, it is true, he set forth at the beginning of each book those things which he was about to say' (John Bodin, *Method for the easy comprehension of history*, trans. Beatrice Reynolds (New York, 1945), 66). For Bodin's criticisms of the rhetorical analysis of history writing see the 'Procemium' (1566 edn, 8; Reynolds, 14). For history-writing as oration see, e.g., Lucian, *How to write history*, 52–5 (*ALC*, 545).

72.15–16 It must be ... modest and short Following Viperano, 2.5 (78–81/77–80): 'just as the statement of the theme ought to be simple, it ought also to be brief [*Atque ut simplex, ita etiam brevis debet esse propositio*]' (79/78).

72.16–18 You must not profess ... arrogant a promise *Ars poetica*, 136–9, a passage referred to at **30.39–40**: 'you are not to begin as the Cyclic poet of old: "Of Priam's fate and famous war I'll sing." What will this boaster produce in keeping with such mouthing? Mountains will labour, to birth will come a laughter-rousing mouse!' Viperano also cites these lines (80).

72.18–20 if Lucan ... not unreprovable On Daniel and Lucan see **12.12–13n.** and **19.24–31n.** Daniel was frequently compared to Lucan by his contemporaries: see, e.g., Meres, *Palladis tamia* (1598), 281ʳ; Guilpin, *Skialetheia* (1598), E1ʳ ('a Lucanist'); and Camden, *Remaines* (1605), 6 ('our *Lucan*'). The 97-line proem to Lucan's *Pharsalia* was imitated closely in the 56-line proem to Daniel's *Civil wars* (1595). Lucan's lacks an invocation since for him Caesar is muse enough (1.63–6); Daniel, similarly, invokes 'no muse but' Queen Elizabeth (ll. 25–6). As Viperano observes, the first 7 lines of Lucan's proem are the *propositio* proper, the rest a digression (81).

72.20–2 It needs … attention at his hands   Cf. Viperano: 'The reader, of course, should not be held up by words in the statement of theme. Once he has learned the conclusion and scope of the events, he hurries on to the narrative' (78).

72.22–30 The invocation … proved offensive   Scott is close to Viperano, but parts company from him in his insistence on a Christian framework; Viperano is only discussing classical poetry and therefore has no problem recommending an invocation to the gods or the Muses (80).

72.25–6 né si comincia … *Pastor fido*   Guarini, *Il pastor fido* ('The faithful shepherd'), 1.1.26: 'And without Prayer no work is well begun', in Fanshawe's 1647 translation.

72.28 Every good … father of lights   James 1:17; Scott cites a later verse in James 1 at **31.8–12**. This translation seems to be Scott's own compressed paraphrase, though the wording coincides exactly with Ralph Brownrig, *Twenty five sermons* (1664), 279. Both the Vulgate and the Greek New Testament match the more expansive form of Geneva and other English versions: 'Every good giving [gift in some translations], and every perfect gift is from above, and commeth downe from the Father of lightes'.

72.34–73.3 the invocation of Josuah Sylvester … proposition or argument   Sylvester had published fragments of his Du Bartas as early as 1592, but in 1598 he published an extended portion of *La seconde sepmaine* as *The second weeke or childhood of the world*. His own interjections are honestly marked in italics; in this case eighteen lines translating Du Bartas's opening (of which around six lines might be called the invocation) are followed by a forty-line invocation in Sylvester's voice, including a digression wishing that other contemporary English poets would follow his example in writing on divine themes (Snyder, I, 316–17). Scott may not have been the only one to criticise Sylvester for this imbalance. When his translation of the first Week appeared in 1605, the balance between Du Bartas (12 lines) and a similar supplement (14 lines) was better. Despite this criticism, Scott in his translation of Du Bartas nevertheless imitates Sylvester's practice in adding his own, indented, interjections, though they are shorter – four lines in this case.

73.3–4 Now some join … Homer and Bartas   Cf. Viperano, 2.5: 'Now the Greeks, of course, combined the invocation and statement of theme, and the Latins separated them' (80). (i) Homer, *Iliad*, 1.1: 'The wrath sing, goddess, of Peleus' son, Achilles'; *Odyssey*, 1.1–2: 'Tell me, Muse, of the man of many devices, driven far astray after he had sacked the sacred citadel of Troy', etc. (ii) Du Bartas, in Scott's translation: 'O Thou that guid'st the course of the flame-bearinge spheares; [margin: 'Invocation'] | The waters fomye bitt, Seas sov'reigne, you that beares, | That mak'st the Earth to tremble, whose worde onely byndes, | And slackes th'unruly raynes, to thy swifte postes the wyndes; | Heave up my soule to thee, my spiritts dull refyne, | And, with a curious skill, enrich this worke of myne; | O father graunte to me, that in a gratious phraze, [margin: 'Argument'] | To all posteritye, the wordles Berth I maye blaze', etc. (British Library, Add. MS 81083, 53ʳ, 1–8).

73.4–5 other have beside . . . as Virgil Referring to the spurious four lines, possibly written by Virgil at a draft stage and subsequently rejected, that are found before 'Arma virumque cano' in some early texts. For Virgil's opening see **52.16–19n.** and **69.29n.**

73.5–7 some again . . . *Faerie Queene* Canto 1 of *The faerie queene* begins *in medias res*, but is preceded by a separate 4-stanza proem which imitates Virgil's opening (including the spurious addition) closely and includes both proposition and invocation (of pagan muse and gods, to Scott's disapproval, before turning to Queen Elizabeth).

73.7–8 some have neither . . . *Arcadia* The *Arcadia* begins, in imitation of Heliodorus, *in medias res*; the work is prefaced by Sidney's dedication to his sister.

73.11–12 For the whole . . . proportionable and beautiful *Poetics*, 1450b34–1451a6; see also **35.23–5n.**, and cf. *Poetics*, 1459a17–b7 and Viperano, e.g. 1.9 (25). Scott is essentially transplanting Aristotle's formalist (and organic) analysis of tragedy to the ground of epic, and in doing so is in part following Viperano, who had generalised Aristotle's analysis in his first book, treating the structure and form of the plot or *fabula* (1.8–12) before turning to distinguish epic from tragedy and the other kinds in his second book.

73.12–13 this narration is called a *fable* . . . actions of men Following Viperano's chapter, 1.8, 'De imitatione, sive fabula' ('On imitation, or the story'): 'But the imitation belonging to poetry consists of the fictional representation of human actions, which the Greeks call *myth*, and the Latins at one time fiction, at another story [*Est autem poeticae imitatio . . . humanarum actionum fictio, quam Graeci muthon, Latini tum fictionem, tum fabulam vocant*]' (28–9/23). Scott's 'fable', *fabula* in Viperano and other contemporary translations and discussions of Aristotle, corresponds throughout to Aristotle's *muthos*, 'plot'.

73.14 conveniency and aptness Decorum: see **33.31–36.33** and **57.16–58.13** for Scott's extensive discussions.

73.15–22 which form is called . . . war and in peace All this – including Aristotle's universals – broadly follows Viperano, 1.8 (24), supplemented by his later discussion of the *Aeneid*'s allegory at 2.3 (72).

73.18 universal nature One of Scott's very few authorial second thoughts is found here. The original manuscript reading was 'universal form', but Scott crossed out 'form' ['forme' in the manuscript] and replaced it with 'nature'. The effect is to move the formulation away from Platonic ideas or forms and towards Aristotelian universals. See Textual Introduction, lxxxi.

73.19–22 as we showed above... and in peace   See **19.35–7**.

73.22–6 not all the life... evident unshapeliness   Closely following Viperano, 1.9, 'On the structure of the story' (25–6). (i) *inconvenience*: incongruity, inconsistency (*OED, inconvenience*, n., †1); (ii) *unshapeliness*: although *unshapely* is found by *OED* as early as *c*.1200 (*OED, unshapely*, adj.), the first recorded usage for the noun is an improbably late 1741 (*OED, unshapeliness*, n.); I have found only one instance before Scott, in *Hypnerotomachia. The strife of love in a dreame* (1592), c2^r.

73.26–8 And the artists... excellent poems have not   Viperano, following Aristotle, stresses that poetry deals in fictions, even when there is some basis in fact: 'the historian describes particular events, while the poet... describes the nature of events' (24). Horace, *Ars poetica*, 119 ('Either follow tradition or invent what is self-consistent') is in line with Aristotle, *Poetics*, 1455a34–b1. However unhistorical the subject matter of ancient and Renaissance epic appears to us now, it was thought to be based in actual events. Scott, however, allows for entirely invented plot material within a recognisable, verisimilar, framework ('reference to some place and time being').

73.30–2 though Aristotle say... so narrowly   *Poetics*, 1449b (see further **76.41–77.28n**.). Cf. Viperano, in his chapter on 'Where the narrative in the epic ought to begin' (2.6), which Scott is following closely: 'And although Aristotle may not think that the epic, like tragedy, is to be contracted within some space of time, nevertheless epic poets should begin at the middle or end and not at the beginning of a sequence of events that covers numerous years' (85).

73.32–3 Some will tie... two years' efficiency   Although Viperano twice repeats that epic is not limited in time (30; 75), in the chapter Scott is following here, 2.6, he reports that 'some also confine the events which epics imitate to a fixed interval of time, usually one year or at the most two' (84). On *efficiency* see **76.41–77.1n**.

73.34–5 if it be much longer... too huge and vast   Scott is looking at Aristotle's discussion of the need for unity in epic plot: Homer shows his excellence in not attempting a poem of the entire war, 'even though it had a beginning and an end. For the plot would have been too large and not easy to see as a whole, or if it had been kept to a moderate length it would have been tangled because of the variety of events' (*Poetics*, 1459a31–4). However, Aristotle stops short of insisting on limits to an epic poem's length or to the scale of its chronology, since epic has much greater licence to vary the time, place, and kind of the episodes it narrates (1459b18–31). Cf. also Aristotle's discussion of the amplitude of (tragic) plot (1450b34–1451a15).

73.38–40 the ancient heroical ... and Tasso Cf. Viperano, 2.6 (84); Scott adds Tasso.

73.40–74.4 Sir Philip Sidney ... his whole invention In fact a misreading of the end of Sidney's *Arcadia*, where Sidney lists the various unresolved plot strands that 'may awake some other spirite to exercise his penne in that, wherewith mine is already dulled' (*NA*, 2s3ᵛ; *OA*, 417).

74.6–14 Now for the parts ... which is the resolution Scott's use of the accusative forms of *desis* and *lusis* ('The first he calls δέσιν [*desin*], the other λύσιν [*lusin*]') suggests that he is either following Viperano's chapter 'De fabulae partibus' ('On the parts of the story', 1.12) or thinking in Latin. Compare Viperano (41/36): 'Eas [partes] Aristoteles videtur effecisse duas, Colligationem, et Solutionem: illam *desin*, hanc *lusin* appellavit' ('Aristotle seems to have made out two [parts]: the complication and the resolution. The former he called *a binding*, the latter *a loosening*'). Viperano himself follows Aristotle closely: 'Part of every tragedy is the complication, part the dénouement: the preliminaries and often some of the action proper are the complication, the rest the dénouement. By "complication" I mean the section from the beginning to the last point before he begins to change to good or bad fortune, by "dénouement" the part from the beginning of the change to the end' (*Poetics*, 1455b24–9). The metaphors of pregnancy are not Aristotle's as Scott seems to suggest, and neither are they implicit in the Greek terms *desis* ('binding together') and *lusis* ('loosing', 'solution') or those with which Aristotle glosses them. Scott in fact builds the pregnancy metaphor on a remark in Viperano's earlier discussion of episodes (1.10), perhaps encouraged by Horace's 'twin egg' (see **74.15–16n.**): 'And this is what it seems to me Aristotle meant when he was discussing episodes, that the womb, as it were, of the poem grows from the interpolation of past actions [*praeteritis actionibus interpositis quasi uterum poematis accrescere*]' (36/30).

74.14–18 Your collection or conception ... as it were the heart Loosely following Viperano, 2.6 ('Where the narrative in the epic ought to begin'; see esp. 83–4). Viperano points out that the beginning of an epic is the beginning of the particular story being told (so that the *Iliad* begins with the causes of the wrath of Achilles); even if that particular story is the middle or end of some larger history, it is therefore still correct to say that it begins at the beginning and not in the middle or at the end.

74.15–16 gemino ab ovo 'From the twin egg': *Ars poetica*, 147, before recommending that the poet begin 'in the midst of things': 'Nor does he begin ... the war of Troy from the twin eggs' [*nec gemino bellum Troianum orditur ab ovo*]'. The twin eggs were the eggs from which – after her rape by Zeus in the form of a swan – Leda's offspring Castor and Pollux, and Helen and Clytemnestra were born, so the meaning is 'from the birth of Helen of Troy'.

74.18–20 (as Pindar sang)... resplendently beautiful *Olympian Odes*, 6.4. The ode opens with Scott's favourite metaphor of the poem as building: 'Let us set up golden columns to support the strong-walled porch of our abode | and construct, as it were, a splendid | palace; for when a work is begun, it is necessary to make | its front [*prosōpon*] shine from afar [*tēlauges*, 'far-shining']' (1–4).

74.20–4 Virgil, after this rule... all his frame Following Viperano, 2.6 (85), and cf. Viperano, 1.10 (a chapter on episodes and digressions, 30).

74.21 sea-fare See *OED*, *sea-fare*, n., 2: 'Travel by sea, a sea-voyage. *Obs.* exc. *dial.*' (first recorded usage 1601).

74.36–8 Now (saith Aristotle)... sections and books *Poetics*, 1452b14–27, after Aristotle has discussed *peripeteia*, *anagnorisis*, and *pathos*, and some while before he discusses *desis* and *lusis*: 'So much for the parts of tragedy that one ought to use as qualitative elements. Now for the category of quantity and the quantitative divisions of a tragedy: they are prologue, episode, *exodos*, choral part, the last being divided into *parodos* and *stasimon*.' On discrete quantity see **59.14n**.

74.38–75.1 this division (as Quintilian speaks... what is to come Quintilian, 4.5.22–3, discussing the section of an oration known as the *partitio* or *divisio*, in which the orator enumerates the various points and propositions at issue: 'For it not only makes our arguments clearer by isolating the points from the crowd in which they would otherwise be lost and placing them before the eyes of the judge, but relieves his attention by assigning a definite limit to certain parts of our speech, just as our fatigue upon a journey is relieved by reading the distances on the milestones which we pass. For it is a pleasure to be able to measure how much of our task has been accomplished, and the knowledge of what remains to do stimulates us to fresh effort over the labour that still awaits us.' On *divisio* and *partitio* cf. Quintilian, 7.1.1.

75.2–5 those that attend... rest may be made The reference to a full point suggests that Scott's use of the metaphor of breaking up journeys may also be suggested by Puttenham's analogy between periodic sentence structure and a day's journey in his chapter on caesura (2.5: *Art*, esp. 164), based ultimately on Demetrius: 'Inns at frequent intervals make long journeys shorter, while desolate roads, even when the distance is short, give the impression of length. The same principle applies to clauses' (*On style*, 47).

75.7 unconvenient Inappropriate, unfitting.

75.7–11 the course an ambassador... receipt and entertainment (i) *mikroprepeia*: shabbiness; (ii) *heneka*: on account of, for the sake of. No source identified, though Scott could have encountered the word *mikroprepeia* in a number of places: Aristotle opposes *mikroprepeia* to *megaloprepeia* (grandeur or magnificence, where money is concerned) in *Nicomachean ethics*, 1107b17–20, *Rhetoric*, 1366b18–20, and *Magna Moralia*, 1192a–b; Plutarch describes Solon's encounter with Croesus and the former's judgement of the latter's display of wealth as *mikroprepeia* (Solon, 27.3); Quintilian (4.2.61) has *megaloprepeia* as a stylistic quality (cf. Dionysius, *On literary composition*, 11); and it is Demetrius' term for the grand style (*On style*, 36 and *passim*), with *mikroprepeia* as its opposite (*On style*, 83; cf. 53).

75.8–9 small-seemingness Neither *small-seemingness* nor *small-seeming* is in *OED*; *seemingness* is included with a first recorded usage of 1640 (*OED*, *seemingness*, n.).

75.10 bait Food.

75.10 dorp Village (*OED*, *dorp*, n. = Dutch *dorp*; cf. German *Dorf*, Old English *Þorp*).

75.12 Virgil...precedent Scaliger, 3.96 (regulations specific to epic): 'an author should divide his book into chapters [*libellos*, 'books'] in imitation of nature, which subdivides into parts of parts, all so related that they constitute an organic body. But in doing this, you should so assign each part to its proper place that the book shall seem to have shaped itself inevitably, an achievement perfectly realised only by the divine Maro [Virgil]. If one will read the *Aeneid* attentively, he will see that it conforms to this principle' (144d1–a2; Padelford, 55).

75.12–13 Bartas...*Judith* *Judith* (on which see **19.40–1n.**) is divided into six books.

75.13–14 the *Faerie Queene*...cut into members Six of a projected twelve (or twenty-four) books of *The faerie queene* were published in Spenser's lifetime (1–3 in 1590; 4–6 in 1596), with a fragment of a seventh appearing in 1609. Each book comprises twelve cantos. Sidney's *Arcadia* was originally written in five books or acts; the revised *Arcadia* breaks off in the middle of the third book, with the composite *Arcadia* of 1593 adding an ending from the 'old' *Arcadia* to make up five books as originally planned. In its first printed edition of 1590, the editors subdivided the books into chapters, though these divisions were removed in the 1593 edition, on which all subsequent printings were based.

75.15–16 The numbers...strictly prescribed Nevertheless, epic poems often deal in multiples of six (as Du Bartas recognises in *Judith*): Virgil's *Aeneid* imitates the twenty-four books of Homer's *Odyssey* in Books 1–6 and the twenty-four books of the *Iliad* in Books 7–12. Practice is less consistent for prose romances: Sidney's *Arcadia* has five books or acts to hint at a dramatic affiliation for his plot structure (on act division see **77.29–78.1**). Heliodorus' *Aithiopika* has ten books; Achilles Tatius' *Leukippe and Kleitophon* has eight; Longus' *Daphnis and Chloe* four.

75.17–18 for your style . . . rich and high   For the association between epic and the grand style see, e.g., Viperano, 2.3 (73); and cf. **57.20.**

75.18–24 your verse . . . as in the ancient   *Poetics*, 1459b31–5: 'The heroic verse was found suitable from experience. For if anyone were to make a narrative *mimēsis* in any other metre or in many metres, it would be obviously unsuitable, as the heroic metre is the steadiest and most weighty of all.' Scott's preference is for the English hexameter as an equivalent for the Greek and Latin hexameter. Epic poets in Italian and French also use a long line (11- and 12-syllable respectively), but because metres in those languages are not foot-based but only syllabic, the analogy to the classical line is less clear.

75.24 (as we showed above)   See **61.32–62.15.**

75.26 proroguing   Deferring.

75.28–36 the heroical . . . complete in himself   Scott is thinking of such contemporary epic poets as Spenser and Daniel. The Italian epic poets – whom Spenser imitates – write in the *ottava rima* 'staff' (on that term see **62.35–63.4n.**) or stanza (ababababcc), which Daniel uses in pentameter form in the *Civil wars* (1595–1609). This, with its combination of cross rhyme and couplet, is what Scott describes as 'the two last verses immediately answering in likeness of sound . . . after the former crossed variety'. The *Faerie queene* stanza (ababbcbc$_{10}$c$_{12}$) is a cross between this and rhyme royal (ababbcc). Epic stanzas are divided from each other by white space, and are sometimes individually numbered ('set alone, as though he were complete in himself').

75.36–9 when the rhyme . . . somewhat light, yet used   A comparison of fourteener couplets, as used by Arthur Golding in his translation of Ovid's *Metamorphoses* (1565; 1567), with pentameter (or heroic) couplets. At the time that Scott was writing, George Chapman was oscillating between the two forms. One of his early efforts at translation from the *Iliad*, *Achilles shield* (1598; see **53.1–2n.**) used pentameter couplets, but that had been immediately preceded by *Seaven bookes of the Iliades of Homere, prince of poets* (1598), which was in fourteener couplets, as was his complete *Iliads* (Books 1–12, 1609; complete 1611). He then reverted to pentameter couplets for *Homer's Odysses* (Book 1–12, 1614; complete 1615). Though the longer fourteener lines can tend to break into two short lines, as William Webbe observes (*ECE*, I, 268–9), the argument for them in translation of classical epic on the simple grounds of equivalent syllable count is strong, since the classical hexameter would have between 13 and 17 syllables. Many contemporary poems were written in pentameter couplets, including such 'light' epyllia as Marlowe's *Hero and Leander* (printed 1598). See also **61.29n.**

75.40–76.2 common error . . . best attain unto   In fact Quintilian, 2.8.1–15, countering the opposite view of Cicero in *De officiis*, 1.31.110–14.

76.3 under-kind   See **69.17–18n.**

76.4–7 he hath a subject...(as Aristotle saith)   That is to say, if the heroic poem is based on history, it can improve upon that history in the interests of better achieving the goal of delighting, teaching, and moving. A vague reference to Aristotle on the general truths of poetry versus the particularities of history, *Poetics*, 1451a–b (on which see **11.21–4n.**).

76.8–9 it is a part...answerable to the whole   A second reference to the popular genre of the epyllion or short narrative poem. See **20.32–3n.**

76.9–10 matter of knowledge...poet undertakes   See **12.10–15n.** and **20.9–25.**

76.14–17 the first of affinity...by personating   Viperano makes the same points in his chapter on tragedy (2.9, esp. 93–4).

76.24 resemblancing   *OED* records no verbal noun form. See †*resemblance*, v. (first recorded usages: 1603 for the verb; 1652 for the adjective *resemblancing*).

76.26–33 For their formal parts...to be shunned   Scott follows Viperano and Scaliger. The parts of tragedy and of comedy are the subjects of separate chapters in Viperano (2.10 and 2.15), although he points out that they are the same (125). Scaliger treats them side by side (1.9) before pointing out the differences in a separate chapter (1.11). Viperano observes that the tragic prologue differs from the comic, the latter being separated from the play itself (103).

76.33–6 the fables or subjects...comedies both   For this point see, e.g., *Poetics*, 1456a10–19, 1459b2–7.

76.36–9 as Aristotle saith...of the tragedy   *Poetics*, 1448b38–1449a2: Homer's '*Margites* bears the same relation to comedy as the *Iliad* and *Odyssey* do to tragedy'. Scott's second use of this passage: see **18.7–9n.**

76.37–9 Dametas...Parthenia   (i) Dametas and Clinias: characters in the *Arcadia*, a clownish shepherd (see **35.38–36.1n.**) and a scheming political agent; they are made to fight a comical duel in Book III, (ii) Braggadocchio: a boastful knight in Spenser's *Faerie queene*, in reality an inept coward. (iii) Dido: in *Aeneid* 1 and 4, her suicide out of love for Aeneas being a tragic story; there is also a character in the revised *Arcadia* called Dido, but even Scott is unlikely to expect us to think of her before Virgil's heroine. (iv) Argalus and Parthenia: see **32.33–4n.** for the early part of their story, which ends with the deaths of both lovers, explicitly presented as a tragedy by Sidney, 'the rarenes of the accident, matching together (the rarely matched together) pittie with admiration' (*NA*, 2cr; Skretkowicz, 399).

76.39–40 those parts...delivery   i.e. *desis* and *lusis* (first discussed at **74.6–35**).

76.41–77.26 All must be . . . as at large Sir Philip Sidney discovers   Scott builds on what in Sidney had been the first coherent statement in English of the neo-Aristotelian doctrine of the unities of action, time, and place, as formulated in Castel-vetro's Italian translation and commentary, *Poetica d'Aristotele vulgarizzata et sposta* (Vienna, 1570; Basle, 1576). Aristotle makes fundamental to his account of tragedy the necessity of a unity of action – that is, the requirement that a tragedy should represent a single, whole, complete, continuous sequence of events (*Poetics*, 1449b, 1450b–1451a). He prefaces this section of his discussion with some remarks on the differences between epic and tragedy, in which he remarks that tragedy attempts 'as far as possible to keep to the limit of one revolution of the sun or not much more or less, while epic is unfixed in time'. He says nothing of the place of the action. The plays Aristotle knew, and those Greek and Roman (and Renaissance neoclassical) comedies and tragedies that came after him, clearly observe conventions that amount to unities of action, time, and place, but it was Castelvetro who stated clearly that 'tragedy . . . must have as its subject an action accomplished in a small area of place and in a small space of time' (*Poetica* (1570), 109; translation from Weinberg, I, 509). Sidney's emphasis is on 'place and time' (*DP*, 45; see further **77.23–8n.**) and he gives an amusing account of absurd breaches of these two unities in much practice (*DP*, 45–6). Unity of action is only implicit. Scott's is a more careful harmonising of Aristotle and the new Italian thinking. First comes Aristotle's 'one revolution of the sun' rule ('one day's efficiency', **76.41–77.1**), then the observation that a play with more than a single action breaks the rule of time (**77.12–20**), and then the inference from the unity of time of a unity of place (**77.23–8**). Where Sidney marginalises the Horatian and Aristotelian requirements of unity of action, Scott's more thorough Aristotelianism makes an organic formal unity central to poetry throughout his treatise.

76.41–77.1 one day's efficiency   The rule of unity of time derived from *Poetics*, 1449b12–14. *OED* does not describe the sense of *efficiency* clearly operative here, from Latin *efficio*, to effect, complete. Cf. 'two years' efficiency' (**73.33**), but note also that included among 'the laws of comedy' discussed on stage in the Induction to Ben Jonson's *Every man out of his humour* (produced in August or September 1599 but not printed until 1600), is the rule 'that the whole argument fall within compass of a day's efficiency' (*CWBJ*, I, 271).

77.1–4 you must begin . . . than all I say   Cf. Sidney: 'they must not (as Horace saith) begin *ab ovo*, but they must come to the principal point of that one action which they will represent' (*DP*, 46). See *DP*, 44–8 for Sidney's reflections on tragedy and comedy.

77.5–11 this single birth . . . recovery and contentation   (i) *peripeteia*: *Poetics*, 1452a22–9 (and see **39.11–16n.**); (ii) *catastrophe*: the term is not used by Aristotle; it was first used formally to describe the conclusion of a comedy by Evanthius and Donatus (see Wessner, I, 22 and 28; Preminger, 305 and 307–8), though Scott may also have encountered it in Scaliger (15b-c1) or Viperano, 2.10 (107), or even Erasmus, *Adagia*,

1.2.36; see further **77.31–4n.**; (iii) *episodes*: *Poetics*, 1455b12–16 (episodes should be relevant and brief); (iv) *error*: see Aristotle's suggestions for the kind of plots that make for pity and fear (*Poetics*, 1452b34–1453a12, esp. 1453a7–10: '[the man] who is not pre-eminent in moral virtue, who passes to bad fortune not through vice or wickedness, but because of some piece of ignorance [*hamartia*]'). Scott's 'error' probably comes from a Latin translation or paraphrase. See, e.g., 'sed propter errorem aliquem eorum', in Isaac Casaubon (ed.), *Operum Aristotelis . . . nova editio*, 2 vols. (Lyon, 1590), II, 379. Although the alternative of 'overthrow . . . or recovery' seems to go against our idea of tragedy, Aristotle does consider, with some apparent self-contradiction, tragedies with happy endings as well as those with the expected deaths and downfalls (*Poetics*, 1453a–1454a).

77.5–6 by one turn . . . change of fortune   The wording brings together Aristotelian tragic theory and the idea, classical in origin but achieving popularity in the middle ages, of the wheel of fortune (personified as a sort of goddess), rather as Chaucer does in *The monk's tale* (VII (B) 1991–8, 2397–8; cf. prologue, 1973–7, for Chaucer's famous definition of tragedy).

77.12–20 If it be above one act . . . shun the like   The scribe here gives us a long string of clauses separated by semicolons, so the modern punctuation can only be tentative: those clauses might be related to each other in a number of ways.

77.12 above one act   i.e. more than one single action or continuous sequence of events, following Aristotle, *Poetics*, 1449b24–5.

77.15–17 It will not be . . . especially be observed   On verisimilitude see **34.18–35.13**. *Truthlike* (= Latin *verisimilis*; see **34.30n.**) is a word close to Scott's sources: the word is first cited in *OED* from Drant's 1567 translation of Horace's *Ars poetica* (*Horace his arte of poetrie, pistles, and satyrs Englished*, A4ʳ); *truthlikeness* is first cited from Sidney's *Arcadia* (*NA*, x6ᵛ; Skretkowicz, 325), and is probably a Sidneian coinage.

77.17 palpable   Obvious: the sense is probably that a plot with too many episodes will be simplistic in its delivery and so the audience, in their 'receipt' of it, will not learn anything.

77.19 through   *OED*, *through*, adj., †2: 'Going through or affecting the whole of something'.

77.22 posting   Hastening (the original sense of *post* is travelling fast with relays of horses: *OED*, *post*, v.²).

77.23–8 This error . . . where he is, etc.   Scott's reference is to the *Defence*, after Sidney's praise of *Gorboduc* (on which see **38.2–4n.**):

yet in truth it is very defectuous in the circumstances, which grieveth me, because it might not remain as an exact model of all tragedies. For it is faulty both in place and time, the two necessary companions of all corporal actions. For where the stage should always represent but one place, and the uttermost time presupposed in it should be, both by Aristotle's precept and common reason, but one day, there is both many days and many places inartificially imagined. But if it be so in *Gorboduc*, how much more in all the rest, where you shall have Asia of the one side and Afric of the other, and so many other under-kingdoms, that the player, when he cometh in, must ever begin with telling where he is, or else the tale will not be conceived? (*DP*, 44–5)

77.31–4 they are cut ... now handled kinds Greek plays were not divided into acts and scenes. Roman grammarians analysed Greek plays into the four parts of *protasis* (proposition), *epitasis* (intensification: the plot thickens), *catastasis* (establishing, heightening), and *catastrophe* (overturning, conclusion). Both Scaliger (1.9, 15b–c1) and Viperano (2.10) summarise this analysis, with Viperano preferring it to the five-act division of 'the Latins' (108) because the latter can appear arbitrary (109; cf. Scaliger, 14c–d2). Scott, in preferring the act–scene division, draws heavily on Viperano's demonstration of its compatibility with the four-part division of Greek drama (see **77.34–6n.**).

77.34–6 An act ... without evident change Following Viperano, 2.10 (108), and influenced also by his equation of each act with a stage of the alternative analysis, *protasis*, *epitasis*, etc. (109).

77.36–7 distinguished ... between every act Cf. Viperano, 108.

77.38–9 in the comedy ... clownish representations Cf. Viperano, 2.15 (127–8), for the separation of comic acts by introduction of mimes, music, or song, instead of the tragic chorus.

77.39–40 Horace ... five acts *Ars poetica*, 189–90.

77.40–78.1 each act is subdivided ... ten scenes in one act Both points follow Viperano, 2.10 (108–9).

78.1–6 If you will precisely ... contentfully pleasant Following Viperano, 2.10 (109), with an eye on the parallel analysis of comedy in 2.15 (127). Scott made the autograph addition 'in the fifth' to the manuscript, as a clarification.

78.7 differences and properties For this logical vocabulary see **5.24–31n.**, and cf. **68.30**.

78.9–11 The subject ... sad events Compare Scott's earlier definition (see **23.31–34n.**).

78.12–16 as Sir Philip Sidney . . . astonishing admiration   Cecropia has died in a fall from the roof, backing away from her furious son Amphialus; he has attempted suicide, and Sidney deliberately describes the aftermath, as Scott recognises, in the language of Aristotelian tragic theory: 'a pittifull spectacle, where the conquest was the conquerors overthrow, and self-ruine the onely triumph of a battaile, fought betweene him and himselfe. The time full of danger, the person full of worthines, the maner full of horror, did greatlie astonish all the beholders . . .' (*NA*, 2E3^r; Skretkowicz, 442). Cf. **18.25–8n.** and **69.9–10n.** for the relations of pity and fear to wonder and **76.37–9n.** for Sidney's translation of the Aristotelian formula into 'admiration and commiseration'. For 'astonishing admiration' cf. **43.36**.

78.14 fact   Deed, crime.

78.17–18 our beholding . . . some kind of pleasure   *Poetics*, 1448b (see **13.5–14n.** and **28.12–17n.**).

78.21 dreadfulness and commiseration   Another version of Aristotle's fear and pity (*Poetics*, 1449b27); cf. 'fear and compassion', **23.33** and **78.10**. Again, Scott is notable for sidestepping Sidney's revisionist 'admiration and commiseration' formula and following Aristotle more closely.

78.25 insolent   Extravagant, unusual (*OED*, *insolent*, adj. and n., †3, †6).

78.26–30 The verse . . . longer metre   Relatively few contemporary tragedies are written in Scott's preferred form of pentameter couplets, though much neoclassical drama of the later seventeenth century would be. The French tragedies that Scott and his contemporaries admired, such as those of Robert Garnier and Pierre Matthieu (see **45.8–25n.**), were in alexandrine couplets, and this may account for his preference. The alexandrine is only two syllables longer than pentameter – hardly 'much a longer metre'. Scott is thinking more of neo-Senecan tragedy (especially closet and university plays, though some such plays were publicly performed) than of tragedies for the contemporary stage, which tend to be in blank verse with occasional couplets. Among the former, Mary Sidney's *Antonius* (1592, translated from the French of Robert Garnier) and Daniel's companion piece *Cleopatra* (1594) provide examples of tragedies in blank verse and cross rhyme respectively. Kyd's *Cornelia* (1594, also translated from Garnier) takes a more varied approach, with a mixture of blank verse, cross rhyme, and couplets. Thomas Nuce's *Octavia* (1566), a translation from Seneca in pentameter couplets, was included in the influential *Seneca his tenne tragedies* (1581); the other nine plays in that collection are in couplets, but in the longer fourteener line.

78.33–9 the comedy . . . difficulties and disgraces   Compare the definition at **23.34–6**.

78.34–5 Tully... manners and conversation   Donatus reports that 'comoediam esse Cicero ait imitationem vitae, speculum consuetudinis, imaginem veritatis' ('Cicero affirms comedy to be an imitation of life, mirror of society, image of truth') in *De comoedia*, included as part of the standard introductory materials to the works of Terence (Wessner, I, 22; Preminger, 305). The judgement (which resembles in form Cicero's definition of history in *De oratore*, 2.9.36, quoted by Sidney, *DP*, 14; cf. **16.17–19n.**) is also reported by Viperano (129/130). Scott's 'manners and conversation' (conversation in the sense of 'society, social relations'), translates *consuetudo*. Cf. Scott's poem on comedy as 'the common errors' glass', **24.1–8.** 'Cicero's definition' was cited on stage in 1599 in Jonson's *Every man out of his humour*, 3.1.414–16 (*CWBJ*, I, 346); cf. **76.41–77.1n.** Cicero discusses laughter and wit at length in *De oratore*, 2.58.234–71.289.

78.35–6 the persons... civiller societies   *Civiller* probably implies an urban rather than a rustic setting (*OED*, *civil*, adj., n., and adv., †9: 'Civic, municipal; urban').

78.37 sportfulness   The *OED*'s first recorded usage is in Sidney's discussion of the proper effects of tragedy and comedy (*DP*, 46).

78.38 gullish   Foolish, simple, pertaining to those easily deceived (*OED*, *gullish*, adj. and *gull*, n.³), and hence perhaps also 'deceiving, false'.

78.39–79.9 Sir Philip Sidney... without pleasure, without use   An extended passage in Sidney, beginning from a discussion of tragicomedy:

So falleth it out that, having indeed no right comedy in that comical part of our tragedy, we have nothing but scurrility unworthy of any chaste ears, or some extreme show of doltishness, indeed fit to lift up a loud laughter, and nothing else, where the whole tract of a comedy should be full of delight, as the tragedy should be still maintained in a well-raised admiration . . . But I speak to this purpose, that all the end of the comical part be not upon such scornful matters as stir laughter only, but, mixed with it, that delightful teaching which is the end of poesy. And the great fault even in that point of laughter, and forbidden plainly by Aristotle, is that they stir laughter in sinful things, which are rather execrable than ridiculous; or in miserable, which are rather to be pitied than scorned. For what is it to make folks gape at a wretched beggar, and a beggarly clown; or, against law of hospitality, to jest at strangers, because they speak not English so well as we do? . . . But rather a busy loving courtier, and a heartless threatening Thraso, a self-wise-seeming schoolmaster, a wry-transformed traveller: these if we saw walk in stage names, which we play naturally – therein were delightful laughter and teaching delightfulness.   (*DP*, 47–8)

The reference is to Aristotle, *Poetics*, 1449a32–7:

Comedy is, as I said, a *mimēsis* of people worse than are found in the world – 'worse' in the particular sense of 'uglier', as the ridiculous is a species of ugliness; for what we find funny is a blunder that does no serious damage or an ugliness that does not imply pain, the funny face, for instance, being one that is ugly and distorted, but not with pain.

79.9–21 Of all things most hateful . . . in passion or mockery A standard criticism of stage drama in puritan attacks on the theatre. See, e.g., Philip Stubbes's *Anatomie of abuses* (1583), L5^{r-v}. By 1606, the authorities had created an 'Act to Restrain Abuses of Players', prohibiting spoken profanity in any stage production (see Janet Clare, *'Art made tongue-tied by authority': Elizabethan and Jacobean dramatic censorship* (Manchester, 1990), 103–4).

79.22–8 the unbecoming forms of behaviour . . . almost fully reckons them Amalgamating, reordering, and slightly rewording Sidney's two lists: 'what is to be looked for of a niggardly Demea, of a crafty Davus, of a flattering Gnatho, of a vainglorious Thraso' (*DP*, 27); and 'a busy loving courtier, and a heartless threatening Thraso, a self-wise-seeming schoolmaster, a wry-transformed traveller', from the passage Scott has just examined (*DP*, 48; see **78.39–79.9n.**). Scott adds one further character from the plays of Terence: Chremes. A 'smell-feast' is 'One who scents out where feasting is to be had; one who comes uninvited to share in a feast; a parasite, a greedy sponger' (*OED, smell-feast*, n., 1a). Terence's characters are: (i) Thraso, a soldier in *Eunuchus*; (ii) Gnatho, a parasite in *Eunuchus*; (iii) Demea, an old man in *Adelphoe*; (iv) Chremes, probably the old man in *Andria* (also an old man in *Heautontimorumenos* and a young man in *Eunuchus*, as well as an ungenerous old man in the *Arcadia*); (v) Davus, a crafty slave in *Andria*. 'Sordid' is presumably meant in the sense 'Of persons, their character, etc.: Inclined to what is low, mean, or ignoble; *esp.* moved by selfish or mercenary motives; influenced only by material considerations' (*OED, sordid*, adj. and n., 6, first recorded usage 1636; related to sense 5, first recorded usage 1611). Cf. Lodge, 'A defence of poetry' (1579), for a similar list of Terence's exemplary characters (*ECE*, I, 82).

79.30–1 The number . . . neglected metre Developing a point introduced at **64.12–14**. Scott's thinking is perhaps as much influenced by the bewildering and apparently prosaic metrics of Terence's Latin comedies, and by the practice of translating classical and neoclassical comedy into English prose, as by practice on the modern stage, where prose was indeed used in much comedy, sometimes mixed with verse. For examples of translated comedies see Gascoigne's *Supposes* (1573, after Ariosto), *Terence in English* (1598), a parallel text of Terence's plays, or Warner's 1595 translation of Plautus' *Menaechmi* (see **39.30–3n.**), all in prose. The idea that metre might be deliberately lax ('neglected') is an important one for understanding dramatic practice.

79.31–2 For the action . . . Aristotle seems to say In a passage in which Aristotle ranks the different components of tragedy: 'for a work is potentially a tragedy even without public performance and players' (*Poetics*, 1450b18–19; cf. 1453b1–8 and 1462a17–18).

79.32–4 if the statesmen and divines . . . unlawfulness of the acting Scott glances at the possibility of state censorship of plays, which might be a matter for statesmen or divines (or divines who were ministers of state). Scott would have had recent knowledge of the 'Bishops' Ban' on the publication of satire and some other categories of literary work issued by John Whitgift, Archbishop of Canterbury, and Richard Bancroft, Bishop of London, on 1 June 1599, which involved the calling in of books by Nashe and Harvey and the burning of books of satires by Guilpin, Marston, and Hall, among others. For this episode and its relation to Essex and the political tensions of 1599–1600 see Cyndia Susan Clegg, *Press censorship in Elizabethan England* (Cambridge, 1997), 198–217. Cf. **24.37–9n.**

79.40 shepherdish   *OED*, †*shepherdish*, a.: 'Pertaining to or like shepherds; pastoral' (first recorded usages from Sidney's *Arcadia*).

79.40–80.3 sometimes by conference . . . pastoral lyric   Cf. **21.4–10** and the chart on **69** for this classification: some pastoral poems are quasi-dramatic dialogues, though without need for staging or much in the way of action implied, as the *Eclogues* of Virgil; others are in one voice only, and therefore resemble lyric.

80.1 boorish   Rustic.

80.3–9 sometime beyond the immediate . . . ravening soldiers   A standard view of pastoral: see **21.4–14n.**; also, e.g., Viperano, 3.8 (151), Puttenham, 1.18 (*Art*, 127–8), and Sidney's two versions of the commonplace, the first the direct source here: 'Is the poor pipe disdained, which sometimes, out of Meliboeus' mouth, can show the misery of people under hard lords or ravening soldiers, and again, by Tityrus, what blessedness is derived to them that lie lowest from the goodness of them that sit highest; sometimes, under the pretty tales of wolves and sheep, can include the whole considerations of wrongdoing and patience' (*DP*, 26); and 'sometimes under hidden formes uttering such matters, as otherwise they durst not deale with' (*NA*, B2^r; Skretkowicz, 24). The manuscript of the *Model* reads 'raving' for 'ravening', but the intended quotation of Sidney makes emendation straightforward.

80.12–16 The phrase and style . . . fertile common conceit   It was a common criticism that pastoral characters spoke too well. See Jonson's complaints 'that Sidney did not keep a decorum in making everyone speak as well as himself', 'That Guarini in his *Pastor Fido* kept not decorum in making shepherds speak as well as himself could', and that 'Lucan, Sidney, Guarini make every man speak as well as themselves, forgetting decorum; for Dametas sometimes speaks in grave sentences' (*Informations to William Drummond of Hawthornden* (*c*.1618–19), in *CWBJ*, v, 360, 362, 388). Scott's inclusion of a gardener in the list of pastoral types follows on from his discussion of the gardener scene in *Richard II* in his earlier section on pastoral (see **22.23–5n.**).

80.16–18 The verse . . . artificially natural   This view helps to explain Scott's evident preference for 'Lamon's tale' (Ringler, OP 4) – which, with its simple diction and *ottava rima* form, is the most 'artificially natural' of Sidney's pastoral poems – over those (the majority of the eclogues in the *Arcadia*) that experiment in some way with poetic form, through use of classical metres, complex rhymes and rhyming patterns, and so forth. These other pastoral poems only figure when Scott is discussing versification (esp. **60.35–63.4**). For 'Lamon's tale' see **55.1–3n**. ('his pattern of pastorals'), and **65.30–1** ('that excellentest pattern of the pastoral'). Cf. **22.11–12n**.

80.17 uncuriously   'In a plain or unelaborate manner' (*OED, uncuriously*, adv., †1).

80.20–30 as Quintilian saith . . . reform manners   Quintilian, 12.7.1–2: 'A good man will undoubtedly prefer defence to prosecution, but he will not have such a rooted objection to the task of accuser as to disregard his duty towards the state or towards individuals and refuse to call any man to render an account of his way of life [*ut aliquem ad reddendam rationem vitae vocet*]. For the laws themselves would be powerless without the assistance of advocates equal to the task of supporting them . . . Therefore . . . his conduct will be governed not by a passion to secure the punishment of the guilty, but by the desire to correct vice and reform morals [*non poenae nocentium cupidus, sed emendandi vitia corrigendique mores*]'. Prosecutions were always brought privately in ancient Rome, and were often explicitly political.

80.30 ripped up   Raked up, brought into discussion (*OED, rip, v.*¹, sub-entry on *to rip up*, 3).

80.32–3 touch . . . untouched   i.e. to the reproach (*OED, touch*, n., †17) of those as yet unaccused (*OED, touch*, v., †19).

80.33–4 Quintilian . . . quod intelligitur   Quintilian, 1.3.17: '[I will not linger on this subject;] it is more than enough if I have made my meaning clear'. Quintilian is discussing excessive corporal punishment in elementary education and 'the opportunity not infrequently offered to others by the fear thus caused in the victims'.

80.35–6 iambic satire . . . satirical epigram   For these distinctions see **24.33–25.18**.

80.36 gibingly sportful   Mocking in jest.

80.40 sordid   Low, coarse, rough (*OED, sordid*, adj. and n., †4, 5).

80.41 untrimmed   Not carefully arranged or dressed (*OED, untrimmed*, adj., 1).

80.41 plausible   Acceptable, agreeable, pleasing (*OED, plausible*, adj. and n., †1).

80.41–81.1 The metre . . . uneven and untoward   For both Gascoigne (*SRLC*, 246) and Puttenham (*Art*, 149, 165) riding rhyme is the name for Chaucer's rhyming couplets and therefore for a loose, metrically irregular kind of pentameter couplet.

81.2–5 a sonnet . . . in the last verses A good definition of the sonnet, a word more often used in Scott's day of short poems in general than of the fourteen-line form in particular. Cf. Gascoigne: 'Some think that all poems (being short) may be called sonnets . . . but yet I can best allow to call those sonnets which are of fourteen lines, every line containing ten syllables' (*SRLC*, 245). Most satirical epigrams, however, are not in sonnet form, but the epigram and the sonnet are often immediate neighbours in Renaissance poetics, and that may explain Scott's connection of the two. See, e.g., Sébillet, 2.1–2 (Goyet, 99–106, esp. 105), and Peletier, 2.3–4 (Goyet, 268–71).

81.6–7 the lyric . . . large jurisdiction See 25.19–29.30.

81.9–11 too long a career . . . prosecute the particulars Scott, nearing his treatise's end, imitates the start of the final section of Sidney's *Defence*, on contemporary English writing: 'But since I have run so long a career in this matter, methinks, before I give my pen a full stop . . .' (*DP*, 41). Most of the early meanings of 'career' concern horses – a gallop at full stretch, a racecourse, etc. *OED* finds a new figurative sense post-Sidney, first illustrated from Shakespeare in 1600: 'Rapid and continuous "course of action, uninterrupted procedure" (Johnson); formerly also, The height, "full swing" of a person's activity' (*OED*, *career*, n., 4).

81.11–13 as the cosmographers . . . enrounds itself *Enround*: *OED*, †*enround*, v., 1, '*trans*. To surround, encircle'. For the spherical form of water see Archimedes, *On floating bodies*, 1, proposition 2; and cf. Aristotle's argument for the sphericity of the earth in *De caelo* ('On the heavens'), 297a–298a. For a full contemporary account of arguments for the sphericity of the earth see Nathanael Carpenter, *Geographie* (1625), esp. 38–43.

81.14 *eadem . . . totius* 'The same rule governs the whole and the part'. A commonplace of logic (as often ' . . . totius et partis') originating in its Latin form in Albertus Magnus' thirteenth-century explication of Aristotle's *Topics* (*Topica*, 5.2.8, in Augustus Borgnet (ed.), *Opera omnia*, 38 vols. (Paris, 1890–9), II, 415); the relevant passage in Aristotle is *Topics*, 135a20–2. The maxim is also found in a long list of *Sententiae ex Aristotele* spuriously attributed to the Venerable Bede (*Opera Bedae Venerabilis*, 8 vols. (Basle, 1563), II, 229).

81.23 entreated of Treated, handled (*OED*, *entreat*, v., †1)

81.26 where some manuary . . . bodily representations That is, 'where some manual art adds material representations to the words' (*OED*, †*manuary*, n. and adj., B1: 'Of or relating to the hand; performed by or with the hands; = manual'; *OED*, *join*, v.¹, †4: add, annex; *OED*, *bodily*, adj., †1: material, physical).

81.28–9 *emblem . . . court and camp* The emblem consists of an image, often together with a motto, and in emblem books is typically supplemented with explicatory verses. The impresa (the Italian word originally means 'undertaking,

attempt'; cf. *enterprise*) always combines image and motto and has specifically military associations, although also amorous ones (so Scott's mention of the court as
context might refer to tilting and military display at court, or to more amorous kinds of
chivalric performance). Puttenham deals with imprese at length in a late insertion into
his book on poetic form, 2.12, a long chapter on 'proportion in figure' that includes
shape poetry (*Art*, esp. 190–6). Treatises on imprese printed in England, in part or
whole translated from continental sources, include Samuel Daniel's *The worthy tract
of Paulus Jovius, contaying a discourse of rare inventions, both militarie and amorous called
imprese* (1585), a translation of Paolo Giovio's *Dialogo dell'imprese militari et amorose*
(Rome, 1555), and Abraham Fraunce's *Insignium, armorum, emblematum, hieroglyph-
icorum, et symbolorum, quae ab Italis imprese nominantur, explicatio* (1588). Sidney was
celebrated for his *imprese*, and includes many within the *Arcadia*. The manuscript
spelling here is 'Imprese', which is the Italian plural form. Since the word elsewhere
is anglicised (**29.29** and **37.32**), it is hard to know if Scott intended the Italian spelling
here, or a plural form.

81.29 artisan   Artist.

81.30–1 portraiture as the body . . . word as the soul   A common image in emblem
and impresa literature. See, e.g., Samuel Daniel, *The worthy tract of Paulus Jovius*
(1585), B3ᵛ–4ʳ.

81.33 fantastical air   *Air* means both breath (*OED*, air, n.¹, †7a) and melody, tune
(*OED*, air, n.¹, 10–11); the latter sense is encouraged by 'fantastical': a 'fantasia' or
'fantasy' was a relatively unstructured piece of music.

81.35 objected to   Brought before (see **12.38n.**).

81.37–9 there must be . . . things represented   As discussed by Giovio and others
(Daniel, *The worthy tract*, B4ʳ: 'an *Impresa* is accounted unperfect when the subject or
body beare no proportion of meaning to the soule, or the soule to the body').

81.39 But this too large a field for me to ear in   *Ear*: plough. Cf. Sidney's 'the
largest field to ear, as Chaucer saith' (*DP*, 33) and Chaucer, 'The knight's tale', 28 (I
(A) 886).

81.41–82.6 one so nobly famous . . . to all posterity   i.e. Sir Henry Lee, who as
the Queen's champion created the annual Accession Day tilts at which Sidney, Essex,
and others competed both at tilting and in the creation of imprese and accompanying
spectacles. Lee also liked to see imprese and emblems in the visual art he commissioned.
See Introduction, xxxii–xxxiii and lxiv–lxv.

82.8–9 if Quintilian will . . . necessary to his art   Quintilian, 12.1.1: 'The orator
then, whom I am concerned to form, shall be the orator as defined by Marcus Cato, "a
good man skilled in speaking" [*vir bonus dicendi peritus*]. But above all he must possess

the quality which Cato places first and which is in the very nature of things the greatest and most important, that is, he must be a good man' (and cf. 1.pr.9). Quintilian then examines this proposition at length, 12.1.1–45. For the historical separation of rhetoric from moral philosophy, which both Cicero and Quintilian wished to reverse, see Cicero, *De oratore*, 3.15.56–19.73 and Quintilian, 1.pr.10–20. Scott copies Quintilian in turning (again) to the question of the poet's/orator's own ethical nature at the very end of his treatise.

82.11–13 sugared meats... *vulgar philosopher* Cf. Sidney's 'the poet is the food for the tenderest stomachs; the poet is indeed the right popular philosopher' (*DP*, 18); for the digestive metaphor see **20.20n.**, **32.8–11n.**, and **47.33–6n.**

82.12 unjudicious *OED* labels this word '? *Obs.*', i.e. possibly obsolete (and therefore perhaps never current); first recorded usage 1614 (*OED*, *unjudicious*, adj.).

82.19–25 They want the life... consent of the mind Paraphrasing Quintilian, 12.1.29 (and cf. 6.2.26–8); see also **45.5–7n.** and **66.1–3n.**

82.25–7 as one saith... outwardly affect The 'one' here is Sidney's Musidorus, talking to the cross-dressed Pyrocles: 'to take this womanish habit (without you frame your behaviour accordinglie) is wholie vaine: your behaviour can never come kindely from you, but as the minde is proportioned unto it' (*NA*, D5ᵛ; Skretkowicz, 71). Cf. **16.9–11**, **26.3–4**, and **70.5–6** for other uses of this episode.

82.30 efficacy See **43.20–4n.**

82.33–5 Now if any... love of her Cf. **15.35–8n.**; in both cases Scott draws on Sidney and his sources: 'the form of goodness (which seen, they cannot but love)' (*DP*, 24); 'if the saying of Plato and Tully be true, that who could see virtue would be wonderfully ravished with the love of her beauty' (*DP*, 29); Plato, *Phaedrus*, 250d, followed in Cicero, *De finibus*, 2.16.52 and *De officiis*, 1.5.15 (citing Plato in each case).

82.36–9 what an indignity... never meeting together How could poets talk of their poetry teaching readers to be virtuous if they were vicious themselves?

82.40–1 these swinish generation... so goodly pearls Proverbial (*ODEP*, 617; Tilley, P 165) but for Scott doubtless attached in his mind to its source, in the Sermon on the Mount: 'Give ye not that which is holy, to dogs, neither cast ye your pearles before swine, least they tread them under their feete, and turning againe, all to rent you' (Matthew 7:6).

83.1–2 The poet being thus disposed... qualified by virtue Cf. the end of Viperano, 1.3 ('De poeta'): 'We therefore seek this kind of poet and artist: one prepared by nature, educated by art [*informatum ab arte*], perfected by experience and imitation of the greatest geniuses, and finally one endowed with some divine and heavenly impulse' (17/11). On this passage in Viperano cf. **8.9–13n.**

83.4–5 as Horace saith . . . nec lucidus ordo   *Ars poetica*, 41: 'neither speech will fail him, nor clearness of order'. *Ordo* ('order') serves as a fitting last word on this most organised of treatises. On *order* and *ordo* in relation to Scott's logical method, cf. **5.2–36n.** and see Introduction, lxvi–lxix.

APPENDIX 1
THE DEDICATION TO SCOTT'S DU BARTAS

The following is a diplomatic transcript of the dedicatory epistle to Scott's uncle George Wyatt that prefaces Scott's partial translation of the first two days of Du Bartas's *La sepmaine*. The Du Bartas translation follows on from the *Model* in British Library, Add. MS 81083 (see Textual Introduction, lxxii–lxxv). The epistle is in the hand of the scribe of the *Model*, with the exception of Scott's signature at the end. It is included as a specimen of the orthography of Scott's scribe, as a further example of Scott's prose, and because of its reference to, and points of contact with, the *Model*.

Conventions: double hyphen ('=') replaced by single hyphen; thorn ('y') replaced by 'th'; line fillers omitted; lineation preserved.

[51^r]

To the worthye Gentleman my very good
Vncle George Wiatt Esquier.

That Respect & interest (good vncle) wch by Nature & kyndnes you may
challenge in mee, & honour of those partes I cannot doe lesse then see &
salute in you, mee thinckes discharge mee of all feare, in the vnder-
takinge any testification of loue & gratefullnes, & consequentlye
ease my Pen at this tyme of all excuses, which are but the Euidences
of a selfe-guiltye faultines, and thus Emboldned by Presumption
on your knowen indifferent good inclination, without farther insi-
nuatinge coulours wrought vsually to dazle the eyes & steale into
the conceipte of those are misaffected with ignorance or indisposition,
I propose this hazarde of my Credite, as a small brooke out of thy cleere
fountaine of affection to pay tribute to your discerninge vertue.
Whereto if I coulde suite anythinge worth regarde, I should thinke
my litle labour much well rewarded. Howsoeuer I can but assure you, I haue lymited the verye beinge & pride of this (what
you will) of myne to your likinge & acceptation, as verye well
pleased it shall therewithall growe out of fashion & all manner
of vse, wherein that I may not doe iniurye to his incomparable father, (whose honour I soe much honour) I may intreate, in this
translation, to be admitted to partake of the vse of good Polycra-
tidas his resolution, whoe when he came as Embazadour from
the Spartans to certein neighbour states, and was demaunded,
whether his busynes were Publike or pryuate, made answere,
Yf wee obteyne that wee come for, then our affaires are Publike, Yf

not, they are priuate motions onely, thus (sayth the reporter) he
woulde haue the honour of obteyninge be cast on the Citye & publike
state, the disgrace of repulse light on him as a priuate person? So
I desire yf you shall finde in anythinge this version faithfull
and worthe acceptance, you would take it in that parte to be
Bartas, the Prince of Poets his owne message, sent to thy worlde
for verye good purpose, and I knowe not howe vndertaken
by mee to deliuer you? but where otherwise, let the impu-

                                                                    tation

[51ᵛ]

imputation of any vnworthynes fall on mee, the vnequall
Interpreter, whoe shall neuer be sorye to haue redeemed the
idlest of my very younge yeares in aduenturing, by worsinge
soe vnreachable an author to better my selfe, and thoroughe
both to take occasion to acknowledge a dett, which if I cannot paye, you may perceiue I cannot but remember.
Nowe in the revisinge this my translation, I easely acknowledge my selfe faultye of much hast; (as onely hauinge one
vacation to spend about it, and my discourse of the Arte of
Poesy, as your selfe can best wittnesse); of some carelessnesse
(as beinge besydes the mayne scope and bent of my necessarye
more fruitefull studyes, and noe greate parte of my no greate
hopes); and of a greate deale of ignorance, whereby yf my
youth be misled with a good meaninge, I may challenge thᵉ
benefite of excuse, at least as farre as the schoole Diuines
graunt, whoe agree that ignorance excuseth a Tanto though
not a Toto, maketh the fault lesse thoughe it cleane wipe it
not out, Thus Committinge both it and my selfe for it to your
approoued fauourable Censure and prayinge for the increase
of your comfort & content in this lyfe and happynes in that to
come I remayne;

                                                    Your most respectfully
                                                    affectionate Nephew
                                                        Will: Scott.

APPENDIX 2
SCOTT'S LETTER TO CECIL

This is a transcript of William Scott's letter to Robert Cecil of 1605, preserved in the state papers in the National Archives at Kew (SP 91/1, 203–4). The undated letter is addressed to Cecil as Earl of Salisbury, and so must postdate 4 May 1605, though the events described in any case take the *terminus a quo* on into June 1605. Scott claims some kinship with Cecil. Cecil had been married to Elizabeth Brooke (1562–97), daughter of William Brooke, tenth Baron Cobham (1527–97). The Brookes are the 'Kentish unhappie howse' to which Scott rather tactlessly refers: Elizabeth Cecil's younger brother George Brooke (1568–1603) was executed for treason for his part in the Bye plot; his older brother Henry, eleventh Baron Cobham (1564–1619) was simultaneously involved in the separate Main plot, and though spared the scaffold was held in the Tower for many years and attainted. Scott's great-grandmother was Elizabeth Brooke, daughter of Thomas Brooke, eighth Baron Cobham, and wife of Sir Thomas Wyatt. For the context of the letter see Introduction, xxi–xxv. The letter is in a scribal secretary hand with certain passages in italic script. It includes autograph corrections, and is signed in Scott's italic hand.

Conventions: contractions and abbreviations silently expanded; i/j and u/v regularised; line fillers omitted; lineation not retained but paragraphing as in original; italic retained; deletions and insertions (some authorial) incorporated silently. Latin quotations, and one obscure Russian term, are glossed, but no further annotation is attempted.

[203^r]

Right Honourable:

Because of the strange accidentes (strange even to prodigeousnes) falling out this yeere of Sir Thomas Smyths negotiacions in Russia, and because of the manifold differing surmises and rumers thereon, me thinkes it worth labour to doe somewhat to assure and informe the world of soe important an affaire; importing indeede the chainge and utter convercion of that state, whose largenes of Territories equalles the Third parte of Europe (it self being a Composicion of Asia and Europe both) for absolutnes of govermente one above all other (I thinke), and for opulencie (especially in the Cheife) not behinde the mightiest, in trafficqe and commerse besides beneficiall to all Christendome; The Duty to yowr Lordshippe as a publike parson together with the Bande of some neerenes to that bloode to which yowr Lordshippe hath bin allide, I meane that Kentish unhappie howse of which one may saye, –

Heu domus antiqua! quam iniquo domino dominaris?[1]

---

[1] 'Alas, ancient house! How unrighteous the master who now owns you!' (adapted from Cicero, *De officiis*, 1.39.139).

theis regardes call me to Particularize yowr Lordship and appropriate the discourse to yowr Lordships eye, the faultes and wantes which my diligence could not prevent yowr Lordships noble curtesies will cleere, as Coming from amynde devoted to charge the uttermost of his least abillities with yowr Lordships service and satisfacion, which if I Cane be so happy to reach to in any degree I shall thinke my paynes and tymes spent (otherwise lost) of precious fruite, my self being yet (as I may saye) amaide from the world, unaffianced to it or any superior power in it, and this being the maidenhoode of my travell, the first fruites of my reducing my study to matter of accion; The summe and argumente of the discourse is the Image of the ambassadors negotiacion, the discription of the Landes and Territories under and adjoyning to the Russe Empier, the mappe of their mannors and facions and last the story of theis Two last confercions in govermente, or rather in the governers, of all which (dedicated to yowr Lordshippe in private) I thought good to offer this summery following Comprizing the breefe of the mayne or Cardenall accident that fell out betwene theis turns (as understanding by Sir Thomas Smyth yowr Lordships desire that waye) till the larger Can be trancescribed.

The death of the Kinge or great Duke of Moscovia, his sonnes and wives after him fell out thus and arose after this facion to owr sight. Some Twelve daies after Sir Thomas his arivall at Moscua Citie, and Fowre after his magnificent receipt for Audience, the quelling newes of this newe Challenger *Dmetree Ivannowich* (as he is called) of the howse of *Bealla*, thought to be murthered, Comes to Courte, that he hath invaded the kingedome out of the partes of *Letto* supported (as it after proves) with some Three Thowsand *Powles* joyned with Sixe Thowsand *Russe Cassacks* (as they call their people living upon the *Volgae* bodderrer-like and wildlie by pray of Beastes and some tymes merchandizes) some fewe *Chiurkasse Tarters* etc; all noe great strangth, The Duke sendes out an Army of one or two hundred Thowsand men against this Competitor; two incounters are; th'one before Christmas wherein Borise had the worst, not much, by reason the batle was fought before a beseidged Casstell, which sallied on the Enemyes trenches, so as in the heate of execucion they were called back, which made the Battell litle better then doutfull, and the losse almost equall, this salley was the worke of *Pewter Pheodorewich Basman* (after mencioned). The second battell was after Christmas wherein the Challenger was broken and utterly discomfited, Eight Thowsand the half of his Army (for he never was above Seaventeene Thowsand united) slayne, and taken, his Artillerry all and most of his Cullers woone, and wholy had bin exstingguished but for the spoyle and soldiers werines that Contineued porsuite and excecucion Eight verst[2] or myles; After this my Lord ambassador had his Honourable dispatch, we taking joyrney by wynter or sled waye, just before Easter, and taking this interprise to be a *Jesuitisme* (that broode so swarminge in Polande) likelie to vanishe quickly: yet we Cleerely sawe the great Duke thunder stricken and spake as much; the next newes followed us within Three weekes and was the death of *Borise*

---

[2] 'A *Verst*, signifies a Myle' (*Sir Thomas Smithes voiage and entertainment in Rushia* (1605), M3ᵛ).

Peior est, mortis modus ipse, morte[3]

Conscivit sibi mortem:[4] a strange thinge without any newe losse or hazard the Army whole not a noble fallen awaye, not a peece of any worth taken the Enemy standing on his defence, rallyde in garison onely, and in such places as a mans nayles would scratche the walles doune, at this tyme he poysned himself, and for feare onely of treason of others he betrayde himself and kingdome, and thereby hath deflowred all the faire name and reputacion of his wisdome vallor etc.

[203ᵛ]

Yet the Prince standes after him, his Mother assistant in the Betwene tymes; the Nobles sworne to him and the people; then Noble generall duke *Methisloskei* is called home to be assured and advised with all, whilest the forenamed *Pewter* (of great service in this warr, rewarded and honored for it by *Borise* with the place of a Counseller, Viceregency of *Vobscoe* etc) was sent in his roome: a few daies past, this *Pewter revolted*, and carred over some Fyfty or Sixty Thowsand men, by traine, by force, with the Artillery to the Enemy that nowe was in a Contemtable weaknes; then a practised uprore or two in the Mussco, where in most of great note are assaulted and the prince with his mother almost violensed, but there upon forced they are to sequester themselves by privatnes, till the nowe approching victers pleasure was knowne, in the meane tyme himself and mother poysned (his onely Sister escaped the Cupp) and prostituted to be seene as authors of their owne Death, lastly with oulde *Borise*, diged out of his grave, basely, reprochfully interd: Nowe is *Dmetree I Ivanowich of all Rossia selfe-upholder* arived to the throne roiall, and if it weare well saide of him *Veni Vidi Vici*,[5] I may saye, he pretended (I should haue saide) Challenged, came, and possessed.

The knott of Difference and Difficulty is whether this person Regnant be the true heire or *Supposititius*, an Imposter, a matter too reverently highe to be rashly adventred one; much more peremtorily resolved onely a word or two that may serve as a Clew to leade yowr Lordshippe oute of the Darke Laberynth toward the light, that tyme (according to his nature) will Cleerely manifest: Ould *Ivan Basilowich*, finding the blood roiall straitned to his hande, after the Turkish manner, and Continuing in that Course dyed and left two onely Chilldren of his owne behinde, the eldest *Pheodor* growen up and married in his life tyme, the youngest (by a Sixte wife) *Dmetree one* yeere ould; the eldest softly and simple witted which was Cause that *Borise* (his wifes brother) was called to Courte (he and all his name having bin without note before and without use all *Ivans* tyme) Called he was by *Bodan Bielskoi and* the *Shalcaloves*, to stande on the beame gainst the nobles that nowe (as is woont in such tymes and States) lift up their wrongd shoulders, and begyn to shake at their shakells; so is it brought about that at the daye of Coronnation *Borise* (before private) is seene next the Kinge or Duke, at his right hand, Carries his septer etc, upon this is made Counseller, Master of his majesties horse, of his ordinance, Controller of his howse (indeede of the state) prince

---

[3] 'Worse is the manner of death than death itself'   [4] 'He killed himself'
[5] 'I came, I saw, I conquered' (Caesar's words of his campaigns in Pontus: see Commentary, 67.26n.).

of *Cazan*, Landes and fees given him in excese, as the whole sheire of *Vagha*, yelding some twenty or Thirty thowsand markes a yeere etc; but before this Coronnation or this interesting *Borise* in the state, the Child *Dmetree* is sent (in princely sorte) with the Queene mother and her father of the name of *Nagayes*, to a place remote some 250 verst: here the Child, in the Sixte or 7th yeere (as I remember) of *Pheodor* is murthered the matter open, and the Child projected to be seene with remarkable circomstances in the sequell nowe saieth this (or the generall fame of this) before the sending doune, the Child was changed and another kept and killed in his roome; the Conveyance by the abovesaide *Bodan* too (yet living) *Andrea Shalcalove* and *Pewter Clechenine*, controller (both nowe dead) Conveyed he was into *Poland*, and nowe thence, after twenty yeeres, restored; Yf it be demaunded, why so rather he was Changed, before any dreame of ambision in *Borise* (the author of the death); how at any tyme Conveyed out of that state out of which a fly goes not without leave; how kept unrevealed till within Three yeeres, for so long onely the *Pole saith* he was knowen with them; before he served and beggd; how never acknowledged nor cleaved to by any of note till all was pored one him by devine Fate and judgemente, not by *Bodan* himself, whoe stoodd out with the Last? theis questions will hardly be aunswered, or the aunswere beeleft; yf the Change were after wardes, why was not the Changelings favoure knowen or why did the gentleman ruine themselves and posterity, with soe hedlong an execucion; Indeede the face and phisnomy of this somwhat leades men arye and *vox populi* not *Vulgi* but *Universi*[6] goes all one waye: onely *Victrix causa Diis Placuit;*[7] they doe as god will have it, and have noe obstinatt Catoes amongst them; neither will I be one to give approbation to Pompeis cause when *Ceasar* is victor; of all this and much more I am reddy to give account, and this is all I Can suddenly saye referring it to yowr Lordships highe Judgement, that Can make more out of theis slight drauftes and lineamentes [204^r] of so great an affaire, then I Can; drawe it to parfecter forme; humbly submiting it to yowr Lordships favourable acception, and humbling my self with all as the

Unworthy devoted servaunt of yowr Lordship

Will: Scott

[postscript]
The sequell and newes at owr Coming was, the treason of one of the Suskoys, a howse of great blood, and his pardon wherein the Cleargy had a finger, it is saide and thought a preperation to their dounefall. A merchant executed for wordes against the personall right of the possesor. that *Gregory Mycoolen* (the last into England) was to be sent into *Poland* about matter of mariadge, *Pewter Basman with ayde* against the Turke but it

---

[6] 'The voice of the people'... 'of the multitude'... 'of everybody'.
[7] 'The victorious cause pleases the gods' (Lucan, *Pharsalia*, 1.128).

is like to light on Duke *Charles* whoe hath prevented the *Russe* (they saye) and taken *Ivangorod* to assure *Narve*; indeede hee is wakefull and sed also to be before Rye.

[superscription, 204ᵛ]
To the noble Earle of Salisburye

[endorsement, 204ᵛ]
Will: Scott to my lord concerning Russia

APPENDIX 3
SCOTT'S WILL

A transcript of the probate copy of William Scott's will: Diocese of Canterbury, Archdeaconry Court will register, CCA-DCb/PRC/17/60, 399^r–400^v.

Conventions: raised letters lowered, contractions and abbreviations expanded, supplied letters italicised; line-fillers and catchwords ignored and lineation not retained; corrections and deletions incorporated silently; some missing parentheses supplied in square brackets.

In the name of god Amen I William Scott of Braborne in the Countye of Kent gent of good and perfecte memorye (Thanckes be gyu*en* vnto god) and in good state of health make and ordeyne this my laste will and testament in wryhtinge the second daye of Iune in the yeare of our Lord christ 1615 [(]I beinge then readye to take my Ioyrney into the partes beyond the Seas) in manner and forme followeinge, First for my soule I bequeath the same to the Father of Spirittes, the holye trinitye sole author both of my being and Feyth (the instrument of my Salvation) perfecte god and man Christe Iesus As alsoe of my redemption, trustinge onlye for the forgyvenes of my synnes both originall and actuall, of frayltye and presumption and for my iustifica*ci*on in the sole and sufficient mercye and merrittes of my Saviour perfecte god and man Christe Iesus, prayinge him to graunt me the rest of my earthly Pilgramadge his supernaturall grace and repentance, that may both enable and warrant me the hartye invocation of him by the Style of Abba Father, the god of Abraham and his seed after him, in the remna*u*nt of my race, alsoe imprecatinge at his hand a fleshlye hart that may yeld merelye to submitt to the sole sufficient selfe aucthorized word of god as the infallible rule of religious lyfe and beleefe and in a subordinate degree therevnto to my nurslinge mother the Church of England Orthodox and Apostolike, the happye beloved spouse of Christe and a member of the Catholicke Church (the piller of veritye to whome I pray god contynew her good estate, and bewtifye her more and more in this militarye vale till he bringe her perfectlye to triomph ou*er* death and hell, As for this frayle prison of my bodye I bequeath yt to the earth from whence yt came and [(]yf I dye in England) to be buryed among my Ancestors in Braborne, for my goodes and worldlye estate I will and devyse yt by this my laste testament in mann*er* and forme followinge. First I will and bequeath seaven acres of ground in Fau*er*sham in the Countye of Kent, [(]beinge that w*h*ich was gyven me w*i*th my wife at or before my marryage, of my father in lawe William Tomlyn Iurat of Fau*er*sham) vnto Barbara my deare and most lovinge wyfe duringe her n*atu*rall lyfe and to the yssue of her, and my bodye (yf any be) and for default of such to the yssue of her the sayd Barbara and theire heires for eu*er*, It*em* I will and bequeath the Brewhouse at Feu*er*sham wherein the sayd William Tomlyn Iurate dwelleth w*i*th all the landes orchardes Closes barnes stables dovehouse and all appurtennaunces thereto belonginge, to the sayd William Tomlyne for his naturall lyfe, vppon Condicion that all the moneyes I stand bound in for him any waye, or that he ys any waye indebted vnto me for be dischardged and after his lyfe vnto my sayd wyfe, duringe her naturall lyfe, and after to the yssue of her and me (yf god send any) and theire heires for euer and in default of such heires to the heires of the sayd Barbara, Item for all my leases and rentes, I will them and devyse them to my sayd wyfe Barbara duringe her naturall lyfe, yf theire terme laste soe longe except onelye one lease of a ferme gyven me duringe thirtye yeares yf she lyve soe longe by Sir Henrye Lee late knight of the noble order of the Garter, which lease I will to goe to the supplyeinge of one rent chardge or anuitye graunted me by my lovinge kinsman Edward Scott of Postlinge Esquire duringe her lyfe, both to beginn at my death which rent chardge or anuitye of Edward Scott I purpose not to make vse of, nor that she shall, soe as my will ys that yf my sayd wyfe within three monethes after my death doe not release the same rent chardge, that then the sayd Edward Scott shall take the benefitt of that lease of Sir Henrye Lees guifte, For the rest of my goodes stocke plate and Chattelles my dettes dischardged I will and bequeath them to my sayd lovinge and deare wyfe Barbara, for the plate I will yt duringe her widdowhood onelye yf she marrye agayne and have yssue by me, I will yt to the vse of the yssue that may be yf yt please god of our bodyes, Item my will ys that for one x^{li} of my wyves Ioynture she within three monethes of my death release yt to my brother For which she ys supplied by one Rent chardge of Sir Iohn Scott Knight of vi^{li} per annum owt of Aldington and the rest owt of the lease of Sir Henry Lees and of this my laste will I make and ordeyne my sayd wyfe my sole Executrix, and my sayd Cozen Edward Scot of Postlinge Esquier my Cozen George Rooke of Horton Monarchorum gent and my Cozen Kennett of Feuersham gent I request to be ouerseers of this my laste will; written with my owne hand all ouer this daye of my Iourney abouesayd and hereto haue sett my hand and seale the sayd daye and yeare, Per me William Scotte Read Sealed and published the daye within written In the presence of Iohn Smyth George Rooke William Wrandle./

[proved 12 August 1617, Barbara Scott judged to be the relict and executrix]

INDEX